Great
Lovers *of the* Movies

Great Lovers *of the Movies*

JANE MERCER

Filmographies researched by Sandy Graham
Picture research by Sheila Whitaker

HAMLYN
London · New York · Sydney · Toronto

This book is dedicated to my mother, Biddy Gardner,
whose passion for the movies inspired my own – in
loving memory of all those Friday nights in the two
and sixes.

Published by
The Hamlyn Publishing Group Limited
London · New York · Sydney · Toronto
Astronaut House, Feltham, Middlesex, England

© Copyright The Hamlyn Publishing Group Limited 1975
ISBN 0 600 34454 1

Printed in England by
Jarrold and Sons Limited, Norwich

Acknowledgments
Many people have helped in the preparation and
writing of this book, offering advice, suggestions,
sources, anecdotes and general encouragement.
Apart from Sandy Graham,
whose filmographies form a vital part of the
text, and Heather Noon, who typed the manuscript,
I would like to thank my own
personal gallery of heart-throbs:
John Baxter, DeWitt Bodeen, Carlos Clarens,
John Gillett, Clyde Jeavons,
John Kobal, Hans Saaltink and Ken Wlaschin.
A great debt of gratitude is
also due, as with any project of
this kind, to the Information
and Documentation department of the
British Film Institute and to the Stills
Collection of the National Film Archive,
and I must also thank Sheila Whitaker,
past Stills Officer of the collection,
who did the picture research
(aided by John Raisbeck).

Title spread illustrations: (left) 'seventies superstar,
Robert Redford, and (right) Clark Gable, King of Hollywood
for three decades, seen here with Lana Turner in *Honky Tonk*
(1941).

Contents

Introduction

Any selection of the most attractive and appealing screen actors is bound to upset someone somewhere, even if personal susceptibility is only one of the criteria employed. I therefore make no apology for omissions or errors in this roster of Hollywood heart-throbs. My personal preference in fact took third and last place when it came to choosing twenty-odd names from among the many men who have projected what Elinor Glyn coyly called 'It' and what later, and more forthright, generations of film-goers came to recognize as sex-appeal. The first criterion was based purely on numbers – I chose actors who evoked a powerful and consistent emotional response from large numbers of female film-goers. Secondly, I took account of the way in which the stars concerned were projected by their studios and by the press; and lastly I made a choice which included all those men who over the years have turned me on – on celluloid.

The fact that all of them, if not American by birth, were American by profession – specifically Hollywood stars – is partly the result of a conscious decision but mainly the natural and inevitable shape for a book of this kind. Stardom, as Alexander Walker points out in his fascinating study of the phenomenon, is essentially a creation of Hollywood and yet, because of the dominance of American films in world markets since the end of the First World War, the stars themselves reflect an international response – the hopes, fantasies and desires of the global cinema-goer. The home-grown product of countries like Britain, France and Italy has always been informed by the Hollywood image – sometimes with a deliberate and intense imitation and sometimes less obviously, though no less surely. The Europeans, Jean Gabin, Gérard Philipe, Marcello Mastroianni, Dirk Bogarde (at the start of his career) and latterly Sean Connery and Michael Caine, all have their own special brand of 'national' appeal. They are, however, shaped largely in answer to demands created by the charisma of Hollywood stars – and judged by their standards. Similarly, the late 'sixties and early 'seventies 'Black is Beautiful' vogue produced modishly ethnic stars like Richard Roundtree, who, like Sidney Poitier before him, was none the less firmly rooted in the Hollywood tradition of male sex-appeal.

What then is this tradition? It is essentially that of the manly man who can show deep emotion and tenderness towards women (or more precisely a woman – emotional promiscuity is a far more damning quality than the physical variety in screen heroes) and still retain the respect and admiration of his fellow men by his physical strength and courage. Douglas Fairbanks Sr sketched the outlines of this prototype, though it must be admitted that while his on-screen image was full of swash-buckling romance, it was a bit short on the man-woman variety. Interestingly, one of the cinema's earliest and greatest heart-throbs was a totally different type of man. Valentino's exoticism, which caused such hysterical adulation among female film-goers, won him the dislike and suspicion of the male part of the audience and yet his brief film career influenced the character of succeeding male stars considerably and beneficially, for he introduced the missing element into the handsome, tough, brave mould – passion. The later lovers and swashbucklers of the Silent era – John Gilbert, Ramon Novarro, Ronald Colman and John Barrymore – could be ardent in their wooing and romantic in their love-making without alienating male cinema-goers and this leavening of passion in the basic formula was undoubtedly Valentino's greatest legacy to the American cinema.

With the coming of Sound, and the Depression, the public felt the need for a different, more down-to-earth screen hero. The introduction of speech into films made redundant the flamboyant fantasy world of the Great Lovers of the 'twenties. Their large romantic gestures and exaggerated emotional reactions were quite at odds with the matter-of-factness of everyday speech – sometimes laughably so, as John Gilbert found. More importantly, the poverty and misery of the early 'thirties did not, as the First World War had done, evoke a desire for purely escapist entertainment. Audiences wanted, if not total realism, at least some kind of mirror (romanticized to a degree) of the society in which they lived. Directors like John Ford, Preston Sturges and, above all, Frank Capra gave it to them, and the stars of their films in the 'thirties were very much the product of prevailing social attitudes – Gable, Cooper, Fonda, Stewart and Tracy. In the New Deal society of the 1930s they played, again and again, the rugged stubborn, stoic heroes who were for the people against the heartlessness of big money, big power and small-mindedness – democratic characteristics sometimes strangely at odds with their own right-wing attitudes, especially in the case of Cooper. At this stage in American history there was still room for the individual to influence society, and these heroes, viewed from today's standpoint, have an almost mythic simplicity in their approach to major problems. They had left the sophistication and surface glamour of the early heart-throbs behind; they were the products not of big cities but of small-town, rural America – Gable from Ohio, Fonda from Nebraska, Stewart from Pennsylvania, Tracy from Wisconsin and Cooper from Montana.

With the coming of such actors as Gary Cooper and Clark Gable we are well into the era of the star-system. This studio-dominated structure could be ruthless, vicious and destructive, but it did have one great saving virtue – it tended to preserve its survivors for extraordinarily long periods. On the distaff side, Bette Davis and Joan Crawford are the living proof of this, and on the other side (the weaker sex perhaps) Cary Grant and Henry Fonda are still with us, though the two giants of the three decades from the coming of Talkies to 1960 are sadly both dead. As recently as 1968, in a nation-wide American television popularity poll organized by Variety, Cooper and Gable were among the actors whose movies continued to give most pleasure to millions.

Of the leading heart-throbs in Hollywood who rose to prominence during the 'thirties, only Cary Grant really broke away from the system to any extent – and even then he divided his time between two studios, Columbia and RKO, rather than operating in a completely free market. Gable (MGM), Cooper (Paramount) and Bogart (Warner Brothers) all worked within the confines of long-term contracts at some period in their careers and felt the benefits as well as the disadvantages. Robert Taylor, Tyrone Power and Alan Ladd were the last generation of stars produced by the system – things changed radically after the Second World War and rising new stars were reluctant to make the same kind of commitment to one studio. Only Rock Hudson, in post-war years, conformed to the pattern and in the post-Brando American cinema he seemed an anachronism – highly successful, but somehow out of place.

If Rock Hudson was the last of the old-style male movie stars, then Paul Newman was undoubtedly the first of a new breed of Hollywood star. While basically in the main tradition of Gable, Cooper and Tracy and the other great figures who came to fame in the 'thirties, Newman was a new type of screen-actor because he was, as it were, filtered through Brando. Brando was and is unique, but things were never quite the same in the star set-up after his advent. In his acting, he placed, for the first time since the bravura style of the Silent era, great emphasis on the body as a dramatic medium. Male stars had stripped off in the intervening years. Gable started it and Alan Ladd was always taking off his shirt, but Brando really used his body as much as, and sometimes more than, his voice and facial expressions to show emotion. His reputation as a non-conformist rebel also enhanced the newness of his image. It is perhaps a moot point whether he created the new attitudes and stereotypes or whether he himself was the product of the times, of the changed mores and values of the post-war world. Either way, he radically altered audiences' expectations of and reactions to men on the screen, and nearly all the major male stars who rose to prominence in Hollywood after him owe a large part of their style and appeal to him. Apart from Newman, there were McQueen, Beatty, Hoffman, Nicholson and, of course, James Dean.

Another result of Brando's dominance among Hollywood men during the 'fifties was the emergence in the 'sixties of the star as first and foremost an actor – and only secondarily as a heart-throb or object of fan worship. Among today's big box-office names, Newman and McQueen, Redford and of course Brando himself have won laurels for their acting ability, and their dramatic skill has been a factor at least as important as their personal style in their success.

Towards the end of the 'sixties the wheel turned full circle and the age of the Hollywood superstar dawned – the modern equivalent of the heyday of the Silent cinema when Valentino and Fairbanks were as revered as royalty and far more adored. It is ironic that the word 'superstar' should have been coined (by the Andy Warhol circus in New York) at precisely the moment when the old, established star-system was in its death throes. However, the label, which was conceived largely in high-camp jest, turned out to be immensely prophetic. The big names of the late 'sixties and early 'seventies have turned out to be quite spectacularly 'super' in terms of popularity, box-office drawing-power and earning capacity. Films like *Bullitt, Dirty Harry, Butch Cassidy and the Sundance Kid, The Sting* and *The Great Gatsby* have made Newman, McQueen, Redford and Eastwood into international stars, international sex symbols – and very rich men. Like Gable and Cooper, and before them Valentino and Fairbanks, they are the product of the cinema audiences' imagination and every time a ticket is bought for one of their films they are not only sustained in their pre-eminence but their image and appeal is given the only vote of confidence whose validity the film world has never questioned.

Movies change technically; they mirror changing social, economic and political situations; the industry which produces them undergoes periodic upheavals. But because what actually ends up on the screen reflects the dreams and aspirations of millions of people, the men – and women – who embody them will always attract, fascinate and tantalize us.

Douglas Fairbanks

Douglas Fairbanks Sr was a folk-hero of mythic proportions. That he seems less than this to all but a few, while Chaplin, his fellow giant of those early days in Hollywood, remains an internationally known and revered artist, is in part due to his relatively early death in 1939. But it also says something about the durability of comedy, as opposed to action and romance, in terms of the public's acceptance of Silent film. We laugh *with* Chaplin, Keaton and Harold Lloyd but often *at* the heroes and heroines of the more solemn dramas. Fairbanks's place at the head of this roster of romantic screen actors is mainly due to chronology – he was the first screen hero to achieve the status of a national – and later international – idol, but it is also due to the unique screen personality he created at a time when films dealt largely in stereotypes. He was an amazing blend of straightforward directness and fantasy escapism – as exemplified in his swashbuckling, which, as one critic has pointed out, started 'with the stuff of ordinary athletics and ended with the feats of a *chanson de geste*'. In contrast to some of the other names in this book, Douglas Fairbanks was not only a heart-throb. His appeal was much wider than that – some biographers have intimated that it rested mainly with small boys, whose emulation of his acrobatics caused a national outbreak of broken bones and sore extremities, but this is to underestimate totally his undeniable and strong romantic appeal, which probably reached its apotheosis when he married Mary Pickford in 1920. America's 'Little Sweetheart' and 'Doug' made the most romantic couple of the century – mobbed by thousands of admirers wherever they went, including the Union of Soviet Socialist Republics.

Douglas Fairbanks was born Douglas Elton Ulman in Denver, Colorado, on 23 May, 1883. His father, H. Charles Ulman (the H stood for Hezekiah), was a New York lawyer who had gone to Denver to look after his mining interests but he played a fairly brief part in young Douglas's life, leaving his wife and children when Doug was five. His mother was a far more important and influential figure. Born Ella Adelaide Marsh, she had been a typical Southern belle at the time of her first marriage to wealthy New Orleans businessman, John Fairbanks, by whom she had a son, John Jr. It was at this time she first met Mr Ulman, who was her husband's lawyer. They were to be much closer later, when, after the death of J. Fairbanks, she made a disastrous second marriage to a Mr Wilcox, who apparently treated her very badly, and Charles Ulman arranged her divorce from him. They married and moved to Denver soon afterwards. Both Douglas and his elder brother Robert were born there and both seemed to have thoroughly enjoyed and pro-

fited (especially Douglas) from the healthy, outdoor life they led in what was still, to all intents and purposes, a frontier town. After H. Charles Ulman's defection, John Fairbanks Jr became the father-figure in the family and Ella reverted to her first married name, which she also gave to Douglas and Robert. The closeness of the family circle probably owed much to their father's absence. All three boys were devoted to their mother and remained so until her death, and in later years Douglas was quick to absorb both his half-brother and Robert into his mushrooming career in movies, John to look after the finances and Robert to employ his engineering skills in the creation of ever-more daring and exciting stunts and special effects. In this Fairbanks showed not only a strong family affection but sound business sense, for both brothers played an important part in the creation of Doug's financial and film empire.

Alongside a boyish love of practical jokes (which stayed with him throughout his life, symbolized by the electrically wired chair in his Hollywood office, controlled by a button beneath his desk) and an ever-increasing athleticism, the young Douglas Fairbanks developed an interest in acting – especially in Shakespeare. It was, perhaps, this name which sanctified his new-found passion in the eyes of his mother, who was immensely puritanical in most respects – when he was twelve she had him marched off to sign the pledge, and, apart from the occasional sherry, he never did touch strong drink. She, in fact, encouraged his aspirations by enrolling him in the town's drama school, which was held every Saturday in a local theatre and which organized a season of summer stock each year. Doug's love of the theatre was partly responsible for his move to New York in spring 1900 with his mother. His two brothers had left home – John to marry and work as a salesman with the Morey Mercantile Company, and Robert to study engineering. Earlier Doug had met Frederick Warde, whose touring company played in Denver each year, and had elicited an offer of a part some day. Now he joined Warde's company and made his first speaking stage appearance in 'Hamlet', which played in Duluth in the autumn of 1900 and won the following review in a local paper: 'Mr Warde's supporting company was bad, but worst of all was Douglas Fairbanks as Laertes.' Acting, he decided after this, was not for him – so he quit.

He spent a brief time at Harvard – mostly in the gymnasium – waiting to take the entrance examination. His enthusiasm for athletics remained, even if his theatrical ambitions had foundered. He never sat the exam. Instead, with two friends, he crossed to Liverpool on a cattle-boat and bummed around Europe till his money ran out and then returned the same way. Back in New York he tried his luck as a clerk in a Wall Street brokerage firm – looked the part but couldn't quite grasp the minutiae of the job – then in a hardware store where he found the technical jargon equally incomprehensible and finally had a whirl at studying law – without much success. By this time, 1902, he had decided to give the stage another go and this time was much more successful.

His dark good looks (his mother, with her deeply ingrained Southern attitudes, had been ashamed of his 'darkness' at birth), his vitality and physical prowess fitted him ideally for the rôle of breezy, athletic, juvenile romantic lead – and as such he soon achieved a modest success on Broadway, despite the comment of Minnie Dupre, an actress with whom he appeared in 'A Rose O'Plymouth Town' in 1902, that she thought he 'had a bad case of St Vitus Dance'. Between 1910 and 1915 he was an established Broadway stage-star and as such, in 1914, attracted the attention of Harry Aitken of the newly formed Triangle Film Company. Triangle (comprising D. W. Griffith, Thomas H. Ince and Mack Sennett) had sent Mr Aitken to sign up big stage names in a bid to increase the box-office appeal of their films by 'respectabilizing' them and Aitken picked on Fairbanks, among several others, because of his 'splendid humanness' he later said. He offered Fairbanks a starting salary of $104,000 a year ($2,000 per week) and Doug was sorely tempted – not just by the money but also perhaps by a sense of adventure, for he must have known that his career as an athletic juvenile lead had a limited life-span. He hesitated though and it was during this period of uncertainty in the autumn of 1914 that he first met Mary Pickford – by then already well launched into her spectacular film-career. Doug and his wife (he had married in 1907 and Douglas Jr was born in 1909) met Mary and her husband, actor Owen Moore, at the house of some mutual friends. According to his biographers, Ralph Hancock and Letitia Fairbanks (Doug's niece), in addition to the emergence of their mutual attraction Doug and Mary also discussed at some length the invitation issued to him by Aitken. Doug finally decided to go into films – although he went with some of the actor's traditional scorn for the entertainment which had started off in penny arcades, and when a friend commented on the size of his promised salary he rejoined, 'I know, but the movies!'

Once on the West Coast, in the spring of 1915, Doug reported to D. W. Griffith for his first film role as the hero of *The Lamb* (1915). His bounce and athleticism did not go down too well with Griffith, who, by this time, was increasingly preoccupied with creating a slower, more emotive style of acting for the camera. He thought Doug would be far more at home in a Mack Sennett movie. However, thanks to Aitken's faith in his discovery, and the intervention of Griffith's 'fixer' Frank Woods, Douglas Fairbanks soon found his own very special niche in films. The husband-and-wife team of John Emerson (director) and Anita Loos (writer), who was still in her teens, harnessed and directed the irrepressible energy, sense of fun and acrobatic talents which Griffith could not use. Doug made eleven films for Triangle in 1916, mostly (as Alistair Cooke says in his excellent Museum of Modern Art

monograph on Fairbanks) 'melodramas decorated by acrobatics', and aided by Emerson and Loos sketched in the outlines of the character which was to make him one of Hollywood's greatest, most popular stars: a young, ingenuous and uncomplicated fellow, gallant to women and rooted firmly and affectionately in the American scene, but with a well-developed sense of the ridiculous and pretentious. Later in 1916 he broke away from Triangle, taking Emerson and Loos with him and adding his brothers Robert and John to the payroll, and the year was also eventful in other ways. His beloved mother died and his emotions were even more confused by his growing involvement with Mary Pickford. He was growing in popularity all the time, too, and was already well on his way to becoming a national idol. In contrast to Valentino, throughout his career he won female hearts without alienating male ones. His obvious good humour, air of clean living and robust health aroused no jealousy or envy in American men – rather a ready and admiring acceptance of him as 'the dashing embodiment of a very American ideal'.

The titles of his films during the next few

Douglas Fairbanks: 'The cracker-barrel gymnast', who, according to Alistair Cooke, became 'a fly-by-night missionary in fancy dress'.

DOUGLAS FAIRBANKS
(LE VOLEUR DE BAGDAD)

years reflect this persona – *Down to Earth, Wild and Woolly* (1917), *A Modern Musketeer, Mr Fix-It, He Comes Up Smiling* (1918), and *The Knickerbocker Buckaroo* (1919). He was a clean-living, moral hero in all these, but none the less his handsome tanned profile, good physique and flashing smile had a considerable romantic appeal for most red-blooded American women.

In 1920 another ingredient was added to the already potent mix – romance. For in that year, reflecting their business union (together with Chaplin and Griffith) in United Artists in 1919, he and Mary Pickford married. They had weathered the storms of a double divorce but emerged unscathed as the world's most romantic couple, the first (and perhaps last) Hollywood royal couple and the living proof that happy endings were not the prerogative of fairy-stories and their modern equivalent, screen romances. Their European honeymoon was a triumphant progress through unprecedented hordes of admirers and fans who turned out in their thousands to pay homage to the 'Little Sweetheart' and her Prince Charming.

After this, Doug's film career moved into its second and, to most people, most famous phase – that of the swashbuckling hero of costume-dramas. This started with *The Mark of Zorro* (1920) and reached its height with *Robin Hood* (1922), *The Thief of Bagdad* (1924) and *The Black Pirate* (1926), in all of which Doug swashed and buckled clad in tights and thigh-high boots and wielding a variety of weapons from a straightforward duelling sword to a Mexican bull-whip. These films added nothing to his established image although they enabled him to exercise his talent as a film-producer, a role which he took very seriously. They blunted the sharp edge of the Loos/Emerson character and intensified the romantic aspects – social comment gave way to the post-war need for escapist fantasy and Doug's historical extravaganzas, whether by chance or design, satisfied and fed upon a national desire for nostalgia and romance.

The Black Pirate marked the peak of his creative life. He was forty-three when it was made and from this period onwards his film-career moved slowly downhill and the decline was mirrored in the gradual break-up of his private life. Increasingly restless, driven almost by demons, he travelled the world with a male entourage, and his absences and the relationships formed during them led to the break-down of his marriage to Mary Pickford. After their divorce, in 1936, he married an English-woman, Sylvia, Lady Ashley, and a year later announced that he had retired from acting.

One bright aspect of the last years of his life was his relationship with Doug Jr, and he was planning to produce a film, *The Californian*, starring his son when he died of a heart-attack in his sleep in December 1939. There is a theory that a lifetime of gymnastics and athletics had left him muscle-bound and this had impeded the circulation of his blood. 'He had not so much died, some of his friends thought,' says John Baxter in 'Stunt', 'as run down.' True or not, Hollywood had lost a great star and its earliest major heart-throb.

Robin Hood (1922) was probably the peak of Doug's popularity and success. Elephantiasis of the creative spirit was setting in – even he was awestruck by the enormous castle built especially for the film. His Maid Marian was Enid Bennett.

One of Fairbanks's biographers called him 'The Fourth Musketeer'. It was certainly a role which appealed to him, and in 1918 he made *A Modern Musketeer* – a forerunner to his famous costume-pictures of the 'twenties.

The Thief of Bagdad (1924) was Doug's most financially rewarding film, and like the other adventure-romances was highly praised. A contemporary reviewer wrote that it was 'an entrancing picture, wholesome and beautiful'.

The Mark of Zorro (1920) was the first swashbuckler of them all, and Doug's first excursion into the world of costume adventure. Here he crosses swords with Robert McKim.

The Three Musketeers (1921) fulfilled Fairbanks's ambition to play D'Artagnan in a full-blown version of the Dumas novel. It was a huge success.

The Black Pirate (1926) was Doug's finest costume-film. The print is beautifully tinted and for once he was not dwarfed by magnificent and oversized sets.

Fairbanks in a pre-tights and sword film, *He Comes Up Smiling* (1919), one of the many Loos/Emerson vehicles which made him Mr Average American.

The King and Queen of Hollywood. Fairbanks and Pickford in their first, and last, film together, *The Taming of the Shrew* (1929). It was his first Talkie.

Douglas Fairbanks

The Lamb. 1915. TRIANGLE/FINE ARTS. W. Christy Cabanné, supervised by D.W. Griffith. With Seena Owen, Lillian Langdon, Monroe Salisbury, Kate Toncray, Alfred Paget.
Double Trouble. 1915. TRIANGLE/FINE ARTS. W. Christy Cabanné, supervised by D.W. Griffith. With Margery Wilson, Tom Kennedy, Gladys Brockwell, Olga Grey, Kate Toncray, Monroe Salisbury.
His Picture in the Papers. 1916. TRIANGLE/FINE ARTS. John Emerson, supervised by D.W. Griffith. With Loretta Blake, Clarence Handyside.
The Habit of Happiness. 1916. TRIANGLE/FINE ARTS. Allan Dwan, supervised by D.W. Griffith. With Margery Wilson, Dorothy West, George Fawcett.
The Good Bad Man. 1916. TRIANGLE/MUTUAL. Allan Dwan, supervised by D.W. Griffith. With Bessie Love, Joe Singleton, Mary Alden, Sam de Grasse.
Reggie Mixes In. 1916. TRIANGLE/FINE ARTS. W. Christy Cabanné, supervised by D.W. Griffith. With Bessie Love, Joseph Singleton, W.E. Lowry, Frank Bennett.
Flirting with Fate. 1916. TRIANGLE/FINE ARTS. W. Christy Cabanné, supervised by D.W. Griffith. With Jewel Carmen, Howard Gaye, Lillian Langdon, W.E. Lawrence.
The Mystery of the Leaping Fish. 1916. TRIANGLE/KEYSTONE. John Emerson, supervised by D.W. Griffith. With Alma Rubens, Bessie Love, A.D. Sears.
The Half Breed. 1916. TRIANGLE/FINE ARTS. Allan Dwan, supervised by D.W. Griffith. With Alma Rubens, Jewel Carmen,

Shades of *Tom Jones*? By the time he made *The Gaucho* (1927) Fairbanks was beginning to show signs of slowing down physically – he was, after all, by then in his mid-forties. With him here is Lupe Velez.

Sam de Grasse.
Manhattan Madness. 1916. TRIANGLE/FINE ARTS. Allan Dwan, supervised by D.W. Griffith. With Jewel Carmen, George Beranger, Warner P. Richmond.
American Aristocracy. 1916. TRIANGLE/FINE ARTS. Lloyd Ingraham, supervised by D.W. Griffith. With Jewel Carmen, Charles de Lima, Albert Parker.
The Matrimaniac. 1916. TRIANGLE/FINE ARTS. Paul Powell, supervised by D.W. Griffith. With Constance Talmadge, Winifred Westover, Fred Warren.
The Americano. 1916. TRIANGLE/FINE ARTS. John Emerson, supervised by D.W. Griffith. With Alma Rubens, Spottiswoode Aitken, Lillian Langdon, Carl Stockdale, Tom Wilson.
In Again Out Again. 1917. FAIRBANKS/ARTCRAFT-PARAMOUNT. John Emerson. With Arline Pretty, Bull Montana, Albert Parker.
Wild and Woolly. 1917. FAIRBANKS/ARTCRAFT-PARAMOUNT. John Emerson. With Eileen Percy, Sam de Grasse.
Down To Earth. 1917. FAIRBANKS/ARTCRAFT-PARAMOUNT. John Emerson. With Eileen Percy, Gustav von Seyffertitz, Charles Gerrard, Bull Montana.
The Man from Painted Post. 1917. FAIRBANKS/ARTCRAFT-PARAMOUNT. Joseph Henabery. With Eileen Percy, Frank Campeau, Herbert Standing, Monte Blue.
Reaching For the Moon. 1917. FAIRBANKS/ARTCRAFT-PARAMOUNT. John Emerson. With Eileen Percy, Eugene Ormonde, Richard Cummings, Frank Campeau.
A Modern Musketeer. 1918. FAIRBANKS/ARTCRAFT-PARAMOUNT. Allan Dwan. With ZaSu Pitts, Marjorie Daw, Kathleen Kirkham, Tully Marshall, Frank Campeau.
Headin' South. 1918. FAIRBANKS/ARTCRAFT-PARAMOUNT. Arthur Rosson, supervised by Allan Dwan. With Katharine MacDonald, Frank Campeau.
Mr Fix-It. 1918. FAIRBANKS/ARTCRAFT-PARAMOUNT. Allan Dwan. With Wanda Hawley, Marjorie Daw, Katharine MacDonald, Frank Campeau.
Say! Young Fellow. 1918. FAIRBANKS/ARTCRAFT-PARAMOUNT. Joseph Henabery. With Marjorie Daw, Frank Campeau, Edythe Chapman, James Neill.
Bound in Morocco. 1918. FAIRBANKS/ARTCRAFT-PARAMOUNT. Allan Dwan. With Pauline Curley, Edythe Chapman, Frank

Campeau, Tully Marshall.
He Comes Up Smiling. 1918. FAIRBANKS/ARTCRAFT-PARAMOUNT. Allan Dwan. With Marjorie Daw, Herbert Standing, Bull Montana, Albert MacQuarrie, Frank Campeau.
Arizona. 1918. FAIRBANKS/ARTCRAFT-PARAMOUNT. Douglas Fairbanks, supervised by Albert Parker. With Marjorie Daw, Marguerite de la Motte, Theodore Roberts, Kate Price, Frank Campeau, Raymond Hatton, Kathleen Kirkham.
The Knickerbocker Buckaroo. 1919. FAIRBANKS/ARTCRAFT-PARAMOUNT. Albert Parker. With Marjorie Daw, William Wellman, Edythe Chapman, Frank Campeau, Albert MacQuarrie.
His Majesty the American. 1919. FAIRBANKS/UNITED ARTISTS. Joseph Henabery. With Frank Campeau, Lillian Langdon, Marjorie Daw.
When the Clouds Roll By. 1919. FAIRBANKS/UNITED ARTISTS. Victor Fleming. With Kathleen Clifford, Frank Campeau, Ralph Lewis, Daisy Robinson.
The Mollycoddle. 1920. FAIRBANKS/UNITED ARTISTS. Victor Fleming. With Wallace Beery, Ruth Renick, Betty Boulton, George Stewart, Albert MacQuarrie, Charles Stevens.
The Mark of Zorro. 1920. FAIRBANKS/UNITED ARTISTS. Fred Niblo. With Marguerite de la Motte, Noah Beery, Charles Hill Mailes, Claire McDowell, Robert McKim, George Periolat.
The Nut. 1921. FAIRBANKS/UNITED ARTISTS. Ted Reed. With Marguerite de la Motte, Barbara La Marr, Charles Chaplin, Gerald Pring, William Lowery, Morris Hughes.
The Three Musketeers. 1921. FAIRBANKS/UNITED ARTISTS. Fred Niblo. With Marguerite de la Motte, Barbara La Marr, Adolphe Menjou, Leon Barry, George Siegmann, Eugene Pallette, Mary MacLaren, Nigel de Brulier, Lon Poff.
Robin Hood. 1922. FAIRBANKS/UNITED ARTISTS. Allan Dwan. With Enid Bennett, Wallace Beery, Sam de Grasse, Willard Louis, Alan Hale, Paul Dickey, William Lowery.
The Thief of Bagdad. 1924. FAIRBANKS/UNITED ARTISTS. Raoul Walsh. With Julanne Johnstone, Anna May Wong, Snitz Edwards, Charles Belcher, Brandon Hurst.
Don Q, Son of Zorro. 1925. FAIRBANKS/UNITED ARTISTS. Donald Crisp. With Mary Astor, Jack McDonald, Donald Crisp, Warner Oland, Jean Hersholt, Lottie Pickford Forrest.

The Black Pirate. 1926. FAIRBANKS/UNITED ARTISTS. Albert Parker. With Billie Dove, Donald Crisp, Sam de Grasse, Tempe Piggott, Anders Randolf, Charles Stevens.
The Gaucho. 1927. FAIRBANKS/UNITED ARTISTS. F. Richard Jones. With Lupe Velez, Eve Southern, Mary Pickford, Gustav von Seyffertitz, Michael Vavitch, Nigel de Brulier.
The Iron Mask. 1929 (re-released in 1954). FAIRBANKS/UNITED ARTISTS. Allan Dwan. With Marguerite de la Motte, Belle Bennett, Stanley Sandford, Leon Barry, Gino Corrado, Dorothy Revier, William Bakewell, Nigel de Brulier, Rolfe Sedan, Vera Lewis, Ulrich Haupt, Lon Poff.
The Taming of the Shrew. 1929 (revised version in 1966). FAIRBANKS/UNITED ARTISTS. Sam Taylor. First Talkie. With Mary Pickford, Edwin Maxwell, Joseph Cawthorn, Glyde Cook, Dorothy Jordan, Geoffrey Wardwell.
Reaching for the Moon. 1931. FAIRBANKS/UNITED ARTISTS. Edmund Goulding. With Bebe Daniels, Edward Everett Horton, Bing Crosby, June MacCloy, Claud Allister, Jack Mulhall, Helen Jerome Eddy.
Around the World in 80 Minutes. 1931. FAIRBANKS/UNITED ARTISTS. Victor Fleming and Douglas Fairbanks. With Victor Fleming, crew and various celebrities as themselves.
Mr Robinson Crusoe. 1932. FAIRBANKS/UNITED ARTISTS. Edward Sutherland. With William Farnum, Maria Alba, Earle Browne.
The Private Life of Don Juan. 1934. LONDON FILMS. Alexander Korda. With Merle Oberon, Benita Hume, Binnie Barnes, Heather Thatcher, Melville Cooper, Owen Nares, Gibson Gowland.

Other appearances: an extra in **Intolerance** (1916); several Liberty Loan bond-selling shorts, including **Sic 'Em Sam** (1918); a compilation film about Chaplin, **The Funniest Man In The World** (1967); and a film about Fairbanks/Pickford careers, **Birth of a Legend** (1966) directed by Matty Kemp.

Rudolf Valentino

If you asked someone to pick a single name to epitomize the Hollywood heart-throb it would undoubtedly be that of Rudolph Valentino, even if he or she had never seen a single film of his. Valentino's international and enduring fame is such that his name has become synonymous with the Great Lover. He died in 1926 and, nearly fifty years on, it is almost impossible to understand the overwhelming impact he had on women, an impact which lasted not only his lifetime, but for many years after his death. No male film-star since has evoked such hysterical adulation, or exercised such a powerful emotional sway over his fans.

Valentino was the natural successor to Fairbanks in some ways, although on the face of it you couldn't find two more different types of male star. Fairbanks is in the mainstream of Hollywood heart-throbs, all-male, husky Americans, not given to wild excesses of passion and languorous poses. Valentino was a major and influential aberration in this tradition. His appeal was the natural extension of the desire for romantic escapism in post-First World War society which made Fairbanks the swashbuckler such a success. With the Depression and the 'thirties the demand for a handsome Mr Average American returned and the women of America gave up their dalliance with dark-eyed foreign exoticism to return to the more proper though less erotic arms of the home-grown product. Valentino had, however, left a strong imprint on the screen heroes that followed. Thanks to him, they could be passionate without embarrassment, coping with a certain degree of ardent emotion without feeling that their virility was impugned. He did not create the Latin Lover type. There were plenty of them, cast as the Other Man in the 'adultery-dramas' of post-war years. He was, however, the first to make the romantic 'villain' powerfully attractive yet basically reassuring to women. He was, in Alexander Walker's phrase, 'the seducer who could be trusted to act like a gentleman' – in the end. In *The Sheik* (1921), probably his most famous film, this ambivalence is clear throughout. The sheik is in fact the Earl of Glencaryll, and the story ends not only happily, but legally. In the meantime, however, Valentino gives a performance redolent with suppressed brutality. The assumption behind his rough wooing of Lady Diana Mayo (Agnes Ayres) is that she, despite her protestations of innocence and fear, knows exactly what he wants and will eventually come to love what she most hated, once she has succumbed to his powerful and dominant embrace. A generation of increasingly liberated American ladies thrilled at the sight of this unconventional and erotic wooing and, presumably were in total sympathy with Lady Diana's final, total submission to her sheik – a double irony in view of the matriarchal pattern of American society and Valentino's own apparent preference for strong, domineering women, of whom Natacha Rambova, his second wife, is a classic example.

If Valentino's screen persona shows an interesting contrast to his real personality, then an even more fascinating schizoid situation is unearthed when it comes to the story of his early life. For there are two very distinct versions. The more popular and glamorous account, on which at least two hagiographical biographies are based, was the joint creation of Valentino and a Photoplay writer, Herbert Howe who, in 1923, ghosted the Valentino story for his magazine. The other is given, less romantically, in Irving Shulman's biography of Valentino. One thing is common to both however – Rodolpho Alfonzo Raffaelo Pierre de Filibert Guglielmi di Valentino d'Antonguolla was born in Castellaneta in Southern Italy in 1895.

In the Photoplay version his lengthy name is explained in terms of descent from ancient nobility and his father is described as a retired cavalry captain, living on the remains of ancestral estates and devoting himself to the study of military philosophy and the practice of veterinary medicine. After not-very-successful spells at a number of schools and colleges, the young Rodolpho disgraced himself on a trip to Paris by spending the family's holiday finances in boulevard cafés and on the ladies, losing even the last small amount on the gaming-tables at Monte Carlo. Having thus established himself as the black sheep of the family, he was dispatched by his despairing mother to find another life in the New World with $4,000 dollars in his pocket.

It seems far more likely that he in fact came from good, solid peasant stock and that his father's skills as a vet lifted his family slightly above the other inhabitants of Castellaneta. The visit to Paris has an air of myth and no records remain of the schools and colleges he claims to have attended. What is certain is that, after proving a rebellious and intractable adolescent, he was sent to America by his family in December 1913, according to Irving Shulman, travelling steerage and carrying in the lining of his coat 'the addresses of two Castellanetan families who would receive him in New York and one American dollar'.

The story of him being befriended by three wealthy and aristocratic young Frenchmen on his arrival has an equally apocryphal feel, but he did become a gardener, first on a Long Island private estate and then in Central Park. Picking bugs off bushes did not appeal to him at all and he finally found employment, at the age of twenty, as a male dancer in New York's nightclubs. He graduated from dancing 'gigolo' to the staff of Maxim's, where respectability of a sort was his as one of their exhibition-dancers-cum-instructors. It was as a result of the contacts he made there that he met Bonnie

Glass, one of the most popular exhibition dancers of her day, and replaced her partner Clifton Webb who had, ironically, gone off to pursue a career in films.

The romantic version cloaks this period with a mantle of distinguished poverty and distressed masculinity and hints at a great love denied, à propos Valentino's involvement in the de Saulles divorce case, a famous scandal, which ended with Mrs de Saulles, a Latin-American beauty, shooting her wealthy husband. Evelyn de Saulles was one of Valentino's society dancing-partners at Maxim's and his evidence featured largely in the case against de Saulles when Mrs de Saulles obtained her divorce. Shortly afterwards he found himself in trouble with the police. All reference to his arrest and charge disappeared from the New York police files when it became obvious that he was a rising Hollywood star, but according to Shulman the folder which once contained the details remains, together with a reference to his arrest in the New York Times Index for 1919, under his then name of Rodolpho Guglielmi.

New York, Valentino decided, wasn't the place for him at that time so he took a job with a touring company of actors and made his way to San Francisco. There he got work in a small theatre, but the future was not looking too bright when he made the acquaintance of a successful young movie-actor called Norman Kerry who persuaded Valentino that his future also lay in films. With nothing at all to lose and more than he had ever imagined possible to gain, Rudolph Valentino set off for Hollywood.

Kerry's friendship and generosity sustained him through the hard early weeks and months and in 1918 he got his first film part as a $5-a-day extra, in *Alimony*. From this he went on into a series of small parts, getting more money, but never able to break out of the 'villain' roles he was inevitably offered. Among these was the part of a romantic young man who turns out to be the villain of the piece in Clara Kimball Young's *Eyes of Youth* (1919) and, though he didn't and couldn't have realized it at the time, it was this performance that launched him, not only as a great star but also as the Great Lover.

It was Valentino's physical grace and muted, almost delicate approach to acting which attracted the attention of June Mathis. Miss Mathis, an *eminence grise* at Metro who selected most of their properties and played a large part in the scripting and casting, was looking for a young actor to play the role of Julio in *The Four Horsemen of the Apocalypse*. Based on the Ibañez novel of the same name, the film told the story of a young Latin-American ne'er-do-well who is living it up in Paris, oblivious to the great destructive forces unleashed in Europe with the First World War, whose conscience at last compels him to play his part and make his sacrifice within the grand design. The part of Julio was originally only of moderate importance, but Rex Ingram, the director chosen by June Mathis, quickly came to share her opinion of Valentino's special appeal and changed the emphasis of the original

screen-play to give prominence to Julio. It was Valentino's first starring role and after a sensational New York première the prints of the film which gave him featured billing were quickly recalled and returned with his name in the star position. *Four Horsemen* was the most successful film of 1921 and it made $4½ million for Metro (one of top box-office grossers of the 1920s, according to Variety). Metro, however, obviously did not grasp what a hot property Valentino was and, when he asked for a $100-a-week pay rise, they refused. He made three more films for them in 1921, one with Ingram (*The Conquering Power* based on Balzac's 'Eugénie Grandet'), *Uncharted Seas* directed by Wesley Ruggles, and another with the great actress Nazimova, playing Armand to her Camille. This was a fateful role for him because it was through Nazimova that he met his second wife, Natacha Rambova. His first marriage to actress Jean Acker (curiously another of Nazimova's protégées) in December had lasted less than a day – the groom found himself locked out of the bride's room on the wedding night! Natacha, born Winifred Shaughnessy in Salt Lake City, was the step-daughter of cosmetics millionaire Richard Hudnut, but after a concentrated steeping in European culture became the designer for all Nazimova's films and adopted a name suited to

Rudolph Valentino – 'a simple Italian boy who tried to live up to his screen image as the great masculine lover and destroyed himself in the process'. Norman Zierold in his book on *Garbo*.

Death and suffering played an important part in the creation of Valentino's image. In *Blood and Sand* (1922), he dies after a dazzling career in the bull-ring.

her artistic temperament. Domineering, cold and very beautiful, her involvement with Valentino and his rise to fame and fortune were not entirely unconnected with her own over-riding ambition. She continually tried to force his career into the mould of Great Art, despising its overwhelming success in terms of popular art, and after their marriage in 1923 she interfered constantly and outrageously in his work.

After *Camille* he and June Mathis took themselves off to Paramount. The powers-that-were at Paramount must have been delighted at their good fortune. Not only had they acquired a rapidly rising new star, but, quite by chance, they had just the property to hasten him on his way – *The Sheik*.

'The Sheik' by Edith M. Hull was almost universally recognized as a rather bad pulp-novel, despite its high sales-figures, and Valentino as Sheik Ahmed Ben Hassan had little to do except emote powerfully, erotically, and menacingly. This he did to perfection and in consequence became an even bigger star and caused a nation-wide outbreak of 'sheik-mania' largely among the young female sector of the population, though his patent-leather hairstyle and novel way of love-making did show signs of catching on with the young men. *The Sheik* (1921) earned over $2 million and raised Valentino's weekly salary ($500 when he moved to Paramount) to $1,250.

He made a couple more films for Paramount – including *Beyond the Rocks* (1922) with Gloria Swanson and a script by Madame Elinor Glyn – before his next great success, *Blood and Sand*, adapted from another Ibañez novel. This tragic story of a bull-fighter and his loves gave him scope once more to do some real acting and was very successful. Even Natacha's high artistic criterion was met, and, spurred on by her, Valentino demanded from Paramount that in order to maintain a high standard of starring vehicle for his talents he should have complete control over his films, from the choice of the property right through the production. Paramount refused and Valentino and Natacha went off to New York in high dudgeon, from whence Valentino conducted his defence against Paramount's charges of a broken contract. Debts piled up, the case dragged on and life was not cheerful when George Ullman, a PR man who subsequently became Valentino's business manager, suggested that the couple should go on a seventeen-week coast-to-coast tour giving tango exhibitions sponsored by the Mineralava Beauty Clay Company Limited. Reluctant at first they finally agreed and the tour was a tremendous success, both financially and in terms of their obvious crowd-drawing power. This latter may have been instrumental in forcing Paramount to come to terms with their errant star. They offered him a salary of $7,500 a week and complete artistic control of his films, but he would be working for an independent producer, J.D. Williams, with Paramount distributing. Valentino accepted, and in late 1923 started work on *Monsieur Beaucaire*. The film was not a great success, though Natacha's

lavish sets and costumes were universally noted. Her influence on Valentino was also more marked, leading James Quirk the editor of Photoplay to comment: 'Rudy is trying to be an actor at the expense of the personality that made him a sensation.'

Her interference increased in Valentino's next two films, *A Sainted Devil* (1924) and *Cobra* (1925), both of which were very disappointing at the box-office. This, together with his wife's arrogant attitudes, brought Valentino to the parting of the ways with Paramount and Williams. He was then offered a fabulous deal by United Artists ($10,000 per week plus a percentage) on one condition – that Natacha was completely excluded from his films. He agreed, reluctantly, and not long afterwards she left him.

Valentino made two films for United Artists: *The Eagle* (1925) with Vilma Banky, and *The Son of the Sheik* (1926) also with Banky, in which he played a dual role – the original sheik and his son. Both were extremely successful, especially the latter which was a box-office smash. Alexander Walker in his book 'Stardom' comments that *The Son of the Sheik* is an advance on the 'simple eroticism' of *The Sheik* in that the accent is on sado-eroticism – not passionate love but passionate hatred.

Valentino, the great star and even greater lover was back on form – at least as far as the box-office was concerned. In other respects things were definitely not right. In August 1926, while visiting New York, he went into hospital after collapsing in the small hours. The hospital was besieged by crowds – mostly women – and the situation took on the aspect of a three-ring circus as all the cranks and publicity-seekers in the city realized that the eyes of the nation at least, if not the world, were focused on Valentino's hospital bed. He died on 23 August, apparently of peritonitis resulting from a perforated ulcer, and his lying-in-state, funeral service, and last journey back to the West Coast for burial made the scenes at the hospital seem quite orderly in comparison. There was a scuffle over a group of fascist Black Shirts who wanted to guard the body; Pola Negri, his most frequent companion on public occasions was conspicuously and beautifully grief-stricken, and even Jean Acker turned up, claiming that a reconciliation had been in the air.

When he died, Valentino was $200,000 in debt, having earned over $5 million during his film-career, and his affairs were in a massive tangle. George Ullman faithfully sorted things out and actually got the estate into profit – only to be sued for mismanagement by Valentino's nephew. The financial wrangles went on for years.

So, too, of course, did interest in and adulation of Valentino. The amazing necrophiliac worship which he evoked has its roots in his own interest in spiritualism and psychic affairs – something he shared with Natacha. Most of the remaining Valentino commemoration societies and fan-clubs are based on some form

One of Valentino's early films was *All Night* (1918) with Carmel Myers. His career as a professional dancing-partner undoubtedly informed his performances as the sexy Other Man in films like this.

For the most part *The Four Horsemen of the Apocalypse* (1921) dealt with pre-First World War café society in Paris. Only towards the end does the debonair seducer become the doomed hero of the trenches.

of psychic communion with the Great Lover's soul. On a more practical level, there was a search immediately after his death for a Valentino replacement. Various names were tossed about, among them Gable, George Raft, and Anthony Quinn. A Fox movie with Tyrone Power as Valentino was announced but never came to anything, and in 1957 a biopic starring Anthony Dexter and Eleanor Powell did appear – and flopped. Some of his films were reissued in 1938, very successfully, but a 1973 revival of *Blood and Sand* in London did not re-launch a Valentino vogue.

Valentino's name lives on, however, and that it does so with such strength and persistence is a tribute not only to the uniqueness of his romantic screen persona but to the pleasure he brought to millions of women during his brief career.

In *Camille* (1921), Valentino
played Armand opposite
the Russian-born actress
Nazimova. His wife-to-be,
Natacha Rambova (alias
Winifred Hudnut) designed
the sets.

Lady Diana (Agnes Ayres) actually asks her abductor, in *The Sheik* (1921), 'Why have you brought me here?' He obviously thinks it a foolish question – and the audience was never in any doubt.

The Young Rajah (1922) carried the exoticism of *The Sheik* to extremes. Valentino was a bit swamped in the sumptuous trimmings but his fans lapped it up. His companion is Wanda Hawley.

Valentino with Gloria Swanson in *Beyond the Rocks* (1922), scripted by Elinor Glyn. They played lovers seen in flashbacks to various points in history.

Valentino's fans found him a little hard to take in the powdered wigs and beauty-spots which he sported in *Monsieur Beaucaire* (1924), though here Bebe Daniels seems to find him pretty irresistible.

Rudolf Valentino

Alimony. 1918. FIRST NATIONAL. Emmett J. Flynn. With Josephine Whittel, Lois Wilson.

A Society Sensation (UK title: **The Little Duchess**). 1918. UNIVERSAL. Paul Powell. Billed as M. Rudolph de Valentina. With Carmel Myers, Alfred Allen, ZaSu Pitts.

All Night. 1918. UNIVERSAL. Paul Powell. With Carmel Myers, Charles Dorian, Mary Warren.

The Delicious Little Devil. 1919. UNIVERSAL. Robert Z. Leonard. With Mae Murray, Harry Rattenbury, Richard Cummings.

A Rogue's Romance. 1919. VITAGRAPH. James Young. With Earle Williams, Brinsley Shaw, Herbert Standing, Katherine Adams, Maude George.

The Homebreaker. 1919. INCE-PARAMOUNT. Victor Schertzinger. With Dorothy Dalton, Douglas MacLean, Edwin Stevens.

Virtuous Sinners. 1919. PIONEER. Emmett J. Flynn. With Norman Kerry, Wanda Hawley, Harry Holden, Bert Woodruff.

The Big Little Person. 1919. UNIVERSAL. Robert Z. Leonard. With Mae Murray.

Out of Luck. 1919. GRIFFITH-ARTCRAFT-PARAMOUNT. Elmer Clifton, supervised by D. W. Griffith. With Dorothy Gish, Ralph Graves, Raymond Carrow, George Fawcett, Porter Strong, Kate V. Toncray.

Eyes of Youth (UK title: **The Love of Sunya**). 1919. EQUITY. Albert Parker. With Clara Kimball Young, Milton Sills, Edmund Lowe, Gareth Hughes, Pauline Starke, Sam Southern, Ralph Lewis.

The Married Virgin. 1920 (re-released as **Frivolous Wives** in 1922). FIDELITY. Joseph Maxwell. With Vera Sisson, Edward Jobson, Frank Newburg.

An Adventuress. 1920 (re-released as **The Isle of Love** in 1922). REPUBLIC DISTRIBUTING COMPANY. Fred J. Balshofer. With Julian Eltinge, Virginia Rappe, Leo White.

The Cheater. 1920. METRO. Henry Otto. With May Allison, King Baggott, Frank Currier, Harry van Meter.

Passion's Playground. 1920. FIRST NATIONAL. J. A. Barry. With Katharine MacDonald, Norman Kerry, Nell Craig, Edwin Stevens, Alice Wilson, Virginia Ainsworth, Howard Gaye.

Once to Every Woman. 1920. UNIVERSAL. Allen J. Holubar. With Dorothy Phillips, William Ellingford, Margaret Mann, Emily Chichester, Elinor Field, Robert Anderson.

Stolen Moments. 1920. PIONEER. James Vincent. With Marguerite Namara.

The Wonderful Chance. 1920. SELZNICK. George Archainbaud. With Eugene O'Brien, Martha Mansfield, Tom Blake.

The Four Horsemen of the Apocalypse. 1921. METRO. Rex Ingram. With Alice Terry, Josef Swickard, John Sainpolis, Alan Hale, Wallace Beery, Stuart Holmes, Jean Hersholt, Mabel van Buren, Nigel de Brulier.

Uncharted Seas. 1921. METRO. Wesley Ruggles. With Alice Lake, Carl Gerard, Fred Turner, Charles Hill Mailes, Rhea Haines.

The Conquering Power. 1921. METRO. Rex Ingram. With Alice Terry, Ralph Lewis, Eric Mayne.

Camille. 1921. METRO. Ray C. Smallwood. With Nazimova, Arthur Hoyt, Zeffie Tillbury, Rex Cherryman, Edward Connelly, Patsy Ruth Miller.

The Sheik. 1921. PARAMOUNT. George Melford. With Agnes Ayres, Adolphe Menjou, Walter Long, Lucien Littlefield, George Wagner, Patsy Ruth Miller, R. R. Butler.

Moran of the Lady Letty. 1922. PARAMOUNT. George Melford. With Dorothy Dalton, Walter Long.

Beyond The Rocks. 1922. PARAMOUNT. Sam Wood. With Gloria Swanson, Alec B. Francis, Edythe Chapman, Gertrude Astor, Mabel van Buren.

Blood and Sand. 1922. PARAMOUNT. Fred Niblo. With Lila Lee, Nita Naldi, Walter Long, Charles Belcher, George Feld, Rosa Rosanova, Leo White.

The Young Rajah. 1922. PARAMOUNT. Philip Rosen. With Wanda Hawley, Pat Moore, Charles Ogle, Fanny Midgely, Robert Ober, Josef Swickard.

Monsieur Beaucaire. 1924. PARAMOUNT. Sidney Olcott. With Bebe Daniels, Doris Kenyon, Lois Wilson, Lowell Sherman, Paulette du Val.

A Sainted Devil. 1924. PARAMOUNT. Joseph Henabery. With Nita Naldi, Helena d'Algy, Dagmar Godowsky, Jean del Val, George Seigmann, Louise Lagrange.

Cobra. 1925. PARAMOUNT/RITZ-CARLTON. Joseph Henabery. With Nita Naldi, Casson Ferguson, Gertrude Olmstead, Claire de Lorez, Eileen Percy, Lillian Langdon, Henry Barrows, Rosa Rosanova.

The Eagle. 1925. UNITED ARTISTS. Clarence Brown. With Vilma Banky, Louise Dresser, Albert Conti, James Marcus, George Nichols, Carrie Clark Ward.

Son of the Sheik. 1926. UNITED ARTISTS. George Fitzmaurice. With Vilma Banky, Agnes Ayres, George Fawcett, Montagu Love, Karl Dane, Bull Montana.

In *The Eagle* (1925), Valentino had another exotic setting – that of Imperial Russia. He played a bandit with a heart of gold and acted with his customary grace and smouldering looks.

Ramon Novarro

In retrospect Ramon Novarro seems to stand in the shadow of Valentino – at least in the league-table of heart-throbs. It seems likely that this was partly true at the time in terms of their relative merits as Great Screen Lovers. Novarro was frequently touted as a rival to Valentino, or even as his successor, in the fan-magazines of his day. However, when it comes to looking at him as a romantic actor, this rather facile assessment comes unstuck for his was a totally different screen personality, and appeal.

Superficially he had the same dark good looks and his inclusion (along with Antonio Moreno) in the roster of Latin Lovers that sprang up after Valentino's success in *The Sheik* was inevitable. He also had a feel for dashing costume roles: his eponymous hero in *Scaramouche* (1923), taken from Sabatini's swashbuckling story, was immensely successful. But his good looks were more boyish, more light-hearted than those of Valentino – a kind of half-way house between the erotic exotic and the clean-living American; sexy but touching, and often with a definite twinkle in his eye. Although he lived to the (relatively) ripe age of sixty-nine and was making films as late as 1960 (*Heller in Pink Tights*) he is indisputably of the Silent and early Talking era, the peer of Valentino, Fairbanks, John Gilbert and John Barrymore.

He was born on 6 February, 1899, in Durango, Mexico, the son of a well-to-do dentist, and the eldest of thirteen children. Like Valentino, his full set of names (fourteen in all) is an impressive roll-call but until he became Ramon Novarro, he contented himself with Jose Ramon Gil Samaniegos. According to DeWitt Bodeen, Dolores del Rio, also a native of Durango, was a distant cousin, though they didn't meet till years later in Hollywood when both had become film-stars. The family moved to Mexico City where Ramon attended college and became a film-fan. This passion led him at last to Hollywood where he arrived on Thanksgiving Day 1916 with his brother Mariano and ten dollars between them. Political upheavals in Mexico brought the rest of the family up to Los Angeles shortly afterwards and there his father, who had retired due to failing eyesight, died. Ramon, the eldest, became the head of the family and breadwinner-in-chief. His many jobs at this time included delivering groceries, singing in cafés and being an usher in a concert hall until he joined the Marion Morgan Dance Troupe and toured the Orpheum circuit in a ballet called 'Attila and the Huns'. He often danced professionally after this, sometimes with his sister Carmen, and began to get small parts as an extra. Early appearances were as a shepherd in the early sequences of *The Hostage* (1917), starring Wallace Reid, and in two DeMille films, *Joan the Woman* (1917) and Mary Pickford's *The Little American* (1917), but he was totally unsuccessful in his attempts to impress producers into giving him a contract, despite taking over twenty screen-tests.

Again according to Mr Bodeen (whose 1967 article on Novarro in Films in Review is an invaluable source of information), he actually managed, through bribery and sheer nerve, to secure a screen-test with D. W. Griffith. The great man kept him waiting, in full make-up, all day before giving him a brief test which resulted only in silence. Goldwyn, after giving him a featured part in a 1922 romantic comedy called *Mr Barnes of New York*, declined to offer him a contract, and even the break when it did come was, alas, a false start.

He was offered the lead, also in 1922, in *The Rubaiyat of Omar Khayyam*, an independent production put together by a talented art director, Ferdinand Pinney Earle. This was shelved, however, and not issued until 1925 (retitled *A Lover's Oath*), by which time Ramon Samaniegos had become Ramon Novarro and was well on the way to success and stardom. Sadly, Ramon returned to working as an extra and dancing professionally with Carmen.

It was these activities which created the legend of how he got his real big break. He and Carmen tangoed together as part of the background in *Four Horsemen of the Apocalypse* (1921) while most eyes were riveted on the hero, Julio (Valentino). However, one pair of eyes, or so the story goes, were not exclusively on Valentino – those of the film-director, Rex Ingram, who noticed the striking, graceful Mexican extra. He remembered him when the time came to make good his boast (made when extremely irritated by a display of Valentino's temperament during the filming of *The Conquering Power* and repeated to a United Press reporter as late as 1949) that he could take any extra from the floor and make him as big a star as Valentino. It's a good story but the truth, as is nearly always the case, is less sensational, swift and quotable.

What actually happened, according to Novarro himself, was that a friend of his who had just completed a part in one of Ingram's films suggested that he should go and see Ingram who was reported to be not averse to casting an unknown as the villainous Rupert of Hentzau in his next picture, *The Prisoner of Zenda*. Getting past the Metro casting-director proved an impossible task however, and Ramon was leaving dejected when, with a real stroke of luck, he ran into a screen-writer called Mary O'Hara. She was on the lot to help her friend Earle with the cutting of the ill-fated *Rubaiyat*, and had, as it happened, just completed the screen-play of 'The Prisoner of Zenda'. She persuaded Earle, who was a friend of Ingram's, to write a letter of introduction for Ramon, and this got him as far as an interview. His problems were not over, though. Ingram told him frankly that the actor he had in mind for the part was taller and older – and blond. Happily Ramon, with remarkable foresight, had brought along his make-up kit, and after getting Ingram to sketch his ideas on the back of Earle's letter, he set to work. Four screen-tests and a monocle (to make him look older) later, the part of Rupert was his.

The Prisoner of Zenda (1922), starring Alice Terry (Ingram's wife), Barbara La Marr, Lewis Stone and Ramon Samaniegos, was a great success – as was Ramon himself. 'A decided find and an entirely new type,' declared Photoplay in July 1922, which must have raised a wry grin from Ramon. It had taken five years and appearances in bit parts and as an extra in nearly a hundred films to get him launched properly on his film-career – but at last he had made it, the journeyman years were over. And Photoplay at least did him the service of not judging him simply as a Latin Lover or a Valentino type. Ingram was delighted with his find and signed him to a personal contract for $125 a week, changing his name at the same time. Samaniegos was a bit of a mouthful. Novarro came from his mother's side of the family.

In his next film for Ingram, *Trifling Women* (1922), Ramon played a tragi-romantic lover, again with La Marr and Stone. Sam Goldwyn got to see the film before it was released and promptly offered Ramon a contract at $2,000 a week. It made his deal with Ingram look like peanuts but loyalty won the day and he declined the offer. Later he told Bodeen, 'Mr Ingram had given me my break and the least I could do was stay with him.'

He made three further films for Rex Ingram, all co-starring Alice Terry, and he and the Ingrams became firm friends. *Where the Pavement Ends* (1923) starred him as a native boy in love with a missionary's daughter (Alice Terry), who when he realizes the impossibility of his love drowns himself in a waterfall. This tragic story, beautifully shot in Florida and Cuba, established him as a romantic star with international appeal and the enthusiastic worship of the public forced Ingram to recall the prints and refashion the ending. Exhibitors had the choice of two conclusions – the original or the Mk II 'happy' version, in which the 'native' is discovered to be a well-tanned Caucasian who can thus safely aspire to his loved one's hand and heart. *Scaramouche* (1923) was equally successful and really established him in the top ranks of Hollywood stars. By the time Ramon made *The Arab* (1924), a straight spin-off from the success of *The Sheik*, Ingram was paying him $500 a week. He travelled to North Africa with the Ingrams to make the film and it was after this that he and Ingram parted company.

The break was absolutely amicable. Ingram decided to remain in North Africa and Europe, making films in the studios in Nice, and eventually took up the Muslim faith. Ramon returned to America. Towards the end of his life he recalled his work with Ingram with pride and affection, 'I enjoyed every moment I worked for Rex Ingram and there wasn't a day I didn't learn something new.'

Back in Hollywood, he signed a contract with Metro-Goldwyn for $10,000 a week – after protracted negotiations lasting five months. Louis B. Mayer is alleged to have offered him a job as head of the MGM legal department if he ever decided to quit acting. He made three films for Metro-Goldwyn – *Thy Name is Woman* and *The Red Lily* (1924) and *The Midshipman* (1925) – before he made the film by which he is most remembered.

Ben Hur (1926) was based on a novel by Lew Wallace which had been frequently, and popularly, adapted for the stage. This first screen version was being made in Italy with Charles Brabin directing and George Walsh playing the lead when Irving Thalberg, Mayer's right-hand man, decided to replace them with Fred Niblo and Ramon Novarro respectively. The film, which was completed in California (the chariot scene was shot there), cost between $5 and $6 million and was then the most expensive film ever made. Ultimately *Ben Hur* grossed $4½ million and was still playing to full houses as late as 1959 when the sound version, starring Charlton Heston, was released. It was an

Just a Valentino substitute? Ramon Novarro's screen-career may have started out like that but his appeal and screen persona were very different from that of The Sheik.

immediate box-office triumph and pushed Ramon up to even dizzier heights of popularity.

In fact this was the peak of his career both in terms of creativity and popularity, although he went on to make over twenty more films during the pre-war years and made a brief comeback as a character actor in the early 'fifties. The following year saw him in what was probably his second most popular film, *The Student Prince*, with Norma Shearer, in which, according to Picturegoer, they both gave of 'their flawless acting and radiant charm'. After this, however, he never quite retained his pre-eminent position among the Hollywood stars, though he remained on the roster of top-ranking stars for some time, and continued to exert tremendously powerful box-office appeal over female film-goers. In the late 'twenties and early 'thirties, Renée Adorée was a frequent co-star in such films as *A Certain Young Man* and *Forbidden Hours* (both 1928 and both Silent), *The Pagan* (1929), in which he sang but did not speak, and *Call of the Flesh* (1930), in which he did both.

His transition to Talkies was not very smooth. Picturegoer and MGM expressed disappointment and in later life he voiced a dislike for all his Sound films. His flagging career was given a boost when he co-starred with Garbo in *Mata Hari* (1932), a service which she also rendered (though for different reasons) to John Gilbert in *Queen Christina*. Perhaps because of this MGM signed him up for a second seven-year contract in 1933. During the next couple of years he made half a dozen films for them, including a remake of *The Arab*, called *The Barbarian* (1933) and *The Cat and the Fiddle* (1934) with Jeanette MacDonald. But he didn't regain his public and his box-office drawing power was obviously on the wane. The *coup de grâce* was a schmaltzy Ruritanian frolic called *The Night Is Young* (1935), in which he co-starred with British stage-star Evelyn Laye. Plans for a sequel were stillborn and Ramon's MGM contract was terminated.

A lengthy period of travel, unrest and experiment followed. He went to London where he sang, successfully, at the Palladium and appeared, disastrously, in a stage musical, 'A Royal Exchange', in 1935. He returned to Hollywood, where he produced, wrote and directed a Spanish-speaking feature film *Contra la Corriente*, before making a couple of disappointing romantic comedies for Republic. After these he cancelled his contract and retired to a fifty-acre ranch near San Diego.

Then, in 1940, he went back to Europe and starred in a French comedy made in Italy called *La Comedie de Bonheur*. Michel Simon, Micheline Presle and the young Louis Jourdan were also in the film and Ramon took over the direction when the exigencies of war forced Marcel l'Herbier, the French director, to return to Paris. Later, the war also caused Novarro to return to Hollywood once more, whence he travelled to Mexico to make *La Virgen Que Forjo una Patria* (1942).

In 1949 he made his comeback as a character actor in John Huston's *We Were Strangers* and followed this up the same year with the part of a Mexican police inspector in Don Siegel's *The Big Steal* and that of a wealthy Mexican in *The Outriders* (1950), a Civil War Western. He played another Latin American, an army colonel in Richard Brooks's *Crisis* (1950), and his last film role was that of a gangster posing as a businessman in George Cukor's *Heller in Pink Tights* (1960).

After that he appeared on television occasionally and lived quietly in his home at Laurel Canyon. He drank a lot and was frequently picked up by the Los Angeles police for drunken driving. He was wealthy and had never married, and these two facts combined tragically in his brutal death in October 1968 at the hands of two young hustlers, brothers, who killed him in an attempt to find out where he kept his money. They were sentenced to life imprisonment in 1969.

Like Valentino, Ramon Novarro's memory continues to inspire worship in the hearts of the women and men who first found him a heart-throb in the 1920s. The British Ramon Novarro Film Club was founded in 1928 and in 1968, after his death, the Club's newsletter said this to its readers: 'No star has nor . . . will be as faithful to his fans as Ramon Novarro was.' If a film-star's immortality can be judged in terms of his fans' fidelity, then Novarro must emerge from Valentino's shadow to stand with him as one of the Silent screen's greatest heart-throbs.

Still billed as Ramon Samaniegos, Novarro played the baddie, Rupert of Hentzau, in *The Prisoner of Zenda* (1922). Barbara La Marr obviously finds the monocle a mite sinister.

Trifling Women (1922) reunited Novarro and La Marr. She played a lethal vamp and he was one of her victims.

Where the Pavement Ends (1923) was the film that really launched Novarro as a heart-throb. Alice Terry played the missionary's daughter whom he loves so desperately.

25

The Arab (1924) was an unashamed piece of cashing-in on the Sheik craze, distinguished only by the fact that it was actually shot in North Africa. Alice Terry co-starred again.

Novarro hoped at one point that Rex Ingram would be asked to direct *Ben Hur* (1926), but the job went to Fred Niblo. The film was a huge success.

'When I saw Mr Novarro as Scaramouche,' said Pola Negri when the film was released in 1923, 'I took off my hat to him.'

Novarro's early ambition was to be a singer. Unfortunately for him, his was the Silent version of *The Student Prince* (1927), though he and Norma Shearer won plaudits for their performances.

Ramon Novarro

A Small Town Idol. 1921. ASSOCIATED PRODUCERS. Earle C. Kenton. With Ben Turpin, James Finlayson, Marie Prevost, Charles Murray.

Mr Barnes of New York. 1922. GOLDWYN. Victor Schertzinger. Billed as Ramon Samaniegos. With Tom Moore, Naomi Childers, Anna Lehr.

The Prisoner of Zenda. 1922. METRO. Rex Ingram. Billed as Samaniegos. With Lewis Stone, Alice Terry, Robert Edeson, Barbara La Marr, Malcolm McGregor, Ed Connelly, Lois Lee.

Trifling Women. 1922. METRO. Rex Ingram. With Barbara La Marr, Lewis Stone, Ed Connelly, Hughie Mack, Pomeroy Cannon.

Where the Pavement Ends. 1923. METRO. Rex Ingram. With Alice Terry, Ed Connelly, Harry T. Morey.

Scaramouche. 1923. METRO. Rex Ingram. With Alice Terry, Lewis Stone, Julia Swayne Gordon, Lloyd Ingraham, William Humphrey, Otto Matiesen, George Seigmann.

Thy Name Is Woman. 1924. METRO-GOLDWYN. Fred Niblo. With Barbara La Marr, William V. Mong, Wallace MacDonald, Robert Edeson, Claire McDowell, Edith Roberts.

The Arab. 1924. METRO-GOLDWYN. Rex Ingram. With Alice Terry, Gerald Robertshaw, Alexandresco, Maxudian, Adequi Miller, Jean de Limur.

The Red Lily. 1924. METRO-GOLDWYN. Fred Niblo. With Enid Bennett, Wallace Beery, Frank Currier, Rosemary Theby, Mitchell Lewis, Emily Fitzroy, George Periolat, Milly Davenport.

A Lover's Oath. 1925. ASTOR. Ferdinand Pinney Earle. With Kathleen Key, Edwin Stevens, Frederick Warde, Hedwig Reicher, Snitz Edwards, Charles A. Post, Arthur E. Carewe.

The Midshipman. 1925. METRO-GOLDWYN. W. Christy Cabanné. With Harriet Hammond, Wesley Barry, Margaret Seddon, Crawford Kent, Maurice Ryan, Harold Goodwin, William Boyd, Gilbert Roland.

Ben Hur. 1926. MGM. Fred Niblo. With Francis X. Bushman, May McAvoy, Claire McDowell, Kathleen Key, Carmel Myers, Nigel de Brulier, Mitchell Lewis, Leo White, Frank Currier, Charles Belcher, Betty Bronson, Dale Fuller, Winter Hall.

Lovers? 1927. MGM. John M. Stahl. With Alice Terry, Ed Martindel.

The Road to Romance. 1927. MGM. John S. Robertson. With Marceline Day, Marc McDermott, Roy D'Arcy, Cesare Gravina, Bobby Mack, Otto Matiesen, Jules Cowles.

The Student Prince. 1927. MGM. Ernst Lubitsch. With Norma Shearer, Jean Hersholt, Gustav von Seyffertitz, Phillippe de Lacy, Edgar Norton, Bobby Mack, Ed Connelly, Otis Harlan.

Across to Singapore. 1928. MGM. William Nigh. With Joan Crawford, Ernest Torrence, Frank Currier, Dan Wolheim, Duke Martin, Ed Connelly, James Mason.

A Certain Young Man. 1928. MGM. Hobart Henley. With Marceline Day, Renée Adorée, Carmel Myers, Bert Roach, Huntley Gordon, Ernest Wood, Willard Louis.

Forbidden Hours. 1928. MGM. Harry Beaumont. With Renée Adorée, Ed Connelly, Albert Vaughn, Roy D'Arcy.

The Flying Fleet. 1929. MGM. With Ralph Graves, Anita Page, Ed Nugent, Caroll Nye, Sumner Getchell, Gardner James, Alfred Allen.

The Pagan. 1929. MGM. W.S. Van Dyke. With Renée Adorée, Dorothy Janis, Donald Crisp.

Devil May Care. 1929. MGM. Sidney Franklin. First Talkie, With Dorothy Jordan, Marion Harris, John Miljan, William Humphrey.

In Gay Madrid. 1930. MGM. Robert Z. Leonard. With Dorothy Jordan, Lottice Howell, Claude King, Eugene Besserer, William V. Mong, Beryl Mercer, Nancy Price, Herbert Clark, David Scott, George Chandler, Bruce Coleman.

Call of the Flesh. 1930. MGM. Charles J. Brabin. With Dorothy Jordan, Renée Adorée, Ernest Torrence, Nance O'Neil, Mathilde Comont, Russell Hopton.

Daybreak. 1931. MGM. Jacques Feyder. With Helen Chandler, Jean Hersholt, C. Aubrey Smith, William Bakewell.

Son of India. 1931. MGM. Jacques Feyder. With Madge Evans, Conrad Nagel, Marjorie Rambeau, C. Aubrey Smith, Mitchell Lewis, John Milgan, Nigel de Brulier.

Mata Hari. 1932. MGM. George Fitzmaurice. With Greta Garbo, Lionel Barrymore, Lewis Stone, C. Henry Gordon, Karen Morley, Alex B. Francis, Blanche Federici, Edmund Breese, Helen Jerome Eddy, Frank Reicher.

Huddle. 1932. MGM. Sam Wood. With Madge Evans, Una Merkel, Ralph Graves.

The Son-Daughter. 1932. MGM. Clarence Brown. With Helen Hayes, Lewis Stone, Warner Oland, Ralph Morgan.

The Barbarian (UK title: **A Night in Cairo**). 1933. MGM. Sam Wood. With Myrna Loy, Reginald Denny, Louise Closser Hale, C. Aubrey Smith, Hedda Hopper.

The Cat and the Fiddle. 1934. MGM. William K. Howard. With Jeanette MacDonald, Frank Morgan, Charles Butterworth, Jean Hersholt.

Laughing Boy. 1934. MGM. W.S. Van Dyke. With Lupe Velez, William Dickenson, Chief Thunderbird, Ruth Channing.

The Night Is Young. 1935. MGM, Dudley Murphy. With Evelyn Laye, Charles Butterworth, Una Merkel, Henry Stephen, Edward Everett Horton, Rosalind Russell.

The Sheik Steps Out. 1937. REPUBLIC. Irving Pichel. With Lola Lane, Gene Lockhart, Kathleen Burke.

A Desperate Adventure. 1938. REPUBLIC. John H. Auer. With Marian Marsh, Margaret Tallichet, Eric Blore.

La Comedie de Bonheur (Italian title: **Ecco La Felicita**). 1940. DISCINA. Marcel l'Herbier. With Michel Simon, Jacqueline Delubac, Micheline Presle, Louis Jourdan.

La Virgen Que Forjo una Patria. 1942. FILMS MUNDIALES. Julio Bracha. With Gloria Marin, Domingo Soler, Julio Villareal.

We Were Strangers. 1949. COLUMBIA. John Huston. With Jennifer Jones, John Garfield, Pedro Armendariz, Gilbert Roland.

The Big Steal. 1949. RKO. Don Siegel. With Robert Mitchum, Jane Greer, William Bendix, Patric Knowles.

The Outriders. 1950. MGM. Roy Rowland. With Joel McCrea, Arlene Dahl, Barry Sullivan, Claude Jarman Jr, James Whitmore, Jeff Corey.

Crisis. 1950. MGM. Richard Brooks. With Cary Grant, José Ferrer, Paula Raymond, Signe Hasso, Gilbert Roland, Leon Ames, Antonio Moreno, Teresa Celli.

Heller in Pink Tights. 1960. PARAMOUNT. George Cukor. With Sophia Loren, Steve Forrest, Anthony Quinn, Margaret O'Brien, Eileen Heckart, Edmund Lowe, George Mathews.

Novarro is also said to have appeared in **La Sevillana** (also known as **Sevilla de Mis Amores**) and **Le Chanteur de Seville**, both foreign versions of **Call of the Flesh** (1930); he apparently directed the former and co-directed the latter. DeWitt Bodeen claims that **Contra La Corriente** (1936), a Spanish-speaking feature, was written, produced and directed by Novarro.

Novarro in *Mata Hari* (1932) with Garbo. He played a young Russian lieutenant betrayed by her.

John Barrymore

John Barrymore, quite apart from being the 'Great Profile' and, like Valentino, a Great Lover, was an actor of distinction. Like Fairbanks he had made this reputation on the stage (though with even greater success than Doug) before he moved on to celluloid, and once there his preference was for character roles rather than tragi-romantic heroes. The public, however, was captivated by his stunning good looks (especially the left profile) and the magnetism of his personality, and so, at least during the 'twenties, his ebullience and sheer acting skill were trimmed and forced into the confines of the by-then traditional screen-hero. Unlike Novarro and Gilbert, he did make the hazardous crossing from Silent to Sound pictures safely, which was really only to be expected after his long and successful stage-career. As a heart-throb though, he was essentially a Silent star – for it was during the 'twenties that he played his most romantic roles. With the coming of Sound he began to switch over to the character parts which he preferred and in which he gave a series of superb performances – his years as a heart-throb, ironically, drew to a close just as he reached the peak of his screen-career.

With a nice sense of timing for a great romantic star, John Barrymore was born on St Valentine's Day 1882 in the Philadelphia home of his maternal grandmother, Louisa Drew. Mrs Drew, who had been a celebrated actress since the age of nine, was the proprietress of the Arch Street Theater, Philadelphia, and John was the third child of her younger daughter Georgianna (the first two were Ethel, who was born in 1875, and Lionel, born in 1878). His father, Maurice, was an Englishman, born Herbert Blythe, who was educated at Harrow and Lincoln College, Oxford, where he read law and became the British Amateur light-weight boxing champion. He then took to the stage – to the great distress of his family. Soon after his arrival in New York he met John Drew, also an actor, as befitted the eldest child of Louisa Drew, and on a visit to the family home fell in love with and married Georgie.

According to John Barrymore's excellent and witty biographer Gene Fowler (in 'Goodnight, Sweet Prince'), he inherited much of his immensely complicated and contradictory personality from his father: 'sudden exploits of generosity and equally fitful moods of self-centred arrogance', as well as his father's 'epic frailties' – not just the taste for alcohol, the restless spirit and the thoughtlessness but also his 'capricious tendencies for self-ruination'. Commentators on John Barrymore's career who believe in astrology have commented on the coincidence of Gemini rising at the time of his birth and what seemed, in later life at least,

a definite Jekyll-and-Hyde quality in his character, though it seems only sensible to point out that very heavy drinkers tend to exhibit this sort of schizoid behaviour.

In 1889 the family moved to New York, and it was here that Georgie's ill-health became a cause for concern. Her death in 1892 in California, where she had been sent for her health with Ethel as her companion, was a tragic blow to her family. The children, especially John, were very hard hit – more so, perhaps, than Maurice, who remarried fairly shortly afterwards. Another emotional deprivation occurred in 1897 when Grandmother Drew also died. John's drinking, fairly heavy even at first, dates from this period – he was fifteen.

Both John and Lionel were not over-keen on following family tradition in their choice of career (though Ethel started acting at a tender age) and in addition to a fairly active pursuit of wine and women John dabbled in art and journalism – without any great success. Rather like the young Fairbanks, he finally resigned himself to the stage and made his Broadway début in 1903. The same year saw the third, and most distressing, of the family tragedies. Maurice Barrymore suffered a complete mental breakdown and was admitted to the psychopathic ward at Bellevue. From there he was moved to a private sanitarium, where he died in 1905. In later life, the remembrance of his father's tragic end haunted John, especially when he began to have serious trouble with his lines, and feared for his own sanity.

His stage breakthrough came in 1909 in 'The Fortune Hunter', when he was hailed as a brilliant light comedian. This was followed, in 1910, by his first marriage – to a young society girl, Katherine Harris – which got off to an inauspicious start when he announced at the

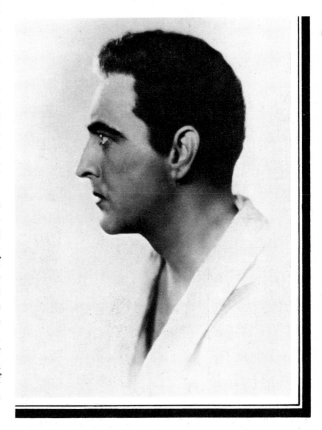

Marshall Neilan's *The Lotus Eater* (1921) was filmed in Florida.

wedding breakfast that he was off almost immediately on tour with 'The Fortune Hunter'! His career marked time for the next few years during which, according to Fowler, 'he smelled more of alcohol than fame'. However, on a trip to Italy by himself in 1914 (the marriage was very shaky by this time), he met an old friend, playwright Edward Sheldon, who persuaded him to try his talents in more serious parts. He had a success in a Broadway melodrama called 'Kick In' on his return and then really came into his dramatic kingdom as the tragic hero of John Galsworthy's 'Justice' in 1916. It was at this time that Katherine began divorce proceedings and John was once more a free man when he undertook his next role – the straight romantic hero in 'Peter Ibbetson', adapted from the George du Maurier novel. The part established him as a romantic actor of tremendous appeal – he became a matinée-idol overnight and thus began his career as a heart-throb.

Barrymore had, in fact, already begun the film-career that was to combine with his sex-appeal so successfully later. In 1913 he had made his first film, *An American Citizen* (1914), partly out of curiosity but also for the money – an ever-present and pressing consideration for him at this time. It was a Famous Players two-reeler farce and on the strength of it Adolf Zukor offered him a contract. The film's director, J. Searle Dawley, later said that they hoped 'to make a Chaplin out of him', and certainly the eleven films he made for Famous between 1914 and 1919 were all farces in which, *à la* Fairbanks, he exhibited his talents for slapstick and gymnastics. His early screen image was rather Gallic – debonair, charming and mustachioed. He filmed during the day, appearing in the theatre at night. The films, usually adaptations of hit stage-comedies, were well received but they were very much a sideline. However, he liked the work and respected its achievements – 'the moving picture is not a business, it is an art'.

His stage-career and his work in films both moved on to a higher and more serious plane around 1920 when he had a greater film success than ever before, in a drama, not a comedy, *Dr Jekyll and Mr Hyde*, and caused a sensation with his stage portrayal of Gloucester in 'Richard III', the first of his two famous Shakespearean roles. He made it a hat-trick, and placed an almost intolerable strain on himself, by marrying for the second time in the middle of all this. His bride was a poetess who wrote under the name of Michael Strange and who, says Fowler, had 'the face of a Romney portrait and the spirit of a US marine'. Later Barrymore is alleged to have commented ruefully, 'I never married any of my wives – they married me.' It was a stormy relationship, not strengthened by the terrible flop, in 1922, of 'Claire de Lune', a drama written by Michael (who produced a daughter around the same time) in which he played the lead.

This wreck of his talent was salvaged spectacularly by the choice of his next stage part,

Hamlet. He was at the peak of his stage-career and 'Hamlet' played to packed and avid audiences on both sides of the Atlantic. For, after a long run of one hundred and one performances on Broadway, Barrymore travelled to London where, with the help of Constance Collier – his co-star in 'Peter Ibbetson', he arranged for the production to be put on at the Haymarket Theatre in 1925. It played for twelve triumphant weeks.

Just before going to London, however, John had made his first film with Warner Brothers, *Beau Brummel* (1924). His co-star was Mary Astor, then only seventeen, and their work together launched them into an intermittent though impassioned romance which lasted until he met his third wife. His marriage to Michael Strange was virtually over by then. He was also at the peak of his romantic beauty at this time and popularity of the film in general and Barrymore in particular led to Warner Brothers offering him a contract, which he signed on his return from England.

It was a particularly advantageous contract for, apart from being financially generous ($76,250 per picture for seven weeks' work, anything over to be charged as overtime at the rate of $7,625 a week, and payment of his travelling expenses to Hollywood, the cost of a four-room suite at a Los Angeles hotel, all his meals and a car and chauffeur), it also gave him control over the stories he appeared in and the co-stars with whom he appeared. News of this must have been especially galling to Valentino, who saw Barrymore gain without the slightest effort the privilege he had fought so long and hard and at such personal cost to obtain.

Warners wanted his first film to be *Don Juan* with Mary Astor, but she was busy at First National and so he started on *The Sea Beast* (1926), an adaptation of Herman Melville's novel 'Moby Dick'. In accordance with the film-going public's adulation of and demand for romantic Barrymore, a love interest was written into the script and the heroine was played by Dolores Costello – the great love of Barrymore's life and eventually his third wife. He fell in love with her at first sight when she came to the Warners lot with her mother and sister for a screen-test. Their off-screen romance lent their on-screen love-scenes a particular passionate intensity, especially since their affair was not an easy, or fulfilled one. Mrs Costello (wife of Maurice Costello, an even earlier heart-throb) viewed their relationship with vast suspicion. Barrymore was forty-three and still married to, though legally separated from, Michael. Dolores was nineteen and obviously had a bright future ahead of her. Mrs Costello chaperoned her daughter with the unwinking vigilance of Cerberus and in consequence John must have seized on their screen embraces with particular fervour!

Barrymore's next film was *Don Juan* (1926), with Mary Astor as originally planned. She came to the film with hopes of continuing their romance, but soon apparently realized that it was not to be and Barrymore's final words on the subject to her were, allegedly, 'I'm just a son of a bitch.' Yet another romantic role followed, in a screen version of 'Manon Lescaut', *When a Man Loves* (1927), but this time with Dolores playing the heroine. Barrymore bent over backwards to make her performance outstanding, so much so that Ethel, seeing a preview, was shocked to see how her brother threw his part away and concentrated all attention on Dolores.

After this, he switched studios, from Warners to United Artists. Again he acted mainly to advance Dolores's career, planning to take her with him as a co-star. He signed the contract without any consultation and then discovered that it was far less advantageous financially than his previous one and, anyway, Dolores was firmly contracted to Warner Brothers. She could not move without massive legal penalties which United Artists were understandably very unwilling to incur. The three films he made with United Artists were pretty well the romantic mixture as before and none advanced his career much – all were Silent, and audiences were increasingly being seduced by Sound. *The Beloved Rogue* (1927) was the story of François Villon; *Tempest* (1928) was set during the Russian Revolution, with Barrymore in uniform and in prison; and *Eternal Love* (1929), his last Silent film, directed by Ernst Lubitsch was a tale of Swiss lovers finally overtaken by an avalanche. Perhaps the deprivation of not being able to work with Dolores was what tipped the matrimonial scales for Barrymore (he had at one time determined not to marry again). Whatever impelled him, in June 1928 he nerved himself to ask Michael for a divorce and five months later he and Dolores were married. During this period he continued to drink heavily with occasional lapses into sobriety. His other great pleasure in life, apart from Dolores and drink, was his boat 'The Mariner', bought with advice and assistance from Douglas Fairbanks. The newly-weds spent a three-month honeymoon cruising on her.

On their return Barrymore started work again – with Warner Brothers. He had re-signed with them for five pictures in two years and he started off auspiciously with an appearance in Technicolor, as Richard III, in Warners' *Show of Shows* (1929), in which the studio's stars went through their vocal paces. It was a marvellous Talkie début and launched him effortlessly into his career as a Sound star. This second Warner contract did not produce much of note – a Sound remake of *The Sea Beast*, with Joan Bennett (Dolores had retired into motherhood), and two versions of the Svengali story, of which the first, *Svengali* (1931), was the better, enabling Barrymore to indulge his taste for character parts.

Barrymore's most creative and impressive years in films were 1932 and 1933. Though he moved away from the Great Lover image, his early films in this period maintained his heart-throb appeal – especially *Grand Hotel* (1932), in which he played opposite Garbo in the romantic role of the Baron, the charming, debonair jewel-thief. Garbo took to him immediately and said later that she admired him for possessing the 'divine madness' of the great artist. This greatness was much in evidence at this time in films such as *State's Attorney* (1932), *Topaze* (1933), *Reunion in Vienna* (1933), and nowhere more dramatically than in George Cukor's 1932 film, *A Bill of Divorcement*. In it he played a man who escapes from a mental institution to find his wife (Billie Burke) divorced from him and about to remarry. His daughter (Katharine Hepburn in her screen début), fearing that his illness is hereditary, breaks off her own engagement to devote herself to caring for him. How far his father's fate influenced his playing of the role is unknown, but he gave a magnificent performance.

Counsellor at Law (1933), William Wyler's film about a rags-to-riches Jewish lawyer, marked the start of Barrymore's tragic downhill slide. It was during the reshooting of a scene from this film that he completely lost his lines and after fifty-six consecutive takes still could not find them. He played the scene perfectly the next morning – despite having been up most of the night calming a hysterical and drunk John Gilbert, who was a neighbour – but it was a straw in the wind and the repetition of the memory-failure during a screen-test for a proposed film of his Hamlet put paid to that project. His last great screen performance was in Howard Hawks's *Twentieth Century* (1934), the Hecht and MacArthur satire in which he played an egomaniac theatrical producer. In May 1934 Barrymore started on an RKO film, *A Hat, A Coat, A Glove*, but he was ill, drinking heavily and going through emotional traumas as his third marriage broke up, and he left the part, which was finally played by Ricardo Cortez.

There followed two years in the wilderness, both professionally and personally, before Barrymore returned to films as Mercutio in Cukor's 1937 *Romeo and Juliet*. He never again had a long-term starring contract and was increasingly dependent on prompt cards to get

Barrymore in *Sherlock Holmes* (1922) with Carol Dempster, filmed in England and Switzerland as well as in America. He went to Hollywood to make his next film.

him through his scenes, but he seemed driven by a desperate need to keep working – as well as by financial troubles. These years saw a fourth, frenetic and financially draining marriage, a misguided and pathetic return to the theatre, and towards the end a radio show which at least solved the problem of forgotten lines but which made a mockery of his former grandeur – and constant heavy drinking. He finally died of bronchial pneumonia in Hollywood's Presbyterian Hospital on 29 May, 1942.

Barrymore made *Beau Brummel* (1924) between his New York success in 'Hamlet' and its repetition in London. The arrogance of the ascendant fop and the pathos of his decline offered him fine dramatic opportunities. With him here is Carmel Myers.

The Great Profile, 1924.

Barrymore coached Dolores Costello personally for her role in *The Sea Beast* (1926). According to her sister, Helene, 'They fell in love with the sudden violence of an earthquake.'

Don Juan (1926) was the first film with a synchronized score. It also had a plethora of beautiful girls, one of whom was Dolores's sister and another the rejected Mary Astor.

JUNE 25¢

CLASSIC
PICTORIAL of SCREEN AND STAGE

Barrymore surrounded by men – an unusual sight, but the right profile is still well to the fore in this scene from *The Tempest* (1928).

The World's Leading Moving Picture Magazine N. S. E.

PHOTOPLAY

July 25c

Hattie
of
Hollywood
by
SAMUEL MERWIN

TEMPEST INMAN

Greatest Story of Movie Life Ever Written

Valentino in *The Four Horsemen of the Apocalypse* (1921).

Lobby-card for Fairbanks's *The Thief of Bagdad* (1924).

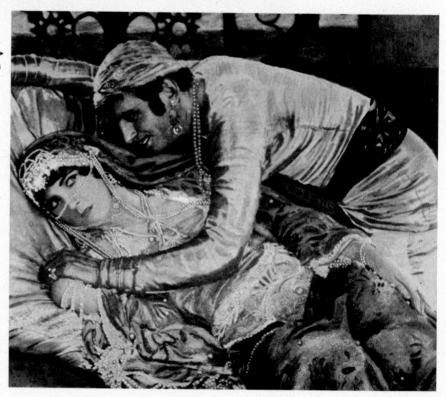

Barrymore wanted to do a
straightforward life of
François Villon, but the
script of *Beloved Rogue*
(1927) was cobbled together
to avoid charges of
plagiarization from an
existing play. The lady is
Marceline Day.

An American Citizen.
1914. FAMOUS PLAYERS. J.
Searle Dawley. With
Evelyn Moore, Ernest
Truex, Wellington Playter.
The Man from Mexico.
1914. FAMOUS PLAYERS.
Thomas Heffron. With
Pauline Neff, Harold
Lockwood, Wellington
Playter.
Are You A Mason? 1915.
FAMOUS PLAYERS. Thomas
Heffron. With Helen
Freeman, Harold
Lockwood, Charles
Dickson.
The Dictator. 1915.
FAMOUS PLAYERS. Oscar
Eagle. With Charlotte
Ives, Ruby Hoffman, Ivan
Simpson.
The Incorrigible Dukane.
1915. FAMOUS PLAYERS.
James Durkin. With W.T.
Carleton, Helen Weir,
Stewart Baird, William
MacDonald.
Nearly A King. 1916.
FAMOUS PLAYERS. Frederick
Thompson. With Katherine

← The Sound version of *The
Sea Beast* was actually
called *Moby Dick* (1930)
and Joan Bennett took
the role previously played
by Dolores Costello, by
this time the third
Mrs Barrymore.

As a jewel-thief and
charmer extraordinary,
Barrymore managed to
up-stage most of the cast
of *Grand Hotel* (1932)
but not Garbo! ↓

Harris, Russell Bassett.
The Lost Bridegroom.
1916. FAMOUS PLAYERS.
James Kirkwood. With
Katherine Harris, Ida
Darling, Edwin Sturgis, H.
Kirkland, Jack Dillon.
The Red Widow. 1916.
FAMOUS PLAYERS. James
Durkin. With Flora
Zabelle, Lillian Tucker,
John Hendricks, George E.
Mack.
**Raffles, the Amateur
Cracksman.** 1917.
LAWRENCE WEBER PHOTO-
DRAMA COMPANY. George
Irving. With Frank
Morgan, Evelyn Brent,
Christine Mayo, Nita
Allen, Mathilda Brundage,
Frederick Perry, H.
Cooper Cliffe.
On the Quiet. 1918.
FAMOUS PLAYERS-LASKY/
PARAMOUNT. Chester
Withey. With Lois
Meredith, J. W. Johnston.
Here Comes the Bride.
1919. FAMOUS PLAYERS-
LASKY/PARAMOUNT. John S.
Robertson. With Faire
Binney, Frank Losee,
Frances Kaye, Alfred
Hickman.
The Test of Honor. 1919.
FAMOUS PLAYERS-LASKY/
PARAMOUNT. John S.
Robertson. With Marcia
Manon, Constance Binney,
Robert Schable, J. W.
Johnston, Bigelow Cooper.
Dr Jekyll And Mr Hyde.
1920. FAMOUS PLAYERS-
LASKY. John S. Robertson.
With Martha Mansfield,
Brandon Hurst, Charles
Lane, J. Malcolm Dunn,
Cecil Clovelly, Nita Naldi,
George Stevens.
The Lotus Eater. 1921.
FIRST NATIONAL. Marshall
Neilan. With Colleen
Moore, Anna Q. Nilsson,
Ida Waterman, Frank
Currier.
Sherlock Holmes (UK
title: **Moriarty**). 1922.
GOLDWYN. Albert Parker.
With Roland Young, Carol
Dempster, Hedda Hopper,
Peggy Bayfield, Gustav
von Seyffertitz, Anders
Randolf, Robert Schable,
William Powell, Reginald
Denny, David Torrence,
Lumsden Hare, Louis
Wolheim.
Beau Brummel. 1924.
WARNER BROTHERS. Harry
Beaumont. With Mary
Astor, Willard Louis,
Irene Rich, Alec B. Francis,
Carmel Myers.
The Sea Beast. 1926.
WARNER BROTHERS. Millard
Webb. With Dolores
Costello, George O'Hara,
Sam Baker, Sojin.
Don Juan. 1926. WARNER
BROTHERS. Alan Crosland.
With Mary Astor, Willard
Louis, Estelle Taylor,
Warner Oland, Montagu
Love, Helene Costello,
Jane Winton, Myrna Loy,
Phyllis Haver, Nigel de
Brulier, Hedda Hopper.
When A Man Loves (UK
title: **His Lady**). 1927.
WARNER BROTHERS. Alan
Crossland. With Dolores
Costello, Sam de Grasse,

Warner Oland, Eugenie
Besserer.
The Beloved Rogue. 1927.
UNITED ARTISTS. Alan
Crosland. With Conrad
Veidt, Marceline Day, W.
Lawson Butt, Henry
Victor, Slim Summerville.
Tempest. 1928. UNITED
ARTISTS. Sam Taylor. With
Camilla Horn, Louis
Wolheim, George Fawcett,
Ulrich Hapt.
Eternal Love. 1929.
UNITED ARTISTS. Ernst
Lubitsch. With Camilla
Horn, Victor Varconi,
Hobart Bosworth, Evelyn
Selbie, Mona Rico.
The Show of Shows. 1929.
WARNER BROTHERS. John
Adolfi. First Talkie. With
all-star cast.
General Crack. 1930.
WARNER BROTHERS. Alan
Crosland. With Lowell
Sherman, Marian Nixon,
Armida, Hobart Bosworth.
The Man from Blankleys.
1930. WARNER BROTHERS.
Alfred E. Green. With
Loretta Young, William
Austin, Emily Fitzroy, Dick
Henderson, Dale Fuller,
Louis Carver.
Moby Dick. 1930. WARNER
BROTHERS. Lloyd Bacon.
With Joan Bennett, Lloyd
Hughes, May Boley,
Walter Long, Tom O'Brien,
Nigel de Brulier, Noble
Johnson, William Walling,
Virginia Sale, Jack Curtis,
John Ince.
Svengali. 1931. WARNER
BROTHERS. Archie Mayo.
With Marian Marsh,
Bramwell Fletcher, Donald
Crisp, Lumsden Hare,
Carmel Myers.
The Mad Genius. 1931.
WARNER BROTHERS.
Michael Curtiz. With
Donald Cook, Marian
Marsh, Carmel Myers,
Charles Butterworth, Luis
Alberni, Boris Karloff.
Arsène Lupin. 1932. MGM.
Jack Conway. With Lionel
Barrymore, Karen Morley,
John Miljan, Tully
Marshall, Henry Armetta.
Grand Hotel. 1932. MGM.
Edmund Goulding. With
Greta Garbo, Lionel
Barrymore, Joan Crawford,
Wallace Beery, Lewis
Stone, Jean Hersholt,
Robert McWade, Rafaela
Ottiano.
State's Attorney (UK
title: **Cardigan's Last
Case**). 1932. RKO. George
Archainbaud. With Helen
Twelvetrees, William Boyd,
Jill Esmond, Mary Duncan.
A Bill of Divorcement.
1932. RKO. George Cukor.
With Katharine Hepburn,
Billie Burke, David
Manners, Bramwell
Fletcher, Henry
Stephenson, Paul
Cavanagh, Elizabeth
Patterson.
**Rasputin and the
Empress** (UK title:
**Rasputin, the Mad
Monk**). 1932. MGM. Richard
Boleslawski. With Ethel
Barrymore, Lionel
Barrymore, Diana
Wynyard, Ralph Morgan,

C. Henry Gordon, Edward
Arnold.
Topaze. 1933. RKO. Harry
D. D'Arrast. With Myrna
Loy, Albert Conti, Luis
Alberni, Jobyna Howland,
Jackie Searle.
Reunion in Vienna. 1933.
MGM. Sidney Franklin.
With Diana Wynyard,
Frank Morgan, Henry
Travers, May Robson,
Eduardo Ciannelli, Una
Merkel.
Dinner at Eight. 1933.
MGM. George Cukor. With
Lionel Barrymore, Billie
Burke, Marie Dressler,
Jean Harlow, Wallace
Beery, Lee Tracy, Edmund
Lowe, Madge Evans, Jean
Hersholt.
Night Flight. 1933. MGM.
Clarence Brown. With
Lionel Barrymore, Clark
Gable, Helen Hayes,
Robert Montgomery,
Myrna Loy.
Counsellor at Law. 1933.
UNIVERSAL. William Wyler.
With Bebe Daniels, Onslow
Stevens, Melvyn Douglas,
Isabel Jewell, Thelma
Todd.
Long Lost Father. 1934.
RKO. Ernest B. Schoedsack.
With Helen Chandler,
Donald Cook, Alan
Mowbray, Claude King.
Twentieth Century. 1934.
COLUMBIA. Howard Hawks.
With Carole Lombard,
Walter Connolly, Roscoe
Karns.
Romeo and Juliet. 1936.
MGM. George Cukor. With
Norma Shearer, Leslie
Howard, Edna May Oliver,
Basil Rathbone, C. Aubrey
Smith, Andy Devine, Ralph
Forbes, Reginald Denny,
Conway Tearle.
Maytime. 1937. MGM.
Robert Z. Leonard. With
Jeanette Macdonald,
Nelson Eddy, Tom Brown,
Lynn Carver.
**Bulldog Drummond
Comes Back.** 1937.
PARAMOUNT. Louis King.
With John Howard, Louise
Campbell, Reginald Denny,
E. E. Clive, John Sutton.
Night Club Scandal. 1937.
PARAMOUNT. Ralph
Murphy. With Lynne
Overman, Charles
Bickford, Louis Campbell,
J. Carrol Naish.
**Bulldog Drummond's
Revenge.** 1938.
PARAMOUNT. Louis King.
With John Howard, Louis
Campbell, Reginald Denny,
E. E. Clive, John Sutton.
True Confession. 1937.
Paramount. Wesley
Ruggles. With Carole
Lombard, Fred
MacMurray, Una Merkel,
Porter Hall, Edgar
Kennedy, Lynne Overman,
Fritz Feld, Hattie
McDaniel.
Romance in the Dark.
1938. PARAMOUNT. H. C.
Potter. With Gladys
Swarthout, John Boles,
Claire Dodd, Fritz Feld,
Curt Bois.
**Bulldog Drummond's
Peril.** 1938. PARAMOUNT.
James Hogan. With John

Howard, Louis Campbell,
E. E. Clive, Porter Hall,
Elizabeth Patterson, Nydia
Westman, Halliwell
Hobbes.
Marie Antoinette. 1938.
MGM. W. S. Van Dyke. With
Norma Shearer, Tyrone
Power, Robert Morley,
Anita Louise, Joseph
Schildkraut, Gladys
George, Henry Stephenson,
Cora Witherspoon,
Reginald Gardiner, Henry
Daniell, Alma Kruger,
Joseph Calleia.
Spawn of the North. 1938.
PARAMOUNT. Henry
Hathaway. With George
Raft, Henry Fonda,
Dorothy Lamour, Louis
Platt, Akim Tamiroff,
Lynne Overman, Fuzzy
Knight.
Hold That Co-Ed (UK
title: **Hold That Girl**).
1938. TWENTIETH CENTURY-
FOX. George Marshall.
With George Murphy,
Marjorie Weaver, Joan
Davis, Jack Haley, Ruth
Terry, Donald Meek.
The Great Man Votes.
1939. RKO. Garson Kanin.
With Peter Holden,
Virginia Weidler,
Katherine Alexander,
Donald MacBride.
Midnight. 1939. PARA-
MOUNT. Mitchell Leisen.
With Claudette Colbert,
Don Ameche, Francis
Lederer, Mary Astor,
Elaine Barrie, Hedda
Hopper, Rex O'Malley.
The Great Profile. 1940.
TWENTIETH CENTURY-FOX.
Walter Lang. With Mary
Beth Hughes, Gregory
Ratoff, John Payne, Anne
Baxter, Lionel Atwill.
The Invisible Woman.
1941. UNIVERSAL. Edward
Sutherland. With Virginia
Bruce, John Howard,
Charles Ruggles, Oscar
Homolka, Donald
MacBride, Edward Brophy.
World Premiere. 1941.
PARAMOUNT. Ted Tetzlaff.
With Frances Farmer,
Eugene Pallette, Virginia
Dale, Ricardo Cortez, Sig
Rumann, Don Castle,
Fritz Feld.
Playmates. 1941. RKO.
David Butler. With Kay
Kyser, Lupe Velez, Ginny
Simms, May Robson, Patsy
Kelly, Peter Lind Hayes,
George Cleveland, Alice
Fleming.

John Gilbert

When Valentino died his place as *the* Great Lover of the screen was immediately filled by John Gilbert, whose throbbing on-screen ardour had already won him fame and popularity as a heart-throb in films like Elinor Glyn's *His Hour* (1924) and Stroheim's *The Merry Widow* (1925). He was, however, a Latin Lover with a difference. He smiled a great deal rather than smouldering, and, instead of a smooth shining cap of hair close to his head, he sported an unruly, appealing mop of dark curls. His love-making lacked Valentino's menace but more than compensated for this by its impetuosity and sincerity. For, as Alexander Walker says, while Valentino was a romantic by adoption, John Gilbert was 'a romantic by conviction'. His was an impulsive passionate temperament off-screen as well as on, and this conveyed itself to audiences, who were captivated by the powerful display of sensibilities allied to his obvious physical charms. If he had any menace, it was perhaps in the rakishness of his moustache (grown to counter-balance a rather bulbous nose). The quality contrasted appealingly with his youthful impatience and sincerity in love-making. It was an intriguing combination.

Sadly, however, John Gilbert is nowadays more remembered for his collapse as a great star than for the high points of his career. The laughter of the audience when he uttered his first words on the screen ('I love you, I love you, I love you') in *His Glorious Night* (1929) and his subsequent stampede into self-doubt, disillusionment, drink and death, at the age of thirty-eight, are a well-established part of the Hollywood myth. It seems all too appropriate that such a fate should be the lot of the twentieth-century Olympians, the Hollywood superstars. Only in a bizarre world like Hollywood could the mere act of speech have entailed such a terrible downfall, and yet there is of course far more to it than that – as we shall see later.

John Gilbert was born John Pringle (like Fairbanks he adopted the name of one of his mother's other husbands) in Logan, Utah, in 1897. His father was leader of a small theatrical company and his mother one of his actresses. He had an unsettled childhood and early adolescence, moving about the States with the company, attending (briefly) a military college in California, and then working as a rubber-goods salesman. He was mad about the movies, however, and in 1915, when he was eighteen, persuaded his father to write to an old friend who was directing for Triangle. To his delight he was taken on as an extra at Inceville, Santa Monica, where he graduated eventually to bit parts and in 1917 to the lead in *Princess of the Dark*. The plot of the film has a double irony in view of his subsequent career for in it he played a crippled boy in love with a blind girl who,

when she recovers her sight, takes one look at him and recoils in disgust, leaving him to die of a broken heart. But he was mostly, in these pre-Valentino days, cast as the villain or the Other Man.

In 1918 Triangle changed hands and his acting contract was dropped. He turned to script-writing and was taken on by a new company called Paralta, who used several of his scripts. But these were the lean years for him. He volunteered for military service and was rejected by both the navy (on physical grounds) and the air force (on educational grounds). The army was not so choosy but before he could report for duty the war ended. His first marriage swiftly foundered and ended in divorce.

In 1919 came his breakthrough – one of his scripts, *The Great Redeemer* (1920), caught the attention of director Maurice Tourneur, then at the height of his career. He hired Gilbert to rewrite it, to assist him direct it and to star in it. Two further films working with Tourneur at Paramount established him as a Hollywood name and he was offered the chance to direct on his own. His first effort was not a success and he signed a three-year acting contract with Fox in 1921. If not quite so lean as earlier times, these were not happy years for him. He liked none of the films he did, saying later that they were all 'cheaply made and badly done'. They included *Shame* (1921) with Anna May Wong, *The Count of Monte Cristo* and *Honor First*, both with Renée Adorée, and yet another attempt to cash in on the sheik craze, *Arabian Love* (all three in 1922).

He had married again – a young actress called Leatrice Joy who at this time was well on the road to stardom. The disparity in the progress of their careers caused a vast amount of marital disharmony and, on Gilbert's side, drinking. They were divorced in 1924 with some acrimony, though when Gilbert achieved fame and fortune they became friends.

Towards the end of the Fox contract, in 1924, Gilbert's career started on an upsurge with such films as *Just Off Broadway*, *The Wolf Man* with Norma Shearer and *The Lone Chance*. When his contract expired, Thalberg at MGM offered him a five-year contract, convinced that he had a star of great potential on his hands – especially in view of the resounding success of Valentino's dark exotic looks. MGM concentrated on highlighting Gilbert's romantic, swashbuckling characteristics, and, as chance would have it, his first film for them was *His Hour*, an adaptation of Elinor Glyn's novel. The High Priestess of Romance decided to take a hand in the transformation of Gilbert into a Great Lover, much as she had proffered advice and assistance (ghosting articles for fan-magazines) to Valentino himself. Gilbert played a passionate Russian aristocrat, all flashing teeth and eyes, unruly locks and boudoir athletics, and went down very well with audiences, especially the ladies. He played lead parts in three more films in quick succession – *He Who Gets Slapped* and *The Snob* (both 1924), and *The Wife of the Centaur* (1925) – before, in

1925, he made the two films which assured his place among the Hollywood greats.

First he played Prince Danilo in Erich von Stroheim's version of *The Merry Widow* (1925), opposite Mae Murray. The film was one of the year's biggest box-office successes: a particularly praiseworthy achievement, one might be forgiven for thinking, for a screen musical – with no music! But greater things were in store – in the shape of King Vidor's mammoth production of *The Big Parade* (1925), in which Gilbert played Jim Apperson, the Average Man, in uniform (without the moustache) but not the spick-and-span outfit of Ruritanian romances. His part required positively ill-fitting kit and plenty of grime and sweat. Vidor wasn't keen on Gilbert for the part originally. Not only did he feel that he was too smooth and sophisticated an actor, but, according to Vidor himself, he felt it was unfair to expect Gilbert to change his screen image so drastically just as it was becoming well established. Thalberg insisted, however, and the film – and Gilbert's performance – were outstandingly successful.

Two lavish costume-dramas, *La Bohème* with Lillian Gish and *Bardelys the Magnificent* (both 1926), set the seal on his stardom. Fan-mail poured in, and his name was constantly in the gossip columns. Valentino's sudden death brought the heir-apparent into the limelight – Gilbert was King of the Heart-Throbs and in 1927 a fitting consort for him appeared in the shape of Greta Garbo.

Theirs was one of the most widely publicized of all screen liaisons, both on and off the set. Garbo's reputation as a lover of silence and solitude was well under way by this time. Gilbert's off-screen personality has been variously described as unpredictable, dynamic, tempestuous and convivial. 'Obviously,' as Norman Zierold says in his biography of Garbo, 'he was the perfect companion for a recluse.' Clarence Brown, the director of their first film together, *Flesh and the Devil* (1927), declared himself convinced of their immediate and mutual passion: 'They are in that blissful state of love so like a rosy cloud.' This and similar remarks made during the film launched it on a tidal wave of publicity which not only made Garbo into a great star but which certainly introduced a new and electrifying type of love-making to the screen. Quite apart from the fact that the love-scenes were among the first in which both man and woman are daringly horizontal, Gilbert and Garbo undoubtedly evoked a strong erotic aura and created a singular sexual relationship in which her powerful sensuality feeds on his passive, sensitive emotions. Gilbert's acting had its roots in a tremendously passionate intensity and when it was matched by Garbo's deeply felt emotionalism they made the audience feel like voyeurs. This film and their next two together, *Love* (1927) and *A Woman of Affairs* (1929), established them as the greatest romantic screen-couple the world has ever known.

Their off-screen affair finally foundered in 1929, but not before both had enjoyed a great deal of the 'difference' in each other. Gilbert drew Garbo out of her shell, introduced her to a wide and interesting new circle of acquaintances, charmed her with his flamboyant life-style and proposed several times. She in turn alternately charmed and infuriated him with her unpredictability, reticence and candour – and kept on turning him down. On one occasion he is said to have persuaded her to elope with him to Mexico. At Santa Ana, however, where they stopped for lunch, she took fright and locked herself in the ladies room of a near-by hotel before taking the train back to Hollywood alone. By the time they came to film *A Woman of Affairs* it was all over, and Garbo is alleged to have said, 'God, I wonder what I ever saw in him. Oh well, I guess he was pretty.' Gilbert consoled himself by marrying Ina Claire, a successful stage-actress.

The years 1927 to 1929 were golden ones for Gilbert. In addition to his films with Garbo, he made several other successful movies – *The Show* with Renée Adorée, *Twelve Miles Out* with Joan Crawford, *Man, Woman and Sin* with Jeanne Eagels (all 1927), and *The Cossacks* (1928). During the filming of the latter he displayed *par excellence* his penchant for living his parts to the hilt off-screen and peopled his house with expatriate Russians who served quantities of vodka and caviar and played balalaika music at mealtimes. These too were the years when Sound was in the air – a challenge that became ever larger and ever more insistent. Gilbert's last Silent film, *Desert Nights*, was released in 1929 and it was obvious that he could remain silent no longer. The craze for Talking pictures was sweeping the country.

He signed an amazingly munificent new contract with MGM in 1929 and started work on his first Sound film, an adaptation of

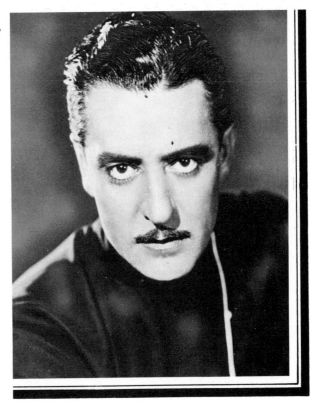

John Gilbert, the Great Lover whose declaration, 'I love you, I love you, I love you,' brought his career crashing down about his ears.

Tolstoy's *Redemption* (1930). It was a heavy film and, faced with the undeniable fact of Gilbert's light, rather high voice, the studios decided to shelve it temporarily. He in fact made his Talkie début in *The Hollywood Revue of 1929*, with Norma Shearer in the balcony scene from 'Romeo and Juliet'. It was not exactly a howling success, but neither was it total failure. This fate was reserved for his first starring appearance in a Talking film – *His Glorious Night* (1929), a lightweight romance based on Ferenc Molnar's play 'Olympia'. The audience reactions ranged from embarrassed titters to downright hearty laughter and Gilbert's bright star began its tragic and swift eclipse.

This terrifying public response to their once-adored idol undoubtedly did not rest solely on the quality of his voice which was, as later films confirmed, a soft, pleasant and quite acceptable tenor. His downfall seems in retrospect to have had two main causes – a deep and increasingly bitter rift with MGM in general and Louis B. Mayer in particular, and the totally differing techniques involved in acting for Silent and Sound films.

The generous terms of Gilbert's new MGM contract (four pictures – two a year for a quarter of a million dollars each) and the extraordinary lack of any kind of voice test can both be traced to his innocent part in an abortive business manœuvre by Nicholas Schenk, head of MGM's East Coast financial operations. Schenk wanted to sell a controlling interest in MGM to William Fox over the heads of the West Coast studio bosses, especially Mayer. It was essential for him to have a superstar of Gilbert's drawing-power to bargain with but Gilbert, his MGM contract drawing to a close, was thinking of joining United Artists. To keep him, Schenk offered an amazingly advantageous deal, without consulting Mayer or Thalberg. The Fox negotiations fell through and a large part of Mayer's resentment when he found out about it must have been directed at Gilbert. There is also a story that Mayer, a firm believer in matriarch worship, once physically set about Gilbert when he heard him refer to his own mother casually as a whore. Neither incident tells the whole story though. Mayer may have been vengeful and mother-fixated, but he had too much business acumen deliberately to kill the goose that had been laying the golden eggs.

The real cause seems, sadly, to have been Gilbert's own inability to adapt the bravura acting style and flamboyant screen image which had brought him such glory in the Silent days to the more restrained and realistic demands of Talking pictures. In Alexander Walker's words, 'speech made some of the most potent archetypes of the Silent movies into obsolete caricatures almost overnight', and the Great Lover was the first to go. The overblown, romantic gestures of earlier days seemed ridiculous alongside the sense of reality induced by lifelike dialogue.

Gilbert's acting, and indeed his life, had never been marked by any great restraint.

A silly script and primitive sound-recording methods combined with an out-dated acting technique, which he probably couldn't and wouldn't have changed, to bring to a close his reign as one of Hollywood's greatest romantic stars.

He marked time, humiliated and with his self-confidence seeping rapidly away, till his contract expired, making films such as *Gentleman's Fate* and *The Phantom of Paris* (both 1931) with good directors, good recording equipment and good parts. But the stuffing seemed to have been knocked out of him by that one fateful event. He was drinking heavily and, ironically, his stage-trained wife was doing very well – they divorced in 1931. He married again in 1932 but that too ended in divorce in 1934.

Then came his last big chance. Garbo descended like a *dea ex machina* from a year's sabbatical in Sweden and insisted on him as her leading man in *Queen Christina* (1933). She rejected Fredric March, the young Laurence Olivier and, despite her good experience with him in *Grand Hotel*, Barrymore. Her loyalty reflected her gratitude to the man who had enabled her to rise to the heights – and perhaps a gentle affection for a past love. By then, however, his confidence was so dissipated and his downward path so marked that even this golden opportunity to re-establish himself passed him by. He was competent, no more, in the part. His last film, *The Captain Hates the Sea* (1934), gave him fourth billing as a drunken Hollywood writer attempting, vainly, to dry out and restore his creative impulses. He died in 1936, ostensibly of a heart-attack, but in fact of alcohol, forgotten by the thousands of fans who, had he died seven years earlier, might have given him a farewell to rival that of Valentino.

John Gilbert's influence on the screen lovers of the 'thirties and 'forties was incalculable. He created a fresh pattern for romantic heroes – that of wholesome strength and direct, sincere passion which won over rather than alienated the male sector of his audiences. He didn't make them feel inadequate as Valentino had done. His tragedy is that ultimately he himself felt inadequate – and that he could not bear.

Gilbert (a dashing Russian nobleman) threatens Aileen Pringle in *His Hour* (1924). Most of the film, however, was spent wooing her – intensely and impetuously.

King Vidor's *The Big Parade* (1926) 'dirtied' Gilbert up, gave him a chance to show his acting ability and broke box-office records, grossing $5 million world-wide.

By the time he made *The Merry Widow* (1925) with Mae Murray, directed by Erich von Stroheim, Gilbert had reached quite dizzy heights of success. 'The whole thing became too fantastic for me to comprehend,' he wrote in 1928. ↓

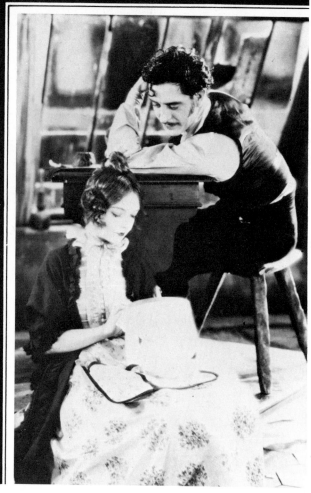

Gilbert and Lillian Gish in
La Bohème (1926). 'Oh
dear,' Miss Gish later
reported herself as
thinking during filming,
'I've got to go through
another day of kissing
John Gilbert.'

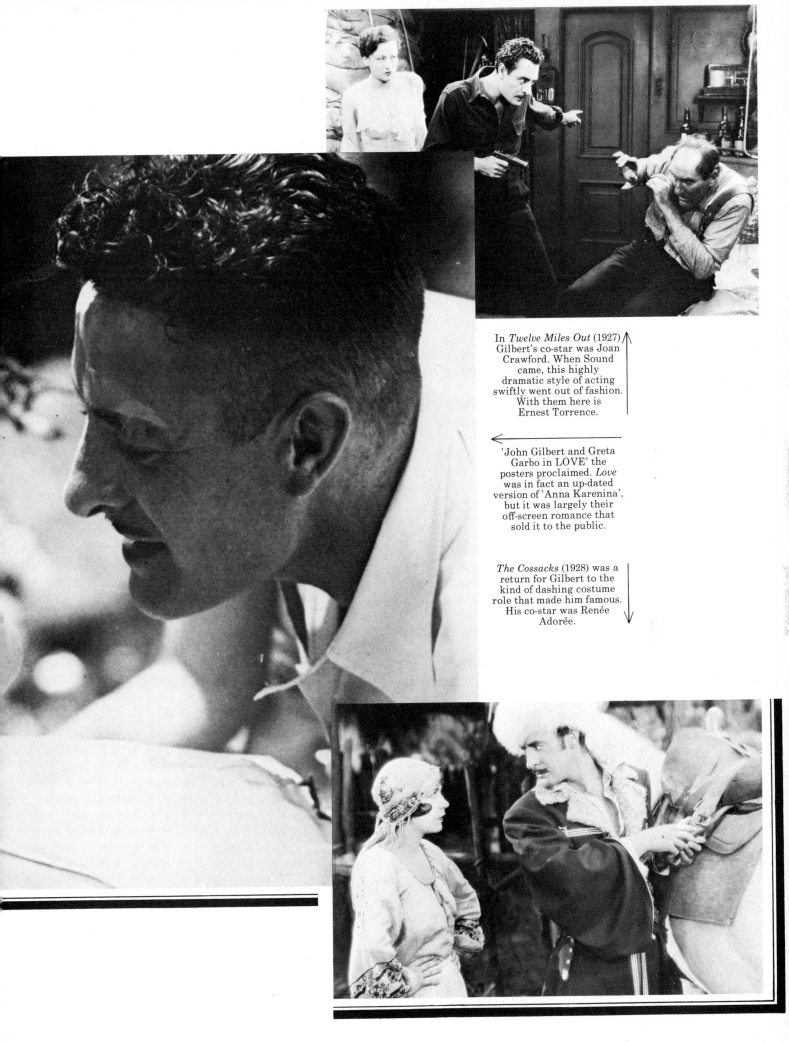

In *Twelve Miles Out* (1927)
Gilbert's co-star was Joan
Crawford. When Sound
came, this highly
dramatic style of acting
swiftly went out of fashion.
With them here is
Ernest Torrence.

'John Gilbert and Greta
Garbo in LOVE' the
posters proclaimed. *Love*
was in fact an up-dated
version of 'Anna Karenina',
but it was largely their
off-screen romance that
sold it to the public.

The Cossacks (1928) was a
return for Gilbert to the
kind of dashing costume
role that made him famous.
His co-star was Renée
Adorée.

By the time Garbo and Gilbert made *A Woman of Affairs* (1929), their romance was fading fast, and it showed in this adaptation of Michael Arlen's novel 'The Green Hat', though not in this picture.

This time the billing read 'Greta Garbo in *Queen Christina* with John Gilbert'. Six years earlier, in *The Flesh and the Devil*, the positions had been reversed, but by 1933 Gilbert was a major casualty of the coming of Sound and although only thirty-six was a bare three years away from his death.

John Gilbert

Hell's Hinges. 1916. INCE-TRIANGLE. William S. Hart. With William S. Hart, Clara Williams, Jack Standing, Alfred Hollingsworth, Robert McKim, Louise Glaum, Jean Hersholt.
Bullets and Brown Eyes. 1916. TRIANGLE (INCE). Scott Sidney. With William Desmond, Jean Hersholt.
The Apostle of Vengeance. 1916. TRIANGLE (INCE). Cliff Smith. With William S. Hart, Jean Hersholt.
The Phantom. 1916. TRIANGLE (INCE). With Frank Keenan, Enid Markey.
The Eye of the Night. 1916. TRIANGLE (INCE). With Margery Wilson, William H. Thompson.
Shell 43. TRIANGLE. Reginald Barker. With H. B. Warner, Enid Markey.
Princess of the Dark. 1917. TRIANGLE. Charles Miller. With Enid Bennett, Alfred Vosburg.
Happiness. 1917. TRIANGLE. With Enid Bennett, Andrew Arbuckle.
The Millionaire Vagrant. 1917. TRIANGLE. Victor Schertzinger. With Charles Ray, Sylvia Breamer.
Hater of Men. 1917. TRIANGLE. With Bessie Barriscale, Charles K. French.
The Mother Instinct. 1917. TRIANGLE. Roy William Neil and Lambert Hillyer. With Margery Wilson.
The Devil Dodger. 1917. TRIANGLE. With Roy Stewart, Caroline Wagner.
Golden Rule Kate. 1917. TRIANGLE. With Louise Glaum, Gertrude Claire.
Doing Her Bit. 1917. TRIANGLE.
Nancy Comes Home. 1918. TRIANGLE (INCE). With George Pearce, Myrtle Lind.
Sons of Men. 1918. PARALTA. With J. Warren Kerrigan.
Three X Gordon. 1918. PARALTA. Ernest C. Warde. With J. Warren Kerrigan, Lois Wilson, Don Bailey.
Shackled. 1918. PARALTA. With Lawson W. Bett.
More Trouble. 1918. ANDERSON-BRUNTON COMPANY. Ernest C. Warde. With Frank Keenan, Joseph Dowling, Jack Rollins.
Wedlock. 1918. APEX FILMS. Wallace Worsley. With Louise Glaum, Bessie Barriscale.
The Mask. 1918. TRIANGLE. With Claire Anderson.
The Dawn of Under-standing. 1918. VITAGRAPH. David Smith and Charles R. Seeling.

With Bessie Love.

The White Heather. 1919. TOURNEUR-HILLER/WILK. Maurice Tourneur. With Mabel Ballin, Spottiswoode Aitken, Gibson Gowland.

The Busher. 1919. TRIANGLE (INCE). Jerome Storm. With Charles Ray, Colleen Moore, Margaret Livingstone.

Widow By Proxy. 1919. FAMOUS PLAYERS-LASKY. Walter Edwards. With Marguerite Clark, Nigel Barrie, Gertrude Claire.

The Red Viper. 1919. TYRAD PICTURES. Jacques Tyrol. With Ruth Stonehouse, Gareth Hughes, Irma Harrison.

Heart O' the Hills. 1919. FIRST NATIONAL. Joseph de Grasse and Sidney Franklin. With Mary Pickford, Sam de Grasse, Claire McDowell, William Bainbridge.

Should A Woman Tell? 1919. METRO. John E. Ince. With Alice Lake, Jack Mulhall, Lydia Knott, Richard Headrick.

The Servant in the House. 1920. FILM BOOKING OFFICE. Jack Conway. With Clara Horton, Jean Hersholt.

The Great Redeemer. 1920. METRO. Maurice Tourneur and Clarence Brown. Gilbert co-wrote script. With House Peters, Marjorie Daw, Joseph E. Singleton, Jack McDonald.

The White Circle. 1920. FAMOUS PLAYERS-LASKY/PARAMOUNT. Maurice Tourneur. Co-adapted by Gilbert. With Janice Wilson, Jack McDonald, Spottiswoode Aitken.

Deep Waters. 1920. FAMOUS PLAYERS-LASKY/PARAMOUNT. Maurice Tourneur. Screen-play by Gilbert. With Barbara Bedford, Florence Deshon, Jack McDonald, Henry F. Woodward.

Shame. 1921. FOX. Emmett J. Flynn. With Mickey More, Frankie Lee, George Siegmann, Anna May Wong.

Ladies Must Live. 1921. FAMOUS PLAYERS-LASKY/PARAMOUNT. George Loane Tucker. With Robert Ellis, Mahlon Hamilton, Betty Compson, Leatrice Joy, Hardee Kirkland, Gibson Gowland.

Gleam O'Dawn. 1922. FOX. John Francis Dillon. With Barbara Bedford, James Farley, John Gough, Wilson Hummel.

Truxton King. 1923. FOX. Jerome Storm. With Ruth Clifford, Mickey Moore, Otis Harlan, Frank Leigh.

Arabian Love. 1922. FOX. Jerome Storm. With Barbara Bedford, Barbara La Marr, Herschel Mayall.

The Yellow Stain. 1922. FOX. John Francis Dillon. With Claire Anderson, John P. Lockney, Mark Fenton, Robert Daly.

Honor First. 1922. FOX.

Jerome Storm. With Renée Adorée, Hardee Kirkland, Shannon Day, Wilson Hummel.

The Count of Monte Cristo. 1922. FOX. Emmett J. Flynn. With Renée Adorée, Estelle Taylor, Virginia Brown Faire, Robert McKim, George Siegmann, Spottiswoode Aitken.

Calvert's Valley. 1922. FOX. John Francis Dillon. With Sylvia Breamer, Philo McCullough, Herschel Mayall.

The Love Gambler. 1922. FOX. Joseph Franz. With Carmel Myers, Bruce Gordon, Cap Anderson, William Lawrence.

The Glory of Love. 1923. MAURICE TOURNEUR PRODUCTIONS. Maurice Tourneur. With Lon Chaney, Mildred Manning, J. Farrell MacDonald.

The Madness Of Youth. 1923. FOX. Jerome Storm. With Billie Dove, George K. Arthur, Donald Hatswell, Julanne Johnston.

Saint Elmo. 1923. FOX. Jerome Storm. With Bessie Love, Barbara La Marr, Warner Baxter.

The Exiles. 1923. FOX. Edmund Mortimer. With Margaret Fielding, John Webb Dillon, Betty Bouton.

Cameo Kirby. 1923. FOX. John Ford. With Gertrude Olmstead, Jean Arthur, Alan Hale, Eric Mayne.

A California Romance. 1923. FOX. Jerome Storm. With George Siegmann, Estelle Taylor.

Just Off Broadway. 1924. FOX. Edmund Mortimer. With Marian Nixon, Pierre Gendron, Trilby Clark.

The Wolf Man. 1924. FOX. Edmund Mortimer. With Norma Shearer, Eugene Pallette, Thomas Mills, Alma Francis.

A Man's Mate. 1924. FOX. Edmund Mortimer. With Renée Adorée, Thomas Mills, Patterson Dial, Wilfred North, James Neill, Jack Giddings.

Romance Ranch. 1924. FOX. Howard Mitchell. With Virginia Brown Faire, John Miljan, Bernard Seigel, Evelyn Selbie.

The Lone Chance. 1924. FOX. Howard Mitchell. With Evelyn Brent, John Miljan, Edwin Booth Tilton.

His Hour. 1924. MGM. King Vidor. With Aileen Pringle, Emily Fitzroy, Lawrence Grant, Dale Fuller.

He Who Gets Slapped. 1924. MGM. Victor Seastrom. With Norma Shearer, Lon Chaney, Tully Marshall, Ford Sterling.

The Snob. 1924. MGM. Monta Bell. With Norma Shearer, Conrad Nagel, Phyllis Haver, Hedda Hopper.

Wife of the Centaur. 1924. MGM. King Vidor. With Eleanor Boardman, Aileen Pringle, Kate Price.

The Merry Widow. 1925. MGM. Eroch von Stroheim. With Mae Murray, Roy D'Arcy, Tully Marshall, Albert Conti, George Fawcett, Josephine Cromwell.

The Big Parade. 1925. MGM. King Vidor. With Renée Adorée, Hobart Bosworth, Claire McDowell, Claire Adams, Robert Ober, Tom O'Brien, Karl Dane, Rosita Marstini.

La Bohème. 1926. MGM. King Vidor. With Lillian Gish, Renée Adorée, Roy D'Arcy, Edward Everett Horton, Karl Dane, Valentina Zimina.

Bardelys the Magnificent. 1926. MGM. King Vidor. With Eleanor Boardman, Roy D'Arcy, Emily Fitzroy, George K. Arthur, Karl Dane, Theodore von Eltz.

Flesh and the Devil. 1927. MGM. Clarence Brown. With Greta Garbo, Lars Hanson, Barbara Kent, William Orlamond, George Fawcett, Eugenie Besserer, Marc McDermott, Marcelle Corday.

The Show. 1927. MGM. Tod Browning. With Renée Adorée, Lionel Barrymore, Edward Connelly, Gertrude Short.

Twelve Miles Out. 1927. MGM. Jack Conway. With Joan Crawford, Eileen Percy, Ernest Torrence, Edward Earle, Gwen Lee, Dorothy Sebastian, Paulette Duval.

Love. 1927. MGM. Edmund Goulding. With Greta Garbo, Philippe de Lacey, George Fawcett, Emily Fitzroy, Brandon Hurst.

Man, Woman and Sin. 1927. MGM. Monta Bell. With Jeanne Eagels, Gladys Brockwell, Marc McDermott, Margaret Lee, Charles K. French.

The Cossacks. 1928. MGM. George Hill. With Renée Adorée, Ernest Torrence, Nils Asther, Paul Hurst, Dale Fuller, Mary Alden.

Four Walls. 1928. MGM. William Nigh. With Joan Crawford, Carmel Myers, Robert E. O'Connor, Louis Natheaux.

Masks of the Devil. 1928. MGM. Victor Seastrom. With Eva von Berne, Ralph Forbes, Alma Rubens, Theodore Roberts, Frank Reicher, Polly Ann Young.

A Woman of Affairs. 1929. MGM. Clarence Brown. With Greta Garbo, Douglas Fairbanks Jr, Lewis Stone, John Mack Brown, Dorothy Sebastian, Hobart Bosworth.

Desert Nights. 1929. MGM. William Nigh. With Mary Nolan, Ernest Torrence.

The Hollywood Revue of 1929. 1929. MGM. Charles

Reisner. First Talkie. With all-star cast.

His Glorious Night. 1929. MGM. Lionel Barrymore. With Catherine Dale Owen, Nancy O'Neil, Hedda Hopper, Gustav von Seyffertitz.

Redemption. 1930. MGM. Fred Niblo. With Eleanor Boardman, Renée Adorée, Conrad Nagel, Claire McDowell, Nigel de Brulier.

Way for a Sailor. 1930. MGM. Sam Wood. With Wallace Beery, Jim Tully, Leila Hyams, Polly Moran, Doris Lloyd.

Gentleman's Fate. 1931. MGM. Mervyn Le Roy. With Leila Hyams, Anita Page, Louis Wolheim, Marie Prevost, Ralph Ince, John Miljan.

The Phantom of Paris (French title: **Cheri Bibi**). 1931. MGM. John Stuart Robertson. With Leila Hyams, Lewis Stone, C. Aubrey Smith, Jean Hersholt.

West of Broadway. 1932. MGM. Harry Beaumont. With Madge Evans, Lois Moran, Frank Conroy, Ralph Bellamy, Gwen Lee, Ruth Renick, Hedda Hopper.

Downstairs. 1932. MGM. Monta Bell. Screen-play by Gilbert. With Virginia Bruce, Olga Baclanova, Paul Lukas, Reginald Owen.

Fast Workers. 1933. MGM. Tod Browning. With Virginia Cherrill, Muriel Kirkland, Mae Clarke, Robert Armstrong, Sterling Holloway.

Queen Christina. 1933. MGM. Rouben Mamoulian. With Greta Garbo, Lewis Stone, Ian Keith, Elizabeth Young, C. Aubrey Smith, Reginald Owen, Akim Tamiroff, Cora Sue Collins.

The Captain Hates the Sea. 1934. COLUMBIA. Lewis Milestone. With Tala Birrell, Wynne Gibson, Helen Vinson, Akim Tamiroff, Victor McLaglen, Walter Connolly, Donald Meek, Alison Skipworth.

Ronald Colman

If the coming of Sound broke John Gilbert, it was the making of Ronald Colman. His striking Latin looks were a passport to fame in the immediate post-Valentino years when, together with Gilbert, he was tipped as Valentino's most likely successor. They both made it to fame and fortune independently anyway, but curiously, whereas Gilbert revelled in his Great Lover parts, Colman was constantly cast against type. His roles in the swashbuckling costume-dramas which Goldwyn put together as vehicles for him and Vilma Banky reveal a basic misconception about the true nature of his screen personality. He was not, despite his physical qualities, a passionate, extrovert Latin-Lover type. He was more than that – he was pre-eminently a 'romantic' screen personality.

It was his voice that brought him to the heights and kept him there. He was the only one of the popular screen lovers of the 'twenties who not only crossed safely over into the Sound era, but built an even greater and more successful career on the strength of it. Speech added an extra dimension to Ronald Colman's screen image. His voice matched his appearance and true style – graceful, reserved, charming and, above all, gentlemanly – and enabled him to concentrate on these qualities.

Talkies revealed him as an actor whose technique (overlaid in the 'twenties by the Silent picture's demand for dramatic, often over-emphatic gesture and heavily registered emotion) was in fact perfectly suited to the new medium. His restraint and power of understatement were reinforced by the gentleness and cultured Englishness of his voice. Sound took him to a peak of popularity, next only to Garbo. He was voted the top male star in the States in 1927, 1928 and 1929, and in 1932 British women voted him No. 1 in a popularity poll organized by a women's magazine.

Colman was exclusively a Hollywood star, though born an Englishman, in Richmond, Surrey, in 1891. He came from a solid middle-class background (his father was a reasonably well-off silk-importer) but his father's death when Ronald was only sixteen put paid to the family's plans of Oxford for him; instead he took a job with a shipping line and dabbled in amateur dramatics in his spare time. He spent four years, from the age of eighteen to twenty-two, in the London Scottish Regiment before returning to clerical work but, with the outbreak of war in 1914, rejoined the regiment. He was one of Kitchener's Contemptibles (the first 10,000 British soldiers to fight in France) and survived the First Battle of Ypres. His luck, however, did not last and at Messines he not only fractured an ankle but was badly gassed. His damaged lungs gave him trouble for the rest of his life and it is thought that their condition may have contributed to the special quality of his voice – like Donat, who suffered with severe asthma, the timbre had a strange, indefinable fragility.

Invalided out of the Army with a military decoration in 1916, Colman thought briefly about following an uncle into the Diplomatic Service but plumped for the stage when stage-producer Lena Ashwell asked him to play a tiny part in her version of Tagore's 'The Maharanee of Arakan' at the London Coliseum. He was an Indian herald, blacked-up and silent – save for a trumpet. After this Gladys Cooper gave him a small, but speaking part in her production of 'The Misleading Lady', in which she and George du Maurier played the leads, and thus Colman was launched on his stage-career. Like Barrymore he ran an embryo screen-career in harness with, but subordinate to, his theatrical life. His first film appearance was for pioneer film-maker George Dewhurst, who persuaded him (for £1 a day, not counting Sundays) to play the lead in a two-reeler comedy. Colman did not seem particularly to

Ronald Colman – the transition from Silent to Sound films meant for him the change from dashing Latin Lover to perfect English gentleman.

enjoy the experience and was frankly appalled by the end-product. Happily for him it was never released.

Undeterred by this, however, he appeared in several other films and was finally asked by Cecil Hepworth ('the D.W. Griffith of Britain') to take a part in one of his films. Hepworth was sufficiently impressed to persuade Colman to give up the stage and join his company, making moving pictures. He offered him a fixed contract – one of the first to be signed in Britain that paid even when the actor was not filming. For Hepworth, Colman made such films as *Anna the Adventuress* (1920), with Alma Taylor. Then he switched to another film-company, Broadwest, making among others *A Son of David* (1920), in which he played a Jewish prize-fighter, but gradually he moved back to the stage, where he acted in 'The Live Wire', 'The Great Day', and 'The Little Brother'. During this period, in September 1919, he married his first wife, Thelma Raye. (They separated in 1925 but did not obtain a divorce until 1934.)

It was Thelma who encouraged him to try his luck in America when it became apparent that the post-war Depression was hitting the theatre as well as the nascent film-industry. They couldn't afford two tickets so he set off alone with less than £10 to his name but with two letters of introduction – one of them to D.W. Griffith. It was not easy to get a break and he was down to near-starvation level when he got a small part in 'The Dauntless Three', which folded after only a few days. However, other small parts followed, including one in a film called *Handcuffs or Kisses* (1921) made on the East Coast and a role in 'East is West' which toured coast to coast. In Los Angeles he tried his luck with the studio casting-directors to no avail and returned to New York.

Then came the break he had been waiting for. In 1922 he landed the part of the Other Man in 'La Tendresse' with Ruth Chatterton and Henry Miller and was an immediate success. Film-director Henry King and Lillian Gish, who were just off to start work on *The White Sister* in Italy, heard about him and went to see the play. Colman's darkly handsome looks were in his favour as well as his acting ability for he would 'photograph Italian' and King wanted just this. He offered Colman the part of the leading man. Both Ruth Chatterton and Miller advised him to accept. For the first time he was in the hands of a really professional director who not only took great pains with film but also in coaching his young lead in the niceties of screen-acting. Lillian Gish, too, must have been a fine example for him with her dedication and consummate skill. The film was released in 1924 and was a great success. Ronald Colman was hailed as a bright new star.

He went on to make a second film with King and Gish, *Romola* (1925), based on George Eliot's novel with Dorothy Gish and William Powell. This too was a box-office hit. While he was filming, Sam Goldwyn had offered him the lead in *Tarnish* with May McAvoy and it was released ahead of *Romola* in September 1924.

On the strength of this Goldwyn gave him a long-term contract and Colman made six films in 1925, most of them on loan to other companies such as Metro-Goldwyn (*The Sporting Venus*) and Warner Brothers (*Lady Windermere's Fan*, directed by Ernst Lubitsch). For Goldwyn he made two good weepies, *Stella Dallas* (remade in 1937 with Barbara Stanwyck), which re-united him with Henry King, and *The Dark Angel*, which starred opposite him for the first time Goldwyn's new Hungarian import, tall, blonde and beautiful Vilma Banky. It was a prototype Colman role about a war-blinded English officer nerving himself up to sacrifice the love of his life. Both films were enormously successful.

His greatest success during the Silent period, however, was *Beau Geste* (1926). Like *The Four Horsemen of the Apocalypse* before it, the film was one of the decade's top ten grossers, and not only established Colman as a great star but also as an immensely skilled and talented actor. In his portrayal of Geste he created a remarkable blend of reality and romanticism and added another important aspect to the screen persona that was finally to emerge in the 'thirties, that of 'the idealist-action hero' (Julian Fox in *Films and Filming*).

After this, Goldwyn lent him out no longer and concentrated on building up the Banky-Colman team into a massive box-office draw in such costume-romances as *The Night of Love* (1927) and *Two Lovers* (1928), directed by Fred Niblo. However, the first film the team made together was not a historical extravaganza but a modern Western, *The Winning of Barbara Worth* (1926), in which he and a gangling new-comer called Gary Cooper competed for the affections of Miss Banky. Colman apparently advised Cooper on the playing of the death-bed scene, 'Easy does it, old boy. Good scenes make good actors. Actors don't make a scene' – advice which Cooper obviously took very seriously. Although Colman was not particularly well cast as the townie who wins the girl in the end, the film went down extremely well with the public and took Cooper to stardom.

In 1928 Goldwyn decided to try doubling his investment and split the screen lovers up, putting Banky with a young Englishman called Walter Byron in *The Awakening* (1928) and teaming Colman with Lili Damita in *The Rescue* (1929). Neither film was very successful and by this time the phenomenon of Sound was upon them. Colman's smooth transition into Talking pictures was as much the result of Goldwyn's personal shepherding of him through the hazards and pitfalls of the new medium as it was of his own mellifluous tones. Two factors inspired Goldwyn's choice of *Bulldog Drummond* (1929) as Colman's first Talkie. Firstly, he was playing an Englishman and not only did that solve the minor problem of accent, but it also matched the public's concept of Colman as an English gentleman, a part which he had played in films such as *The Dark Angel* and an impression that he conveyed very strongly, even in the midst of swashbuckling.

Secondly, Goldwyn had become aware that the old Silent romantic style was far too over-blown and florid, both in what was said and more particularly how it was said. With the sad spectacle of John Gilbert before him, he decided to avoid heavy romance for Colman, casting him instead as the modern gentleman-adventurer, witty, charming and chivalrous. The love interest was kept to a minimum and thus Colman's audience appeal was maintained, indeed intensified, with no hint of an embarrassed giggle from the spectators. The mould for his future roles had been created. In fact the film was an outstanding critical and box-office success and received Oscar nominations in several categories.

Colman made seven films for Goldwyn in the next four years, including in 1930 *Raffles* with Kay Francis and *The Devil to Pay* with Myrna Loy and Loretta Young, and in 1931 *The Unholy Garden* with Fay Wray and *Arrowsmith*, directed by John Ford. *Arrowsmith* was based on Sinclair Lewis's Nobel-prize-winning novel in which Colman played the title role of a young doctor caught up in a possible outbreak of bubonic plague. It was another great personal success for him and strengthened further his powerfully appealing screen image. In 1935 he and Goldwyn quarrelled. The Goldwyn publicity-machine suddenly issued damaging statements about Colman's behaviour on set, including an accusation of doing his love scenes 'fortified by a considerable amount of alcohol'. He sued for libel and $2 million in damages, and the case was settled out of court. An impasse developed when Colman refused to make any more films for Goldwyn, who in turn would not release him from a contract which had another year to run. The dilemma was resolved when Joe Schenk, who together with Darryl F. Zanuck had just created Twentieth-Century Pictures, persuaded Goldwyn to let him sign Colman.

His first film for Twentieth Century was *Bulldog Drummond Strikes Back* (1934), a rather jokey follow-up to his first great Sound success, in which he again had Loretta Young as his leading lady. This was followed by a biopic about Clive of India and in it he appeared without his moustache for the first time since *Romola* in 1924. *Clive* was released in 1935 and soon afterwards Twentieth Century merged with the Fox Film Corporation. In that year Colman made a rather undistinguished light comedy for the new company, *The Man Who Broke the Bank at Monte Carlo*, before being loaned out to MGM to play the part of Sydney Carton in a new film version of Dickens's *A Tale of Two Cities*. Colman gave one of his finest performances and apparently himself considered it his best film. He returned to Twentieth Century-Fox to make his last film for them, *Under Two Flags* (1936), the fourth screen version of Ouida's romantic Foreign Legion melodrama. His leading ladies were Ros Russell and Claudette Colbert. Surprisingly, especially after his brilliant performance as Carton, Fox did not renew his contract.

As it turned out, however, this was unimportant – the year 1937 was the pinnacle of his screen-career, both as an actor and a star. He gave outstanding performances in two films that were among the most successful of the decade, critically and in terms of box-office – Capra's *Lost Horizon* and John Cromwell's *The Prisoner of Zenda*. In Capra's film of James Hilton's novel, he plays Conway, the man of action, who eventually discovers that he is also a man of peace. He was Capra's ideal for the part and was surrounded by splendid performances from Isabel Jewell, Thomas Mitchell and Edward Everett Horton. *Lost Horizon* now stands among the top money-makers of all time, but the astronomical production costs did not initially endear it to Harry Cohn, the Columbia studio boss. It was, however, a triumph for both Capra and for Colman, whose screen personality seemed to acquire another, subtle layer with the playing of this part. He displayed a heightened 'spirituality' in his acting, a sense of sadness at unfulfilled ideals and a gentle wistfulness in the face of the world's follies. Even his role as Rudolph Rassendyll in *The Prisoner of Zenda*, a film marked by its fast-paced exuberance, was given depth and interest by this intriguing addition to Colman's screen persona. Again Colman was backed by a fine cast, Madeleine Carroll, Raymond Massey, Mary Astor, and Douglas Fairbanks Jr as Rupert of Hentzau.

Curiously, despite signing a seven-year contract with David O. Selznick, who produced *Zenda*, he didn't make any more films for him. Instead he signed a two-picture deal with Paramount, which produced *If I Were King* (1938), another version of the François Villon story, and Kipling's *The Light That Failed* (1940), directed by William Wellman. A similar deal with RKO led to two lightweight comedies, *Lucky Partners* (1940) with Ginger Rogers and *My Life with Caroline* (1941). In 1938 he was married for the second time, to actress Benita Hume, and they stayed married until his death in 1958.

With the outbreak of war he devoted himself to the war effort. First he founded the Franco-

Colman's dark looks won him the part of a young Italian officer playing opposite Lillian Gish in *The White Sister* (1924). The film made him a star.

British War Relief Fund with Charles Boyer and Douglas Fairbanks Jr, and then he became President of the British War Relief Association of Southern California. He appeared in fewer films and was very selective about his roles in an attempt to widen his acting range. He proved himself a versatile actor in such films as George Stevens's *The Talk of the Town* (1942) with Jean Arthur and Cary Grant, Le Roy's *Random Harvest* (1942) with Greer Garson, *Kismet* (1944) with Marlene Dietrich, and *The Late George Apley* (1946).

He finally won his long-deserved Oscar in 1948 – for his Jekyll-and-Hyde role in Cukor's *A Double Life* – and after one more film, *Champagne for Caesar* (1950), a satire on the new television quiz shows, he went into semi-retirement. He did quite a bit of radio and television work during the early and middle 'fifties and made two further film appearances, a guest spot in Mike Todd's *Around the World in 80 Days* (1956) and the lead in *The Story of Mankind* (1957). He died of pneumonia in May 1958, his lung trouble catching up with him at last.

Ronald Colman had never given up his British citizenship. During his screen-career he had come to embody a very special English archetype which, sadly perhaps, is rather unfashionable these days. Quiet, humorous, courageous and dignified, his tremendous appeal lay in his ability to portray deep and moving emotions with restraint and sincerity. The Times said, in its affectionate obituary, 'his good looks and cultured manners made him an impressive hero of the classic English school', and his success seems largely due to the fact that he really did embody the virtues which made his screen personality such a great one.

After Garbo and Gilbert, Colman and Vilma Banky were the greatest romantic duo of the 'twenties. *Night of Love* (1927) was set in seventeenth-century Spain and he, a charming bandit, kidnaps Miss Banky on her wedding night.

Colman played *Bulldog Drummond* (1929) as 'a debonair, witty, overgrown schoolboy' (Julian Fox), an especially apt description since the love-interest, Joan Bennett, was only sixteen at the time.

Colman in 1946.

John Gilbert and Lillian
Gish in *La Bohème* (1926),
from 'Picture Show
Annual' for 1927.

Debonair gentleman by day, and equally debonair amateur safecracker by night, Colman was perfect as *Raffles* (1930), a role that Barrymore played on film as early as 1917.

After his performance as the doctor in *Arrowsmith* (1931), Sinclair Lewis wrote to Colman: 'Thank you for *Arrowsmith*. It completely carried out everything I tried to do in the novel.'

The role for which Colman is best remembered is that of Sydney Carton in *A Tale of Two Cities* (1935). The little seamstress (Isabel Jewell) gives him a farewell kiss.

Douglas Fairbanks Jr as Rupert of Hentzau and Colman as Rudolph Rassendyll in John Cromwell's 1937 version of *The Prisoner of Zenda* – 'one of the purest and noblest fables ever put on film,' according to Jeffrey Richards.

Ronald Colman

The Toilers. 1919. DIAMOND SUPER. Tom Watts. With Gwynne Herbert, Eric Barker, George Dewhurst, Mandra Thew.
A Daughter of Eve. 1919. BROADWEST. Walter West. Colman was unbilled. With Stewart Rome, Violet Hopson, Cameron Carr, Ralph Forster, Edward Banfield, Vesta Sylva.
Snow in the Desert. 1919. BROADWEST. Walter West. With Violet Hopson, Stewart Rome, Poppy Wyndham, Sir Simon Stuart.
A Son of David. 1920. BROADWEST. Hay Plumb. With Vesta Sylva, Arthur Walcott, Poppy Wyndham, Constance Backner.
Anna the Adventuress. 1920. HEPWORTH. Cecil Hepworth. With Alma Taylor, James Carew, Gwynne Herbert, Gerald Ames.
The Black Spider. 1920. B & C (BUTCHER). William J. Humphrey. With Lydia Kyasht, Sam Livesey, C. Hayden Coffin, Bertram Burleigh.
Handcuffs Or Kisses. 1921. SELZNICK. George Archainbaud. With Elaine Hammerstein, Julia

Swayne Gordon, Dorothy Chappell, Robert Ellis, Alison Skipworth.
The Eternal City. 1923. GOLDWYN/FIRST NATIONAL. George Fitzmaurice. Colman was unbilled. With Barbara La Marr, Lionel Barrymore.
The White Sister. 1924. INSPIRATION/METRO. Henry King. With Lillian Gish, Gail Kane, J. Barney Sherry, Charles Lane.
Twenty Dollars A Week. 1924. SELZNICK. Harmon F. Weight. With George Arliss, Edith Roberts.
Tarnish. 1924. GOLDWYN/FIRST NATIONAL. George Fitzmaurice. With May McAvoy, Marie Prevost, Albert Gran, William Boyd.
Her Night of Romance. 1924. FIRST NATIONAL. Sidney A. Franklin. With Constance Talmadge, Albert Gran, Jean Hersholt.
Romola. 1925. INSPIRATION/METRO. Henry King. With Lillian Gish, Dorothy Gish, William Powell.
A Thief in Paradise. 1925. GOLDWYN/FIRST NATIONAL. George Fitzmaurice. With Doris Kenyon, Aileen Pringle, Clause Gillingwater, Alec Francis.
His Supreme Moment. 1925. GOLDWYN/FIRST NATIONAL. George Fitzmaurice. With Blanche Sweet, Jane Winton, Belle Bennett, Anna May Wong.

The Sporting Venus.
1925. METRO-GOLDWYN.
Marshall Neilan. With
Blanche Sweet, Lew Cody,
Edward Martindel, Kate
Price.
Her Sister from Paris.
1925. FIRST NATIONAL.
Sidney Franklin. With
Constance Talmadge,
George K. Arthur,
Margaret Mann, Gertrude
Clare.
The Dark Angel. 1925.
GOLDWYN/FIRST NATIONAL.
George Fitzmaurice. With
Vilma Banky, Wyndham
Standing, Frank Elliott,
Helen Jerome Eddy,
Florence Turner, Charles
Lane.
Stella Dallas. 1925.
GOLDWYN/UNITED ARTISTS.
Henry King. With Belle
Bennett, Alice Joyce, Jean
Hersholt, Lois Moran,
Douglas Fairbanks Jr,
Vera Lewis, Beatrice
Pryor.
Lady Windermere's Fan.
1925. WARNER BROTHERS.
Ernst Lubitsch. With Irene
Rich, May McAvoy, Bert
Lytell, Edward Martindel,
Helen Dunbar.
Kiki. 1926. FIRST NATIONAL.
Clarence Brown. With
Norma Talmadge, Gertrude
Astor, Marc MacDermott,
Mack Swain.
Beau Geste. 1926. PARA-
MOUNT/FAMOUS PLAYERS-
LASKY. Herbert Brenon.
With Neil Hamilton,
Ralph Forbes, Alice Joyce,
Mary Brian, Noah Beery,
William Powell, Victor
McLaglen, Norman Trevor,
Donald Stuart.
**The Winning of Barbara
Worth.** 1926. GOLDWYN/
UNITED ARTISTS. Henry
King. With Vilma Banky,
Charles Lane, Gary
Cooper, Paul McAllister.
The Night of Love. 1927.
GOLDWYN/UNITED ARTISTS.
George Fitzmaurice. With
Vilma Banky, Montagu
Love, Natalie Kingston,
Laska Winter.
The Magic Flame. 1927.
GOLDWYN/UNITED ARTISTS.
Henry King. With Vilma
Banky, Augustino Borgato,
Gustav von Seyffertitz,
Harvey Clark, Shirley
Palmer.
Two Lovers. 1928.
GOLDWYN/UNITED ARTISTS.
Fred Niblo. With Vilma
Banky, Noah Beery, Paul
Lukas, Virginia Bradford,
Nigel de Brulier, Helen
Jerome Eddy.
The Rescue. 1929.
GOLDWYN/UNITED ARTISTS.
Herbert Brenon. With Lili
Damita, Alfred Hickman,
Theodore von Eltz,
Philip Strange.
Bulldog Drummond.
1929. GOLDWYN/UNITED
ARTISTS. F. Richard Jones.
First Talkie. Oscar
nomination. With Joan
Bennett, Lilyan Tashman,
Montagu Love, Lawrence
Grant.
Condemned. 1929.
GOLDWYN/UNITED ARTISTS.
Wesley Ruggles. Oscar
nomination. With Ann

Harding, Dudley Digges,
Louis Wolheim, William
Elmer.
Raffles. 1930. GOLDWYN/
UNITED ARTISTS. Harry D.
D'Arrast and George
Fitzmaurice. With Kay
Francis, Bramwell
Fletcher, Frances Dade,
David Torrence, Alison
Skipworth.
The Devil To Pay. 1930.
GOLDWYN/UNITED ARTISTS.
George Fitzmaurice. With
Loretta Young, Myrna
Loy, Florence Britton,
Frederick Kerr, David
Torrence, Mary Forbes,
Paul Cavanaugh.
The Unholy Garden.
1931. GOLDWYN/UNITED
ARTISTS. George
Fitzmaurice. With Fay
Wray, Estelle Taylor,
Mischa Auer, Tully
Marshall, Lawrence Grant.
Arrowsmith. 1931.
GOLDWYN FOR UNITED
ARTISTS. John Ford. With
Helen Hayes, A. E. Anson,
Alec B. Francis, Richard
Bennett, Myrna Loy,
Beulah Bondi, Russell
Hopton.
Cynara. 1932. GOLDWYN/
UNITED ARTISTS. King
Vidor. With Kay Francis,
Phyllis Barry, Henry
Stephenson, Viva
Tattersall.
The Masquerader. 1933.
GOLDWYN/UNITED ARTISTS.
Richard Wallace. With
Elissa Landi, Juliette
Compton, Halliwell
Hobbes, David Torrence,
Creighton Hale, Helen
Jerome Eddy.
**Bulldog Drummond
Strikes Back.** 1934.
TWENTIETH CENTURY/
UNITED ARTISTS. Roy Del
Ruth. With Loretta Young,
Charles Butterworth, Una
Merkel, C. Aubrey Smith,
E. E. Clive, Halliwell
Hobbes, Warner Oland.
Clive of India. 1935.
TWENTIETH CENTURY/
UNITED ARTISTS. Richard
Boleslawski. With Loretta
Young, Colin Clive, Cesar
Romero, Francis Lister, C.
Aubrey Smith, Lumsden
Hare, Montagu Love, Leo
G. Carroll, Mischa Auer.
**The Man Who Broke the
Bank at Monte Carlo.**
1935. TWENTIETH CENTURY-
FOX. Stephen Roberts. With
Joan Bennett, Colin Clive,
Nigel Bruce, Montagu
Love.
A Tale of Two Cities.
1935. MGM. Jack Conway.
Oscar nomination. With
Elizabeth Allan, Edna May
Oliver, Reginald Owen,
Basil Rathbone, Blanche
Yurka, Donald Woods,
Walter Catlett, H.B.
Warner, Fritz Leiber.
Under Two Flags. 1936.
TWENTIETH CENTURY-FOX.
Frank Lloyd. With
Claudette Colbert, Victor
McLaglen, Rosalind
Russell, Gregory Ratoff,
Nigel Bruce, John
Carradine.
Lost Horizon. 1937.
COLUMBIA. Frank Capra.
With Jane Wyatt, Thomas

Mitchell, Edward Everett
Horton, H. B. Warner,
Margo, John Howard, Sam
Jaffe, Isabel Jewell.
The Prisoner of Zenda.
1937. UNITED ARTISTS. With
Madeleine Carroll,
Douglas Fairbanks Jr,
Mary Astor, C. Aubrey
Smith, Raymond Massey,
David Niven, Lawrence
Grant.
If I Were King. 1938.
PARAMOUNT. Frank Lloyd.
With Frances Dee, Basil
Rathbone, Ellen Drew,
Henry Wilcoxon, Heather
Thatcher, Montagu Love,
Sydney Toles, William
Farnum.
The Light That Failed.
1940. PARAMOUNT. William
Wellman. With Walter
Huston, Ida Lupino,
Dudley Digges, Muriel
Angelus, Ernest Cossart,
Halliwell Hobbes.
Lucky Partners. 1940.
RKO. Lewis Milestone.
With Ginger Rogers, Jack
Carson, Spring Byington,
Harry Davenport, Walter
Kingsford, Leon Belasco.
My Life With Caroline.
1941. RKO. Lewis Milestone.
With Anna Lee, Charles
Winninger, Reginald
Gardiner, Gilbert Roland,
Katherine Leslie, Hugh
O'Connell.
The Talk of the Town.
1942. COLUMBIA. George
Stevens. With Jean Arthur,
Cary Grant, Edgar
Buchanan, Glenda Farrell,
Rex Ingram, Emma Dunn,
Lloyd Bridges.
Random Harvest. 1942.
MGM. Mervyn Le Roy.
Oscar nomination. With
Greer Garson, Philip Dorn,
Susan Peters, Henry
Travers, Reginald Owen,
Bramwell Fletcher,
Melville Cooper.
Kismet. 1944. MGM.
William Dieterle. With
Marlene Dietrich, Edward
Arnold, Joy Ann Page,
James Craig.
The Late George Apley.
1946. TWENTIETH CENTURY-
FOX. Joseph L. Mankiewicz.
With Peggy Cummins,
Vanessa Brown, Percy
Waram, Richard Haydn,
Richard Ney, Nydia
Westman, Edna Best,
Mildred Natwick.
A Double Life. 1948.
UNIVERSAL-INTERNATIONAL.
George Cukor. Received
an Academy Award. With
Signe Hasso, Edmund
O'Brien, Shelley Winters,
Ray Collins.
Champagne for Caesar.
1950. POPKIN-UNITED
ARTISTS. Richard Whorf.
With Celeste Holm,
Vincent Price, Barbara
Britton, Art Linkletter.
**Around the World in 80
Days.** 1956. UNITED
ARTISTS. Michael
Anderson. With all-star
cast, and David Niven and
Cantinflas, Shirley
MacLaine and Robert
Newton in leads.
The Story of Mankind.
1957. WARNER BROTHERS.
Irwin Allen. With all-star

cast, including the Marx
Brothers, Hedy Lamarr,
Vincent Price, Peter Lorre,
Agnes Moorehead, Cedric
Hardwicke, Franklin
Pangborn.

Colman also appeared in
The Live Wire (c. 1918),
which was never released.

If I Were King (1938) was a
remake of another
Barrymore vehicle,
Beloved Rogue (1927), the
story of the poet and
adventurer François
Villon. Though not
terribly credible in the
part, Colman caused a lot
of hearts to flutter. With
him is Henry
Wilcoxon.

Leslie Howard

Like Ronald Colman, Leslie Howard had an appeal as an actor that was essentially English and that increased rather than decreased as he grew older. As C. A. Lejeune wrote of Howard shortly after his death in 1943, he 'was a man of great personal charm which increased with the years'. Both men were substantially the same as their screen personalities, sharing the gently humorous, charming and intelligent but slightly dreamy character of the English gentleman personified.

Unlike the other male stars discussed so far, Leslie Howard did not give up his stage-career when he became a success in films. Indeed he became a widely admired, and adored, leading man through his performances on Broadway long before he even considered making films at all seriously. Even after such box-office draws as *Smilin' Through* (1932) with Norma Shearer and *Of Human Bondage* (1934), he continued to divide his time between stage and screen and achieved the high point of his acting career in the stage version of 'The Petrified Forest' in 1935. In fact his life was pretty much perpetual motion for he moved as freely between England and America as he did between the theatre and the film-studios.

He was temperamentally somewhat of a contradiction – upright, kindly, apparently rather vague, but actually witty, shrewd and, in his acting, precise and technical. Howard manipulated these contrasts fairly ruthlessly for his own benefit, maintaining the woolly-minded professor act to keep unnecessary worries at bay and using a string of apparently tougher people, most notable among them his wife Ruth, to organize him, protect him and generally make life easy for him. It is typical of his brand of overwhelming charm that, far from resenting him for using them in this way, they all seemed, along with his many female fans, to adore him.

Leslie Howard was born in April 1893 in London, the first child of Frank and Lilian Stainer. Frank was a Hungarian by birth though British by nationality, and he had met Lilian while supplementing his meagre clerk's income by playing the piano in the middle-class parlours of South London. Lilian encouraged her son's ambitions as a writer and took her children to the theatre as often as possible. When, after leaving Dulwich College, Leslie went into a bank, she also encouraged him to become involved in the lively amateur-dramatic group in the suburb of South Norwood where the family lived. Leslie hated working as a bank clerk and was snatched away from this fate by the outbreak of the First World War. He enlisted in the cavalry and married (in 1916) Ruth Martin, the daughter of a Regular Army officer. He was invalided back from France in 1917, a severe case of shell-shock. His father was anxious for him to return to the security of

the bank but his mother suggested a far more congenial occupation – that of acting.

So Leslie Stainer became Leslie Howard and tried his luck on the stage, and the exigencies of war brought him just that. The shortage of juvenile leads enabled him to get a part with a touring version of 'Peg O' My Heart' without too much difficulty. After this he established himself fairly rapidly on the London stage in a series of minor roles. It was during this period that he first dabbled in films. His uncle was directing films at a small studio at Bushey in Hertfordshire and there Leslie met a young man called Adrian Brunel, with whom he founded Minerva Films in 1920. The company produced three one-acters and counted C. Aubrey Smith, A. A. Milne and H. G. Wells among its backers before Leslie's burgeoning stage-career caught him up and swept him off to New York to play a small part in 'Just Suppose', a romantic comedy presented by theatrical impresario Gilbert Miller. Leslie set about establishing himself successfully on the New York stage and brought his wife and son over from England. He rented a house out on Great Neck where, according to his daughter's biography, he became very friendly with a neighbour, F. Scott Fitzgerald. The Howards also socialized a lot – and became fringe members of the Algonquin set – Alexander Woollcott, Robert Benchley, Dorothy Parker *et al.* In 1925 he played Napier Harpenden in the stage version of Arlen's 'The Green Hat' with great success, but it was his part in 'Her Cardboard Lover' opposite Jeanne Eagels in 1927 which really turned him into a Broadway matinée-idol. During the next three years his career as a stage-star boomed and he began the sequence of crossings and recrossings of the Atlantic which was to go on through the 'thirties, to play 'Her Cardboard Lover' with Tallulah Bankhead in London in 1928. Gertrude Lawrence was another of his leading ladies, with her first straight part in 'By Candlelight' which they played in both London and New York (not very successfully), and he also appeared in both cities with greater success in 'Berkeley Square', a strange nostalgic play which he was later to film about a man transported in time to the eighteenth century.

His great popularity and prestige at this time caused two of his own plays to be produced in New York, one an original and the other an adaptation of a German play (during the auditioning for which he rejected a young hopeful called Clark Gable on the grounds that 'he has no appeal at all'). They also meant that offers to make films started coming in. Leslie's first venture in films, Minerva, had quietly faded away when it became apparent that his stage-career was taking off. Now he weighed up the various deals offered him and in 1930 signed with Warner Brothers at $5,000 a week to make *Outward Bound*. The film, which was banned by the British censor, was a macabre tale of passengers on a ship who gradually realize that they are dead. Leslie scored a personal hit, and then moved on to MGM to make three more films. *Never the Twain Shall Meet* (1931), in which he rather improbably played a beachcomber, *A Free Soul* (1931) with Norma Shearer, Lionel Barrymore and the earlier rejected Clark Gable, who became a star with this film, and *Five and Ten* (1931) with Marion Davies. None of these did a great deal for his reputation and nor did *Devotion* (1931), which he made for RKO. Leslie and his wife Ruth quite enjoyed life in Hollywood (though one suspects that their hearts were with the country-house in Surrey which they had bought during one of their English sojourns). They socialized with the John Gilberts, the John Barrymores and the younger Fairbankses (Joan Crawford was then married to Douglas Jr), and after *Five and Ten* were fairly frequent visitors at Marion Davies's sumptuous beach-house. However, Leslie was no more enamoured of the actual process of filming than he had been of long runs in the theatre, and it must have been with some relief that he returned to England in the summer of 1931 to make a film with Alexander Korda and enjoy the house in Surrey.

The Korda film was *Reserved for Ladies* (1932), the Sound version of a Silent film in which Adolphe Menjou had played the hero – a kind of Cinderella-in-reverse, a waiter who is mistaken for a prince. It was Korda's first film as director and not a great success. The Howards returned to New York late in 1931, and Leslie began rehearsals for his new Broadway play, 'The Animal Kingdom', which had been written especially with a rising young actress, Katharine Hepburn, in mind. She, however, left the cast before the play opened in New York in January 1932 and the emphasis of the plot was then thrown mainly on Leslie Howard, who won rave reviews for his part. The play had a long run and he agreed to do a film version later that year.

But first he made *Smilin' Through* (1932) with Norma Shearer, a weepy romance strongly rooted in Victorian mysticism, which caused Leslie's fan-mail to rise abruptly. Then came *The Animal Kingdom* (1932) with Ann Harding and Myrna Loy, in one of her first straight roles, and a film with Mary Pickford called *Secrets* (1933). It was her last screen appearance and a rather bizarre one for Leslie who played a cowboy and aged some fifty years in the course of the film. He made *Captured!* (1933) for Warners and the film version of *Berkeley Square* (1933) for Fox, before travelling to England to make *The Lady is Willing* (1934) for Columbia with Binnie Barnes and Cedric Hardwicke. The film was directed by his friend Gilbert Miller, who subsequently produced him in a stage play about the life of Shakespeare ('This Side Idolatry') by Clemence Dane. Neither venture was very successful and Leslie began to consider various film offers. His refusal to co-star with Garbo in *Queen Christina* made headlines. He was quite honest about his reason – he did not want to be outshone ('She has a peculiarly dominating personality on the screen and that is exactly why I declined the part'). He finally agreed to make a film version of Maugham's novel *Of Human Bondage* for RKO if they could purchase the rights. They did and he returned to the States for filming with a relatively unknown Bette Davis (the only American in the cast) as the Cockney waitress, Mildred. The film lifted her to stardom but despite good notices did not do particularly well at the box-office. After this Leslie made *British Agent* (1934) with Kay Francis before yet another trip to England to make his second, and immensely successful, film for Alexander Korda, *The Scarlet Pimpernel* (1934).

Travelling on the same boat with the Howards was playwright Robert Sherwood, who was to complete the film's script. He showed Leslie the text of his new play 'The Petrified Forest' and Leslie immediately saw a marvellous part in it for himself. In fact, his part in *The Scarlet Pimpernel*, that of Sir Percy Blakeney, was one of his most memorable. Merle Oberon played Lady Blakeney, Nigel Bruce the Prince Regent and Raymond Massey the villainous Chauvelin. Leslie was already back in New York, rehearsing 'The Petrified Forest', when the film opened to overwhelming acclaim in London at the end of 1934. 'The finest performance of his career' (Daily Mail), 'the greatest hit of his screen career' (Daily Telegraph), and

The perfect Howard image – the cool, quizzical, pipe-smoking Englishman. New York theatre-critic Brooks Atkinson wrote of his grace, precision and spirit, and eulogized over his 'limpid personality'.

the Picturegoer Gold Medal for 1934 were among the plaudits heaped upon him. Leslie's immensely delicate and fastidious style was especially suited to the part of Sir Percy, revealing as it did his genius for high comedy in which he showed himself to be deft, witty, speedy and above all light of touch.

This success was followed by another, equally resounding, on the other side of the Atlantic when 'The Petrified Forest' opened in January 1935. It was his penultimate Broadway appearance, and his greatest. His portrayal of Alan Squiers, the cynical intellectual who falls in love with an idealistic young girl, won him, according to his daughter, 'the ultimate in critical reviews and public enthusiasm'. After a brief sojourn in England, researching for what was becoming an increasingly important project, his own production of 'Hamlet', he returned to America to film *The Petrified Forest* (1936) with Humphrey Bogart, who had been with him in the stage version, as the gangster who finally shoots him, and Bette Davis as the waitress, Gaby. Warners apparently wanted Edward G. Robinson for the gangster, but Leslie dug his heels in and insisted on Bogart, who was very successful in the part and never forgot Leslie's kindness and support. The plans for 'Hamlet' continued to absorb him, but were kept in the background by another film, *Romeo and Juliet* (1936), which he made, with some reluctance, for MGM. Directed by George Cukor, the film starred Norma Shearer as Juliet and had a prestige cast which included John Barrymore, Basil Rathbone, Edna May Oliver and Ralph Forbes.

Leslie probably overcame his qualms (he was too old for the part, and knew it, and felt as he had with Garbo that his role was overshadowed by the heroine) in order to get some experience in Shakespearean acting for he had never done any before. In the event, the much-planned and eagerly awaited 'Hamlet' which opened in the autumn of 1936 was not the great theatrical event he had hoped. It did, however, cover its costs by a long and assiduous tour across the country which finally took Leslie back to Hollywood and films again. There he made two of the then-popular 'zany' comedies, *It's Love I'm After* (1937) with Bette Davis and Olivia de Havilland and *Stand-In* (1937) with Joan Blondell. Then it was back to England and a film that was to change his career considerably – *Pygmalion* (1938), which he co-directed with Anthony Asquith, with whom he also produced the film. David Lean was the editor. Wendy Hiller was triumphant as Eliza and *Pygmalion* was hailed by The Observer as 'one of the most brilliant jobs ever turned out of a British film studio'. It was this success, probably combined with the realization that his career as a romantic hero was drawing to a close (he was now forty-three), which made him decide to move towards film direction and production.

Meanwhile he returned to America to make more films. Ironically, in view of the resounding success of *Pygmalion* on both sides of the Atlantic, he was offered only one part – that of Ashley in David O. Selznick's mammoth production of *Gone With the Wind* (1939), which he did not want to do. 'I have a hunch it is no good for me,' he wrote to his family in England. 'I'm not nearly beautiful or young enough for Ashley.' His heart really was set on directing by now, but, encouraged by talk of a possible deal with Selznick which would encompass acting and producing/directing, he finally agreed early in 1939. 'Yesterday,' he wrote, 'I put on my Confederate uniform for the first time and looked like a fairy doorman at the Beverley Wiltshire.' In late spring, while waiting to complete retakes on the film, he started work on *Intermezzo* (1939) with Ingrid Bergman – her first Hollywood film. He was associate producer on the picture, a ploy, he suspected, to keep him happy while *Gone With the Wind* was finished, but he did not care what the reason was. By the time *Intermezzo* was completed, the clouds of war in Europe were very black indeed and he, with his family, made his last trip back across the Atlantic to England in late August.

After the outbreak of war in September he devoted all his energies to the war effort, using the medium of radio (he did a weekly morale-boosting broadcast to the States) as well as that of films such as *Pimpernel Smith* (1941), which he produced and directed, Michael Powell's *49th Parallel* (1941), and *The First of the Few* (1942), which he directed and appeared in with David Niven. The British Film Yearbook for 1945 said of him that his work in England during the war was 'one of the most valuable facets of British propaganda'. He died in June 1943, when the plane in which he was returning from a British Council-sponsored lecture tour in Spain and Portugal was shot down by German fighters.

Smilin' Through (1932) was a real four-handkerchief weepie. Howard played Carteret, the lonely old recluse (hence the make-up), and Norma Shearer the dual role of dead love Kathleen and her young niece.

Howard in typical matinée-idol pose with Olivia de Havilland in *It's Love I'm After* (1937), one of the 'zany' comedies popular in the late 'thirties.

Hardly the most romantic picture of Howard, but probably one of the more unusual. Quite why Mary Pickford wanted him to play a cowboy in her last film, *Secrets* (1933), must remain her secret – he thought the idea quite lunatic.

Sir Percy Blakeney was probably Howard's most memorable role. 'In the great tradition of English high comedy,' The Daily Telegraph wrote of *The Scarlet Pimpernel* (1934). Merle Oberon played Lady Blakeney.

'No Bogart, no Howard,' was Leslie's ultimatum to Warner Brothers when the film version of *The Petrified Forest* (1936) was mooted. It was one of his favourite films and reunited him with Bette Davis.

Howard made *Romeo and Juliet* (1936) with Norma Shearer under protest – the poet had his heart and soul in Juliet, he said. With Howard are (right) Benvolio (Reginald Denny) and Balthasar (Maurice Murphy).

Concert-violinist Howard falls in love with his young accompanist (Bergman) in *Intermezzo* (1939) – his last American film, and her first.

Howard really disliked his role as Ashley Wilkes in *Gone With the Wind* (1939). Undoubtedly he realized from the start just how thoroughly he was being up-staged. Here he is with some of the opposition – Vivien Leigh.

Leslie Howard

Outward Bound. 1930. WARNER BROTHERS. Robert Milton. With Beryl Mercer, Alison Skipworth, Douglas Fairbanks Jr, Helen Chandler, Montagu Love, Dudley Digges.

A Free Soul. 1931. MGM. Clarence Brown. With Norma Shearer, Lionel Barrymore, Clark Gable, James Gleason, Lucy Beaumont.

Never the Twain Shall Meet. 1931. MGM. W.S. Van Dyke. With Conchita Montenegro, C. Aubrey Smith, Karen Morley, Mitchell Lewis.

Five and Ten (UK title: **Daughter of Luxury**). 1931. MGM. Robert Z. Leonard. With Marion Davies, Irene Rich, Richard Bennett, Kent Douglas, Halliwell Hobbes.

Devotion. 1931. RKO-PATHÉ. Robert Milton. With Ann Harding, Robert Williams, O.P. Heggie, Louise Closser Hale, Dudley Digges, Alison Skipworth.

Reserved for Ladies (UK title: **Service for Ladies**). 1932. PARAMOUNT BRITISH PRODUCTION. Alexander Korda. With Benita Hume, George Grossmith, Elizabeth Allan, Morton Shelton, Martita Hunt.

Smilin' Through. 1932. MGM. Sidney Franklin. With Norma Shearer, Fredric March, O.P. Heggie, Ralph Forbes, Beryl Mercer, Margaret Seddon.

The Animal Kingdom (UK title: **Woman in His House**). 1932. RKO. Edward H. Griffith. With Anne Harding, Myrna Loy, Neil Hamilton, William Gargan, Henry Stephenson, Ilka Chase.

Secrets. 1933. UNITED ARTISTS. Frank Borzage. With Mary Pickford, C. Aubrey Smith, Blanche Frederici, Doris Lloyd, Herbert Evans.

Captured! 1933. WARNER BROTHERS. Roy Del Ruth. With Douglas Fairbanks Jr, Paul Lukas, Margaret Lindsay, Arthur Hohl, Robert Barrat, J. Carrol Naish.

Berkeley Square. 1933. FOX. Frank Lloyd. With Heather Angel, Valerie Taylor, Irene Browne, Colin Keith-Johnston, Alan Mowbray, Beryl Mercer.

Of Human Bondage. 1934. RKO. John Cromwell. With Bette Davis, Frances Dee, Kay Johnson, Reginald Denny, Alan Hale, Reginald Owen.

The Lady Is Willing. 1934. COLUMBIA. Gilbert Miller. With Binnie Barnes, Sir Cedric Hardwicke, Sir Nigel Playfair, Nigel Bruce.

British Agent. 1934. WARNERS-FIRST NATIONAL. Michael Curtiz. With Kay Francis, William Gargan, Phillip Reed, Irving Pichel, Halliwell Hobbes, J. Carrol Naish, Cesar Romero.

The Scarlet Pimpernel. 1934. LONDON FILMS-UNITED ARTISTS. Harold Young. With Merle Oberon, Raymond Massey, Q.B. Clarence, Walter Rilla, Anthony Bushell, Ernest Milton, Nigel Bruce.

The Petrified Forest. 1936. WARNER BROTHERS. Archie L. Mayo. With Bette Davis, Humphrey Bogart, Genevieve Tobin, Dick Foran, Joseph Sawyer, Porter Hall.

Romeo and Juliet. 1936. MGM. George Cukor. With Norma Shearer, John Barrymore, Edna May Oliver, Basil Rathbone, C. Aubrey Smith, Andy Devine, Ralph Forbes.

It's Love I'm After. 1937. WARNER BROTHERS. Archie L. Mayo. With Bette Davis, Olivia de Havilland, Patric Knowles, Eric Blore, Spring Byington, Bonita Granville.

Stand-In. 1937. UNITED ARTISTS. Tay Garnett. With Joan Blondell, Humphrey Bogart, Alan Mowbray, Marla Shelton, C. Henry Gordon, Jack Carson.

Pygmalion. 1938. MGM (BRITISH). Anthony Asquith and Leslie Howard. With Wendy Hiller, Wilfred Lawson, Marie Lohr, Scott Sunderland, Jean Cadell, David Tree.

Intermezzo – a Love Story (UK title: **Escape to Happiness**). 1939. SELZNICK-INTERNATIONAL/UNITED ARTISTS. Gregory Ratoff. Howard was associate producer. With Ingrid Bergman, Edna Best, John Halliday, Cecil Kellaway, Enid Bennett, Ann Todd.

Gone With the Wind. 1939. SELZNICK-INTER-NATIONAL/MGM. Victor Fleming. With Clark Gable, Vivien Leigh, Olivia de Havilland, Thomas Mitchell, Hattie McDaniell, Victor Jory, Evelyn Keyes, Laura Hope Crews, Butterfly McQueen.

Pimpernel Smith (US title: **Mr V**). 1941. BRITISH NATIONAL/UNITED ARTISTS. Howard produced and directed. With Francis L. Sullivan, Mary Morris, Hugh McDermott, Raymond Huntley, Peter Gawthorn, David Tomlinson.

49th Parallel (US title: **The Invaders**). 1941. ORTUS FILMS/COLUMBIA. Michael Powell. With Raymond Massey, Laurence Olivier, Anton Walbrook, Eric Portman, Glynis Johns, Finlay Currie.

The First of the Few (US title: **Spitfire**). 1942. MISBOURNE-BRITISH AVIATION/RKO. Howard produced and directed. With David Niven, Rosamond John, Roland Culver, Anne Firth, David Horne.

Howard also co-directed a propaganda documentary about the ATS called **The Gentle Sex** and produced another, **The Lamp Still Burns**, as a tribute to nurses.

Gary Cooper

For film-producer Arthur Jacobs, and many others, Gary Cooper 'was the greatest film star there has ever been'. He personified the quiet American. This tall, handsome, soft-spoken hero, slow to anger but lethal when roused, driven by an unshakeable honesty and determination to do the right thing, seemed to grow directly from Cooper's own personality. He did, however, show a surprising flexibility in his acting, especially in the area of light comedy. This tends to be overlooked in the overwhelming appreciation of him as the Westerner *par excellence*. The 'naturalness' in his acting cannot simply be written off as the result of Cooper being a 'personality star'. Over the years he proved himself to be an actor of subtlety and depth, if not of tremendous range.

Cooper was totally a creation of the movies. A film-star long before he became a true actor, he never appeared on the legitimate stage, unlike the other stars discussed so far. He deliberately set narrow limits on the exercise of his art and had an intuitive sense of what was right for him. He knew that his tremendous popularity sprang from his simple, natural screen personality and saw himself as the prototype 'Mr Average Joe American. Just an average guy from the middle of America.' It was a policy that paid off handsomely. He won two Oscars during his career, for fourteen years he was constantly in the box-office top ten, and in 1939 was named by the US Treasury as the nation's highest wage-earner, with an income that year of $482,819.

Cooper was born in the former gold-rush town of Helena in Montana in 1901, the second son of two British immigrants. His father, Charles Cooper, was a judge and owned a large ranch just outside the town where Frank (later Gary) spent a great deal of time, especially after a brief and not-too-successful spell at school in England, before the First World War. A serious car accident, while still at school, damaged his hip and he was told by the doctor that riding was the best therapy. During his convalescence on the ranch he became an expert horseman.

At college he gained something of a reputation as a cartoonist and when, in late 1924, he visited his parents in Los Angeles where the judge was administering the estate of some relatives, his ambition was to join a newspaper in this capacity. He was unsuccessful, however, and took a series of casual jobs (including one as a baby-photographer) before he made his unexpected start in the movies. Walking down Hollywood Boulevard one day he ran into a couple of school-friends, clad in cowboy gear and sporting numerous fresh bruises. They were working as cowboy extras for $10 a day in a Poverty Row studio and persuaded Cooper to join them. Right through 1925 and into 1926

he worked pretty well non-stop as an extra, pushing up his earnings by mastering the art of falling off his horse (for which he earned $5 and later $10 more for each tumble). He was probably in as many as fifty films during this period, including Valentino's *The Eagle* (1925), in which he appeared as a Cossack, and many Westerns such as Tom Mix's *The Lucky Horse-shoe* (1925) and *The Vanishing American* (1925) with Richard Dix and Noah Beery. The uncertainty here is due to the practice of shooting large amounts of action footage which could be cut and recut for several different films.

Then he acquired an agent, who not only changed his name from Frank to Gary (she came from Gary, Indiana) but also got him a bit part in Henry King's *The Winning of Barbara Worth* (1926) with Ronald Colman and Vilma Banky. His break came when the actor hired to play Abe Lee, the unsuccessful suitor for Barbara's hand who dies in Colman's arms, was tied up on another film. He was offered the part and, according to one biographer, his death-scene was most convincing because, under the hot studio lights, he fell asleep. His appeal to movie-goers was immediately apparent and he signed a contract with Paramount at $150 a week. His first film for them was the legendary *It* (1927) with Clara Bow, in which he had a tiny part as a reporter. Miss Bow, however, was very taken with him and asked for him as the male lead in her next picture, *Children of Divorce* (1927). It was his first excursion into romantic movies and he was not good. He found the whole business of love-making in front of the cameras highly embarrassing and he was, in fact, taken off the picture once because of his woodenness.

In his next film, *Arizona Bound* (1927), he was back in the saddle, very much more at home, and he played the hero in two more Westerns that year, *Nevada* (from a Zane Grey story) and *The Last Outlaw*, with Flash the Wonder Horse. Perhaps his most important part in 1927 was his shortest. In William Wellman's *Wings* (1927) he played a tough, experienced flyer who philosophizes to the heroes, 'Buddy' Rogers and Richard Arlen, for two minutes before flying to his death. It was a small but distinguished appearance which greatly enhanced his growing reputation.

That reputation was not based simply on his skill in action pictures and convincingly heroic demeanour – he was well and truly launched as a heart-throb, thanks partly to his off-screen relationship with Clara Bow. A romance which started off as a publicity stunt apparently turned into the real thing, and Cooper became known as the 'It' Boy for a while. Of course his own good looks and particular brand of shy charm as a screen lover had a great deal to do with it as well.

Clara's Bow's place in his off-screen affections was taken, in 1928, by Evelyn Brent, his leading lady in *Beau Sabreur* (1928), a desert drama concocted to use up Paramount's spare footage from the 1926 *Beau Geste*. His other leading ladies on-screen that year included

Fay Wray, Florence Vidor, Esther Ralston, Colleen Moore and Nancy Carroll. Paramount tried to promote Cooper and Wray as 'Paramount's glorious young lovers' – but the public didn't really buy this. In 1929 Cooper started another well-publicized, and fairly turbulent, affair with his co-star in *Wolf Song* (1929), Lupe Velez, which cannot have harmed his romantic image. *Betrayal* (1929) with Emil Jannings and Esther Ralston, in which he played a handsome (curly-haired) Viennese artist, was Cooper's last Silent film. It was a somewhat dated melodrama and was not well received by critics or audiences. However, in his first Talkie, *The Virginian* (1929), Cooper was most successful, making an effortless transition to Sound. Walter Huston played the villain, Trampas, to whom Cooper (in the course of a poker game) addresses a popularly misquoted famous movie line – 'When you call me that, smile!' The Times found him 'everything he should be . . . strong, attractive and serious.'

Cooper made eleven films during the next two years, mostly action pictures, of which the most outstanding were *Morocco* (1930), a Foreign Legion romance with Marlene Dietrich, and *City Streets* (1931) with Sylvia Sidney. Both started off as problem pictures for Cooper. *Morocco*, Josef von Sternberg's American début, remained a problem throughout, mainly because of Sternberg's preoccupation with Dietrich and his habit of directing her in German. Cooper hated him and was furious when he discovered that he and Adolphe Menjou had been given second billing. He vowed never to do another film with Dietrich and later turned down the lead in *Dishonoured* (though in 1936, with Borzage directing, he made *Desire* with her). None the less, he was very successful as Legionnaire Tom Brown, a love 'em and leave 'em character who came across powerfully despite von Sternberg's concentration on Dietrich. *City Streets* was, initially, Paramount's means of disciplining Cooper for making a fuss about money. It was originally intended as a vehicle for Clara Bow with Cooper supporting, but Bow was involved in a court case and newcomer Sylvia Sidney took the part. Directed by Rouben Mamoulian and with an original screenplay by Dashiell Hammett, *City Streets* was an innovatory and immensely successful film. Cooper was marvellous and Sylvia Sidney became a star on the strength of it.

The pace was beginning to tell on Cooper by now. Following severe attacks of 'flu and jaundice, he took himself off to Europe to relax and recuperate, and became involved with the international smart set of the day while in Italy. After a brief return to America to make *His Woman* (1931) with Claudette Colbert, he joined his friends big-game hunting in Africa until news of Paramount's grooming of Fredric March and a newcomer, Cary Grant, as possible replacements sent him hastening back to Hollywood.

During the period 1932 to 1941, Gary Cooper made twenty-four features, of which only four were Westerns. One was *The Plainsman* (1936), Cecil B. DeMille's 'deliciously grandiose' version of the Wild Bill Hickok legend with Jean Arthur as Calamity Jane, but the most notable was probably William Wyler's *The Westerner* (1940) with Walter Brennan as the legendary Judge Roy Bean. These years also saw the first and best screen version of Hemingway's *A Farewell to Arms* (1932) directed by Frank Borzage, with Helen Hayes (Cooper and Hemingway subsequently became good friends), the highly successful *Lives of a Bengal Lancer* (1935) directed by Henry Hathaway, and Frank Capra's *Mr Deeds Goes to Town* (1936). The latter did for Cooper what *It Happened One Night* had done for Gable a year earlier in terms of box-office popularity and critical acclaim (though it didn't win him an Oscar). In 1933 he married New York socialite and aspiring actress, Veronica Balfe.

For Cooper the early 1940s were his peak years. *Meet John Doe* (1941) was another Capra film, more pretentious and less successful than *Mr Deeds*. (In retrospect, the theme of guarding against fascism squares rather oddly with Cooper's statements to the House Un-American Activities Committee in 1947.) But with *Sergeant York* (1941), the true story of a First World War conscientious objector turned hero, he entered a winning streak and gained his first Oscar.

Gary Cooper – 'The greatest film star there has ever been and that includes Gable', according to Hollywood producer Arthur Jacobs. He was certainly the nearest Hollywood ever came to the romantic image of Chaucer's 'parfit gentle knight'.

Howard Hawks directed both this and Cooper's next film, *Ball of Fire* (1941), which was a complete and highly successful change of pace, with him as a sheltered academic confronted by a burlesque dancer called Sugarpuss O'Shea (Barbara Stanwyck). In 1942 *The Pride of the Yankees* cast him as Lou Gehrig, the real-life baseball hero struck down by multiple sclerosis, and many consider this to have been his greatest role. 'If Cooper had left any doubts,' wrote film historian Homer Dickens, 'that he was an actor as well as a screen personality, he eliminated them completely with his splendid, sensitive and many-faceted performance.' In 1943, at Hemingway's special request, he played Robert Jordan in *For Whom the Bell Tolls* with Ingrid Bergman. The film largely ignored the political aspects of the novel and the Spanish Civil War served only as background for the great romance between Cooper and Bergman, who both won Academy Award nominations.

The post-war years saw Cooper's career in the doldrums. His films were competent but relatively undistinguished, though he worked with good directors: Sam Wood in *Saratoga Trunk* (1945), Fritz Lang in *Cloak and Dagger* (1946), Leo McCarey in *Good Sam* (1948) and King Vidor in *The Fountainhead* (1949), the film version of Ayn Rand's best-selling novel. Although the latter was not particularly outstanding (even Vidor admitted later that Cooper was not ideally cast as the architectural genius Howard Roark), it had momentous repercussions in Cooper's private life. He fell in love with his co-star, Patricia Neal, and for several years his marriage went through a very rocky period. He and his wife were legally separated in 1951, but by the end of 1954 had been reconciled and stayed together till his death in 1961.

The year 1952 saw Cooper right back on acting form in Fred Zinnemann's *High Noon*, which brought rave reviews and totally restored his slightly crumbling reputation. Among the first of the new 'adult' Westerns, dealing more with morals than sheer physical courage, the film was the perfect vehicle for the powerful image of the Westerner that Cooper had been building up over the years. His Sheriff Will Kane was cool, courageous, and the embodiment of integrity and determination. It was a magnificently understated performance, winning him his second Oscar and launching him on a run of more successful films, including Aldrich's *Vera Cruz* (1954) with Burt Lancaster, William Wyler's *Friendly Persuasion* (1956) and Delmer Daves's *The Hanging Tree* (1959). As Parkinson and Jeavons said in their 'Pictorial History of Westerns', 'if the Western came to rely on Cooper, he could in turn thank the genre for rescuing him from periodic bad patches.'

Gary Cooper died in May 1961. In 1960 he was awarded an honorary Oscar for his services to the film-industry. He had been one of Hollywood's most enduring stars and had won a tremendous following of both men and women by his consistent portrayal of 'Mr Average Joe American'. John Barrymore once said of him, 'That fellow is the world's greatest actor. He can do with no effort what the rest of us spent years trying to learn: to be perfectly natural.'

The Virginian (1929) was Cooper's Sound début and had him back in what many people came to consider his natural habitat – the saddle. The anxious-looking girl is Mary Brian.

William Wellman's *Wings* (1927) was the most famous war film of the inter-war years and though Cooper's part was tiny, it made a disproportionate impact on audiences. Here he is with comrades Buddy Rogers (left) and Richard Arlen.

Making *Morocco* (1930) with Marlene Dietrich was a painful experience for Cooper, who suffered at the hands of von Sternberg, but his playing of the rakish legionnaire was delightful and very successful.

Cooper was, apparently, as embarrassed as he looks here when filming *Children of Divorce* (1927) with Clara Bow (centre), but their off-screen romance got him noticed and labelled, for a while, as the 'It' Boy. On the right is Esther Ralston.

The delicious Jean Arthur as Calamity Jane woos a dour-looking Wild Bill Hickok (Cooper) in *The Plainsman* (1936).

Hemingway it wasn't, but terribly romantic it undoubtedly was. *For Whom the Bell Tolls* (1943) centred the Spanish Civil War on Cooper's love for Maria (Ingrid Bergman).

Ball of Fire (1941) gave Cooper an opportunity to show his paces in comedy as a shy professor doing research into slang – and Sugarpuss O'Shea (Barbara Stanwyck). Lurking in the wardrobe is Dan Duryea.

Cooper was not very happily cast as architect Howard Roark in *The Fountainhead* (1949). His co-star was Patricia Neal, who also featured strongly in his off-screen life.

Gary Cooper

Films as an unbilled extra:
The Thundering Herd
(1925); **Wild Horse Mesa**
(1925); **The Lucky
Horseshoe** (1925); **The
Vanishing American**
(1925); **The Eagle** (1925);
The Enchanted Hill
(1925); **Watch Your Wife**
(1926). It is also claimed
that he appeared in three
'featurettes': **Tricks**
(1925); **Three Pals** (1925);
Lightnin' Wins (1926).

**The Winning Of Barbara
Worth.** 1926. GOLDWYN/
UNITED ARTISTS. With
Ronald Colman, Vilma
Banky, Charles Lane, Paul
McAllister.
It. 1927. PARAMOUNT.
Clarence Badger. With
Clara Bow, Antonio
Moreno, William Austin,
Jacqueline Gadson, Julia
Swayne Gordon, Elinor
Glyn.
Children of Divorce. 1927.
PARAMOUNT. Frank Lloyd.
With Clara Bow, Esther
Ralston, Einar Hanson,
Hedda Hopper, Norman
Trevor, Julia Swayne
Gordon, Edward
Martindel.
Arizona Bound. 1927.
PARAMOUNT. John Waters.
With Betty Jewel, El
Brendel, Jack Doughtery,

Christian J. Frank.
Wings. 1927. PARAMOUNT.
William Wellman. With
Charles 'Buddy' Rogers,
Richard Arlen, Clara Bow,
Jobyna Ralston.
Nevada. 1927. PARAMOUNT.
John Waters. With William
Powell, Thelma Todd,
Philip Strange, Ernie S.
Adams.
The Last Outlaw. 1927.
PARAMOUNT. Arthur
Rosson. With Betty
Jewel, Jack Luden,
Herbert Prior, Jim Cory.
Beau Sabreur. 1928.
PARAMOUNT. John Waters.
With Evelyn Brent,
William Powell, Noah
Beery, Roscoe Karns.
**The Legion of the
Condemned.** 1928. PARA-
MOUNT. William Wellman.
With Fay Wray, Lane
Chandler, Barry Norton.
Doomsday. 1928. PARA-
MOUNT. Rowland V. Lee.
With Florence Vidor,
Lawrence Grant, Charles
A. Stevenson.
Half A Bride. 1928. PARA-
MOUNT. Gregory La Cava.
With Esther Ralston,
William Worthington,
Freeman Wood, Mary
Doran.
Lilac Time. 1928. FIRST
NATIONAL. George
Fitzmaurice. With Colleen
Moore, Kathryn McGuire,
Burr McIntosh, Eugenie
Besserer.
The First Kiss. 1928.
PARAMOUNT. Rowland V.
Lee. With Fay Wray, Lane

Chandler, Leslie Fenton,
Paul Fix.
The Shopworn Angel.
1929. PARAMOUNT.
Richard Wallace. First
Talkie. With Nancy
Carroll, Paul Lukas,
Emmet King, Mildred
Washington.
Wolf Song. 1929. PARA-
MOUNT. Victor Fleming.
With Lupe Velez, Louis
Wolheim, Constantine
Romanoff.
The Betrayal. 1929. PARA-
MOUNT. Lewis Milestone.
With Emil Jannings,
Esther Ralston, Jada
Welles, Douglas Haig.
The Virginian. 1929.
PARAMOUNT. Victor
Fleming. With Walter
Huston, Richard Arlen,
Mary Brian, Chester
Conklin, Eugene Pallette.
Only the Brave. 1930.
PARAMOUNT. Frank Tuttle.
With Mary Brian, Phillips
Holmes, James Neill,
Morgan Farley, Virginia
Bruce.
Paramount on Parade.
1930. PARAMOUNT. Dorothy
Arzner, Otto Brower,
Edmund Goulding,
Rowland V. Lee, Ernst
Lubitsch, Edward
Sutherland, Frank Tuttle,
etc. With all-star cast.
The Texan. 1930. PARA-
MOUNT. John Cromwell.
With Fay Wray, Emma
Dunn, Oscar Apfel.
Seven Days' Leave. 1930.
PARAMOUNT. Richard
Wallace. With Beryl
Mercer, Arthur Hoyt,
Daisy Belmore.
A Man from Wyoming.
1930. PARAMOUNT. Rowland
V. Lee. With June Collyer,
Regis Toomey, Morgan
Farley, E. H. Calvert.
The Spoilers. 1930. PARA-
MOUNT. Edwin Carewe.
With William 'Stage' Boyd,
Kay Johnson, Betty
Compson, Slim
Summerville.
Morocco. 1930. PARA-
MOUNT. Josef von
Sternberg. With Marlene
Dietrich, Adolphe Menjou,
Ullrich Haupt, Juliette
Compton, Francis
McDonald, Albert Conti.
Fighting Caravans. 1931.
PARAMOUNT. Otto Brower
and David Burton. With
Lili Damita, Ernest
Torrence, Tully Marshall,
Fred Kohler, Eugene
Pallette.
City Streets. 1931.
PARAMOUNT. Rouben
Mamoulian. With Sylvia
Sidney, Paul Lukas,
William 'Stage' Boyd,
Guy Kibbee.
I Take This Woman.
1931. PARAMOUNT. Marion
Gering. With Carole
Lombard, Helen Ware,
Lester Vail, Charles
Trowbridge, Clara
Blandick.
His Woman. 1931. PARA-
MOUNT. Edward Sloman.
With Claudette Colbert,
Douglass Dumbrille,
Averill Harris, Richard
Spiro.
Make Me A Star. 1932.

PARAMOUNT. William
Beaudine. Guest
appearance as himself.
With Stuart Erwin, Joan
Blondell, ZaSu Pitts, Ben
Turpin.
The Devil and the Deep.
1932. PARAMOUNT. Marion
Gering. With Tallulah
Bankhead, Charles
Laughton, Cary Grant,
Paul Porcasi, Juliette
Compton.
If I Had a Million. 1932.
PARAMOUNT. Stephen
Roberts, Norman McLeod,
William Seiter, H. B.
Humberstone, James
Cruze, Ernst Lubitsch,
Norman Taurog. With
Roscoe Karns, Jack Oakie,
Charles Laughton, W. C.
Fields, George Raft, Mary
Boland, Charles Ruggles,
Alison Skipworth, Frances
Dee.
A Farewell to Arms.
1932. PARAMOUNT. Frank
Borzage. With Helen
Hayes, Adolphe Menjou,
Mary Phillips, Jack La
Rue.
Today We Live. 1933.
MGM. Howard Hawks. With
Joan Crawford, Franchot
Tone, Robert Young,
Roscoe Karns, Louise
Closser Hale, Rollo Lloyd,
Hilda Vaughn.
One Sunday Afternoon.
1933. PARAMOUNT. Stephen
Roberts. With Frances
Fuller, Neil Hamilton, Fay
Wray, Roscoe Karns, Jane
Darwell.
Design for Living. 1933.
PARAMOUNT. Ernst
Lubitsch. With Fredric
March, Miriam Hopkins,
Edward Everett Horton,
Franklin Pangborn, Isabel
Jewell, Jane Darwell.
Alice in Wonderland.
1933. PARAMOUNT. Norman
Z. McLeod. With Charlotte
Henry, Cary Grant, W. C.
Fields, Edna May Oliver,
Richard Arlen, Edward
Everett Horton.
Operator 13. 1934.
COSMOPOLITAN/MGM.
Richard Boleslawski. With
Marion Davies, Sidney
Toler, Mae Clarke, Walter
Long, The Mills Brothers,
Jean Parker, Marjorie
Gateson, Sterling
Holloway.
Now and Forever. 1934.
PARAMOUNT. Henry
Hathaway. With Carole
Lombard, Shirley Temple,
Henry Kolker, Charlotte
Granville, Sir Guy
Standing, Akim Tamiroff.
The Wedding Night. 1935.
GOLDWYN/UNITED ARTISTS.
King Vidor. With Anna
Sten, Ralph Bellamy, Sig
Ruman, Helen Vinson,
Walter Brennan.
Lives of a Bengal Lancer.
1935. PARAMOUNT. Henry
Hathaway. With Franchot
Tone, Sir Guy Standing, C.
Aubrey Smith, Monte Blue,
Kathleen Burke, J. Carrol
Naish, Richard Cromwell,
Akim Tamiroff.
Peter Ibbetson. 1935.
PARAMOUNT. Henry
Hathaway. With Ann
Harding, John Halliday,

Ida Lupino, Douglass
Dumbrille, Virginia
Weidler, Dickie Moore,
Donald Meek.
Desire. 1936. PARAMOUNT.
Frank Borzage. With
Marlene Dietrich, John
Halliday, William
Frawley, Akim Tamiroff,
Allan Mowbray.
Mr Deeds Goes to Town.
1936. COLUMBIA. Frank
Capra. With Jean Arthur,
George Bancroft, Douglass
Dumbrille, Lionel Stander,
H. B. Warner, Dennis
O'Keefe, Franklin
Pangborn.
Hollywood Boulevard.
1936. PARAMOUNT. Robert
Florey. An uncredited
appearance. With Pat
O'Malley, Freeman Wood,
Maurice Costello, Francis
X. Bushman, Esther
Ralston.
**The General Died At
Dawn.** 1936. PARAMOUNT.
Lewis Milestone. With
Akim Tamiroff, Madeleine
Carroll, Porter Hall,
William Frawley, Dudley
Digges.
The Plainsman. 1936.
PARAMOUNT. Cecil B.
DeMille. With Jean
Arthur, James Ellison,
Charles Bickford, Anthony
Quinn, Porter Hall, Helen
Burgess, John Miljan,
James Mason.
Souls at Sea. 1937. PARA-
MOUNT. Henry Hathaway.
With George Raft, Frances
Dee, Henry Wilcoxon,
Robert Cummings, Olympe
Bradna, Porter Hall,
Virginia Weidler.
**The Adventures of
Marco Polo.** 1938.
GOLDWYN/UNITED ARTISTS.
Archie Mayo. With Sigrid
Gurie, Basil Rathbone,
Binnie Barnes, Alan Hale,
Lana Turner, Ernest Truex,
George Bambier.
Bluebird's Eighth Wife.
1938. PARAMOUNT. Ernst
Lubitsch. With Claudette
Colbert, Edward Everett
Horton, David Niven,
Hermann Bing, Franklin
Pangborn, Elizabeth
Patterson.
**The Cowboy And The
Lady.** 1938. GOLDWYN/
UNITED ARTISTS. H. C.
Potter. With Walter
Brennan, Merle Oberon,
Patsy Kelly, Fuzzy Knight,
Mabel Todd, Henry Kolker.
Beau Geste. 1939. PARA-
MOUNT. William A.
Wellman. With Ray
Milland, Brian Donlevy,
Robert Preston, Susan
Hayward, J. Carrol Naish,
Broderick Crawford.
The Real Glory. 1939.
GOLDWYN/UNITED ARTISTS.
Henry Hathaway. With
David Niven, Andrea
Leeds, Reginald Owen, Kay
Johnson, Broderick
Crawford.
The Westerner. 1940.
GOLDWYN/UNITED ARTISTS.
William Wyler. With
Walter Brennan, Doris
Davenport, Chill Wills,
Fred Stone, Forrest
Tucker, Dana Andrews,
Paul Hurst.

High Noon (1952) revived
Cooper's flagging career
and crystallized perfectly
his image as the perfect,
quiet – but brave –
Westerner.

Cooper in 1947.

↑ Clark Gable and Vivien
Leigh in *Gone With the
Wind* (1939).

———————————→

Cary Grant in 1947/8.

Northwest Mounted Police. 1940. PARAMOUNT. Cecil B. DeMille. With Madeleine Carroll, Paulette Goddard, Preston Foster, Robert Preston, Lon Chaney Jr, Akim Tamiroff.

Meet John Doe. 1941. WARNER BROTHERS. Frank Capra. With Barbara Stanwyck, Walter Brennan, Edward Arnold, Spring Byington, James Gleason.

Sergeant York. 1941. WARNER BROTHERS. Howard Hawks. Academy Award and New York Film Critics' Award. With Walter Brennan, Joan Leslie, George Tobias, Dickie Moore, Ward Bond, Noah Beery Jr, Howard da Silva.

Ball of Fire. 1941. GOLDWYN/RKO-RADIO. Howard Hawks. With Barbara Stanwyck, Oscar Homolka, Henry Travers, S. Z. Sakall, Dan Duryea, Dana Andrews.

The Pride of the Yankees. 1942. GOLDWYN/RKO-RADIO. Sam Wood. With Teresa Wright, Babe Ruth, Walter Brennan, Dan Duryea.

For Whom the Bell Tolls. 1943. PARAMOUNT. Sam Wood. With Ingrid Bergman, Akim Tamiroff, Arturo de Cordova, Katina Paxinou, Duncan Renaldo, Joseph Calleia.

The Story of Dr Wassell. 1944. PARAMOUNT. Cecil B. DeMille. With Laraine Day, Signe Hasso, Dennis O'Keefe, Paul Kelly, Barbara Britton, Carol Thurston, Carl Esmond.

Casanova Brown. 1944. INTERNATIONAL/RKO. Sam Wood. With Teresa Wright, Frank Morgan, Anita Louise.

Along Came Jones. 1945. INTERNATIONAL/RKO. Stuart Heisler. Produced by Cooper. With Loretta Young, William Demarest, Dan Duryea, Frank Sully.

Saratoga Trunk. 1945. WARNER BROTHERS. Sam Wood. With Ingrid Bergman, Flora Robson, Jerry Austen, John Warburton, Florence Bates.

Cloak and Dagger. 1946. US PICTURES/WARNER BROTHERS. Fritz Lang. With Lilli Palmer, Robert Alda, Vladimir Sokoloff, J. Edward Bromberg.

Unconquered. 1947. PARAMOUNT. Cecil B. DeMille. With Paulette Goddard, Howard da Silva, Boris Karloff, Cecil Kellaway, Katherine DeMille, Ward Bond, Henry Wilcoxon, C. Aubrey Smith.

Variety Girl. 1947. PARAMOUNT. George Marshall. Cooper appears as himself. With all-star cast, including Bing Crosby, Bob Hope, Ray Milland, Veronica Lake.

Good Sam. 1948. RAINBOW/RKO. Leo McCarey. With Ann Sheridan, Ray Collins, Edmund Lowe, Ruth Roman, William Frawley.

The Fountainhead. 1949. WARNER BROTHERS. King Vidor. With Patricia Neal, Raymond Massey, Kent Smith, Robert Douglas.

It's a Great Feeling. 1949. WARNER BROTHERS. David Butler. Cooper guested as himself. With Dennis Morgan, Doris Day, Jack Carson.

Task Force. 1949. WARNER BROTHERS. Delmer Daves. With Jane Wyatt, Wayne Morris, Walter Brennan, Julie London, Jack Holt, Bruce Bennett.

Bright Leaf. 1950. WARNER BROTHERS. Michael Curtiz. With Lauren Bacall, Patricia Neal, Jack Carson, Donald Crisp, Gladys George, Elizabeth Patterson.

Dallas. 1950. WARNER BROTHERS. Stuart Heisler. With Steve Cochran, Raymond Massey, Ruth Roman, Barbara Payton, Leif Erickson, Antonio Moreno.

You're in the Navy Now (original title: **USS Teakettle**). 1951. TWENTIETH CENTURY-FOX. Henry Hathaway. With Jane Greer, Eddie Albert, Millard Mitchell, Jack Webb, John McIntyre, Ed Begley, Lee Marvin.

Starlift. 1951. WARNER BROTHERS. Roy Del Ruth. Guest appearance. With Doris Day, Gordon MacRae, Dick Wesson, Virginia Nelson.

It's a Big Country. 1951. MGM. Charles Vidor, Richard Thorpe, John Sturges, Don Hartman, Don Weis, Clarence Brown and William Wellman. Cooper appeared in Episode 6 directed by Clarence Brown. With all-star cast.

Distant Drums. 1951. US PICTURES/WARNER BROTHERS. Raoul Walsh. With Arthur Hunnicutt, Ray Teal, Richard Webb, Mari Aldon, Robert Barratt.

High Noon. 1952. UNITED ARTISTS. Fred Zinnemann. Academy Award. With Thomas Mitchell, Lloyd Bridges, Katy Jurado, Grace Kelly, Otto Kruger, Lon Chaney Jr, Henry Morgan.

Springfield Rifle. 1952. WARNER BROTHERS. Andre De Toth. With David Brian, Phyllis Thaxter, Phillip Carey, Paul Kelly, Lon Chaney Jr.

Return to Paradise. 1953. UNITED ARTISTS. Mark Robson. With Roberta Haynes, Barry Jones, John Hudson, Moira MacDonald.

Blowing Wild. 1953. US PICTURES/WARNER BROTHERS. Hugo Fregonese. With Barbara Stanwyck, Ruth Roman, Ward Bond, Anthony Quinn.

Garden of Evil. 1954. TWENTIETH CENTURY-FOX. Henry Hathaway. With Richard Widmark, Susan Hayward, Hugh Marlowe, Cameron Mitchell, Rita Moreno.

Vera Cruz. 1954. HECHT-LANCASTER/UNITED ARTISTS. Robert Aldrich. With Burt Lancaster, Denise Darcel, Cesar Romero, Ernest Borgnine, Sarita Montiel.

The Court-Martial of Billy Mitchell. 1955. US PICTURES/WARNER BROTHERS. Otto Preminger. With Rod Steiger, Charles Bickford, Ralph Bellamy, Elizabeth Montgomery, Fred Clark, Darren McGavin.

Friendly Persuasion. 1956. ALLIED ARTISTS. With Dorothy McGuire, Marjorie Main, Anthony Perkins, Richard Eyer, Robert Middleton, Phyllis Love.

Love in the Afternoon. 1957. ALLIED ARTISTS. Billy Wilder. With Audrey Hepburn, Maurice Chevalier, John McGiver.

Ten North Frederick. 1958. TWENTIETH CENTURY-FOX. Philip Dunne. With Diana Varsi, Suzy Parker, Geraldine Fitzgerald, Tom Tully, Stuart Whitman, Barbara Nichols.

Man of the West. 1958. MIRISCH/UNITED ARTISTS. Anthony Mann. With Arthur O'Connell, Jack Lord, John Dehner, Frank Ferguson, Julie London, Lee J. Cobb.

The Hanging Tree. 1959. WARNER BROTHERS. Delmer Daves. With Maria Schell, Karl Malden, George C. Scott, Ben Piazza.

Alias Jesse James. 1959. UNITED ARTISTS. Norman Z. McLeod. Unbilled guest appearance. With Bob Hope, Wendell Corey, Ward Bond, Rhonda Fleming.

They Came to Cordura. 1959. COLUMBIA. Robert Rossen. With Van Heflin, Rita Hayworth, Tab Hunter, Richard Conte, Dick York, Michael Callan.

The Wreck of the Mary Deare. 1959. MGM. Michael Anderson. With Charlton Heston, Emlyn Williams, Michael Redgrave, Virginia McKenna, Cecil Parker, Alexander Knox, Richard Harris.

The Naked Edge. 1961. UNITED ARTISTS. Michael Anderson. With Deborah Kerr, Eric Portman, Diane Cilento, Hermione Gingold, Michael Wilding, Peter Cushing.

Cooper is also supposed to have appeared in **Lest We Forget** (1937).

Clark Gable

'Clark Gable was the king of an empire called Hollywood,' wrote Joan Crawford in 1967. 'The Empire is not what it once was – but the King has not been dethroned, even after death.' Gable had acquired the title of King of Hollywood in 1937 when Ed Sullivan invited readers of his nationally syndicated movie column to nominate a King and Queen of the Movies. Twenty million votes were cast and Gable was elected King by an overwhelming majority. Nobody now remembers who was Queen (she was in fact Myrna Loy) but Gable's title stuck – becoming an established part of the Hollywood mythology. For thirty years the King was one of the most popular male film-stars around, manhandling and loving the screen's greatest beauties from Harlow, Garbo and Norma Shearer to Grace Kelly, Ava Gardner and Marilyn Monroe.

His enduring fame and popularity in a business so short on survival and so long on swift declines rests mainly on one film – *Gone With the Wind* (1939) – in which he played, or rather lived (so interchangeable seem the role and the man), the part of Rhett Butler. During the first decade of his career his reputation was unassailable, but after the war it was less stable. He had trouble finding good scripts and, though his personal popularity and status remained unchanged, his screen appearances varied greatly in quality. It was the re-releases of *Gone With the Wind* which each time launched him on a new wave of popularity and admiration, and Gable himself acknowledged this, saying that the various revivals of the film were 'the only thing that kept me a big star'.

Gable's on-screen personality seemed to mirror very precisely his own off-screen character. He had a directness, a vitality and a strength which appealed to both sexes. For women it made him appear exhilaratingly virile and masterful, a challenge and a threat, a man who in John Kobal's words 'slapped women around with one hand and defended them with the other'. For men his physical toughness, his obvious dislike of the phoney and over-elaborate and his air of having come from honest-to-god small-town America, made him seem like a man's man. A famous early example of his influence over the male sector of the population occurred in *It Happened One Night* (1934) with Claudette Colbert, when he appeared (daringly for those days) without a vest. This confirmed his tough, brawny virility and overnight the men of America rejected their under-shirts. Several underwear manufacturers promptly went out of business, or so the story goes, and Gable won an Oscar and yet more fans.

He was born in Cadiz, Ohio, in 1901, the son of William Gable, an oil wildcatter and his rather frail wife, Addie, who died less than a year after the birth of her son. After a reasonably uneventful childhood and adolescence (his father remarried when he was two and he adored his stepmother), Gable started his acting career in his teens as a call-boy with a stock company in Akron, Ohio. His disappointed father, however, persuaded him to give up the theatre and join him in the Oklahoma oil-fields. Gable hated this period, but later acknowledged that his work there toughened him up, giving him the powerful physique which later played such a vital part in the creation of the Gable persona.

As soon as he was twenty-one and could claim a small legacy from his grandfather, he went back to acting. He joined a travelling company and for two years, till the group went bankrupt, played any and every part he could get his hands on. When the company folded, he worked as a telephone linesman, a lumberjack, a necktie salesman and a reporter before finding his way back to acting through the kind offices of Miss Josephine Dillon, later to be the first Mrs Gable. He met her in Portland, Oregon, where he was working for the telephone company and she was putting on good amateur shows. She took him under her wing, started to give him acting lessons, and, when she left Portland for Los Angeles to open an acting school, Gable went with her. They married in December 1924 – he was twenty-three and she was thirty-six.

Gable worked as an extra in several movies, including Stroheim's *The Merry Widow* starring John Gilbert, but then shifted back to the stage playing, among other sizeable parts, the juvenile lead in Lionel Barrymore's production of 'The Copperhead', which was the start of a lifelong friendship. He moved to Broadway but returned to the West Coast to play the by-then-famous Spencer Tracy part in 'The Last Mile' – that of a condemned man on Death Row. He was a great success, and among those who came backstage to congratulate him was Lionel Barrymore. He persuaded Gable to do a screen-test for MGM wearing a mini-sarong, a hibiscus behind his ear, dark make-up and little else. It was a total disaster. By this time, however, Gable had acquired an agent, Minna Wallis (sister of Hal, the producer), and she got him a small part in a medium-budget Western, *The Painted Desert* (1931), playing a brutish, unscrupulous cowboy. Then he took another screen-test, this time for Warner Brothers. Jack Warner was not impressed. 'What can you do with a guy with ears like that?' he is reported to have said. (Later Milton Berle referred to them as 'the best ears of our lives'.)

Gable was about to pack his bags and return to Broadway when he received *two* film offers – one from RKO, the other from Thalberg at MGM. He accepted the latter and was cast as Constance Bennett's brother-in-law in *The Easiest Way* (1931). Things were looking up, and Gable was noticed in the film.

In fact 1931 was the year of Clark Gable. In it he made twelve films and rose to fame and stardom. He also married for the second time. He and Josephine Dillon had drifted well apart and finally divorced. In the summer of 1931 he married Ria Langham, a thrice-married society lady from Houston, Texas, whom he met in New York. She was seventeen years his senior.

The film that really took Gable to the top was *A Free Soul* (1931), with Norma Shearer, Leslie Howard and Lionel Barrymore. In it, playing a smooth racketeer, he slaps Norma Shearer (a spoilt little rich girl) across the face and slams her down in a chair while telling her exactly what he does and does not want of her. This scene electrified female audiences, who saw a desirable, sexy man treating a desirable 'nice' girl roughly and yet, in a curious way, ardently. That slap marked the end of an era of romantic heart-throbs. From then onwards male stars all showed a degree of toughness and challenge in their attitudes to women which had been totally lacking in the Great Lovers of the previous decade.

After this Gable was much in demand – and not just by the fans. He benefited not only from his own qualities as a screen actor but also from a chronic shortage of young, attractive leading men. Gilbert, Barrymore and Novarro were all on the way out. There were good actresses aplenty in 1931 and Gable acted with some of Hollywood's top female stars during his first year of stardom – often at their request. Joan Crawford was the first to ask for him in *Dance, Fools, Dance* (he made two more films with her in 1931 – *Laughing Sinners* and *Possessed*) followed by Garbo (*Susan Lenox – Her Fall and Rise*) and Norma Shearer.

MGM were stunned by the speed of his rise to stardom. In Gable they had not only an exceedingly hot property, but a cheap and profitable one too. He cost around $4,000 a picture – as opposed to the $150,000 paid to a star like Will Rogers.

In his first 1932 film, *Polly of the Circus* with Marion Davies, in which he played the unlikely part of a clergyman, he took top billing and an unscheduled vacation right in the middle of shooting. He returned only when MGM agreed to raise his salary substantially. Later he also expressed resentment at what he obviously felt to be MGM's high-handed treatment of him. 'My advice has never been asked about a picture,' he told a Photoplay reporter in 1933. 'I walked on the lot one day and was told I was to play *Red Dust* in place of John Gilbert.'

Red Dust (1932), in which he played opposite Jean Harlow, was a box-office sensation. Gable, as a plantation manager in Indo-China, divided his attentions between Harlow the tramp and Mary Astor, a prim newly-wed. Again he played it rough and tough – dunking Harlow in a barrel of water and getting her to take off his dusty boots. Audiences loved his blend of simplicity, arrogance and sheer sex-appeal. Despite the film's great success, MGM did not do much with Gable afterwards, and in 1933 he returned to the studio after a slight illness to find that he had been cast as second lead opposite Joan Crawford and Franchot Tone in *Dancing Lady* (1933). He rowed with the front office about

this apparent down-grading and to teach him a lesson they promptly loaned him out to Columbia for a film called *Overland Bus*. Gable was furious. At that time Columbia was very much a minor studio and MGM had in fact sold them the property, not thinking it good enough for real star treatment. The MGM executives must have kicked themselves later. The film, directed by Frank Capra, starring Gable and Claudette Colbert and renamed *It Happened One Night*, was a smash hit and swept the board at the 1934 Oscar ceremony winning five awards, including one for Gable as Best Actor. Gable's performance had the by-now-familiar but no less exciting blend of sexual assurance and toughness. This enabled him to cut right across class barriers, rudely taking the society lady (Colbert) down a peg or two, and endeared him even more to the average cinema-goer, both male and female, who could identify with his cheerful and frequently brutal disregard for 'Society' conventions. Sex had become, in his hands, the great leveller – in this sense (though not in many other ways) Gable was a democrat. If there is an element of sado-masochism in his treatment of women on the screen, then this 'democratizing' aspect makes it not only palatable but immensely enjoyable.

Gable was MGM's blue-eyed boy from that

Gable – 'He was America's dream of itself, a symbol of courage, indomitable against the greatest odds. But he was also a human being, kind, likeable, a guy right out of the life all around the fans who worshipped him.'
(Ben Hecht)

moment on. Sadly, however, his subsequent pictures did not again achieve this high standard (though he continued to prove a major box-office attraction) until *Mutiny on the Bounty* (1935) with Charles Laughton as Captain Bligh to his Fletcher Christian. Gable was reluctant to take the part initially, fearing that he would look foolish in period costume, but the film was both a critical and commercial success, gaining him another Oscar nomination.

He was also reluctant to appear in another success, *San Francisco* (1936), believing that he would be overshadowed by Jeanette MacDonald, who had specifically asked for him as her leading man. Gable enjoyed making the film, especially acting with Spencer Tracy whom he liked and admired. Shortly after this came his first and greatest disaster, *Parnell* (1937). He was totally miscast as the Irish political leader (Myrna Loy played Kitty O'Shea) and this was the only pre-war Gable film actually to lose money. He hated it and knew that it was quite wrong for him. To counter this he was immediately rushed into *Saratoga* (1937) with Jean Harlow, who, sadly, died during the filming.

In August 1938 Gable signed to do the picture that was to make him a legend for generations of film-goers. When David Selznick first bought *Gone With the Wind*, he announced the leads as Ronald Colman and Tallulah Bankhead, but the overwhelming feeling, both within Hollywood and throughout the nation, was that Gable was Rhett. Filming started in January 1939 with director George Cukor, who was soon replaced by Victor Fleming (the director of three Gable pictures, *Red Dust*, *The White Sister* and *Test Pilot*). He was a faster worker than Cukor, but there is no doubt that Gable influenced this decision. He wanted a sympathetic director in a film in which the heroine had a longer screen-life than he did and could have threatened his impact.

Gone With the Wind was premièred on 15 December, 1939, in Atlanta, Georgia, and Gable with his third wife, Carole Lombard (they married in March 1939), received a huge, almost hysterical welcome when he flew in for the event. The rest is history. What remains something of an enigma is the question of how far Clark Gable took on the role of Rhett Butler and how far Rhett Butler, as a character, was based on Gable himself. Margaret Mitchell, the author of the novel, is alleged to have said that she drew on Gable's personality when she created the character. Certainly, both in the book and in the film, Rhett has many of the qualities inherent in Gable's screen persona. It may be simply that this was one of those rare occasions when the fictional character and the actor's personality complemented each other so perfectly that they became indistinguishable. Whatever the answer, there is no doubt that in *Gone With the Wind* Gable created one of the great film roles of all time. Revivals of the film over the years have proved just how sophisticated and forward-looking Gable's portrayal of Rhett Butler was – his cynicism, brazen

Beauty (Norma Shearer), the Beast (Clark Gable) and Prince Charming (Leslie Howard) in *A Free Soul* (1931). Gable baulked slightly at slapping the boss's wife (Shearer was married to MGM Head of Production, Irving Thalberg) but overcame his scruples and became a star.

sexuality, lack of chivalry and totally amoral attitudes made him not only deeply and enduringly attractive, but they pointed quite clearly to the screen heroes of the post-war years. He was nominated for an Oscar, but the award went to Robert Donat for *Goodbye Mr Chips*.

In January 1942 tragedy struck. The plane carrying Carole Lombard back from a war-bond selling tour crashed with no survivors. Gable was overwhelmed by grief – theirs had been, by all accounts, an extremely happy relationship. As soon as shooting on *Somewhere I'll Find You* (1942) with Lana Turner finished, he enlisted as a private in the US Air Corps. He was forty-one years old. He rose eventually to the rank of captain and spent some time based in England, flying as a gunner (and film cameraman) in missions over the Ruhr and Occupied France.

Sadly, his first post-war film, *Adventure* (1945) directed by Victor Fleming, was not successful. He was teamed with Greer Garson under the banner 'Gable's Back and Garson's Got Him', and he disliked both the film and the slogan. In terms of films, the 'forties and 'fifties were disappointing years for Gable, though his hold over the fans seemed as strong as ever. The only one that really stands out is *Mogambo* (1954), a remake of *Red Dust*, directed by John Ford and set this time in Africa. Gable's co-stars were Ava Gardner and Grace Kelly. He was married twice during this period, briefly (1949–52) to Lady Sylvia Ashley (whose second husband had been Douglas Fairbanks Sr) and then in 1955 very happily to Kay Williams Spreckles, whom he had known for some years and who bore him, posthumously, his only child, a son.

The Misfits (1960) came along at just the right time for Gable. Faced, after a string of undistinguished films, with the choice of playing supporting roles or character parts, or, even worse, retirement, he had a unique opportunity to create a character which, in the words of the film's producer, Frank Taylor, expressed 'the essence of masculinity and virility'. What made, and still makes, *The Misfits* such a marvellously intriguing film is the almost epic quality of the confrontation between Gable as Gay Langland, the epitome of all the strong male qualities he had embodied over the years, and Marilyn Monroe who by that time had herself become the embodiment of a peculiarly evocative combination of female qualities. Roslyn is an insubstantial, immensely complicated and unreachable dream woman before whom Gable's brand of womanizing is quite powerless. He is conquered, magnificently, by her.

Gable died in November 1960, a few weeks after shooting finished. He had, however, seen a rough-cut of the film, and told his wife, 'I think it's the best thing I've done since *Gone With the Wind*.'

Rough, tough and supremely sexy – Gable gives Jean Harlow the runaround in *Red Dust* (1932). The film ran in burlesque houses after its normal theatrical distribution, so lucrative was it.

Garbo asked for Gable for *Susan Lenox* (1931) but during filming he was so overawed that they never really established any on-set *rapport*.

Disciplinary action by MGM put Gable into *It Happened One Night* (1934) with Claudette Colbert. Rakish reporter tames snooty society lady – both won Oscars and the vest manufacturers of America felt the draught.

Gable and Jeanette MacDonald in *San Francisco* (1936), brought together at last by the 1906 earthquake – a most dramatic sequence which has stood the test of time.

Irving Thalberg persuaded Gable to play Fletcher Christian in *Mutiny on the Bounty* (1935) despite Gable's qualms about his lack of English accent and unsuitability for period dress. Thalberg was right.

Gone With the Wind (1939) was another film that Gable was reluctant to do. Happily for him – and us – he changed his mind and created one of the cinema's most enduring and powerful male characters in Rhett Butler, seen here with Hattie McDaniel.

Clark Gable

Various sources make differing claims as to the number of Silent films Gable appeared in. The following films have been located in more than one source: **Forbidden Paradise** (1924); **White Man** (1924); **North Star** (1926). He is also supposed to have appeared as an extra in **Declasse** (1925); **The Johnstown Flood** (1926); **The Pacemakers** (1925); **The Merry Widow** (1925); **The Plastic Age** (1927).

The King meets the Myth. Earthy and aggressively masculine Gable with ethereal, elusive Marilyn Monroe in *The Misfits* (1961) – a truly fitting epitaph for him.

Lana Turner was a popular and profitable co-star for Gable during the war years. Here they are in *Honky Tonk* (1941).

The Painted Desert. 1931. PATHÉ. Howard Higgin. With Bill Boyd, Helen Twelvetrees, William Farnum Jr, Farrell MacDonald.
The Easiest Way. 1931. MGM. Jack Conway. With Constance Bennett, Adolphe Menjou, Robert Montgomery, Anita Page, Marjorie Rambeau, J. Farrell McDonald, Clara Blandick.
Dance, Fools, Dance. 1931. MGM. Harry Beaumont. With Joan Crawford, Lester Vail, Cliff Edwards, William Bakewell, William Holden.
The Finger Points. 1931. FIRST NATIONAL. John

Francis Dillon. With Richard Barthelmess, Fay Wray, Regis Toomey.
The Secret Six. 1931. MGM. George Hill. With Wallace Beery, Lewis Stone, John Mack Brown, Jean Harlow, Marjorie Rambeau, Paul Hurst, Ralph Bellamy.
Laughing Sinners. 1931. MGM. Harry Beaumont. With Joan Crawford, Neil Hamilton, Marjorie Rambeau, Guy Kibbee, Cliff Edwards, Roscoe Karns.
A Free Soul. 1931. MGM. Clarence Brown. With Norma Shearer, Leslie Howard, Lionel Barrymore, James Gleason.
Night Nurse. 1931. WARNER BROTHERS. William Wellman. With Barbara Stanwyck, Joan Blondell, Ben Lyon, Charles Winninger.
Sporting Blood. 1931. MGM. Charles Brabin. With Ernest Torrence, Madge Evans, Marie Prevost, Lew Cody.
Susan Lenox – Her Fall and Rise. 1931. MGM. Robert Z. Leonard. With Greta Garbo, Alan Hale, John Miljan, Jean Hersholt.
Possessed. 1931. MGM. Clarence Brown. With Joan Crawford, Wallace Ford, Skeets Gallagher, Frank Conroy, John Miljan, Marjorie White.
Hell Divers. 1932. MGM. George Hill. With Wallace

Beery, Conrad Nagel, Dorothy Jordon, Marjorie Rambeau, Marie Prevost, Cliff Edwards, John Miljan, Landers Stevens, Reed Howes, Alan Roscoe.
Polly of the Circus. 1932. MGM. Alfred Santell. With Marion Davies, C. Aubrey Smith, Raymond Hatton, David Landau, Ruth Selwyn, Maude Eburne, Guinn Williams, Lilian Elliott.
Strange Interlude. 1932. MGM. Robert Z. Leonard. With Norma Shearer, Alexander Kirkland, Ralph Morgan, Robert Young, May Robson, Maureen O'Sullivan.
Red Dust. 1932. MGM. Victor Fleming. With Jean Harlow, Gene Raymond, Mary Astor, Donald Crisp, Tully Marshall, Forester Harvey, Willie Fung.
No Man of Her Own. 1932. PARAMOUNT. Wesley Ruggles. With Carole Lombard, Dorothy Mackaill, Grant Mitchell, George Barbier, Elizabeth Patterson, Farrell MacDonald.
The White Sister. 1933. MGM. Victor Fleming. With Helen Hayes, Lewis Stone, Louise Closser Hale, May Robson, Edward Arnold.
Hold Your Man. 1933. MGM. Sam Wood. With Jean Harlow, Stuart Erwin, Dorothy Burgess, Muriel Kirkland, Gary Owen, Barbara Barondess, Elizabeth Patterson.
Night Flight. 1933. MGM. Clarence Brown. With John Barrymore, Helen Hayes, Lionel Barrymore, Robert Montgomery, Myrna Loy, William Gargan, C. Henry Gordon, Henry Beresford.
Dancing Lady. 1933. MGM. Robert Z. Leonard. With Joan Crawford, Franchot Tone, May Robson, Winnie Lightner, Fred Astaire, Robert Benchley, Nelson Eddy.
It Happened One Night. 1934. COLUMBIA. Frank Capra. Best Actor Oscar. With Claudette Colbert, Walter Connolly, Roscoe Karns, Jameson Thomas, Alan Hale, Ward Bond, Eddie Chandler.
Men in White. 1934. MGM. Richard Boleslawski. With Myrna Loy, Jean Hersholt, Elizabeth Allan, Otto Kruger, C. Henry Gordon, Russell Hardie, Wallace Ford.
Manhattan Melodrama. 1934. MGM. W.S. Van Dyke. With William Powell, Leo Carillo, Myrna Loy, Nat Pendleton, George Sidney, Isabel Jewell, Muriel Evans, Mickey Rooney.
Chained. 1934. MGM. Clarence Brown. With Joan Crawford, Otto Kruger, Stuart Erwin, Una O'Connor, Marjorie Gateson, Akim Tamiroff.
Forsaking All Others. 1934. MGM. W.S. Van Dyke. With Joan Crawford,

Robert Montgomery, Billie Burke, Charles Butterworth, Frances Drake, Rosalind Russell, Ted Healy, Lillian Harmer, Tom Ricketts.
After Office Hours. 1935. MGM. Robert Z. Leonard. With Constance Bennett, Stuart Erwin, Billie Burke, Harvey Stephens, Katherine Alexander, Hale Hamilton, Henry Travers.
Call of the Wild. 1935. TWENTIETH CENTURY-FOX/ UNITED ARTISTS. William Wellman. With Loretta Young, Jack Oakie, Frank Conroy, Reginald Owen, Sidney Toler, Katherine DeMille, Lalo Encinas, Charles Stevens, James Burke.
China Seas. 1935. MGM. Tay Garnett. With Jean Harlow, Wallace Beery, Lewis Stone, Rosalind Russell, Dudley Digges, C. Aubrey Smith, Robert Benchley, William Henry, Live De Maigret, Soo Yong, Carol Ann Beery, Akim Tamiroff.
Mutiny on the Bounty. 1935. MGM. Frank Lloyd. With Charles Laughton, Franchot Tone, Herbert Mundin, Eddie Quillan, Dudley Digges, Donald Crisp, Henry Stephenson, Francis Lister, Spring Byington, Movita.
Wife Versus Secretary. 1936. MGM. Clarence Brown. With Jean Harlow, Myrna Loy, May Robson, Marjorie Gateson, James Stewart.
San Francisco. 1936. MGM. W.S. Van Dyke. With Jeanette MacDonald, Spencer Tracy, Jack Holt, Shirley Ross, Jessie Ralph, Ted Healy.
Cain and Mabel. 1936. WARNER BROTHERS. Lloyd Bacon. With Marion Davies, Roscoe Karns, Walter Catlett, William Collier Sr, Ruth Donnelly, Pert Kelton, Allen Jenkins.
Love on the Run. 1936.

MGM. W.S. Van Dyke. With Joan Crawford, Franchot Tone, Reginald Owen, Mona Barrie, William Demarest, Donald Meek.

Parnell. 1937. MGM. John M. Stahl. With Myrna Loy, Edna May Oliver, Edmund Gwenn, Alan Marshall, Donald Crisp, Billie Burke, Donald Meek, Montagu Love.

Saratoga. 1937. MGM. Jack Conway, With Jean Harlow, Lionel Barrymore, Frank Morgan, Walter Pidgeon, Una Merkel, Cliff Edwards, Hattie McDaniel.

Test Pilot. 1938. MGM. Victor Fleming. With Myrna Loy, Spencer Tracy, Lionel Barrymore, Samuel S. Hinds, Marjorie Main, Virginia Grey.

Too Hot to Handle. 1938. MGM. Jack Conway, With Myrna Loy, Walter Pidgeon, Walter Connolly, Leo Carillo, Johnny Hines, Virginia Weidler, Betsy Ross Clarke, Henry Kolker, Willie Fung.

Idiot's Delight. 1939. MGM. Clarence Brown. With Norma Shearer, Edward Arnold, Charles Coburn, Joseph Schildkraut, Burgess Meredith, Laura Hope Crewes.

Gone With the Wind. 1939. MGM. Victor Fleming. With Vivien Leigh, Hattie McDaniel, Thomas Mitchell, Leslie Howard, Olivia de Havilland, Laura Hope Crewes, Evelyn Keyes, Butterfly McQueen.

Strange Cargo. 1940. MGM. Frank Borzage. With Joan Crawford, Ian Hunter, Peter Lorre, Paul Lukas, Albert Dekker, J. Edward Bromberg, Eduardo Ciannelli.

Boom Town. 1940. MGM. Jack Conway. With Spencer Tracy, Claudette Colbert, Hedy Lamarr, Frank Morgan, Lionel Atwill, Chill Wills, Marion Martin.

Comrade X. 1940. MGM. King Vidor. With Hedy Lamarr, Oscar Homolka, Felix Bressart, Eve Arden, Sig Rumann.

They Met in Bombay. 1941. MGM. Clarence Brown. With Rosalind Russell, Peter Lorre, Jessie Ralph, Reginald Owen, Matthew Boulton, Eduardo Ciannelli.

Honky Tonk. 1941. MGM. Jack Conway. With Lana Turner, Frank Morgan, Claire Trevor, Marjorie Main, Albert Dekker, Henry O'Neill, Chill Wills, Veda Ann Borg, Douglas Wood, Betty Blythe.

Somewhere I'll Find You. 1942. MGM. Wesley Ruggles. With Lana Turner, Robert Sterling, Patricia Dane, Reginald Owen, Lee Patrick, Charles Dingle.

Adventure. 1945. MGM. Victor Fleming. With Greer Garson, Joan Blondell, Thomas Mitchell, Tom Tully, John Qualen, Richard Haydn, Lina Romay.

The Hucksters. 1947. MGM. Jack Conway. With Deborah Kerr, Sydney Greenstreet, Adolphe Menjou, Ava Gardner, Keenan Wynn, Edward Arnold, Frank Albertson.

Homecoming. 1948. MGM. Mervyn Le Roy. With Lana Turner, Anne Baxter, John Hodiak, Ray Collins, Gladys Cooper, Cameron Mitchell, Marshall Thompson, Lurene Tuttle.

Command Decision. 1948. MGM. Sam Wood. With Walter Pidgeon, Van Johnson, Brian Donlevy, John Hodiak, Charles Bickford, Edward Arnold, Marshall Thompson, Richard Quine.

Any Number Can Play. 1949. MGM. Mervyn Le Roy. With Alexis Smith, Wendell Corey, Lewis Stone, Audrey Totter, Barry Sullivan, Leon Ames, Frank Morgan, Edgar Buchanan, Mary Astor, Marjorie Rambeau.

Key to the City. 1950. MGM. George Sidney. With Loretta Young, Frank Morgan, Marilyn Maxwell, James Gleason, Raymond Burr, Lewis Stone, Raymond Walburn, Pamela Britton.

To Please a Lady. 1950. MGM. Clarence Brown. With Barbara Stanwyck, Adolphe Menjou, Will Greer.

Across the Wide Missouri. 1951. MGM. William Wellman. With Ricardo Montalban, John Hodiak, Adolphe Menjou, Maria Elena Marques, J. Carrol Naish, Jack Holt, Alan Napier, George Chandler.

Callaway Went Thataway. 1951. MGM. Norman Panama and Melvin Frank. Gable plays a cameo role as himself. With Fred MacMurray, Dorothy McGuire, Howard Keel, Elizabeth Taylor.

Lone Star. 1952. MGM. Vincent Sherman. With Ava Gardner, Broderick Crawford, Lionel Barrymore, Beulah Bondi, Ed Begley, James Burke, William Farnum.

Never Let Me Go. 1953. MGM. Delmer Daves. With Gene Tierney, Richard Haydn, Belita, Kenneth More, Theodore Bikel, Anna Valentina, Bernard Miles.

Mogambo. 1954. MGM. John Ford. With Ava Gardner, Grace Kelly, Donald Sinden, Philip Stainton.

Betrayed. 1954. MGM. Gottfried Reinhardt. With Lana Turner, Victor Mature, Louis Calhern, Wilfred Hyde White, Ian Carmichael, Roland Culver.

Soldier of Fortune. 1955. TWENTIETH CENTURY-FOX. Edward Dmytryk. With Susan Hayward, Michael Rennie, Gene Barry, Alex D'Arcy, Tom Tully, Anna Sten.

The Tall Men. 1955. TWENTIETH CENTURY-FOX. Raoul Walsh. With Jane Russell, Robert Ryan, Cameron Mitchell.

The King and Four Queens. 1956. UNITED ARTISTS. Raoul Walsh. With Eleanor Parker, Jo Van Fleet, Jean Willes, Barbara Nichols, Sara Shane.

Band of Angels. 1957. WARNER BROTHERS. Raoul Walsh. With Yvonne de Carlo, Sidney Poitier, Efrem Zimbalist Jr, Rex Reason, Patric Knowles, Torin Thatcher, Andrea King.

Run Silent, Run Deep. 1958. UNITED ARTISTS. Robert Wise. With Burt Lancaster, Jack Warden, Brad Dexter, Nick Gravat, Joe Maross, Mary Laroche.

Teacher's Pet. 1958. PARAMOUNT. George Seaton. With Doris Day, Gig Young, Mamie Van Doran, Nick Adams.

But Not For Me. 1959. PARAMOUNT. Walter Lang. With Carroll Baker, Lilli Palmer, Lee J. Cobb, Barry Coe, Thomas Gomez.

It Started in Naples. 1960. PARAMOUNT. Melville Shavelson. With Sophia Loren, Vittorio De Sica, Marietto.

The Misfits. 1961. SEVEN ARTS-UNITED ARTISTS. John Huston. With Marilyn Monroe, Montgomery Clift, Thelma Ritter, Eli Wallach, James Barton, Estelle Winwood, Kevin McCarthy.

Mogambo (1954) was John Ford's remake of *Red Dust*, with Ava Gardner (the tramp) and Grace Kelly (the lady) fighting over Gable. Though now in his fifties he still looked worth fighting for – shorts and all.

Cary Grant

Two important factors differentiate Cary Grant from all the other heart-throbs – his sheer durability and his unerring gift for light comedy. He rose to stardom at about the same time as Gable, Tracy and Cooper – and, unlike them, is still with us, though he has not made a film since 1967. Not only has he survived, but he does not seem to have changed much either. Whenever his picture appears in newspapers in connection with his business trips for Fabergé (the perfume business of which he became a director in May 1968), it is still the same chunky, handsome and impeccably groomed image that charmed cinema audiences ten, twenty, thirty years ago. The hair may be greying but it is still thick and the features are perhaps a little more rugged, but the essential Grant magic remains untouched by age and time. 'I've been called the longest lasting young man about town,' he wrote in Films and Filming in 1961. The feeling that he has a personal magic talisman to keep not only age, but the world and its problems at bay was reinforced when, during his divorce from actress Dyan Cannon in 1968 (at the age of sixty-four), a number of unsavoury facts about him were produced, ranging from the regular taking of LSD to physical ill-treatment of his wife. Yet his popularity remained undimmed and intact – such is the power of his personality that it can withstand the sort of publicity that would very likely have destroyed, or at least badly dented, the reputation of a lesser mortal.

If one had to choose a single adjective to describe Cary Grant as an actor and heart-throb, it would undoubtedly be the word 'smooth'. From the top of his immaculately coiffured head to the soles of his stylish shoes, he is charm and polish personified and over the years, despite a fairly wide range of parts, he made the consummate playing of light comedy and romance his forte. This is an accomplishment all the more remarkable since the difficulty of its achievement is hidden by the apparent ease of its execution. Yet over the years he became the master of the charmingly inconsequential and elegant romance.

Cary Grant began life as Archibald Leach in Bristol, England, in 1904. His childhood was overshadowed by the disappearance from home, when he was nine years old, of his mother who, according to his avowedly unauthorized biographer, Albert Govoni, had suffered a nervous breakdown. School was not an especially happy experience for young Archibald, whose idea of real pleasure was to be allowed backstage at the Bristol Hippodrome where he knew one of the electricians. There he worked as an unpaid call-boy and general dogsbody in his spare time, before deciding (at the age of thirteen) to devote all his energies to a theatrical career. He ran away from home to join Bob Pender's travelling troupe of young knockabout comedians and acrobats. His first attempt failed, as he was underage for full-time employment, but as it turned out both Pender and his father were Masons and took to one another so that as soon as he reached fourteen Archibald Leach joined Pender's troupe with parental permission and began to learn his trade. In July 1920 the company travelled to New York on board the liner 'Olympic'. A fellow passenger was Douglas Fairbanks Sr, returning from his European honeymoon with Mary Pickford, and, according to legend, he joined the Pender boys for their daily work-out on deck.

The company played successfully in New York and then toured the country on the B. F. Keith vaudeville circuit for six months. Archibald loved America, especially New York, and when his colleagues returned to England in mid-1921 he decided to remain behind and take his chances. They were rather odd chances and included selling neckties, hand-painted by a young man called Orry-Kelly who later won an Oscar for his costume designs, stilt-walking (clad in red, gold, blue and white eight-foot-long trousers) to advertise the Steeplechase Amusement Park on Coney Island, and touring the small-town vaudeville circuits with a mind-reading act.

He decided to quit vaudeville and in 1923 switched to playing in musical comedies. Spotted by an Arthur Hammerstein scout, he was offered the juvenile lead in a new musical comedy, 'Golden Dawn', which opened at the Hammerstein Theatre on Broadway in November 1927. He didn't take Broadway by storm but

Cary Grant – 'consummately romantic and consummately genteel,' wrote Tom Wolfe. He might have added, 'and consummately elegant'.

his notices were kind and he went on to more musical comedies. Among them was 'Boom-Boom' with Jeanette MacDonald. After the show opened in New York, they were both approached by Paramount talent scouts to take screen-tests. Jeanette MacDonald's proved successful and, at the end of the run, she took off for Hollywood and Nelson Eddy. Archibald had about as much luck as Gable had with his first test – 'You're bow-legged and your neck is too thick', the future Hollywood heart-throb was apparently informed.

Undeterred by this, he made his way to the West Coast in late 1931 and got a job – with Paramount – feeding lines to a young film actress who was being given a screen-test. She didn't win a contract but he did. He signed for $450 a week and changed his name to Cary Grant (the Cary from the hero of a short-lived Broadway production in which he had earlier played and the Grant from a studio list of available names). Shortly afterwards, in January 1932, he reached the age of twenty-eight and found himself playing in his first film, *This Is the Night* (1932) with Lili Damita, Thelma Todd and Roland Young.

Like Gable, he found his first year in films extremely busy (though he only notched up seven movies against Gable's amazing 1931 achievement of eleven). None of them catapulted him to instant stardom, but he began to build a solid reputation. In *Blonde Venus* he was little more than handsome background for Dietrich, but in *The Devil and the Deep* with Charles Laughton his original small supporting role, a junior naval officer gallantly resisting the advances of his captain's wife (Bankhead), was rewritten and enlarged at the request of the film's director, Marion Gering. In the film Tallulah transferred her attentions to Gary Cooper and after that Grant began to get parts that were scheduled for Cooper but not taken up by him for one reason or another (notably his extended trip to Africa with the European smart set). *Hot Saturday* won him top billing for the first time, and good reviews – the critic of the New York Herald Tribune referred to him as 'the new Gable-esque leading man . . . a dashing young man who seems destined for that screen popularity which comes when a player can seem a handsome juvenile and still make sense.' He was less well served by *Madame Butterfly* (also directed by Gering – and his last film in 1932), variously described as 'a rather foolish film' and, less charitably, as 'a cinematic abortion'. Certainly one feels that both he and Sylvia Sidney, who played Cio-Cio-San, must have had trouble keeping straight faces.

At this point the legendary Mae West entered Cary Grant's life. She spotted him as he was walking back to the *Butterfly* set, sporting a white naval uniform and a deep tan. 'I saw a sensational looking man,' she later wrote in her memoirs, and, as she was the hottest property in Hollywood at the time, her request for Grant as her leading man in *She Done Him Wrong* (1933) was immediately acceded to by the studio. Not

unnaturally, Mae West dominates the film entirely, but Grant shows to advantage as the hero – 'warm, dark and handsome' were her own immortal words. The film was a box-office smash and established Grant as a star. It seems likely that it also set his feet firmly on the path of light comedy, for he said later, 'I learned everything from her . . . her instinct is so fine, her timing is so perfect, her grasp of situation is right.' He played in another Mae West vehicle the same year, *I'm No Angel*, in which he proved himself almost her match at *double entendres* in the climactic court scene. Apart from this, he did little of note for Paramount for the next couple of years (though he found time to marry and divorce – after barely a year – his first wife, Virginia Cherrill). However, in late 1935 Paramount loaned him to RKO to make *Sylvia Scarlett* (1936) with Katharine Hepburn and George Cukor directing. His was a secondary role, that of a Cockney adventurer who thaws out an icy and mannishly suited Hepburn, but he proved himself an accomplished scene-stealer and Time magazine wrote of his 'superb depiction of the Cockney'. By this time he was getting very fed up with Paramount. They refused to lend him to MGM for *Mutiny on the Bounty* (Franchot Tone got the part) but quite happily let MGM have him to play second fiddle to Harlow in *Suzy* (1936), a First World War flying/espionage drama. When his contract expired at the end of 1936, he made control over his parts a condition of re-signing and when Paramount refused to accept this he decided to take a risk and freelance – a momentous and daring decision at a time when the studio-system dominated Hollywood.

After a brief sojourn in England, he returned to start his career as a Hollywood freelance with a couple of fairly unexciting movies, *When You're In Love* (1937) with Grace Moore and *Toast of New York* (1937), for Columbia and RKO respectively. However, he had pushed his price up to $300,000 a picture and with his next film, *Topper* (1937), began the run of successful comedies that was to make him an immensely popular international star. Hal Roach produced *Topper* (the first and best of the 'Topper' series) for MGM, and Grant and Constance Bennett played the ghosts of the young society couple trying desperately to gain heavenly accreditation. Grant's comic style was now developing rapidly and in *The Awful Truth* (1937) with Irene Dunne he was triumphant. Directed by Leo McCarey for Columbia, this delightful film, which hinges on the rights of access of a young, divorcing couple to their dog, was one of the top box-office earners of the year, established Grant's pre-eminence as a witty, charming and romantic star, and remains a classic of its kind. Equally classic are his next two films, both with Katharine Hepburn, *Bringing Up Baby* and *Holiday* (both 1938). Both were excellent comedies, in which his elegant style and dry wit showed to best advantage when pitted against Hepburn's angular charms and equally astringent personality.

Mae West as Diamond Lil in *She Done Him Wrong* (1933). 'I learned everything from Mae West,' Grant said later ' – well, not quite everything.'

As if to prove his versatility, Grant went on to do two extremely good and popular adventure films. The first was *Gunga Din* (1939), directed by George Stevens and based on a rather haphazard but extremely successful *mélange* of Kipling's 'Soldiers Three' and Dumas's 'The Three Musketeers'. His two companions in the British Indian Army were Victor McLaglen and Douglas Fairbanks Jr, and the film contains some remarkable action sequences. *Only Angels Have Wings* (1939), directed by Howard Hawks, gave him a chance to play a straight dramatic role in this story of mail pilots in Central America, though his wit shines clearly through in his crisp exchanges with Jean Arthur.

In Name Only, his last film in 1939, starred him with Carole Lombard and Kay Francis and was also straight drama but his next film, *His Girl Friday* (1940), saw his return to comedy. This remake of Hecht and MacArthur's 'Front Page Story', directed by Howard Hawks, had Hildy Johnson the reporter transmogrified into a girl (Ros Russell). Grant is reported to have enjoyed making the film so much that in the mid-'fifties he planned to buy the screen rights and do yet another remake, this time with Grace Kelly. Bearing in mind the deliciously acid quality of the relationship between Hildy and her ex-husband/boss (Grant), it seems an unlikely proposition. Another 1940 comedy, *The Philadelphia Story* marks the high point of his art and is the film for which he is probably best remembered. Like *Holiday*, this was a film version of a Philip Barry stage play and it reunited Hepburn and Grant with a superb supporting cast, from James Stewart (who won an Oscar for it) and Roland Young right through to the bit players. It was, of course, very successful at the box-office, as was Grant's next film, *Penny Serenade* (1941), a potential 'weepie' redeemed from soggy sentimentality by George Stevens's direction and deft, sensitive performances by Irene Dunne and Grant – who won for it his first Academy Award nomination.

At this time his name was being constantly linked with that of Woolworth heiress, Barbara Hutton, whom he had met through Gary Cooper's erstwhile companion, the Countess di Frasso. They married in July 1942 (shortly after Grant had legally changed his name and been through the final formalities of becoming an American citizen), and divorced in August 1945. He was subsequently married twice, to Betsy Drake (from 1949 to 1962) and to Dyan Cannon (from 1965 to 1968) who bore him his only child, a daughter Jennifer in February 1966, when he was sixty-two years old.

Also during this period another, and more lasting, relationship began – with director Alfred Hitchcock, like him an expatriate Englishman. His first Hitchcock thriller was *Suspicion* (1941) with Joan Fontaine. She won an Oscar and Grant gave a splendid performance, suggesting very nasty and mysterious depths beneath his congenial, boyish exterior. He became one of Hitchcock's favourite leading men, his casual stylishness making a fascinating contrast to the darker qualities under the surface which Hitchcock hinted at, none too lightly; James Stewart offered a similar dramatic contrast for Hitchcock, who – with extraordinary sleight of hand – used one of Hollywood's nicest 'good guys' to portray a voyeur, in *Rear Window* (1954), and a necrophile in *Vertigo* (1958). Grant made three more films for Hitchcock, *Notorious* (1946) with Ingrid Bergman, *To Catch a Thief* (1955) with Grace Kelly, and *North By Northwest* (1959) with Eva Marie Saint – all immensely popular and successful films.

For the remaining twenty-five years of his screen-career, Grant's achievement was, understandably, patchy. No actor can sustain a continuous high level of performance for even a fifth of that time – but he made enough good, interesting pictures to keep him unchallenged as one of Hollywood's greatest, most durable and most popular stars. Among the high points were the Capra version of *Arsenic and Old Lace* (1944), Clifford Odets's *None But the Lonely Heart* (1944), Howard Hawks's *I Was a Male War Bride* (1949), the same director's *Monkey Business* (1952), with a cameo performance by Marilyn Monroe – and, of course, his films for Hitchcock. *Operation Petticoat* (1959) directed by Blake Edwards was probably his biggest financial success, though critically not especially well received. However, the gap between critical and popular success is often as wide, if not wider, as that between critical and financial success. Many of Grant's later films, dismissed by critics as not being especially noteworthy, continued to give tremendous pleasure to cinema audiences. Into this category come *Indiscreet* (1958) with Ingrid Bergman, *Charade* (1964) with Audrey Hepburn, and *Father Goose* (1964) with Leslie Caron. Perhaps the secret of this continued popularity lies in the fact that in the 'fifties and 'sixties Grant was nearly always better than his material. None of his later films offered him the heaven-sent, almost personally tailored opportunities of those wonderful late 'thirties comedies, but by this time he had polished both his acting style and personal image to such a high degree that subsequent lesser vehicles could bask a little in his reflected glory.

Charles Laughton, Tallulah Bankhead and Cary Grant in *The Devil and the Deep* (1932). He played second fiddle to Cooper in this film, but never again.

Notorious (1946) was Grant's second film for Hitchcock. Ingrid Bergman played the daughter of an American traitor, suspected but ultimately saved by Grant.

With *The Awful Truth* (1937), Cary Grant really came into his own. He and Irene Dunne fought and made up delightfully with the aid of Asta– that lovely dog from the *Thin Man* films.

James Stewart, Cary Grant and Katharine Hepburn at the happy ending of *Philadelphia Story* (1940). Their enjoyment in making the film was evident in the finished product and Hepburn later said of Grant that he had 'a delicious personality'.

Even in drag, in Howard Hawks's *I was a Male War Bride* (1949), Grant managed to look sexily masculine. It's a delightful improbability that Anne Baxter ever began to get away with her plan.

A retired jewel-thief met an American millionairess (Grace Kelly) on the Riviera in *To Catch a Thief* (1955) and the consequence was inevitable, exciting and vastly romantic.

Henry Travers, Jackie Kelk, Marion Burns, Andrew Tombes.
Kiss and Make Up. 1934. PARAMOUNT. Harlan Thompson. With Helen Mack, Edward Everett Horton, Genevieve Tobin, Lucien Littlefield, Mona Maris.
Ladies Should Listen. 1934. PARAMOUNT. Frank Tuttle. With Frances Drake, Rosita Moreno, Edward Everett Horton, George Barbier, Nydia Westman.
Enter Madame. 1934. PARAMOUNT. Elliot Nugent. With Elissa Landi, Frank Albertson, Lynne Overman, Sharon Lynne.
Wings in the Dark. 1935. PARAMOUNT. James Flood. With Myrna Loy, Dean Jagger, Hobart Cavanaugh, Roscoe Karns, Russell Hopton.
Last Outpost. 1935. PARAMOUNT. Charles Barton and Louis Gasnier. With Claude Rains, Kathleen Burke, Gertrude Michael, Akim Tamiroff.
Sylvia Scarlett. 1936. RKO. George Cukor. With Katharine Hepburn, Brian Aherne, Edmund Gwenn, Natalie Paley.
Big Brown Eyes. 1936. PARAMOUNT. Raoul Walsh. With Joan Bennett, Walter Pidgeon, Lloyd Nolan, Isabel Jewell, Alan Baxter.
Suzy. 1936. MGM. George Fitzmaurice. With Jean Harlow, Franchot Tone, Benita Hume, Lewis Stone.
Wedding Present. 1936. PARAMOUNT. Richard Wallace. With Conrad Nagel, Joan Bennett, George Bancroft, William Demarest, Gene Lockhart.
Amazing Quest (of Ernest Bliss) (US title: **Romance and Riches**). 1936. GRANT NATIONAL. Alfred Zeisler. With Mary Brian, Iris Ashley, Peter Gawthorn.
When You're in Love. 1937. COLUMBIA. Robert Riskin. With Grace Moore, Thomas Mitchell, Henry Stephenson, Aline McMahon.
Toast of New York. 1937. RKO. Rowland V. Lee. With Frances Farmer, Edward Arnold, Jack Oakie, Donald Meek.
Topper. 1937. MGM. Norman McLeod. With Constance Bennett, Roland Young, Billie Burke.
The Awful Truth. 1937. COLUMBIA. Leo McCarey. With Irene Dunne, Ralph Bellamy, Alexander D'Arcy.
Bringing Up Baby. 1938. RKO. Howard Hawks. With Katharine Hepburn, Barry Fitzgerald, Charles Ruggles, May Robson.
Holiday. 1938. COLUMBIA. George Cukor. With Katharine Hepburn, Lew Ayres, Edward Everett Horton, Doris Nolan.
Gunga Din. 1939. RKO.

George Stevens. With Douglas Fairbanks Jr, Victor McLaglen, Joan Fontaine, Eduardo Ciannelli, Sam Jaffe, Montagu Love, Abner Biberman.
Only Angels Have Wings. 1939. COLUMBIA. Howard Hawks. With Jean Arthur, Rita Hayworth, Richard Barthelmess, Thomas Mitchell.
In Name Only. 1939. RKO. John Cromwell. With Carole Lombard, Kay Francis, Helen Vinson, Charles Coburn.
His Girl Friday. 1940. COLUMBIA. Howard Hawks. With Rosalind Russell, Helen Mack, Ralph Bellamy, Ernest Truex, Gene Lockhart, Porter Hall, Roscoe Karns, Regis Toomey.
My Favourite Wife. 1940. RKO. Garson Kanin. With Irene Dunne, Randolph Scott, Gail Patrick.
The Howards of Virginia. 1940. COLUMBIA. Frank Lloyd. With Martha Scott, Sir Cedric Hardwicke, Paul Kelly, Richard Carlson, Alan Marshal, Anne Revere.
The Philadelphia Story. 1940. MGM. George Cukor. With Katharine Hepburn, James Stewart, Roland Young, Ruth Hussey, John Howard, John Halliday, Henry Daniell, Virginia Weidler, Mary Nash.
Penny Serenade. 1941. COLUMBIA. George Stevens. With Irene Dunne, Edgar Buchanan, Beulah Bondi, Ann Doran.
Suspicion. 1941. RKO. Alfred Hitchcock. With Joan Fontaine, Sir Cedric Hardwicke, Dame May Whitty, Nigel Bruce, Heather Angel, Leo G. Carroll.
Talk of the Town. 1942. COLUMBIA. George Stevens. With Ronald Colman, Jean Arthur, Glenda Farrell, Edgar Buchanan, Rex Ingram, Emma Dunn.
Once Upon a Honeymoon. 1942. RKO. Leo McCarey. With Ginger Rogers, Walter Slezak, Albert Dekker.
Mr Lucky. 1943. RKO. H. C. Potter. With Laraine Day, Charles Bickford, Henry Stephenson, Gladys Cooper, Alan Carney.
Destination Tokyo. 1943. WARNER BROTHERS. Delmer Daves. With John Garfield, Dane Clarke, Faye Emerson, Alan Hale.
Once Upon a Time. 1944. COLUMBIA. Alexander Hall. With Janet Blair, William Demarest, James Gleason, Ted Donaldson.
Arsenic and Old Lace. 1944. WARNER BROTHERS. Frank Capra. With Priscilla Lane, Raymond Massey, Peter Lorre, Josephine Hull, Jean Adair.
None But the Lonely Heart. 1944. RKO. Clifford Odets. With Ethel

Barrymore, Barry Fitzgerald, Jane Wyatt, George Coulouris, Roman Bohnen, Dan Duryea.
Night and Day. 1946. WARNER BROTHERS. Michael Curtiz. With Alexis Smith, Jane Wyman, Mary Martin, Ginny Simms, Monty Woolley, Eve Arden.
Notorious. 1946. RKO. Alfred Hitchcock. With Ingrid Bergman, Claude Rains, Louis Calhern, Moroni Olsen.
The Bachelor and the Bobby-Soxer. 1947. RKO. Irving Reis. With Shirley Temple, Myrna Loy, Rudy Vallee, Harry Davenport, Johnny Sands.
The Bishop's Wife. 1947. RKO. Henry Koster. With Loretta Young, David Niven, Elsa Lanchester, Monty Woolley, Gladys Cooper, James Gleason.
Mr Blandings Builds His Dream House. 1948. SELZNICK/RKO. With Myrna Loy, Melvyn Douglas, Louise Beavers, Reginald Denny.
Every Girl Should Be Married. 1948. RKO. Don Hartman. With Betsy Drake, Franchot Tone, Eddie Albert, Diana Lynn, Alan Mowbray.
I Was a Male War Bride. 1949. TWENTIETH CENTURY-FOX. Howard Hawks. With Ann Sheridan, Randy Stewart, Marion Marshall.
Crisis. 1950. MGM. Richard Brooks. With José Ferrer, Ramon Novarro, Signe Hasso, Antonio Moreno, Gilbert Roland, Paula Raymond.
People Will Talk. 1951. TWENTIETH CENTURY-FOX. Joseph L. Mankiewicz. With Jeanne Crain, Walter Slezak, Hume Cronyn, Finlay Currie, Sidney Blackmer.
Room for One More. 1952. WARNER BROTHERS. Norman Taurog. With Betsy Drake, Iris Mann, Lurene Tuttle, George 'Foghorn' Winslow.

Monkey Business. 1952. TWENTIETH CENTURY-FOX. Howard Hawks. With Ginger Rogers, Marilyn Monroe, Charles Coburn, Hugh Marlowe, George 'Foghorn' Winslow.
Dream Wife. 1953. MGM. Sidney Sheldon. With Deborah Kerr, Walter Pidgeon, Bruce Bennett, Buddy Baer, Betta St John.
To Catch a Thief. 1955. PARAMOUNT. Alfred Hitchcock. With Grace Kelly, John Williams, Jessie Royce Landis, Charles Vanel.
The Pride and the Passion. 1957. UNITED ARTISTS. Stanley Kramer. With Sophia Loren, Frank Sinatra, Theodore Bikel.
An Affair to Remember. 1957. TWENTIETH CENTURY-FOX. Leo McCarey. With Deborah Kerr, Neva Patterson, Richard Denning, Cathleen Nesbitt, Robert Q. Lewis.
Kiss Them for Me. 1957. TWENTIETH CENTURY-FOX. Stanley Donen. With Suzy Parker, Jayne Mansfield, Ray Walston, Larry Blyden, Leif Erickson.
Indiscreet. 1958. WARNER BROTHERS. Stanley Donen. With Ingrid Bergman, Phyllis Calvert, Cecil Parker, Megs Jenkins, David Kossoff.
Houseboat. 1958. PARAMOUNT. Melville Shavelson. With Sophia Loren, Martha Hyer, Harry Guardino, Eduardo Ciannelli, Paul Peterson.
North by Northwest. 1959. MGM. Alfred Hitchcock. With Eva Marie Saint, James Mason, Leo G. Carroll, Jessie Royce Landis, Martin Landau.
Operation Petticoat. 1959. UNIVERSAL-INTERNATIONAL. Blake Edwards. With Tony Curtis, Dina Merrill, Arthur O'Connell, Joan O'Brien, Gene Evans, Dick Sargent.
The Grass Is Greener.

1960. UNIVERSAL-INTERNATIONAL. Stanley Donen. With Deborah Kerr, Jean Simmons, Robert Mitchum, Moray Watson.
That Touch of Mink. 1962. UNIVERSAL-INTERNATIONAL. Delbert Mann. With Doris Day, Gig Young, Mickey Mantle, Yogi Berra.
Charade. 1964. UNIVERSAL-INTERNATIONAL. Stanley Donen. With Audrey Hepburn, Walter Matthau, James Coburn, George Kennedy, Ned Glass.
Father Goose. 1964. UNIVERSAL-INTERNATIONAL. Ralph Nelson. With Leslie Caron, Trevor Howard.
Walk, Don't Run. 1966. COLUMBIA. Charles Walters. With Samantha Eggar, Jim Hutton.

Such a familiar Grant 'face'. If it sounds churlish to say that his range of acting ability was fairly limited, it must be said that he deployed his talents superbly for over thirty years of film-making.

Charles Boyer

Charles Boyer was in fact an anachronism – the last of the Great Lovers in an era which had found a new type of screen heart-throb altogether, the rugged, All-American Male of the 'thirties, personified in stars such as Clark Gable and Gary Cooper. Boyer's appeal and style were in many ways an extension of the sensual, romantic tradition of the 'twenties and Silent pictures – the tradition of early Novarro and Colman, of Valentino and John Gilbert. That he became a heart-throb at all at this point in movie history is a slight mystery, though his immense acting ability has a great deal to do with it. Perhaps he evoked a nostalgic response in his female fans – a gratefully seized-upon escape into the make-believe romanticism of earlier, happier times. This is borne out by his appearance during the war years in virtually nothing but 'women's pictures', cinematic novelettes in which he played second string to a powerful female star. By this time the brief revival of the Great Lover that he had generated with films like *Mayerling* (1936), *The Garden of Allah*

Charles Boyer – the last of the Great Lovers, complete with sexy accent, bedroom eyes and genuine acting ability. His recent role in *Stavisky* (1974) has won him enthusiastic notices.

(1936), and *Algiers* (1938) was truly over.

Another explanation for this apparently incongruous reversion to the heart-throbs of an earlier decade was probably Boyer's genuine exoticism. Initially a terrible handicap both in practical terms and in the less tangible areas of box-office popularity and audience appeal, his looks, accent and general style finally became a tremendous asset. In fact, his initial importation to Hollywood, from a highly successful stage- and film-career in France and Germany, was to make French-language versions of Hollywood hits for European distribution. He did a couple of these before the studios switched to the cheaper device of subtitles and he moved on, gradually and at times painfully, to a career in Hollywood films proper.

There has been some investigation of the varying degrees of success of the different ethnic groups of Hollywood immigrants and, rather surprisingly, the French (who, after all, according to popular legend virtually created L'Amour and the figure of the Great Romantic Lover) are relatively low in the league-table. In the days of Silent films, nationality and language, of course, were not important – which was probably just as well in view of Valentino's early, heavy Italian accent – but Sound was an altogether different proposition. This is why, in any roster of major heart-throbs, Boyer and, to a lesser extent, Chevalier are the only Frenchmen to appear among the post-Silent picture-stars. French actors such as Gérard Philipe and Jean Gabin achieved world-renown, but their true popularity lay mainly in France. Boyer was the only 'foreign' actor to achieve outstanding success in the inter-war years as a Hollywood, and therefore international, heart-throb.

Charles Boyer was born in Figeac in South-Western France in August 1899, the son of a prosperous salesman of farm machinery. From a very early age he seems to have taken an interest in acting, and he was encouraged in his dramatic activities by his parents, although they were not happy when he finally decided to make acting his career. They gave in, however, on condition that he finished his formal education first, and he complied with their request by attending classes at the Sorbonne where he gained a degree in philosophy. Then he promptly enrolled at the Paris Conservatoire to study drama. He made his stage and film débuts in the same year, 1920, when he had a small part in Marcel L'Herbier's film *L'Homme du Large* and in the play 'Les Jardins de Murcie'. Success at this time came relatively quickly. By 1922 he was a leading Parisian stage-star and matinée-idol, adored by women of all ages, and, under the guidance of Sacha Guitry's producer/director Henri Bernstein, he consolidated this success throughout the decade. Not only his stage parts, but his film roles too, got larger and he had already attracted the attention of Hollywood when he signed a contract with UFA, the giant German film production company, to make French versions of German features in Berlin. MGM approached UFA shortly after

"In your arms...I have no yesterdays!"

A Metro-Goldwyn-Mayer PICTURE

Greta GARBO Conquest Charles BOYER

Lobby-card for *Conquest* (1938).

Mayerling (1936) made audiences, especially female audiences, sit up and take notice of Boyer. This tale of tragic passion amongst the crowned heads of Europe (his co-star was Danielle Darrieux) was remade in 1968 with Omar Sharif and Catherine Deneuve.

Boyer had made the very successful *La Barcarolle d'Amour* (1929) for them, and offered to buy up his contract.

This first move to the American film business was a definite failure. He made French versions of *The Trial of Mary Dugan* (1929) and *The Big House* (1930) before subtitles made him redundant, and he then had the unnerving and (after his hectic career in Europe) unaccustomed experience of sitting around doing nothing. MGM could not cancel his contract, nor could they find him anything to do, as they felt his English was not good enough for major roles. Finally they cast him as a chauffeur in Jean Harlow's *Red-Headed Woman* (1932); this embittered Boyer so much that he asked for his footage to be deleted and for his release from the contract which had become such a burden to him.

He returned to Europe – to UFA to do French versions of two Conrad Veidt films and then back to Paris – and popular stardom again. In 1934 he played the lead in *La Bataille* (he had had a small part in a 1921 stage production) and an English version, *The Battle* (*Thunder in the East* in the US), was also produced. It seems that he had improved his English during this period, for on the strength of his performance in this English version Twentieth Century were sufficiently impressed to persuade him to return to Hollywood.

Unfortunately his first film for them, *Caravan* (1934) with Loretta Young, in which he played a gipsy violinist, was a resounding flop. A disheartened Boyer once more asked for a release from his contract and prepared to return to Paris. Producer Walter Wanger, however, gave him another chance to make his mark in Hollywood. He offered Boyer a featured role in *Private Worlds* (1935) with Claudette Colbert and Joel McCrea, as the superintendent of a mental hospital. Some concentrated language study brought his English up to scratch and this time American audiences were impressed. So was Wanger. He signed Boyer to a personal contract with a clause which allowed him to make one film a year in France. The turning-point had come and Boyer said later of the film, 'It made me in America. It was my first real motion picture.' This probably does less than justice to his films for UFA, but certainly in terms of his Hollywood career he was right. At this time, too, he married. His bride was an English actress, Pat Patterson, and they are still married today.

His first film for Wanger under the new contract was *Break of Hearts* (1935) with Katharine Hepburn, in which he played a fashionable young conductor. Then came *Shanghai* (1935), in which he played a Eurasian boy, hopelessly in love with Loretta Young. After this, Boyer took advantage of the special clause in his contract to return to Paris where he made *Mayerling* (1936) for Anatole Litvak. He played the Crown Prince Rudolph (the part played in the 1968 version by Omar Sharif) opposite Danielle Darrieux and was a tremendous success, not only in France but everywhere else too. This film really established him with

British and American audiences (hitherto not over-enamoured of his charms) as a Great Lover in the tradition of Valentino. His dark good looks, brooding 'bedroom' eyes and intriguing accent made him irresistible, and where he had the edge over Chevalier in heart-throb terms was in the seriousness of his passion. He was intense where Chevalier was arch, and, though not lacking in humour, he did act with sincerity whereas Chevalier tended to frolic.

On his return to Hollywood, he followed up his success in *Mayerling* by appearing in *The Garden of Allah* (1936) with Marlene Dietrich. It was a deliberate return to the smouldering sheik-lover image created by Valentino and was widely publicized (not least because it was among the first Technicolor live-action films ever made). This was followed by Frank Borzage's *History is Made at Night* (1937), in which he co-starred with the delightful Jean Arthur. Here his undoubted acting ability had a freer range and his performance was masterly in its passionate restraint and humour. Borzage was probably the greatest romantic director in American cinema in the pre-war era, and in films like *Man's Castle* (1934) with Tracy and Loretta Young had perfected a touching formula with lovers managing to savour a few moments of great happiness in the face of danger and disasters. John Kobal speaks of *History* as the peak of Borzage's 'exalted romanticism' and refers to it as one of 'the two romantic highlights' of the 'thirties – the other being McCarey's *Love Affair* (1939), which also starred Charles Boyer. Before this, however, he made four other films, two of them his most famous – *Conquest* (1937) with Garbo and *Algiers* (1938) with Hedy Lamarr. Between these, his gift for comedy was displayed again in *Tovarich* (1937), which reunited him with Claudette Colbert and Anatole Litvak.

Conquest saw him as the Emperor Napoleon Bonaparte, playing opposite Greta Garbo as Marie Walewska (the film's UK title is *Marie Walewska*). In Britain readers of Picturegoer voted him Best Actor of the Year on the strength of the film and the New Yorker was moved to comment that Garbo had at last found a leading man who gave 'more to the interest and vitality of the film' than she did. Then came a film in France, *Orage* (1938) with Michèle Morgan, before he returned to Hollywood to make *Algiers*. This was the American version of a French film starring Jean Gabin called *Pepé-le-Moko*, the story of the passion of a gangster chief for a beautiful society girl. It was also Hedy Lamarr's American début and the film was a sensation, establishing her as a much-sought-after Hollywood leading lady and pushing Boyer to the pinnacle of his success as a romantic actor. This was, as many film-historians have pointed out, the movie in which Boyer is supposed to have invited Hedy to 'come wiz me to ze Casbah'. In fact he never said the line, but this was absolutely the spirit of the film and the man he was playing. (Other examples of apt misquotation abound – Mae West's 'Come up and see me sometime' and

Garbo's 'I want to be alone' being prime examples.)

Despite Boyer's enormous popularity, Wanger chose this moment to close the star's contract, apparently because exhibitors warned him that they wouldn't book foreign actors. Whether this was through an overdeveloped sense of chauvinism or a quite misguided analysis of what constituted box-office success is not certain, but Wanger is reputed to have waxed excessively indignant when Boyer went on blithely making immensely successful movies such as *Love Affair* (1939) and *When Tomorrow Comes* (1939), both with Irene Dunne.

Boyer had returned to France to make *Le Corsaire* when war broke out. He joined the French army but was advised by the government that he would serve his country best as a propagandist in Hollywood and so returned to the States early in 1940. He became an American citizen in 1942 and throughout the war years devoted much of his time and energies to the war effort, especially the cause of the Free French.

His films throughout the 'forties saw a gradual decline from his peak of romantic stardom, though he appeared with many of Hollywood's leading ladies. He starred with Bette Davis in *All This and Heaven Too* (1940), with Margaret Sullavan in *Back Street* (1941) and *Appointment for Love* (1941), Olivia de Havilland in *Hold Back the Dawn* (1941), Joan Fontaine in *The Constant Nymph* (1943), Ingrid Bergman in a 1944 remake of Thorold Dickinson's *Gaslight*, and then again with Irene Dunne in *Together Again* (1944), a pale reflection of their earlier films together.

Boyer's career as a heart-throb was virtually over by the end of the war. He appeared in a screen version of Graham Greene's novel 'The Confidential Agent' with Lauren Bacall in 1945, and in 1946 made *Cluny Brown* for Ernst Lubitsch, playing a Czech refugee opposite Jennifer Jones. The following year saw another adaptation of a famous modern literary work, *A Woman's Vengeance* taken from Aldous Huxley's play 'The Giaconda Smile'. Huxley himself was on hand during the filming and a letter to Anita Loos in July 1947 complains of delays in shooting when an unnamed actor, whom one must assume, I think, was Boyer, 'began throwing his temperament around' and insisting on right-profile shots only. Later in the year, however, writing to a friend about a stage production of the play, he said, 'Boyer knew how to create an atmosphere of tenderness, very simply and without any sentimentality.' Despite this, the film was not very successful and nor was *Arch of Triumph* (1948) with Ingrid Bergman.

At this point Boyer wisely decided to give up Hollywood for a while. He began an American stage-career in the Broadway production of Sartre's 'Les Mains Sales', and when he did return to films it was as a character actor in films like *The Thirteenth Letter* (1951) and *The Happy Time* (1952). During the 'fifties he filmed mainly in France (though like Colman he too

had a cameo role in Todd's *Around the World*), appearing with such leading ladies as Martine Carole, Sophia Loren and Brigitte Bardot, but continued to work in America on the stage and in television. He was one of the co-founders of Four Star Playhouse on American television and appeared with Gladys Cooper, Robert Coote and David Niven in a successful television series called 'The Rogues' which was also seen in Britain.

Boyer continued to work steadily through the 'sixties too, usually in Hollywood-financed films made in Europe such as *The Four Horsemen of the Apocalypse* (1962), *How to Steal a Million* (1966) and *The Madwoman of Chaillot* (1969). He has, however, returned occasionally to Hollywood – successfully for *Barefoot in the Park* (1967), unmemorably for *The April Fools* (1969) directed by Stuart Rosenberg with Jack Lemmon and Catherine Deneuve, and disastrously for Charles Jarrott's musical version of *Lost Horizon* (1972). The disaster was really the film rather than Boyer personally, but it was a case of everyone going down (at least in critical terms) with the ship. In 1974 he was seen in Alain Resnais's film *Stavisky*, the story of the great French swindler of the 'twenties and 'thirties. Boyer plays Baron Raoul, Stavisky's only real friend, and Richard Roud, writing from Cannes Film Festival, said that 'Belmondo (Stavisky) is better than one expected, but Charles Boyer is even finer as the ruined Baron.'

Boyer as Napoleon. He was probably the best popular impersonator of Bonaparte to grace the screen – and a fitting mate for Garbo in *Conquest* (1938).

Boyer and Irene Dunne surprised, in Leo McCarey's *Love Affair* (1939), the ultimate in glamorous shipboard romances, tinged with tragedy but happily resolved in the end.

Algiers (1938) consolidated Boyer's international popularity and fame as a romantic screen-idol and launched Hedy Lamarr as a Hollywood star. His accent was so intriguing, especially to the ladies.

Boyer with Ingrid Bergman in the 1944 remake of Thorold Dickinson's *Gaslight*. Strong stuff, but his career as a romantic star was on the wane.

Charles Boyer

L'Homme du Large. 1920. Marcel L'Herbier. With Jacques Catelain, Marcelle Pradot, Roger Carl.
Chantelouve. 1921. Georges Monca and Rose Pansini. With Jean Toulout, Yvette Andreyor.
Le Grillon du Foyer. 1922. Jean Manoussi. With Marcel Vibert, Suzanne Dantis.
L'Esclave. 1923. Georges Monca and Rose Pansini.
La Ronde Infernale. 1927. Luitz-Morat. With Jean Angelo, Blanche Montel.
Le Capitaine Fracasse. 1928. Alberto Cavalcanti. With Pierre Blanchar, Lien Dyers, Pola Illery, Leon Courtois.
La Bacarolle d'Amour (French version of **Barcarole o Brand in Der Opera**). 1929. UFA. Henri Roussel. With Simone Cerdan, Annabella.
Le Procès de Mary Dugan (French-language version of **The Trial of Mary Dugan**). 1929. Marcel de Sano. With Huguette Duflos, Françoise Rosay.
Revolte dans la Prison (French-language version of **The Big House**). 1930. Paul Fejos. With André Berley, André Burgère, Mona Goya.
The Magnificent Lie. 1931. PARAMOUNT. Berthold Viertel. With Ruth Chatterton, Ralph Bellamy, Stuart Erwin, Françoise Rosay.
Tumultes (French-language version of **Sturme Der Leidenschaft**). 1931. UFA. Robert Siodmak. With Claire Tambour, Florelle, Armand Bernard.
The Man from Yesterday. 1932. PARAMOUNT. Berthold Viertel. With Claudette Colbert, Clive Brook, Andy Devine, Alan Mowbray.
Red-Headed Woman. 1932. MGM. Jack Conway. With Jean Harlow, Chester Morris, Lewis Stone, Leila Hyams, Una Merkel, Henry Stephenson, May Robson.
FPI Ne Repond Plus (French-language version of **FPI Antowortet Nicht**). 1932. UFA. Karl Hartl. With Jean Murat, Daniela Darola.
Moi et l'Imperatrice (French-language version of **Ich und Die Kaiserin**). 1933. UFA. Friedrich Hollaender. With Lillian Harvey.
The Only Girl (US title: **Heart Song**; English-language version of **Moi et l'Imperatrice**). 1933. FOX-GAUMONT BRITISH-UFA.

Friedrich Hollaender. With Lillian Harvey, Mady Christians, Ernest Thesiger, Maurice Evans.
L'Epervier (US title: **Les Amoureux**). 1933. PAX FILMS. Marcel L'Herbier. With Natalie Paley, Pierre Richard-Willm, George Grossmith.
Le Bonheur. 1934. PATHÉ-NATHAN PRODUCTION. Marcel L'Herbier. With Gaby Morlay, Michel Simon, Paulette Dubost, Jean Toulout, Jacques Catelain.
La Bataille. 1934. LEON GARGANOFF PRODUCTIONS. Nicolas Farkas. With Annabella.
The Battle (English-language version of **La Bataille**). 1934. LEON GARGANOFF PRODUCTIONS. Nicolas Farkas. With Merle Oberon, John Loder, Betty Stockfeld, V. Inkijinoff, Miles Mander, Henri Fabert.
Liliom. 1934. ERICH POMMER PRODUCTION. Fritz Lang. With Madelaine Ozeray, Pedro Alcover, Odette Florelle, Henri Richard, Mimi Funes.
Caravan. 1934. FOX. Erik Charrell. With Loretta Young, Jean Parker, Phillips Holmes, Louise Fazenda, Eugene Pallette, C. Aubrey Smith, Noah Beery.
Caravane (French-language version of **Caravan**). 1934. FOX. Erik Charrell. With Annabella, Conchita Montenegro.
Private Worlds. 1935. WALTER WANGER PRODUCTION/PARAMOUNT. Gregory LaCava. With Claudette Colbert, Joel McCrea, Joan Bennett, Helen Vinson, Esther Dale, Sam Hinds.
Break of Hearts. 1935. RKO. Philip Moeller. With Katharine Hepburn, John Beal, Jean Hersholt, Sam Hardy, Inez Courtney.
Shanghai. 1935. WALTER WANGER/PARAMOUNT. James Flood. With Loretta Young, Warner Oland, Fred Keating, Charley Grapewin, Alison Skipworth.
Mayerling. 1936. PAX FILMS. Anatole Litvak. With Danielle Darrieux, Suzy Prim, Jean Dax, Gabrielle Dorziat, Vladimir Sokoloff.
The Garden of Allah. 1936. SELZNICK/UNITED ARTISTS. Richard Boleslawski. With Marlene Dietrich, Basil Rathbone, C. Aubrey Smith, Tilly Losch, Joseph Schildkraut, John Carradine.
History Is Made at Night. 1937. WALTER WANGER/PARAMOUNT. Frank Borzage. With Jean Arthur, Leo Carillo, Colin Clive, Ivan Lebedeff, George Meeker.
Conquest (UK title: **Marie Walewska**). 1937. MGM. Clarence Brown. With Greta Garbo,

Reginald Owen, Alan Marshal, Henry Stephenson, Leif Erickson, Dame May Whitty, C. Henry Gordon.

Tovarich. 1937. WARNER BROTHERS. Anatole Litvak. With Claudette Colbert, Basil Rathbone, Morris Carnovsky, Isabel Jeans, Anita Louise, Melville Cooper, Montagu Love.

Algiers. 1938. WALTER WANGER/UNITED ARTISTS. John Cromwell. With Hedy Lamarr, Sigrid Gurie, Joseph Calleia, Gene Lockhart, Johnny Downs, Alan Hale.

Orage. 1938. TRI-NATIONAL FILMS. Marc Allegret. With Michèle Morgan, Lisette Lanvin, Robert Manual, Jean-Louis Barrault.

Love Affair. 1939. RKO. Leo McCarey. With Irene Dunne, Lee Bowman, Maria Ouspenskaya, Astrid Allwyn, Maurice Moscovich.

When Tomorrow Comes. 1939. UNIVERSAL. John M. Stahl. With Irene Dunne, Barbara O'Neil, Onslow Stevens, Nydia Westman.

All This and Heaven Too. 1940. WARNER BROTHERS. Anatole Litvak. With Bette Davis, Jeffrey Lynn, Barbara O'Neil, Virginia Weidler, Helen Westley, Henry Daniell, George Colouris, Montagu Love, Ann Todd.

Back Street. 1941. UNIVERSAL. Robert Stevenson. With Margaret Sullavan, Richard Carlson, Frank McHugh, Tim Holt.

Hold Back the Dawn. 1941. PARAMOUNT. Mitchell Leisen. With Olivia de Havilland, Paulette Goddard, Victor Francen, Walter Abel, Curt Bois, Billy Lee, Rosemary DeCamp, Nesto Paiva, Mitchell Leisen, Brian Donlevy, Richard Webb, Veronica Lake.

Appointment for Love. 1941. UNIVERSAL. William A. Seiter. With Margaret Sullavan, Rita Johnson, Eugene Pallette, Ruth Terry, Reginald Denny, Cecil Kellaway.

Tales of Manhattan. 1942. TWENTIETH CENTURY-FOX. Julien Duvivier. With all-star cast.

The Constant Nymph. 1943. WARNER BROTHERS. Edmund Goulding. With Joan Fontaine, Alexis Smith, Brenda Marshall, Charles Coburn, Peter Lorre, Dame May Whitty, Jean Muir, Joyce Reynolds, Montagu Love.

The Heart of a Nation. 1943. PAUL GRATZ. Julien Duvivier. Boyer as narrator. With Louis Jouves, Suzy Prim, Michèle Morgan.

Flesh and Fantasy. 1943. UNIVERSAL. Julien Duvivier. Boyer co-produced. With Barbara Stanwyck, Charles Winninger.

Gaslight. 1944. MGM. George Cukor. With Ingrid Bergman, Joseph Cotten, Dame May Whitty, Angela Lansbury.

Together Again. 1944. COLUMBIA. Charles Vidor. With Irene Dunne, Charles Coburn, Mona Freeman, Jerome Courtland, Elizabeth Patterson, Charles Dingle.

Confidential Agent. 1945. WARNER BROTHERS. Herman Shumlin. With Lauren Bacall, Victor Francen, Wanda Hendrix, George Colouris, Peter Lorre, Katina Paxinou.

Cluny Brown. 1946. TWENTIETH CENTURY-FOX. Ernst Lubitsch. With Jennifer Jones, Peter Lawford, Helen Walker, Reginald Owen, C. Aubrey Smith, Richard Haydn.

A Woman's Vengeance. 1948. UNIVERSAL-INTERNATIONAL. Zoltan Korda. With Ann Blyth, Cedric Hardwicke, Mildred Natwick, Jessica Tandy.

Arch of Triumph. 1948. UNITED ARTISTS. Lewis Milestone. With Ingrid Bergman, Charles Laughton, Louis Calhern, Roman Bohnen.

The Thirteenth Letter. 1951. TWENTIETH CENTURY-FOX. Otto Preminger. With Linda Darnell, Michael Rennie, Constance Smith, Françoise Rosay.

The First Legion. 1951. UNITED ARTISTS. Douglas Sirk. With William Demarest, Barbara Rush, Lyle Bettger, Leo G. Carroll.

The Happy Time. 1952. COLUMBIA. Richard Fleischer. With Louis Jordan, Linda Christian, Marsha Hunt, Kurt Kasznar, Bobby Driscoll.

Thunder in the East. 1953. PARAMOUNT. Charles Vidor. With Alan Ladd, Deborah Kerr, Corinne Calvert, Cecil Kellaway.

Madame De . . . 1953. FRANCO LONDON/ARLAN. Max Ophüls. With Danielle Darrieux, Vittorio de Sica.

Nana. 1954. ROITFELD/TIMES. Christian-Jaque. With Martine Carol, Walter Chiari, Jacques Castelot, Noel Roquevert.

La Fortuna de Essere Donna. 1955. LUX FILM. Alessandro Blasetti. With Sophia Loren, Marcello Mastroianni, Nino Besozzi, Titina de Filippo.

The Cobweb. 1955. MGM. Vincente Minnelli. With Richard Widmark, Lauren Bacall, Gloria Grahame, Lillian Gish, John Kerr, Oscar Levant, Rommy Rettig.

Paris-Palace Hôtel (US title: **Paris Hotel**). 1956. SPERA-RIZZOLI/FILMS-AROUND-THE-WORLD. Henri Verneuil. With Françoise Arnoul, Roberto Risso, Michèle Philippe, Tild Thamer, Julien Carette.

Around the World in 80 Days. 1956. UNITED ARTISTS. Michael Anderson. Boyer made a guest appearance. With all-star cast.

Une Parisienne. 1957. UNITED ARTISTS. Michel Boisrond. With Brigitte Bardot, Henri Vidal, Noel Roquevert, Nadia Gray.

Maxime. 1958. RAOUL PLONQUIN/COCINOR PRODUCTIONS. Henri Verneuil. With Michèle Morgan, Arletty, Felix Martin.

The Buccaneer. 1958. PARAMOUNT. Anthony Quinn. With Yul Brynner, Inger Stevens, Charlton Heston, Claire Bloom, E. G. Marshall.

Fanny. 1961. WARNER BROTHERS. Joshua Logan. With Leslie Caron, Maurice Chevalier, Horst Buchholz, Baccaloni, Lionel Jeffries, Raymond Bussieres, Victor Francen.

The Four Horsemen of the Apocalypse. 1962. MGM. Vincente Minnelli. With Glenn Ford, Ingrid Thulin, Lee J. Cobb, Paul Henreid, Paul Lukas, Yvette Mimieux, Karl Boehm.

Les Demons de Minuit. 1962. UNIDEX. Marc Allegret and Charles Gerard. With Pascale Petit, Maria Mauber, Charles Belmont, Berthe Grandval.

Love Is a Ball. 1963. UNITED ARTISTS. David Swift. With Hope Lange, Glenn Ford, Ricardo Montalban, Ruth McDevitt, Georgette Anys.

Adorable Julia. 1964. SEE-ART FILMS/WEINER-MUNDUS. Alfred Weidenmann. With Lilli Palmer, Thomas Fritsch, Jean Sorel, Ljuba Wetilsch, Jeanne Valerie, Charles Regnier, Tilly Lavenstein.

A Very Special Favor. 1965. LANKERSHIM/UNIVERSAL. Michael Gordon. With Rock Hudson, Leslie Caron, Walter Slezak, Dick Shawn, Larry Storch, Nita Talbot.

How To Steal a Million. 1966. TWENTIETH CENTURY-FOX. William Wyler. With Peter O'Toole, Audrey Hepburn, Eli Wallach, Hugh Griffith, Fernand Gravet.

Is Paris Burning? 1966. PARAMOUNT. René Clement. With Jean-Paul Belmondo, Leslie Caron, Jean-Pierre Cassel, George Chakiris, Alain Delon, Kirk Douglas, Glenn Ford, Gert Frobe, Yves Montand, Anthony Perkins, Simone Signoret, Robert Stack, Marie Versini, Skip Ward, Orson Welles, Bruno Cremer, Claude Dauphin, Michel Piccoli, Claude Rich, Jean-Louis Trintignant.

Casino Royale. 1967. COLUMBIA. John Huston, Ken Hughes, Val Guest, Robert Parrish, Joe

McGrath. Boyer makes a guest appearance.

Barefoot in the Park. 1967. PARAMOUNT. Gene Saks. With Robert Redford, Jane Fonda, Mildred Natwick, Herbert Edelman.

The Day the Hot Line Got Hot. 1968. COMMONWEALTH UNITED ENTERTAINMENTS. Etienne Perier. With Robert Taylor, George Chakiris, Dominique Faber, Gerard Tichy, Marie DuBois.

The April Fools. 1969. WARNER PATHÉ. Stuart Rosenberg. With Catherine Deneuve, Jack Lemmon, Peter Lawford, Jack Weston, Myrna Loy, Harvey Korman, Sally Kellerman.

The Madwoman of Chaillot. 1969. WARNER BROTHERS. Bryan Forbes. With Katharine Hepburn, Claude Dauphin, Edith Evans, John Gavin, Paul Henreid, Oscar Homolka, Margaret Leighton, Guilietta Massina, Nanette Newman, Richard Chamberlain, Yul Brynner, Donald Pleasence, Danny Kaye.

Lost Horizon. 1972. COLUMBIA-WARNER. Charles Jarrott. With Peter Finch, John Gielgud, Liv Ullman, Sally Kellerman, George Kennedy, Michael York, Olivia Hussey, Bobby Van.

Stavisky. 1974. EURO-INTERNATIONAL PRODUCTIONS. Alain Resnais. With Jean-Paul Belmondo, François Perier, Claude Rich, Anny Duperey.

Errol Flynn

'He had a mediocre talent, but to the Walter Mittys of the world he was all the heroes in one magnificent, sexy, animal package.' The writer was Jack L. Warner, in his memoirs, and the man of whom he spoke was Errol Flynn – the screen's greatest swashbuckler and, according to Warner, 'One of the most charming and tragic men I have ever met.' Flynn was undoubtedly one of the most beautiful men ever to grace the screen, and, though as an actor he seems to have been limited (he complained of lack of opportunity to try a wider range of parts), as the gallant, virile hero of romantic costume-dramas he was unique – the swashbuckler supreme. His detractors tend to dwell on his later years when drink and self-disgust had taken their toll. By that time he was an object of ridicule for precisely the two aspects of his life which had made him a great star – his amorous propensities and his screen heroics. His admirers talk of him as possessing overwhelming grace and style (poetic is a word that crops up frequently in assessments of his screen image), and in films such as *The Adventures of Robin Hood* (1938) and *The Sea Hawk* (1940) it is undeniable that he projects a remarkable physical presence – a powerful blend of good looks, confident charm, romantic chivalry and tremendous sex-appeal.

In the post-war years the film genre that had been Flynn's making and his main career-vehicle fell from grace and that affected Flynn profoundly. Perhaps the fact of so much real-life wartime heroism, performed often without grace and gallantry but with a lot of blood and pain, had dulled the cinema-goers' appetite for the almost ritualized, and certainly unreal, heroics of the costume-drama. Flynn himself grew to dislike the swashbuckling romances that made him famous and it is sad that he did not live long enough to see their rehabilitation. Olivia de Havilland, his co-star in eight films, also rather disliked them and, unhappy playing second-fiddle in every picture, broke up their screen partnership. Years later, however, in Paris in the late 'fifties she saw *Robin Hood* again and realized how good the film actually was. She wrote to tell Flynn so, but tore the letter up feeling he would think her silly. He died a few months later, notorious rather than famous, remembered more for his off-screen peccadilloes and scandals than for his on-screen performances – a youthful, athletic roisterer who had become a sad, tormented man, physically much older than his fifty years.

Flynn's image as an adventurer was firmly rooted in fact. His late adolescence and early twenties had been stuffed with such exotic incident that the Warner Brothers' publicity machine was faced with a rather bizarre task. Instead of having to create a suitably dashing and exciting background for their new star, their main problem was to present his real-life experiences in a credible light. Gold-mining, copra-farming, crocodile-hunting and dodging head-hunters in New Guinea, combined with gambling and opium-smoking in Macao and a stint with the Royal Hong Kong Volunteers fighting the Japanese in China, all made a pretty heady brew. Flynn's actual career prepared him perfectly to be a screen adventurer. He had lived by his wits and his charm (and often by the skin of his teeth) with no specific ambition, skill or training. By the time he reached Hollywood he had the face, figure, façade and flair that were perfect qualifications for a Hollywood heart-throb of heroic proportions.

Errol Flynn was born in Tasmania in June 1909. His mother was the daughter of a sea-captain and his father a distinguished marine biologist, and it seems likely that Errol inherited his deep and abiding love of the sea from both sides of the family. However, none of his father's academic prowess seemed to have rubbed off on him for, though he excelled at sport, Errol was expelled from most of the schools he attended both in Australia and England. There seems to have been no normal, happy relationship at all between him and his mother. She found him rebellious and difficult; he found her cold and hard. Perhaps in these early, unhappy confrontations lay the seeds of his later inability to settle down with any one woman even when he could acknowledge his need for the stability that such a relationship could bring.

He left his last school when he was sixteen and worked as a clerk in Sydney till he left for New Guinea early in 1926. After brief stints as a trainee district-officer and manager of a copra plantation, he and a partner ran a small charter-schooner. Flynn first appeared on celluloid at this time when a film-crew hired the boat to take footage of the Sepik River and shot pictures of him 'tangling with a crocodile for fun and sport' (as he later wrote in his autobiography, 'My Wicked, Wicked Ways'). After a short career as a gold-miner, a brief return to Australia, purchase of another boat and a return voyage on her to New Guinea where he managed a tobacco plantation for a while, Flynn had his first real taste of film-making. An Australian producer/director Charles Chauvel offered him the part of Fletcher Christian in his feature *In the Wake of the Bounty* (1933). He accepted, enjoyed the experience and determined to make his way to England to pursue an acting career there. This he did, with a friend, a Dutch doctor, his boon companion in the numerous hilarious and hair-raising adventures that befell him *en route*, all described in detail in his autobiography.

Flynn arrived in London in 1933 and after drawing a total blank in the job stakes there, finally obtained a place in a repertory company in Northampton where he stayed for four and a half years. He became a reasonably accomplished actor during this period and finally made it to the West End. There he was asked to take part in a cops-and-robbers film, *Murder at*

Monte Carlo (1934), to be made at Warner Brothers' Teddington studio. On the strength of it, he was offered a six-month contract at $150 a month and promptly set sail for America – and Hollywood.

After a couple of supporting parts, his big chance came. Warners, emboldened by the recent success of film costume-dramas, decided to try their luck (as did MGM with *Mutiny on the Bounty*) and chose as their vehicle Rafael Sabatini's *Captain Blood*, a Silent version of which had been made in 1923 by Vitagraph (a company subsequently acquired by Warners). Robert Donat was scheduled to play the name part, a young physician who in the late seventeenth century is unfairly convicted of treason, sent to Jamaica as a slave and escapes to become first a pirate and then Governor of Jamaica. Donat had to cancel at the last minute, however, and Michael Curtiz, who had previously used Flynn in a small part, tested him. He was a natural for the role and despite an initial nervousness he gained in confidence and stature so visibly that the first two weeks' shooting was redone. He had just the right blend of innocence, sincerity, gallantry and impudence for the part. In addition, his teaming with another newcomer, Olivia de Havilland, produced exactly the right screen chemistry.

Captain Blood (1935) was a great success and it made Flynn into a star virtually overnight. It also proved to Warners that not only had they found a money-spinning formula, but they had its best exponent in the person of Errol Flynn. The team that worked on *Blood*, Flynn, de Havilland, Michael Curtiz and Erich Korngold (who wrote the score) were to work together again and again, equally successfully. From this time Errol Flynn was a Hollywood star of the first magnitude, adored by a large public, courted by his studio and the press, and very well paid. The peak years for Flynn were 1936 to 1942 and film after film confirmed his popularity and appeal. Among them were *The Charge of the Light Brigade* (1936) with de Havilland and David Niven, *The Adventures of Robin Hood* (1938) again with de Havilland, *The Private Lives of Elizabeth and Essex* (1939) with Bette Davis, *The Dawn Patrol* (1938) with Niven again, *Dodge City* (1939) his first Western, directed by Curtiz, *The Sea Hawk* (1940) arguably his finest costume-picture, and *They Died with Their Boots On* (1941), the life of General Custer, directed by Raoul Walsh and co-starring, for the last time, Olivia de Havilland.

This was the period too, when Flynn could, and did, enjoy the fruits of his success to the full. He had married, shortly after his arrival in Hollywood, French actress Lili Damita. They did not divorce till 1942, but Flynn was hardly a constant husband and during these years his reputation as a ladies' man with an almost boundless appetite for hedonism matured. He was, in all probability, a man of quite ordinary sexuality, and an insight into the man rather than the myth is given by his deep but quiet affection for Olivia de Havilland who said later,

'I had a crush on him, and later found he did for me.' This hardly sounds like the Great Stud, a reputation he endured light-heartedly and perhaps even enjoyed. What turned his initially fairly jokey reputation as a modern Casanova horribly sour was his arrest and trial in November 1942 for statutory rape.

The affair was nothing like as dramatic as it sounds. However, the effects of the whole business on Flynn himself were tragic and damaging. He was charged with having sexual intercourse with two girls under the Californian legal age of consent – eighteen. Both girls had questionable backgrounds, there was a strong feeling that a new DA was making Flynn a scapegoat for the whole Hollywood community – and he was acquitted – but the experience left deep scars and had immensely sad side-effects. He had been liked, laughed at a little, never perhaps taken too seriously before the trial but now, with the court reports offering light relief to a nation at war, he became a figure of fun, ridiculed and unrespected. 'In like Flynn' became a popular phrase and even the titles of his films became fair game, especially *They Died with Their Boots On* following a trial revelation that he had made love with his socks on. After this it was pretty well downhill all the way. He made some interesting films but none of the calibre of earlier years, his drinking took over more and more, and his health and appearance suffered accordingly. His tarnished reputation kept him constantly in trouble with women – who challenged his sexual prowess – and men, who challenged his bravery and physical strength. The divorce settlement with Lili

'He was a charming and magnetic man, but so tormented,' wrote Olivia de Havilland of Errol Flynn after his death.

Damita proved to be a terrible financial drain on him. 'My problem,' he quipped, 'lies in reconciling my gross habits with my net income.' Another of his *bon mots* was 'Women won't let me stay single and I won't let myself stay married', and he proved the truth of this by marrying for the second time in 1943. His bride was Nora Eddington, who had worked on the cigar counter at the Los Angeles Hall of Justice during his trial. They maintained separate establishments (at his insistence), had two little girls and divorced in 1949. His great escape from this time onwards was the sea. He had bought a boat, the 'Sirocco', shortly after his rise to fame and this figured prominently in the rape trial. He sold it, but shortly afterwards bought an ocean-going schooner, the 'Zaca', that in later years was to be his only home for a long period.

Flynn continued to star in major features, but somehow audience enthusiasm was less than it had been. *Objective Burma!* (1945), directed by Raoul Walsh and photographed by James Wong Howe, was a better-than-average war-movie produced during the war. However, the impression it gave of Flynn winning the war single-handed for America did little to endear it to the British public and it was withdrawn from a London cinema after only a week. In 1947 Warners decided to gamble again, with a costume-drama and with Flynn. *The Adventures of Don Juan* (1948) was an unabashed attempt to recapture past glories, but sufficiently knowing to do it slightly tongue-in-cheek. Flynn was thirty-eight and his drinking not only affected his looks and agility but also caused grave problems on the set. Despite this, the finished product was stylish and witty. It did well in Europe but not in the States, though (ironically) reissues of both *The Sea Hawk* and *Robin Hood* were very popular.

In 1950 Flynn was married for the third time, to Patrice Wymore, and in 1952 the Flynns left Hollywood for Europe, where Errol made a couple of costume-pictures, *The Master of Ballantrae* (1953) and *Crossed Swords* (1953) with Gina Lollobrigida, before branching out on his own as a producer. The vehicle he chose was *William Tell*, planned as the first of three features to be made by Flynn and his partner, Barry Mahon, in partnership with Italian producers for United Artists distribution. Flynn was to play the lead, and had put up about $430,000 of his own money. After several weeks of shooting, the Italian backer announced that his money had run out (after contributing only a tiny part of his promised total) and the project folded. At the same time the US Government started to sue Flynn for $840,000 in back taxes.

For the next four and a half years the Flynns drifted around the Mediterranean in the 'Zaca'. Errol continued to make movies in Europe – including a couple with Anna Neagle – until inveigled back to Hollywood to make *Istanbul* (1956). He thought it was going to be shot in Turkey – instead he wound up on Universal's back lot. To his surprise he wasn't as forgotten

and unwanted as he thought, and shortly afterwards was asked to play the part of Mike Campbell, wastrel, charmer, and drinker in Hemingway's *The Sun Also Rises* (1957) with Tyrone Power and Ava Gardner. The part was tailor-made for him and he received excellent notices which effectively launched him into a comeback. His next film was *Too Much Too Soon* (1958), a biopic about John Barrymore's daughter, Diana (played by Dorothy Malone), in which he played John Barrymore himself. They had in fact been great friends before Barrymore's death in 1942 and it was, again, an apt piece of type-casting. It was during the filming of this that he met his last love – fifteen-year-old Beverly Aadland, then a dancer in the cast of *Marjorie Morningstar*. She looked, and acted, older than her years and her youth seemed to give a much-needed boost to Flynn's flagging spirits.

The Roots of Heaven (1958), filmed in Africa for Darryl F. Zanuck, was Flynn's last serious film – again he portrayed a drunk – though in 1959 he made a semi-documentary about Castro's Cuba called *Cuban Rebel Girls*, starring himself and Beverly.

In October 1959 they travelled together to Vancouver to see a Canadian businessman interested in buying the 'Zaca'. While there, Flynn was taken ill with severe back pains. He died on 14 October, officially of a heart-attack, but in fact there were many contributing factors of which alcohol was only one. Bouts of malaria and a tubercular condition, plus chain smoking and frequent use of narcotics, had aged him well beyond his actual years.

Flynn and de Havilland together for the first time on the screen in *Captain Blood* (1935). The chemistry was right and Flynn always looked perfectly at home in period costume.

The Charge of the Light Brigade (1936) teamed Flynn with David Niven and Olivia de Havilland, and gave him yet another opportunity to swash and buckle, this time in the Crimea.

Dawn Patrol (1938) put Flynn and Niven together again in a remake of the earlier, Hawks version. Off-screen they were the greatest of friends – their shared home at Malibu beach was called 'Cirrhosis-by-the-Sea'.

The 1938 version of the *Robin Hood* story, directed by Michael Curtiz and starring Flynn, is undoubtedly the best. What exuberance, what style! Flynn is seen here with faithful followers, Patric Knowles and (centre) Eugene Pallette

The Seahawk (1940) showed Flynn at his most dashing, lithe and romantic. He and director Michael Curtiz worked superbly together and were never better than in this tale of British sea-dogs in Elizabethan days. Flora Robson played the Virgin Queen.

Dodge City (1939) was Flynn's first Western and, although no less dashing in a stetson than in doublet and hose, he somehow didn't look quite so good. With Flynn here (left to right) are Victor Jory, Bruce Cabot, Alan Hall and Douglas Fowley.

The last time Flynn and de Havilland were on the screen together was in *They Died With Their Boots On* (1941). Later she regretted breaking up the partnership and her undervaluation of the films they made together.

Pallette, Alan Hale, Melville Cooper, Patric Knowles, Herbert Mundin.

Four's A Crowd. 1938. WARNER BROTHERS. Michael Curtiz. With Olivia de Havilland, Rosalind Russell, Patric Knowles, Walter Connolly, Hugh Herbert, Melville Cooper, Franklin Pangborn.

The Sisters. 1938. WARNER BROTHERS. Anatole Litvak. With Bette Davis, Anita Louise, Ian Hunter, Donald Crisp, Beulah Bondi, Jane Bryan, Alan Hale, Henry Travers, Patric Knowles.

The Dawn Patrol. 1938. WARNER BROTHERS. Edmund Goulding. With David Niven, Basil Rathbone, Donald Crisp, Melville Cooper, Barry Fitzgerald, Carl Esmond.

Dodge City. 1939. WARNER BROTHERS. Michael Curtiz. With Olivia de Havilland, Ann Sheridan, Bruce Cabot, Frank McHugh, Alan Hale, John Litel, Henry Travers, Henry O'Neill, Victor Jory.

The Private Lives of Elizabeth and Essex. 1939. WARNER BROTHERS. Michael Curtiz. With Bette Davis, Olivia de Havilland, Donald Crisp, Alan Hale, Vincent Price, Henry Stephenson, Henry Daniell, Ralph Forbes.

Virginia City. 1940. WARNER BROTHERS. Michael Curtiz. With Miriam Hopkins, Randolph Scott, Humphrey Bogart, Frank McHugh, Alan Hale, Guinn 'Big Boy' Williams.

The Sea Hawk. 1940. WARNER BROTHERS. Michael Curtiz. With Brenda Marshall, Claude Rains, Donald Crisp, Flora Robson, Alan Hale, Henry Daniell, Una O'Connor, Gilbert Roland, William Lundigan.

Sante Fe Trail. 1940. WARNER BROTHERS. Michael Curtiz. With Olivia de Havilland, Raymond Massey, Ronald Reagan, William Lundigan, Van Heflin, Alan Hale.

Footsteps in the Dark. 1941. WARNER BROTHERS. Lloyd Bacon. With Brenda Marshall, Ralph Bellamy, Alan Hale, Lee Patrick, Allen Jenkins, Lucille Watson, William Frawley, Roscoe Karns.

Dice Bomber. 1941. WARNER BROTHERS. Michael Curtiz. With Fred MacMurray, Ralph Bellamy, Alexis Smith, Robert Armstrong, Regis Toomey, Allen Jenkins.

They Died With Their Boots On. 1941. WARNER BROTHERS. Raoul Walsh. With Olivia de Havilland, Regis Toomey, Stanley Ridges, Arthur Kennedy, Sidney Greenstreet, Walter Hampden, John Litel, Anthony Quinn.

Desperate Journey. 1942. WARNER BROTHERS. Raoul Walsh. With Ronald Reagan, Nancy Coleman, Raymond Massey, Alan Hale, Arthur Kennedy.

Gentleman Jim. 1942. WARNER BROTHERS. Raoul Walsh. With Alexis Smith, Jack Carson, Alan Hale, John Loder, William Frawley, Ward Bond, Minor Watson.

Edge of Darkness. 1943. WARNER BROTHERS. Lewis Milestone. With Ann Sheridan, Walter Huston, Nancy Coleman, Judith Anderson, Helmut Dantine, Ruth Gordon, Charles Dingle, John Beal.

Thank Your Lucky Stars. 1943. WARNER BROTHERS. David Butler. With all-star cast, including Eddie Cantor, Dinah Shore, Bette Davis, Humphrey Bogart.

Northern Pursuit. 1943. WARNER BROTHERS. Raoul Walsh. With Julie Bishop, Helmut Dantine, John Ridgeley, Gene Lockhart, Tom Tully.

Uncertain Glory. 1944. WARNER BROTHERS. Raoul Walsh. With Paul Lukas, Jean Sullivan, Lucille Watson, Faye Emerson.

Objective Burma! 1945. WARNER BROTHERS. Raoul Walsh. With William Prince, James Brown, George Tobias, Henry Hull, Warner Anderson.

San Antonio. 1945. WARNER BROTHERS. David Butler. With Alexis Smith, S. Z. Sakall, Victor Francen, Florence Bates, John Litel, Paul Kelly.

Never Say Goodbye. 1946. WARNER BROTHERS. James Kern. With Eleanor Parker, Lucille Watson, S. Z. Sakall, Forrest Tucker, Donald Woods, Peggy Knudsen, Hattie McDaniel, Tom D'Andrea.

Cry Wolf. 1947. WARNER BROTHERS. Peter Godfrey. With Barbara Stanwyck, Richard Basehart, Jerome Cowan, Geraldine Brooke, John Ridgeley.

Escape Me Never. 1947. WARNER BROTHERS. Peter Godfrey. With Ida Lupino, Eleanor Parker, Gig Young, Reginald Denny, Isobel Elsom, Albert Basserman.

Silver River. 1948. WARNER BROTHERS. Raoul Walsh. With Ann Sheridan, Thomas Mitchell, Bruce Bennett, Tom D'Andrea, Monte Blue.

Always Together. 1948. WARNER BROTHERS. Frederick De Cordova. An unbilled appearance. With Humphrey Bogart, Jack Carson, Dennis Morgan.

The Adventures of Don Juan. 1948. WARNER BROTHERS. Vincent Sherman. With Viveca Lindford, Robert Douglas, Alan Hale, Romney Brent, Ann Rutherford, Robert Warwick.

It's a Great Feeling. 1949. WARNER BROTHERS. David Butler. Guest role with Flynn playing himself.

That Forsyte Woman. 1949. MGM. Compton Bennett. With Greer Garson, Walter Pidgeon, Robert Young, Janet Leigh, Harry Davenport.

Montana. 1950. WARNER BROTHERS. Ray Enright. With Alexis Smith, S. Z. Sakall, Douglas Kennedy, Ian MacDonald, Charles Irwin, Monte Blue.

Rocky Mountain. 1950. WARNER BROTHERS. William Keighley. With Patrice Wymore, Scott Forbes, Guinn 'Big Boy' Williams, Slim Pickens.

Kim. 1950. MGM. Victor Saville. With Dean Stockwell, Paul Lukas, Cecil Kellaway, Arnold Moss, Robert Douglas, Reginald Owen.

The Adventures of Captain Fabian. 1951. SILVER FILMS/REPUBLIC. William Marshall. With Micheline Presle, Vincent Price, Agnes Moorehead, Victor Francen.

Cruise of the Zaca. 1952. WARNER BROTHERS. Errol Flynn. Flynn narrated.

Mara Maru. 1952. WARNER BROTHERS. Gordon Douglas. With Ruth Roman, Raymond Burr, Paul Picerni, Richard Webb, Dan Seymour.

Against All Flags. 1952. UNIVERSAL-INTERNATIONAL. George Sherman. With Maureen O'Hara, Anthony Quinn, Mildred Natwick, Alice Kelly.

The Master of Ballantrae. 1953. WARNER BROTHERS. William Keighley. With Roger Livesey, Anthony Steel, Beatrice Campbell, Felix Aylmer, Mervyn Johns, Charles Goldner, Yvonne Furneaux.

Crossed Swords. 1953. VIVA FILMS/UNITED ARTISTS. Milton Krims. With Gina Lollobrigida, Cesare Danova, Nadia Grey, Roldano Lupi.

Lilacs in the Spring. 1955. EVEREST PICTURES. Herbert Wilcox. With Anna Neagle, David Farrar, Kathleen Harrison, Peter Graves.

The Warriors (UK title: **The Dark Avenger**). 1955. ALLIED ARTISTS/TWENTIETH CENTURY-FOX. Henry Levin. With Joanne Dru, Peter Finch, Yvonne Furneaux, Patrick Holt, Michael Hordern, Noel Willman, Rupert Davies.

King's Rhapsody. 1955. EVEREST PICTURES/BRITISH LION. Herbert Wilcox. With Anna Neagle, Patrice Wymore, Martita Hunt, Finlay Currie, Miles Malleson.

Istanbul. 1956. UNIVERSAL-INTERNATIONAL. Joseph Pevney. With Cornell Borchers, John Bentley, Torin Thatcher, Leif Erickson, Peggy Knudsen, Martin Benson, Nat 'King' Cole.

The Big Boodle. 1957. UNITED ARTISTS. Richard Wilson. With Pedro Armendariz, Rosanne Rory, Gia Scala.

The Sun Also Rises. 1957. TWENTIETH CENTURY-FOX. Henry King. With Tyrone Power, Ava Gardner, Mel Ferrer, Eddie Albert, Juliette Greco.

Hello God. 1958 (made in 1951). CAVALCADE PICTURES. William Marshall. With Sherry Jackson, Joe Muzzuca, Armando Formica.

Too Much, Too Soon. 1958. WARNER BROTHERS. Art Napoleon. With Dorothy Malone, Efrem Zimbalist Jr, Ray Danton, Neva Patterson, Murray Hamilton.

The Roots of Heaven. 1958. TWENTIETH CENTURY-FOX. John Huston. With Juliette Greco, Trevor Howard, Eddie Albert, Orson Welles, Herbert Lom, Paul Lukas.

Cuban Rebel Girls. 1959. EXPLOIT FILMS. Barry Mahon. With John MacKay, Marie Edmund, Jackie Jacklin, Beverley Aadland.

Flynn also appeared in a film made during the filming of **Captain Blood, Pirate Party on Catalina Isle** (1936), and tried to produce **William Tell** (thirty minutes of film apparently exist somewhere).

Humphrey Bogart

Humphrey Bogart is that extraordinary film phenomenon, a star whose popularity, fame and following are much greater nearly twenty years after his death than they ever were during his lifetime. Not only that, but although he had had considerable appeal for audiences while he was alive, it was none the less inconceivable that he would ever be nominated as a heart-throb. One can imagine how horrified Bogey himself would have been by such a suggestion. However, since his death in 1957 and the subsequent cult that has grown up around such films as *Casablanca* (1943) and *The Big Sleep* (1946), he has become one of the most potent male symbols ever to grace the screen. Like Gable and Cooper he appeals to both men and women equally, but his particular brand of world-weariness, cynicism and soft-centred toughness make him especially attractive to women, despite his apparently unpromising physical appearance – he was not handsome but he was very sexy. Like them too his matured screen character reflected the man fairly accurately. Bogart seems to have been genuinely toughminded, cynical, principled and stubborn – all the characteristics of the screen persona which emerged during his middle years, starting with *High Sierra* (1941), and which remained with him till the end. James Agate wrote of him in the early 'forties, 'He has charm and he doesn't waste energy by pretending to act . . . he has an exciting personality and lets it do the work.'

Bogart had an undiplomatic and endearing honesty. He drank heavily, and made no secret of it (he frequently said he didn't trust anyone who didn't drink). He protested vociferously against HUAC's treatment of the Hollywood Ten and supported the Democratic Party and Adlai Stevenson at times when it was unpopular or even, in Stevenson's own words, 'quite perilous' to be seen doing things like that.

His greatest hobby was what he and his cronies called 'needling', an activity with two quite different faces, depending on whether the writer is pro or anti Bogart. For Joe Hyams, whose 1966 biography has the Bacall Seal of Approval in the shape of an introduction by her, the needling was directed only at 'the pompous and opinionated, the proud and pretentious'. Actress Louise Brooks in a curiously schizoid article written for Sight and Sound at about the same time saw it in quite another light. 'During the last ten years of his life,' she wrote, 'driven by his ferocious ambition, Humphrey Bogart allowed himself to be formed into a coarse and drunken bully, a puppet Iago who fomented evil without a motive.' This may seem a little too shrill and it certainly does not square with the amount of affection and respect which Bogart evoked among fellow actors and journalists, but there is no doubt that some of the 'pranks' which he and his companions perpetrated have a coarse, almost brutal quality about them – playing football with someone else's Ming vase for example.

Where all the chroniclers of his life and times agree, however, is that this sport was partly motivated by a desire for publicity. After ten years in Hollywood without the big break, Bogart was only too painfully aware of the value of publicity and, when he realized that his 'tough guy' image was on the way to making him a star, he began to live up to it, to strengthen it in the only way he could – verbally. For there is no doubt – and this perhaps was one of his most endearing characteristics – that faced with physical violence he found discretion to be very much the better part of valour and either charmed or joked his way out of tricky situations.

There seems to be some confusion about the exact date of Bogart's birth. Hyams gives it as Christmas Day 1899 and Lauren Bacall (who presumably should have known) ratifies this. Elsewhere it is given as 23 January, 1899, but all sources seem to agree on the location – New York City. His parents were wealthy professionals – father a doctor and mother a leading magazine and advertisement illustrator (Bogart's first claim to fame was as the Mellins Baby Food baby). Their next-door neighbours were the Brady family. William Brady was a leading theatrical impresario and it was through him that Bogart entered the world of showbusiness shortly after the end of the First World War (he had served briefly in the navy after leaving school under something of a cloud and with very bad marks). He started off as an office boy in Brady's organization and then rose to be a stage manager. He started acting soon after this when the juvenile lead fell ill, and for the next ten years worked fairly steadily, alternating between stage managing and acting. He was usually the romantic juvenile – later he called them his 'tennis anyone' parts. He married twice during this period. He divorced his first wife, Helen Mencken, after a couple of years and in 1928 he married another actress, Mary Phillips, who remained Mrs Bogart until 1937.

In 1930 he was caught up in Hollywood's desperate trawl of Broadway for actors who could help them through the trauma of the Talkies. A Fox talent scout signed him up at $750 a week and he was off to the West Coast. His first film was *A Devil with Women* (1930) with Victor McLaglen, which gave him another 'tennis anyone' part, and his second was a John Ford comedy, *Up the River* (1930) starring Spencer Tracy, also a Broadway émigré but at this stage a more successful one than Bogart. It was the beginning of a lifelong friendship.

He made three more pictures before Fox dropped him. Women, reasoned a studio executive, would never really go for him, what with the scarred upper lip (acquired while in the navy) and the slight lisp. He returned to Broadway in 1931. The Depression was by now in full swing and money was a pressing problem for the Bogarts. After appearing in John van Druten's 'After All', he returned briefly to Hollywood to co-star in *Love Affair* (1931) with Dorothy MacKail and stayed to make a couple of films for Warners, both with Joan Blondell, and both directed by Mervyn Le Roy. None of the films shook his determination that the stage was his rightful *métier* and so he went back to Broadway again.

It was Robert Sherwood's play 'The Petrified Forest' and Leslie Howard (in that order) that finally got his film career properly started. Producer Arthur Hopkins had noticed him playing the villain in 'Invitation to a Murder' and cast him as the gangster, Duke Mantee, in 'The Petrified Forest'. It was a complete change from the sleek, dapper man-about-town parts he had been playing for years and people began to sit up and take notice – especially Leslie Howard, the star of the play. He promised Bogart that if it was ever filmed he would do all he could to ensure that Bogart also played Mantee on the screen. And he was as good as his word. Warners bought the play, but decided to cast Edward G. Robinson as Mantee. Bogart cabled Howard (on holiday in Scotland) and Howard immediately sent Warners an ultimatum – no Bogart, no Howard. The studio capitulated and Bogey never forgot Howard's kindness – his daughter, born in 1954, was named after him. Louise Brooks propounds the theory that Bogart was also deeply influenced by Howard's quiet natural, 'English' style of acting. Brought up in the Broadway tradition of flamboyant showing-off and scene-stealing, she felt that Howard's style, with its subtlety and emphasis on technique, impressed Bogart, who embarked on a long and painful struggle to reconstruct his own style, breaking down the habits of years.

In the period which followed his success in *The Petrified Forest* (1936), Bogart did not get too many opportunities to flex his acting muscles. Warners did not seem to have registered his critical success and box-office popularity as Mantee, and for the next five years used him as a supporting villain in gangster film after gangster film. He was a junior member of what became known as 'Murderers Row' at Warners – Cagney, Robinson, Muni and Raft. 'In my first thirty-four pictures,' Bogart said later, 'I was shot in twelve, electrocuted or hanged in eight and was a jailbird in nine. I was the little Lord Fauntleroy of the lot.' Perhaps not accurate to the letter, but true in spirit!

During this period his second marriage broke up, and in August 1938 he married for the third time – another actress, a hard-drinking bellicose and unconventional blonde called Mayo Methot. They soon became known as 'The Battling Bogarts', and indeed some contemporary observers were of the opinion that it was the fighting that kept the marriage alive. Mayo gave up her acting career when she married, and resentment at this fuelled many of her attacks on Bogart. She was also very jealous

and, if he was a heavy drinker before he met her, under her tutelage his capacity was tremendously enlarged. For a while, however, Bogart seemed to thrive on this tempestuous relationship, even boasting about his wife's wilder demonstrations. He was embattled at the studio too, constantly arguing with Jack Warner, who had at last recognized his growing popularity in gangster roles, but refused to let him try any better parts.

Ironically, when his chance came, it was in the form of another gangster, the tired, ageing killer in Raoul Walsh's *High Sierra* (1941). The important difference was that the part of Roy Earle, the psychopathic killer, gave Bogart a real opportunity to act. George Raft had turned down the film because he refused to die at the end as the script and the Hays Office dictated. For Bogart it was the real breakthrough in terms of critical and public acclaim. On a trip to New York to publicize the film, he and Mayo were trapped in the cinema by fans who jammed the street. He had made it at last – he was over forty and had been in Hollywood on and off for more than ten years.

George Raft was also indirectly responsible for his next great success, the screen version of Dashiell Hammett's *The Maltese Falcon* (1941).

American critic Pauline Kael wrote of Bogart in the late 'sixties, 'There isn't an actor in American films today with anything like his assurance, his magnetism or his style.'

It was John Huston's directorial début and Raft was cagey about working with an untried unknown. Bogart did not share his qualms and the film marked not only his establishment as a star of the first order but also the start of an enduring friendship with Huston. The film is a *tour de force*, with excellent performances from Peter Lorre, Sidney Greenstreet, and Mary Astor, but it is Bogart's triumph first and foremost. His Sam Spade is nonchalant but intense, contemptuous yet courteous, unsmiling but sardonic, and immensely appealing in his loneliness and disillusionment about women and love. He is the Bogart prototype for all the later films – the tough, classy, sexy loner with the voice half-way between a rasp and a lisp.

The film which more than any other exploited the romantic aspect of this character was *Casablanca* (1943), which brought him an Academy Award nomination for his playing of Rick, the embittered expatriate club-owner of no fixed abode and, apparently, no fixed affections. Again he took a risk in accepting the part. Not that the director was untried – Michael Curtiz was one of the great Hollywood work-horse directors who could, and did, turn his hand to anything and everything. The problem lay in the fact that the shooting script gave no indication at all of the shape and direction of the finished film (Hedy Lamarr turned down the Ingrid Bergman part on these grounds). The story was virtually written as they went along, and it was not until the last day that any of the actors knew how it was to end. John Kobal in 'Romance in the Cinema' analyses the film briefly but superbly and makes the interesting observation that 'the actors' uncertainty about the script projected itself into the people's uncertainty about being able to escape, about deciding between love and honour.' Certainly, with each viewing of 'this glorious piece of hokum' the romantic, desperate atmosphere of unpredictability and pervasive danger is unfailingly re-created. Again, the cast was strong – Claude Rains, Paul Henreid, Conrad Veidt, Lorre and Greenstreet and, of course, Ingrid Bergman, exquisitely beautiful in her Orry-Kelly outfits, idealistic and aquiver with suppressed emotion. With the addition of the cynical, abrasive but soft-centred Bogart persona and the haunting theme of Sam playing 'As Time Goes By', you have what many people consider to be the cinema's most romantic film. It made Warners a fortune and Bogart King of the Warners lot.

The same formula was used in Howard Hawks's good but none too exact adaptation of Hemingway's novel *To Have and Have Not* (1945), even down to the piano-player (Hoagy Carmichael this time). The girl in this film was played by a newcomer to Hollywood, an ex-New York model called Lauren Bacall. She was twenty and Bogart forty-five and they fell in love quickly and obviously. (He divorced Mayo on 10 May, 1945, and married Lauren Bacall on 21 May.) The popular theory is that their off-screen romance gives their on-screen relationship something special. In fact Bogart had far more exciting screen relationships with his other leading ladies than he ever had with Bacall – notably Mary Astor, Ingrid Bergman and, above all, Gloria Grahame in *In a Lonely Place* (1950), directed by her then husband Nicholas Ray. The love-scenes in this film have a depth and passion rare in the American cinema. Bacall is just a little too cool, too self-possessed and watchful. This works extremely well in the film she and Bogart made next, Howard Hawks's superb version of Raymond Chandler's novel *The Big Sleep* (1946), where those qualities are perfect for the character she plays, a wealthy insolent divorcée. It was less acceptable in *Key Largo*, John Huston's adaptation of a Maxwell Anderson play about a disillusioned war-veteran, which also starred Claire Trevor, Edward G. Robinson and Lionel Barrymore.

Bogart's mature style and personality show to perfection as Philip Marlowe in *The Big Sleep*, undoubtedly a minor masterpiece, but, as if to prove his range, Bogart's next major film, Huston's *Treasure of the Sierra Madre* (1948), gave him a chance to turn in a fine piece of character acting as the greedy, obsessive prospector, Fred Dobbs.

From 1950 till his death from cancer in January 1957 Bogart made a dozen films. They were a mixed bag, but gave him plenty of opportunities to show the range of his acting ability. Among his most notable roles were those of Captain Queeg in *The Caine Mutiny* (1954) and the veteran Hollywood director in *The Barefoot Contessa* (1954), and highly entertaining, if less applauded, was his 'comic' convict performance with Peter Ustinov and Aldo Ray in *We're No Angels* (1955). The high point of these last years was undoubtedly *The African Queen* (1951), his two-hander with Katharine Hepburn, directed by John Huston. The film won him a Best Actor Oscar and, like *Casablanca*, is a truly romantic Bogart movie, perhaps the most romantic. The material does not look very promising – a drunken layabout and a prim lady-missionary take a decrepit steam-boat down an African river and fire a homemade torpedo at a German gun-boat – but out of it came one of the screen's greatest love-stories. In Katharine Hepburn Bogart found his ideal screen partner. Her personality was as tough and uncompromising as his, but in a quite different, more astringent way, and their relationship in the film was a meeting of giants and just as awe-inspiring.

At Bogart's funeral John Huston summed up the man and the actor when he said, 'He is quite irreplaceable. There will never be anybody like him.'

After appearing as Bogart's moll in *High Sierra* (1941), Ida Lupino refused to act with him in *Out of the Fog* (which she made the same year with John Garfield) – she had had enough of his sharp tongue.

Bogart's screen version of his stage success as gangster Duke Mantee in the Broadway production of *The Petrified Forest* (1936) set the pattern for his 'thirties film career. Leslie Howard and Bette Davis were the lovers. Also here are Charley Grapewin (left) and Dick Foran.

The gang's all here.
Bogart, Peter Lorre, Mary
Astor and Sidney
Greenstreet – and the
strange black bird that
caused all the trouble in
The Maltese Falcon
(1941).

'Here's looking at you, kid.'
Bogart, Bergman and an
atmosphere of unbelievable
but glorious romanticism
combined to make
Casablanca (1943) a
screen classic.

On the facing page:
Bogart in *The Left Hand of
God* (1955).

Robert Taylor and Dana Wynter in *D-Day the Sixth of June* (1956).

Bogart's 'forties films invariably threw up highly memorable lines. In *To Have and Have Not* (1945) it was Bacall's injunction, 'If you want anything, all you have to do is whistle.' In this Caribbean version of *Casablanca*, Hoagy Carmichael (left) played the pianist.

Louise Brooks wrote of Lauren Bacall that she was 'as seductive as Eve, as cool as the serpent', and this sums up perfectly her performance in *The Big Sleep* (1946).

Humphrey Bogart

Bogart as Fred Dobbs in John Huston's *The Treasure of the Sierra Madre* (1948). This desperate and deranged character seems almost like a dry-run for his later Captain Queeg in *The Caine Mutiny* (1954).

Broadway's Like That. 1930. VITAPHONE/WARNER BROTHERS. Murray Roth. With Ruth Etting, Joan Blondell.
A Devil With Women. 1930. FOX. Irving Cummings. With Victor McLaglen, Mona Maris, Luana Alcaniz.
Up the River. 1930. FOX. John Ford. With Spencer Tracy, Claire Luce, Warren Hymer.
Body and Soul. 1931. FOX. Alfred Santell. With Charles Farrell, Elissa Landi, Myrna Loy, Donald Dillaway.
Bad Sister. 1931. UNIVERSAL. Hobart Henley. With Conrad Nagel, Sidney Fox, Bette Davis, ZaSu Pitts.
Women of All Nations. 1931. FOX. Raoul Walsh.

With Victor McLaglen, Edmund Lowe, Greta Nissen, Bela Lugosi.
A Holy Terror. 1931. FOX. Irving Cummings. With George O'Brien, Sally Eilers, Rita LaRoy, James Kirkwood.
Love Affair. 1932. COLUMBIA. Thornton Freeland. With Dorothy Mackail, Jack Kennedy, Halliwell Hobbes, Barbara Leonard.
Big City Blues. 1932. WARNER BROTHERS. Mervyn Le Roy. With Joan Blondell, Eric Linden, Inez Courtney, Guy Kibbee, Lyle Talbot.
Three On a Match. 1932. WARNER BROTHERS (FIRST NATIONAL). Mervyn Le Roy. With Joan Blondell, Warren William, Ann Dvorak, Bette Davis, Lyle Talbot, Glenda Farrell.
Midnight (UK title: **Call It Murder**). 1934. UNIVERSAL (ALL-STAR PRODUCTION). Chester Erskine. With Sidney Fox, O. P. Heggie, Henry Hull, Lynne Overman.
The Petrified Forest. 1936. WARNER BROTHERS. Archie Mayo. With Leslie Howard, Bette Davis, Dick Foran, Genevieve Tobin, Porter Hall, Charley Grapewin.
Bullets or Ballots. 1936. WARNER BROTHERS (FIRST NATIONAL). William Keighley. With Edward G. Robinson, Joan Blondell, Barton MacLane, Frank McHugh.
Two Against the World (UK title: **The Case of Mrs Pembrook**). 1936. WARNER BROTHERS (FIRST NATIONAL). William McGann. With Beverly Roberts, Helen MacKeller, Henry O'Neill, Linda Perry.
China Clipper. 1936. WARNER BROTHERS (FIRST NATIONAL). Ray Enright.

With Pat O'Brien, Beverly Roberts, Ross Alexander, Marie Wilson.
Isle of Fury. 1936. WARNER BROTHERS. Frank McDonald. With Margaret Lindsay, Donald Woods, Paul Graetz, Gordon Hart.
Black Legion. 1937. WARNER BROTHERS. Archie Mayo. With Dick Foran, Erin O'Brien-Moore, Ann Sheridan, Robert Barrat, Helen Flint, Joseph Sawyer.
The Great O'Malley. 1937. WARNER BROTHERS. William Dieterle. With Pat O'Brien, Sybil Jason, Ann Sheridan, Donald Crisp, Frieda Inescort, Henry O'Neill.
Marked Woman. 1937. WARNER BROTHERS (FIRST NATIONAL). Lloyd Bacon. With Bette Davis, Lola Lane, Isabel Jewell, Allen Jenkins, Eduardo Ciannelli, Rosalind Marquis, Mayo Methot.
Kid Galahad. 1937. WARNER BROTHERS. Michael Curtiz. With Edward G. Robinson, Bette Davis, Wayne Morris, Jane Bryan.
San Quentin. 1937. WARNER BROTHERS (FIRST NATIONAL). Lloyd Bacon. With Pat O'Brien, Ann Sheridan, Barton MacLane, Joseph Sawyer, Veda Ann Borg.
Dead End. 1937. GOLDWYN/UNITED ARTISTS. William Wyler. With Sylvia Sidney, Joel McCrea, Wendy Barrie, Claire Trevor, Allen Jenkins, Marjorie Main, Ward Bond, Esther Dale.
Stand-In. 1927. WALTER WANGER/UNITED ARTISTS. Tay Garnett. With Leslie Howard, Joan Blondell, Alan Mowbray, Marla Shelton, C. Henry Gordon, Jack Carson.
Swing Your Lady. 1938. WARNER BROTHERS. Ray Enright. With Frank McHugh, Louise Fazenda, Allen Jenkins, Nat Pendleton, Ronald Reagan.
Crime School. 1938. WARNER BROTHERS (FIRST NATIONAL). Lewis Seiler. With Gale Page, Billy Halop, Bobby Jordan, Huntz Hall.
Men Are Such Fools. 1938. WARNER BROTHERS. Busby Berkeley. With Wayne Morris, Priscilla Lane, Hugh Herbert, Penny Singleton, Mona Barrie, Gene Lockhart.
The Amazing Dr Clitterhouse. 1938. WARNER BROTHERS (FIRST NATIONAL). Anatole Litvak. With Edward G. Robinson, Claire Trevor, Allen Jenkins, Donald Crisp, Ward Bond, Gale Page, Henry O'Neill.
Racket Busters. 1938. WARNER BROTHERS. Lloyd Bacon. With George Brent, Gloria Dickson, Allen Jenkins, Walter Abel, Henry O'Neill, Penny Singleton.

In a Lonely Place (1951) was a highly atmospheric melodrama about lonely people on the fringes of Hollywood. Bogart's relationship with Gloria Grahame had tremendous tension and passion.

Like *Casablanca*, *The African Queen* (1951) was a piece of sheer romantic fantasy and, however unlikely Katharine Hepburn may have seemed as a Bogart co-star, it worked supremely well.

108

Angels With Dirty Faces. 1938. WARNER BROTHERS (FIRST NATIONAL). With James Cagney, Pat O'Brien, Ann Sheridan, George Bancroft.

King of the Underworld. 1939. WARNER BROTHERS. Lewis Seiler. With Kay Francis, James Stephenson, John Eldredge, Jessie Busley.

The Oklahoma Kid. 1939. WARNER BROTHERS. Lloyd Bacon. With James Cagney, Rosemary Lane, Donald Crisp, Ward Bond.

Dark Victory. 1939. WARNER BROTHERS (FIRST NATIONAL). Edmund Goulding. With Bette Davis, George Brent, Geraldine Fitzgerald, Ronald Reagan, Henry Travers.

You Can't Get Away With Murder. 1939. WARNER BROTHERS (FIRST NATIONAL). Lewis Seiler. With Billy Halop, Gale Page, John Litel, Henry Travers.

The Roaring Twenties. 1939. WARNER BROTHERS (FIRST NATIONAL). Raoul Walsh. With James Cagney, Priscilla Lane, Gladys George, Jeffrey Lynn, Frank McHugh, Paul Kelly, Elizabeth Risdon.

The Return of Dr X. 1939. WARNER BROTHERS (FIRST NATIONAL). Vincent Sherman. With Wayne Morris, Rosemary Lane, Dennis Morgan, John Litel.

Invisible Stripes. 1939. WARNER BROTHERS (FIRST NATIONAL). Lloyd Bacon. With George Raft, Jane Bryan, William Holden, Flora Robson.

Virginia City. 1940. WARNER BROTHERS (FIRST NATIONAL). Michael Curtiz. With Errol Flynn, Miriam Hopkins, Randolph Scott, Frank McHugh, Alan Hale.

It All Came True. 1940. WARNER BROTHERS (FIRST NATIONAL). Lewis Seiler. With Ann Sheridan, Jeffrey Lynn, ZaSu Pitts, Una O'Connor, Jessie Busley.

Brother Orchid. 1940. WARNER BROTHERS (FIRST NATIONAL). Lloyd Bacon. With Edward G. Robinson, Ann Sothern, Donald Crisp, Ralph Bellamy, Allen Jenkins, Cecil Kellaway.

They Drive by Night. 1940. WARNER BROTHERS (FIRST NATIONAL). Raoul Walsh. With George Raft, Ann Sheridan, Ida Lupino, Gale Page, Alan Hale, Roscoe Karns.

High Sierra. 1941. WARNER BROTHERS (FIRST NATIONAL). Raoul Walsh. With Ida Lupino, Alan Curtis, Arthur Kennedy, Joan Leslie, Isabel Jewell, Cornel Wilde.

The Wagons Roll at Night. 1941. WARNER BROTHERS (FIRST NATIONAL). Ray Enright. With Sylvia Sidney, Eddie Albert, Joan Leslie, Sig Rumann.

The Maltese Falcon. 1941. WARNER BROTHERS (FIRST NATIONAL). John Huston. With Mary Astor, Gladys George, Peter Lorre, Barton MacLane, Lee Patrick, Sidney Greenstreet, Ward Bond.

All Through the Night. 1942. WARNER BROTHERS (FIRST NATIONAL). Vincent Sherman. With Conrad Veidt, Karen Verne, Jane Darwell, Frank McHugh, Peter Lorre, Judith Anderson, William Demarest, Jackie Gleason, Phil Silvers.

The Big Shot. 1942. WARNER BROTHERS (FIRST NATIONAL). Lewis Seiler. With Irene Manning, Richard Travis, Susan Peters, Stanley Ridges, Howard da Silva.

Across the Pacific. 1942. WARNER BROTHERS (FIRST NATIONAL). John Huston. With Mary Astor, Sidney Greenstreet, Charles Halton, Victor Sen Yung.

Casablanca. 1943. WARNER BROTHERS (FIRST NATIONAL). Michael Curtiz. With Ingrid Bergman, Paul Henreid, Claude Rains, Conrad Veidt, Sidney Greenstreet, Peter Lorre, S. Z. Sakall, Dooley Wilson.

Action in the North Atlantic. 1943. WARNER BROTHERS (FIRST NATIONAL). Lloyd Bacon. With Raymond Massey, Alan Hale, Julie Bishop, Ruth Gordon.

Thank Your Lucky Stars. 1943. WARNER BROTHERS (FIRST NATIONAL). David Butler. Bogart played himself. With Eddie Cantor, Bette Davis, Olivia de Havilland, Errol Flynn.

Sahara. 1943. COLUMBIA. Zoltan Korda. With Bruce Bennett, J. Carrol Naish, Lloyd Bridges, Rex Ingram, Dan Duryea.

Passage to Marseille. 1944. WARNER BROTHERS (FIRST NATIONAL). Michael Curtiz. With Claude Rains, Michèle Morgan, Philip Dorn, Sidney Greenstreet, Peter Lorre, Helmut Dantine, John Loder.

To Have and Have Not. 1945. WARNER BROTHERS (FIRST NATIONAL). Howard Hawks. With Walter Brennan, Lauren Bacall, Dolores Moran, Hoagy Carmichael, Sheldon Leonard.

Conflict. 1945. WARNER BROTHERS (FIRST NATIONAL). Curtis Bernhardt. With Alexis Smith, Sidney Greenstreet, Rose Hobart, Charles Drake.

The Big Sleep. 1946. WARNER BROTHERS (FIRST NATIONAL). Howard Hawks. With Lauren Bacall, John Ridgely, Martha Vickers, Dorothy Malone, Peggy Knudsen, Regis Toomey.

Dead Reckoning. 1947. COLUMBIA. John Cromwell. With Lizabeth Scott, Morris Carnovsky, Charles Cane, William Price, Marvin Miller, Wallace Ford.

The Two Mrs Carrolls. 1947. WARNER BROTHERS (FIRST NATIONAL). Peter Godfrey. With Barbara Stanwyck, Alexis Smith, Nigel Bruce, Isobel Elsom.

Dark Passage. 1947. WARNER BROTHERS (FIRST NATIONAL). Delmer Daves. With Lauren Bacall, Bruce Bennett, Agnes Moorehead, Tom D'Andrea.

The Treasure of the Sierra Madre. 1948. WARNER BROTHERS (FIRST NATIONAL). John Huston. With Walter Huston, Tim Holt, Bruce Bennett, Barton MacLane.

Key Largo. 1948. WARNER BROTHERS (FIRST NATIONAL). John Huston. With Edward G. Robinson, Lauren Bacall, Lionel Barrymore, Claire Trevor.

Knock On Any Door. 1949. SANTANA/COLUMBIA. Nicholas Ray. With John Derek, George Macready, Allene Roberts, Susan Perry, Dewey Martin.

Tokyo Joe. 1949. SANTANA/COLUMBIA. Stuart Heisler. With Alexander Knox, Florence Marly, Sessue Hayakawa, Jerome Courtland, Lora Lee Michael.

Chain Lightning. 1950. WARNER BROTHERS (FIRST NATIONAL). Stuart Heisler. With Eleanor Parker, Raymond Massey, Richard Whorf, James Brown.

In A Lonely Place. 1950. SANTANA/COLUMBIA. Nicholas Ray. With Gloria Grahame, Frank Lovejoy, Carl Benton Reid, Art Smith.

The Enforcer. 1951. UNITED STATES PICTURE/WARNER BROTHERS. Bretaigne Windust. With Zero Mostel, Ted De Corsia, Everett Sloane, Roy Roberts, King Donovan.

Sirocco. 1951. SANTANA/COLUMBIA. Curtis Bernhardt. With Marta Toren, Lee J. Cobb, Everett Sloane, Gerald Mohr, Zero Mostel.

The African Queen. 1951. HORIZON-ROMULUS/UNITED ARTISTS. John Huston. Received an Academy Award. With Katharine Hepburn, Robert Morley, Peter Bull, Theodore Bikel.

Deadline USA (UK title: **Deadline**). 1952. TWENTIETH CENTURY-FOX. Richard Brooks. With Ethel Barrymore, Kim Hunter, Ed Begley, Warren Stevens.

Battle Circus. 1953. MGM. Richard Brooks. With June Allyson, Kennan Wynn, Robert Keith, William Campbell.

Beat the Devil. 1954. SANTANA/ROMULUS/UNITED ARTISTS. With Jennifer Jones, Gina Lollobrigida, Robert Morley, Peter Lorre.

The Caine Mutiny. 1954. KRAMER/COLUMBIA. Edward Dmytryk. With José Ferrer, Van Johnson, Fred MacMurray, Robert Francis, May Wynn, Lee Marvin, E. G. Marshall, Tom Tully, Warner Anderson.

Sabrina. 1954. PARAMOUNT. Billy Wilder. With Audrey Hepburn, William Holden, Walter Hampden, Martha Hyer, Francis X. Bushman, John Williams.

The Barefoot Contessa. 1954. FIGARO/UNITED ARTISTS. Joseph L. Mankiewicz. With Ava Gardner, Edmond O'Brien, Marius Goring, Valentina Cortesa, Rossano Brazzi, Elizabeth Sellars, Bessie Love.

We're No Angels. 1955. PARAMOUNT. Michael Curtiz. With Aldo Ray, Peter Ustinov, Joan Bennett, Basil Rathbone, Leo G. Carroll.

The Left Hand of God. 1955. TWENTIETH CENTURY-FOX. Edward Dmytryk. With Gene Tierney, Lee J. Cobb, Agnes Moorehead, E.G. Marshall, Jean Porter.

The Desperate Hours. 1955. PARAMOUNT. William Wyler. With Fredric March, Arthur Kennedy, Martha Scott, Dewey Martin, Gig Young, Mary Murphy, Richard Eyer, Robert Middleton.

The Harder They Fall. 1956. COLUMBIA. Mark Robson. With Rod Steiger, Jan Sterling, Mike Lane, Max Baer.

Bogart also appeared in **Report from the Front** (1944); **Hollywood Victory Caravan** (1945); **Two Guys from Milwaukee** (1946); **Always Together** (1948); **US Savings Bond Trailer** (1952); **Road to Bali** (1952); **The Love Lottery** (1953).

Robert Taylor

To say that Robert Taylor was predominantly a pretty face sounds suspiciously like belittling him. The fact of the matter is, however, that his face – and fine physique – were his fortune almost exclusively. Hence his popularity with strong women stars (he married one of the strongest, Barbara Stanwyck) and the tremendous box-office appeal, based on his chiselled profile and elegant widow's peak rather than on any quirks of character or real acting ability. There is no doubt that, in the fashion of his day, he was one of Hollywood's most superficially beautiful male heart-throbs. Today his looks seem dated in a way that those of Bogart, Grant, Cooper and even Gable are not. The Valentino-type cap of sleek dark hair, the cupid's bow mouth, the perfectly proportioned face have an unreality, and, above all, an unlived-in look. Where Flynn, who was another 'beautiful' man, scored off Taylor was that behind the boyish charm and incredibly handsome exterior, Flynn, even in his early twenties, had a wealth of experience. The adventurous, carefree spirit which informed his screen character had actually been created by life. One senses in Taylor something of a vacuum behind the gorgeous exterior: not a lack of intelligence or emotion but the placidity of unruffled waters, of a sheltered and relatively untroubled existence.

This is borne out by Taylor's relationship with his studio – MGM. He signed with them when he was twenty-two, straight from drama school (whence he had gone after graduating from college where he studied music), and stayed with them for twenty-six years. In doing so he beat even Gable's record of twenty-four years with the same outfit and although, like Gable, his career was interrupted by war service, his years of servitude were completely unruffled by the customary protests, withdrawals of labour and subsequent suspensions and other sanctions visited on most of the other stars who, like him, were enmeshed in the studio-dominated Hollywood system. He later acknowledged (to Roderick Mann of the Sunday Express) that this system suited him perfectly: 'I was under contract to Metro for 26 years and I wasn't suspended once. I always figured they knew what they were doing so I never complained about my pictures.' No wonder Louis B. Mayer had such a soft spot for him.

The feeling was reciprocal (in 1966 Taylor wrote in Variety that Mayer 'was the most important person in my career') and with good reason. For a young man of modest acting ability but striking good looks, the big studio offered a protection and a backing without which, in the open market, it is doubtful if Taylor's career in films would ever have been more than a forgotten gleam in a talent scout's

The boom year for Taylor was 1936. Among his leading ladies was Joan Crawford, seen here with him in *The Georgeous Hussy* (1936).

eye. The benefits were operative throughout his career, MGM providing the right vehicles, the right co-stars and the right publicity. There were, for example, the two girls smuggled on board the boat on which he travelled to England to make *A Yank at Oxford* (1938) and discovered hiding beneath his bed, courtesy of MGM's publicity department, though the studio can hardly have been quite so directly responsible for the thousands of fans who crowded the quayside at Southampton and the platforms on Waterloo Station. These benefits, however, were never more in evidence than during the period of his decline in the middle and late 'fifties. He was no longer the great box-office attraction he had once been, but MGM continued to star him in expensive, prestige films. 'I was never a good actor, I guess,' he told Roderick Mann in 1962, 'but they sure put me in some good pictures.' Loyalty and docility may be dull qualities but they bring their own rewards – as Robert Taylor surely discovered during his quarter century with MGM.

He was born in August 1911 in Filley, Nebraska, the son of a prosperous grain-merchant who became a doctor late in life, prompted by an ailing wife (who, as often happens in these cases, outlived her husband). There was talk of young Spangler Arlington Brugh (surely the most bizarre 'real' name in Hollywood history) following in father's medical footsteps, but at college (in Clairemont, California) he studied music and played the 'cello. He also joined the college dramatic society and it was while playing in its production of R. C. Sherriff's 'Journey's End' that he was spotted by an MGM casting-director. After graduating, in June 1933, Spangler enrolled in a Hollywood drama school and took up the Metro official's offer of a screen-test. The result was satisfactory but not spectacular. He did not become a star overnight, but he did become Robert Taylor and, in February 1934, signed a seven-year contract with MGM for $35 a week.

Robert Taylor's film début was in *Handy Andy* (1934), a vehicle for Will Rogers, playing Will's daughter's sweetheart. He was then loaned out to Universal for *There's Always Tomorrow* (1934), Binnie Barnes's first American film, returning to MGM for *A Wicked Woman* (1935) before really getting down to business, playing an embezzling bank-clerk in *Buried Loot* (1935), the first of MGM's series of 'Crime Does Not Pay' shorts. It was with his next role, a supporting one as a young intern in *Society Doctor* (1935), that the fan-mail began to trickle in (and Metro raised his money to a munificent $50 a week). The trickle swelled to a torrent four films later when he was chosen by Universal to star opposite Irene Dunne in *Magnificent Obsession* (1935). The film did for Taylor what the 1954 version with Jane Wyman was to do for Rock Hudson. 'I was awful,' Taylor said later of these early years, 'the world's worst actor. But I had a couple of good things going for me: I was a good-looking kid and had a good voice. So I got the breaks.' *Magnificent Obsession* with the part of the playboy-turned-romantic-hero was his first big break. After this he was much in demand as a partner for many of Hollywood's leading ladies. In the next year, 1936, he appeared with Janet Gaynor in Wellman's *Small Town Girl*, with Loretta Young in *Private Number*, with Barbara Stanwyck in *His Brother's Wife* and with Joan Crawford in *The Gorgeous Hussy*.

Then came his second big break – *Camille* (1936), the mismating of a pair of great profiles (though it won Garbo her first Oscar nomination). It seems unlikely that she asked for Taylor as Armand. Far more probable is the theory that MGM saw Taylor as the major box-office draw – he had by then risen very high in national popularity polls. If so, it was ironic that Garbo, who herself had been used earlier in the decade to prop the ailing reputations of such heart-throbs as Novarro and Gilbert, should have had similar support proffered to her.

By now Taylor was firmly established as a ladies' man with tremendous drawing-power at the box-office. Shortly after making *Camille*, he was loaned out to Twentieth Century-Fox to make *This Is My Affair* (1937) with Barbara Stanwyck, who by this time was his off-screen romance too (they married in May 1939 – and divorced in 1952). By now the full popularity of Taylor the heart-throb was obvious to all, especially the MGM executives, and they didn't loan him out again till nearly twenty years and forty pictures later, when he went to Twentieth Century again, for a part in *D-Day the Sixth of June* (1956).

During 1938 and 1939 there was a certain 'toughening-up' of the Taylor image. Whether at his request or because the studio thought it best is not clear, but it was almost certainly the latter. While it was no doubt amazingly good box-office to have thousands of female fans swooning over Taylor, there was always the danger of alienating the male cinema audiences too far for comfort. There were people around who could still remember the backlash of the great Valentino cult. So, in *A Yank at Oxford* (1938) the process started, with Taylor playing a less obviously romantic part, as an arrogant American athlete who falls for an English girl (Vivien Leigh). The film was made in England amidst a barrage of publicity (including the girls under the bed).

The trend continued with *The Crowd Roars* (1938), in which he played a tough but honest boxer fighting against a crooked racket. In between he made a film for Frank Borzage, *The Three Comrades*, about three ex-soldiers running a garage in post-war Germany, with Franchot Tone and Margaret Sullavan. Like all Borzage's films, it was muted and restrained in its emotions, and Taylor showed that with the right direction he had presence and ability independent of his handsome face. However, in *Stand Up and Fight* (1938) he returned to the new, tougher Taylor with a Western in which he fought the baddy (Wallace Beery) and the elements to build a railroad across the Cumberland Gap.

After a couple of rather bad romantic films, *Lucky Night* (1939) with Myrna Loy and *Lady of the Tropics* (1939) with Hedy Lamarr, and a not-very-memorable comedy, *Remember?* (1939) with Greer Garson, he made the film which was his personal favourite. In *Waterloo Bridge* (1940) he was teamed again with Vivien Leigh and sported, for the first time, the moustache which (with occasional disappearances) was to be his hallmark. The film, adapted from a Robert ('Petrified Forest') Sherwood play, was an unashamed tear-jerker about the love of a soldier for a ballerina-turned-prostitute and was immensely popular. He made nine more films before he enlisted in the Navy Air Corps, of which the best remembered are probably *Billy the Kid* (1941), with even *his* looks being overshadowed by the beautiful Technicolor scenery, and, for less happy but more risible reasons, *Song of Russia* (1944). In the latter Taylor played an American conductor (of Tchaikowsky) on tour in Russia who falls for a Russian girl. It seems to have been little more than a rather bumbling piece of propaganda produced in a hurry when Russia joined the Allies, but in 1947 even such a trifle didn't escape the ever-watchful eyes of HUAC members who spotted it and cited it as a major pro-communist film. Louis B. Mayer protested emphatically that it was just a simple boy-meets-girl story, set in Russia at a time when the Allies were calling for support of the Russians embattled at Stalingrad. Taylor appeared before HUAC and said that there had been what he considered to be 'pro-communist points' which did not appear in the final script. He added that all communists, in his opinion, should be forced to live in Russia. After *Song of*

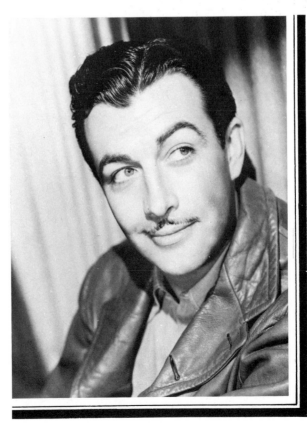

One of the great Hollywood beauties of the 'thirties – Robert Taylor. His fidelity to MGM became legendary and sustained him in his declining years.

Russia he went off to war. During his two years of military service he became a flying instructor, directed several training films, and narrated an Oscar-winning documentary about a US warship called *The Fighting Lady* (1944).

Taylor's post-war films, like those of Gable and Cooper, were not very successful. In fact, with the exception of *Quo Vadis?* (1951), it was pretty well downhill all the way, though it was a fairly gradual decline. In 1955 an MGM biography of Taylor declared that, according to the Hollywood Foreign Correspondents' Association, he had been named as 'the most popular star in all countries abroad'. This sounds a bit like protesting too much, but there is no doubt that he had built up a substantial following over the years. *Quo Vadis?* was intended by MGM to repeat the huge financial success of the Silent version. Taylor played a Roman centurion who falls in love with a Christian (Deborah Kerr), and the popularity of the film (it grossed $11 million) did a great deal to boost his flagging reputation.

He followed this with a Western, *Westward the Women* (1952) directed by William Wellman, and then went into the first of the series of swashbuckling costume-dramas which MGM used to maintain his image and appeal. *Ivanhoe* (1952) was a reasonably faithful adaptation of Scott's novel and starred Elizabeth Taylor, Joan Fontaine and George Sanders. *Knights of the Round Table* (1954), with Ava Gardner and Mel Ferrer, was his next medieval effort. He played Lancelot this time and his third and last knight-in-armour part was the title-role in *Quentin Durward* (1955), another adaptation from Scott with Kay Kendall, Robert Morley and a slightly mind-boggling cast of British actors such as George Cole, Ernest Thesiger and Wilfred Hyde White.

In 1959 Taylor made his last film for MGM, a thriller called *The House of the Seven Hawks*, and then freelanced for the remaining ten years of his life. He also, through his neighbour Dick Powell, became interested in television in 1959, and during the 'sixties was best known, at least in Britain, for his part as Captain Matt Holbrook in 'The Detectives'. The nine films he made after he left MGM are not at all memorable, ranging from Disney's *The Miracle of the White Stallions* (1963) through to Spanish Westerns, *Savage Pampas* (1966), and television-tailored movies like *Return of the Gunfighter* and *Hondo and the Apaches* (both 1967).

When he died in 1969, Robert Taylor had made over seventy films. While he never hit the heights in terms of performance and presence, he none the less exercised considerable sway at the box-office, not least because of his profile and that fetching widow's peak.

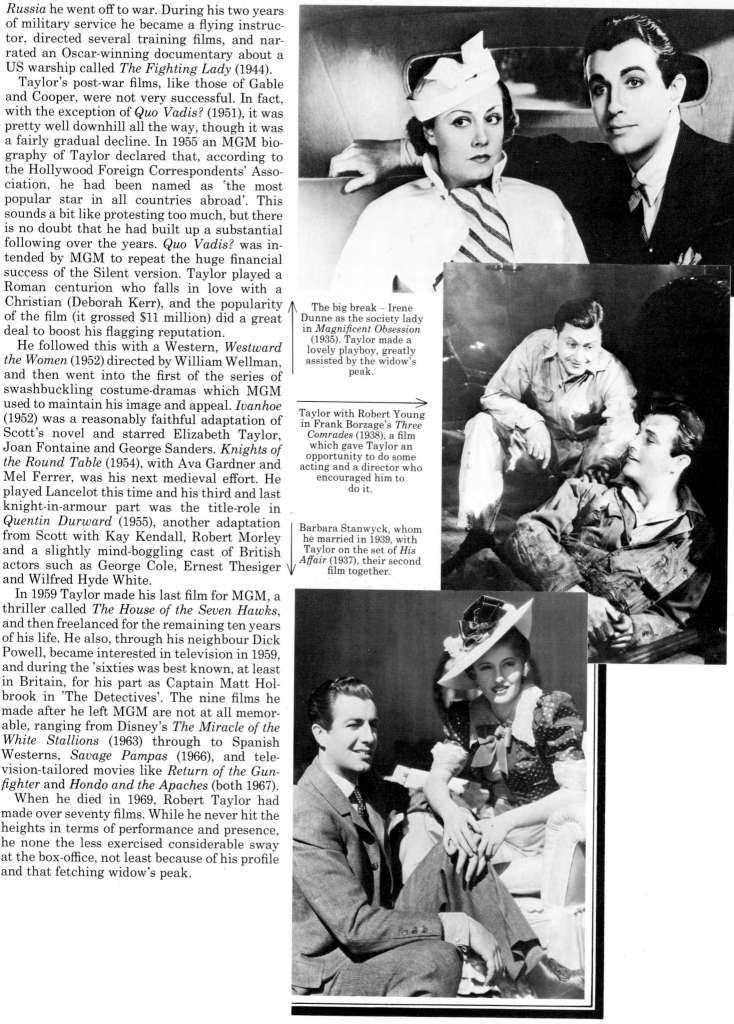

The big break – Irene Dunne as the society lady in *Magnificent Obsession* (1935). Taylor made a lovely playboy, greatly assisted by the widow's peak.

Taylor with Robert Young in Frank Borzage's *Three Comrades* (1938), a film which gave Taylor an opportunity to do some acting and a director who encouraged him to do it.

Barbara Stanwyck, whom he married in 1939, with Taylor on the set of *His Affair* (1937), their second film together.

Taylor with Vivien Leigh in *Waterloo Bridge* (1940). His own favourite film, it was totally implausible and a million miles away from the Thames, but hugely enjoyable.

Taylor and Garbo in *Camille* (1936). 'She was one of the finest and most professional actresses I ever worked with,' he wrote in Variety in 1966.

Yes, it is Robert Taylor, improbable as it may seem, in Wellman's *Westward the Women* (1951).

MGM repaid his long years of good behaviour by sustaining Taylor's declining image in the 'fifties with a series of costume-dramas. *Quentin Durward* (1955) had gorgeous Kay Kendall as a bonus.

This picture of Taylor with Susan Peters gives a very accurate impression of *Song of Russia* (1943). Less funny was its serious examination as a piece of pro-communist propaganda in later years by HUAC.

Robert Taylor

Handy Andy. 1934. FOX. David Butler. With Will Rogers, Peggy Wood, Conchita Montenegro, Mary Carlisle.
There's Always Tomorrow. 1934. UNIVERSAL. Edward Sloman. With Frank Morgan, Binnie Barnes, Lois Wilson, Alan Hale, Elizabeth Young.
A Wicked Woman. 1934. MGM. Charles Brabin. With Mady Christians, Jean Parker, Charles Bickford, Betty Furness, William Henry, Sterling Holloway.
Buried Loot. 1935. MGM. George B. Seitz. With Robert Livingstone, James Ellison.
Society Doctor. 1935. MGM. George B. Seitz. With Chester Morris, Virginia Bruce, Bille Burke, Donald Meek.
West Point of the Air. 1935. MGM. Richard Rosson. With Wallace Beery, Robert Young, Lewis Stone, Maureen O'Sullivan, Rosalind Russell.
Times Square Lady. 1935. MGM. George B. Seitz. With Virginia Bruce, Helen Twelvetrees, Henry Kolker, Isabel Jewell, Nat Pendleton, Jack La Rue.
Murder in the Fleet. 1935. MGM. Edward Sedgwick. With Jean Parker, Ted Healy, Una Merkel, Nat Pendleton, Jean Hersholt.
Broadway Melody of 1936. 1935. MGM. Roy Del Ruth. With Eleanor Powell, Jack Benny, Una Merkel, Buddy Ebsen.
Magnificent Obsession. 1935. UNIVERSAL. John M. Stahl. With Irene Dunne, Charles Butterworth, Betty Furness, Sara Haden.
Small Town Girl. 1936. MGM. William A. Wellman. With Janet Gaynor, James Stewart, Binnie Barnes, Lewis Stone.
Private Number. 1936. TWENTIETH CENTURY-FOX. Roy Del Ruth. With Loretta Young, Basil Rathbone, Patsy Kelly, Joe Lewis, Marjorie Gateson, Jane Darwell.
His Brother's Wife. 1936. MGM. W.S. Van Dyke. With Barbara Stanwyck, Jean Hersholt, John Eldredge, Joseph Calleia.
The Gorgeous Hussy. 1936. MGM. Clarence Brown. With Joan Crawford, Melvyn Douglas, James Stewart, Lionel Barrymore, Franchot Tone, Alison Skipworth, Louis Calhern, Beulah Bondi.
Camille. 1936. MGM. George Cukor. With Greta Garbo, Lionel Barrymore, Henry Daniell, Lenore Ulric, Laura Hope Crews.
Personal Property. 1937. MGM. W.S. Van Dyke. With Jean Harlow, Reginald Owen, Una O'Connor, Cora Witherspoon.
This Is My Affair. 1937. TWENTIETH CENTURY-FOX. William A. Seiter. With Barbara Stanwyck, Victor McLaglen, Brian Donlevy, Sidney Blackmer, John Carradine.
Broadway Melody of 1938. 1937. MGM. Roy Del Ruth. With Eleanor Powell, George Murphy, Sophie Tucker, Buddy Ebsen, Judy Garland, Binnie Barnes.
A Yank at Oxford. 1938. MGM. Jack Conway. With Maureen O'Sullivan, Lionel Barrymore, Vivien Leigh, Edmund Gwenn.
Three Comrades. 1938. MGM. Frank Borzage. With Margaret Sullavan, Robert Young, Franchot Tone, Guy Kibbee.
The Crowd Roars. 1938. MGM. Richard Thorpe. With Maureen O'Sullivan, Edward Arnold, Frank Morgan, William Gargan, Lionel Stander, Jane Wyman.
Stand Up and Fight. 1939. MGM. W.S. Van Dyke. With Wallace Beery, Florence Rice, Helen Broderick, Charles Bickford, Barton MacLane.
Lucky Night. 1939. MGM. Norman Taurog. With Myrna Loy, Joseph Allen, Henry O'Neill, Douglas Fowley, Marjorie Main.
Lady of the Tropics. 1939. MGM. Jack Conway. With Hedy Lamarr, Joseph Schildkraut, Gloria Franklin.
Remember? 1939. MGM. Norman Z. McLeod. With Greer Garson, Lew Ayres, Billie Burke, Reginald Owen.
Waterloo Bridge. 1940. MGM. Mervyn Le Roy. With Vivien Leigh, Virginia Field, Maria Ouspenskaya, C. Aubrey Smith.
Escape. 1940. MGM. Mervyn Le Roy. With Norma Shearer, Conrad Veidt, Nazimova, Felix Bressart, Bonita Granville.
Flight Command. 1940. MGM. Frank Borzage. With Ruth Hussey, Walter Pidgeon, Red Skelton, Paul Kelly, Marsha Hunt, Shepherd Strudwick.
Billy the Kid. 1941. MGM. David Miller. With Brian Donlevy, Ian Hunter, Mary Howard, Gene Lockhart, Lon Chaney Jr, Henry O'Neill.
When Ladies Meet. 1941. MGM. Robert Z. Leonard. With Joan Crawford, Greer Garson, Herbert Marshall, Spring Byington.
Johnny Eager. 1941. MGM. Mervyn Le Roy. With Lana Turner, Edward Arnold, Van Heflin, Robert Sterling, Glenda Farrell.
Her Cardboard Lover. 1942. MGM. George Cukor. With Norma Shearer, George Sanders, Frank McHugh, Elizabeth Patterson, Chill Wills.
Stand By for Action. 1942. MGM. Robert Z. Leonard. With Charles Laughton, Brian Donlevy, Walter Brennan, Marilyn Maxwell.
The Youngest Profession. 1943. MGM. Edward Buzzell. Taylor made an unbilled guest appearance. With Virginia Weidler, Edward Arnold, Agnes Moorehead.
Bataan. 1943. MGM. Tay Garnett. With Thomas Mitchell, George Murphy, Lloyd Nolan, Lee Bowman, Robert Walker, Desi Arnaz, Barry Nelson.
Song of Russia. 1944. MGM. Gregory Ratoff. With Susan Peters, John Hodiak, Robert Benchley, Felix Bressart.
Undercurrent. 1946. MGM. Vincente Minnelli. With Katharine Hepburn, Robert Mitchum, Edmund Gwenn, Marjorie Main, Jayne Meadows, Clinton Sundberg.
The High Wall. 1948. MGM. Curtis Bernhardt. With Audrey Totter, Herbert Marshall, Dorothy Patrick, H. B. Warner, Warner Anderson.
The Bribe. 1949. MGM. Robert Z. Leonard. With Ava Gardner, Charles Laughton, Vincent Price, John Hodiak.
Conspirator. 1949. MGM. Victor Saville. With Elizabeth Taylor, Robert Fleming, Harold Warrender, Marjorie Fielding, Thora Hird, Wilfred Hyde White, Honor Blackman.
Ambush. 1949. MGM. Sam Wood. With John Hodiak, Arlene Dahl, Don Taylor, Jean Hagen.
The Devil's Doorway. 1950. MGM. Anthony Mann. With Louis Calhern, Paula Raymond, Marshall Thompson, Spring Byington.
Quo Vadis? 1951. MGM. Mervyn Le Roy. With Deborah Kerr, Peter Ustinov, Leo Genn, Finlay Currie, Felix Aylmer.
Westward the Women. 1951. MGM. William A. Wellman. With Denise Darcel, Hope Emerson, John McIntire.
Ivanhoe. 1952. MGM. Richard Thorpe. With Elizabeth Taylor, Joan Fontaine, George Sanders, Emlyn Williams, Robert Douglas, Finlay Currie, Felix Aylmer.
Above and Beyond. 1952. MGM. Melvin Frank and Norman Panama. With Eleanor Parker, James Whitmore, Larry Keating, Larry Gates, Marilyn Erskine, Barbara Ruick, Jim Backus.
I Love Melvin. 1953. MGM. Don Weis. Taylor made a guest appearance. With Debbie Reynolds, Donald O'Connor, Barbara Ruick, Howard Keel.
Ride Vaquero! 1953. MGM. John Farrow. With Ava Gardner, Howard Keel, Anthony Quinn, Kurt Kasznar.
All the Brothers Were Valiant. 1953. MGM. Richard Thorpe. With Ann Blythe, Stewart Granger, Betta St John, Keenan Wynn, James Whitmore, Kurt Kasznar, Lewis Stone.
Knights of the Round Table. 1953. MGM. Richard Thorpe. With Ava Gardner, Mel Ferrer, Anne Crawford, Stanley Baker, Felix Aylmer, Maureen Swanson.
Valley of the Kings. 1954. MGM. Robert Pirosh. With Eleanor Parker, Carlos Thompson, Kurt Kasznar, Victor Jory.
Rogue Cop. 1954. MGM. Roy Rowland. With Janet Leigh, George Raft, Anne Francis, Steve Forrest.
Many Rivers to Cross. 1955. MGM. Roy Rowland. With Eleanor Parker, Victor McLaglen, Jeff Richards, Russ Tamblyn, James Arness.
Quentin Durward. 1955. MGM. Richard Thorpe. With Kay Kendall, Robert Morley, George Clunes, Duncan Lamont, Marius Goring, Wilfred Hyde White.
The Last Hunt. 1956. MGM. Richard Brooks. With Stewart Granger, Lloyd Nolan, Debra Paget, Russ Tamblyn.
D-Day the Sixth of June. 1956. TWENTIETH CENTURY-FOX. Henry Koster. With Richard Todd, Dana Wynter, Edmond O'Brien, John Williams.
The Power and the Prize. 1956. MGM. Henry Koster. With Elizabeth Mueller, Burl Ives, Charles Coburn, Sir Cedric Hardwicke, Mary Astor.
Tip on a Dead Jockey. 1957. MGM. Richard Thorpe. With Dorothy Malone, Gia Scala, Martin Gabel, Marcel Dalio, Jack Lord.
Saddle the Wind. 1958. MGM. Robert Parrish. With Julie London, John Cassavetes, Donald Crisp, Royal Dano.
The Law and Jake Wade. 1958. MGM. John Sturges. With Richard Widmark, Patricia Owens, Robert Middleton, Henry Silva.
Party Girl. 1958. MGM. Nicholas Ray. With Cyd Charisse, John Ireland, Lee J. Cobb, Kent Smith, Claire Kelly.
The Hangman. 1959. PARAMOUNT. Michael Curtiz. With Fess Parker, Tina Louise, Jack Lord, Shirley Harmer.
The House of the Seven Hawks. 1959. MGM. Richard Thorpe, With Linda Christian, Nicole Maurey, Gerard Heinz, David Kossoff, Donald Wolfit.
Killers of Kilimanjaro. 1960. WARWICK-COLUMBIA BRITISH. Richard Thorpe. With Anthony Newley, Anne Aubrey, Donald Pleasence, Gregoire Aslan.
The Miracle of the White Stallions. 1963. BUENA VISTA/DISNEY. Arthur Hiller. With Lilli Palmer, Curt Jurgens, Eddie Albert, James Franciscus.
Cattle King. 1963. MGM. Tay Garnett. With Joan Caulfield, Robert Loggia, Robert Middleton, Larry Gates.
A House Is Not A Home. 1964. EMBASSY. Russell Rouse. With Shelley Winters, Cesar Romero, Ralph Taeger, Broderick Crawford, Kaye Ballard.
The Night Walker. 1965. UNIVERSAL. William Castle. With Barbara Stanwyck, Hayden Rorke, Lloyd Bochner, Judith Meredith.
Johnny Tiger (also called **Cry of the Laughing Owls**). 1966. UNIVERSAL. Paul Wendkos. With Geraldine Brooks, Chad Everett, Brenda Scott, Marc Lawrence.
Savage Pampas. 1966. DACA. Hugo Fregonese. With Ron Randell, Marc Lawrence, Ty Hardin, Rosenda Monteros.
Return of the Gunfighter. 1966. KING BROTHERS/MGM. James Neilson. With Chad Everett, Anna Martin.
The Golden Sphinx. 1967. ITALIA/PICASA/COPRO. Luigi Scattini. With Anita Ekberg, Gianna Sera, Jack Stuart, Angel del Pazo.
Hondo and the Apaches. 1967. BATJAC-FENADY/MGM. Lee H. Katzin. With Ralph Taeger, Michael Rennie, Gary Merrill, Noah Beery, Kathie Brown.
Where Angels Go . . . Trouble Follows. 1968. COLUMBIA. James Neilson. With Rosalind Russell, Stella Stevens, Milton Berle, Van Johnson, Binnie Barnes.
The Day the Hot Line Got Hot. 1968. COMMONWEALTH UNITED ENTERTAINMENTS. Etienne Perier. With George Chakiris, Dominique Faber, Gerard Tichy, Marie Du Bois.

Taylor also appeared in **Lest We Forget** (1937); **The Fighting Lady** (1944); and **The Secret Land** (1948).

Alan Ladd

Raymond Chandler once wrote of Alan Ladd that despite being 'hard, bitter and occasionally charming, he is after all a small boy's idea of a tough guy'. Chandler, one feels, should have had a fairly clear perspective on Ladd's image, having written the screen-plays for two of his early successes. On the other hand, without wishing to be too obvious, it must be pointed out that Chandler, being a man, may not have been best qualified to judge Ladd's appeal and certainly not in box-office terms. Male heart-throbs are made into stars not by their fellow men, but by women cinema-goers. They become great stars – like Gable, Bogart and Cooper – if they then extend their appeal to the male population, but initially it is the female vote of confidence that counts. In Alan Ladd's case it counted to the tune of thirty thousand letters flooding into Paramount after the release of *This Gun for Hire* (1942), asking to see more of the beautiful, somnambulant psychopath who, in Richard Schickel's words, 'succeeded in reducing murder to an act as irrelevant as crossing the street'.

By the time he came to stardom – and it was a very rapid rise from the ranks in his case – the notion of the attractive good-bad guy was hardly new. The element of roughness and toughness which entered into the acknowledged appeal of male stars with Gable had found a fruitful area of development in the gangster films of the 'thirties with George Raft, James Cagney, Paul Muni, Edward G. Robinson and, of course, Bogart. With Bogart there emerged the attractive yet ambiguous persona of the man who shifts constantly from the right to the wrong side of the law, from the conventional mores of society to the seedy, shady corners of the underworld. However, in his case, after *The Maltese Falcon* (1941), there is little doubt as to which side he will be on in the end. Ladd carried both the sexual attraction and moral ambiguity even further. He had, when young, the face of a spoiled angel, but was never really on the side of the angels, even when the plot required him to be hero rather than anti-hero. He takes punishment more often than he metes it out, yet when he does so it is with a cool calmness and lack of emotion. Certainly, until the change of direction in his career that came with *Shane* (1953), his appeal as a star lay in the combination of his sensitively modelled, handsome features and the ruthless toughness of his screen image. This somehow produced a sense of pathos, a solitary withdrawn quality which brought out the protective instincts of hundreds of women film-goers as well as being enormously attractive sexually. Curiously, this loner quality was later found in another of the rare blond heart-throbs – Steve McQueen. With *Shane*, a third and equally potent element entered the image – that of wistful disillusion.

Ladd's lack of inches was, from the start, the cause of so many jokes – most of them cruel – that his other outstanding natural asset (apart from his good looks) tended to be overlooked. His voice is as distinctive in its own way as that of Bogart. In fact, as Julian Fox pointed out in a major article on Ladd in Films and Filming in June/July 1972, 'nearly all the great American stars with first rate or distinctive voices have been tough guys'. Cagney, Raft and Edward G. Robinson bear out this thesis. Ladd himself was aware of the value of a distinctive voice in an actor. He worked for nearly three years on a local radio station in Los Angeles in the middle and late 'thirties and said later of this period, 'It was in radio that I learned what a fine instrument the voice is.' Before he became famous he played a bit part in *Citizen Kane* (1941) and the giveaway clue to his identity – cloaked by a pipe and a snap-brim hat – is his unmistakeable voice. He is the reporter who asks all the questions in the last scene of the film.

Despite the jokes, he really was not that small. At around five foot six, there were of course leading ladies for whom he had to stand on boxes, or they in trenches, but with his most famous co-star, petite Veronica Lake, there was no problem at all. 'We were both little people,' she wrote in her autobiography (published in 1968). She went on to say, 'We were a good match for each other.' The public agreed with her. Ladd and Lake were probably the most popular screen couple during the early 'forties. 'Bogart and Bacall were better,' wrote

'I have the face of an ageing choirboy,' Alan Ladd once said, 'and the build of an undernourished featherweight.' He couldn't understand his own success but Darryl Zanuck wondered at his failure to rise to the real heights: 'He stays on top with mediocre films.'

David Shipman in 'The Great Stars', 'but Lake and Ladd came first.' Despite the tremendous popularity now of the Bogarts as a team, there are many who might disagree with him. The on-screen tension between Ladd and Lake is still tremendously powerful, viewed thirty years on. It is largely the result of the cool, wary coupling of two very aloof people – his menacing taciturnity matched by her sullen and provocative don't-touch-me allure. They made only four full features together but theirs was a classic screen relationship – without Lake, Ladd had to establish a new image. Happily he did. Less happily, she did not.

Alan Ladd was born in Hot Springs, Arkansas, in September 1913. His father, an accountant, died when he was three, and his mother took him to Denver, Colorado, where she remarried. The family moved again, to California, during the 1921–2 Depression. Though he was not academically inclined, Ladd shone at athletics, especially swimming (in 1932 he was the West Coast diving champion). His only excursion into acting was in the role of the Lord High Executioner in a high-school production of 'The Mikado', and it was perhaps his success in this that led him, after a succession of odd jobs, to try for a place in Universal Studio's new training-unit for young actors. He was accepted and completed the four-month course – unlike a fellow student, Tyrone Power, who dropped out early on. He did not, however, get any kind of contract as a result and contented himself with working as an extra on films for Paramount, Columbia and Republic. Later he reckoned to have been in 'about 150 pictures if you count advertising shorts'. He also worked on a newspaper, ran a hot-dog stand called 'Tiny's', was a salesman for the National Cash Register Company and finally took a job as a grip at the Warner Brothers studios. This last job, he felt, might be an alternative route into film-acting but it was a forlorn hope. He spent two years as a grip, mainly on the catwalks fixing lights, forty feet above the actors. Twice he fell but in the end it was not the danger but the loneliness of the job which caused him to quit. He still felt drawn towards acting though – watching Errol Flynn practising his fencing for *Captain Blood* (1935) caused stirrings of envy. He enrolled at an acting school and worked in bit parts and on radio. At one stage he was doing twenty radio shows a week and eventually he was offered a contract by the Columbia Broadcasting Company. It was a tempting thought, since his film work had yielded little promise of success. A sailor in Hathaway's *Souls at Sea* (1937), which starred Cooper and Raft, a waiter in *Last Train from Madrid* (1937) starring Lamour and Quinn, and eleventh billing in a Zane Grey story, *Born to the West* (1938) – none of these seemed likely to launch him on a film-career. It was, ironically, the medium of radio which really got him started in 1938.

In one of his radio shows he played two parts – an old man and his son. Sue Carol, an ex-actress (in Silent and early Sound films) turned agent heard the programme and was impressed by both performances. She was even more impressed when she discovered that they were the work of the same actor and wasted no time in persuading Alan Ladd to sign up with her. Immediately she started to sell him around town as hard as she could. Her first efforts were not rewarded. She got him an interview for the lead in *Golden Boy* (1938) but it went to another young hopeful, William Holden. Less ambitious, but more successful, was the part she organized for Ladd in *Rulers of the Sea* (1939), a costume-drama about the early steamship days starring Douglas Fairbanks Jr. It was a small role – that of a seasick voyager who disappeared after the first reel – but he was noticed and talked about. Things were moving and Miss Carol continued to work hard for her protégé. Her influence on his career was tremendous, and long-lived for they married in 1942 (both had been married before and both had a child by a previous marriage – she a daughter and he a son, Alan Ladd Jr, now a film-producer). The marriage endured till his death and as late as 1956 she was still heavily involved in his career, advising him, for example, not to take the part of Jet Rink in George Stevens's *Giant* (1956).

During the next couple of years, with Sue Carol's help, Alan Ladd appeared in increasingly large parts in a dozen films. His first really important part was in an RKO film, *Joan of Paris* (1942), a wartime drama with Michèle Morgan in which (like Cooper in *Barbara Worth*) he made his mark in an affecting death-scene – 'I clipped my words and quietly passed away.' The head of casting at Paramount, urged on by Sue, tested him for the part of Raven, the gunman in the Americanized version of Graham Greene's 'entertainment', 'A Gun for Sale'. He got the part, which carried fourth billing, and after viewing the first day's rushes Paramount hastily offered him a contract.

This Gun for Hire (1942) took him, if not to instant stardom (his journeyman years had been long and pretty arduous), then at least to a height of popularity and success which he and Sue Carol must, at first, have had a hard time believing. As Raven, the beautiful, unemotional psychopathic killer, he was electrifying. Bosley Crowther wrote of Ladd's performance that 'not since Jimmy Cagney massaged Mae Clark's face with a grapefruit has a grim desperado gunned his way into cinema ranks with such violence'. It was, above all, his blond, trench-coated handsomeness that knocked out audiences. Up to then gangsters in films had not been noted for their good looks – fascinating, yes, but rarely handsome. Then there was his weakness for cats – and Veronica Lake. In some theatres audiences hissed as the police moved in on Raven. Readers of the British film magazine Picturegoer awarded him a Gold Medal for his playing of Raven – the only acting award he ever won.

Paramount were quick to cash in on the success of Ladd the good-bad guy – and the

Ladd-Lake chemistry. They put them both, plus Brian Donlevy and William Bendix (who were to become to the Ladd/Lake team what Lorre and Greenstreet were to Bogart) into a remake of Dashiell Hammett's *The Glass Key* (1942). Originally made with George Raft in 1935, this fast-paced and complex thriller gave Ladd another baby-faced gangster role and was a great box-office success – eventually taking over $4 million. Throughout the film he takes a tremendous amount of physical punishment (mainly from Bendix), and this suffering of pain and torture – especially in the later *Two Years Before the Mast* (1946) – became almost as marked a feature of his films as it did later in the films of Brando.

The Glass Key confirmed Paramount's feeling that they now had a full-fledged star on their hands. He played another gangster in *Lucky Jordan* (1942), getting top billing for the first time. Then, after making a guest appearance in *Star Spangled Rhythm* (1942) and filming *China* (1943) for director John Farrow, he joined the air force in January 1943. *China* kept his name before the public while he was away. He played a tough oil man and his co-stars were Loretta Young and William Bendix. That year he won a national poll as America's most popular male star and came 14th in the Motion Picture Herald's annual poll. Invalided out of the air force late in 1943, he was reunited with Loretta Young in *And Now Tomorrow* (1944), a weepie about a society girl being cured of deafness. He was next seen as a tough-guy again in *Salty O'Rourke* (1945), a neat thriller in which he played a compulsive gambler trying to pay off his racing debts. After guest spots in a propaganda short, *Hollywood Victory Caravan* (1945), and an all-star round-up, *Duffy's Tavern* (1945), in which he and Lake sent themselves up nicely, he went on suspension for four months following a row with Paramount about his contract. They finally upped his money to $75,000 a picture but refused to give him story approval. Later, their refusal to let him play the Kirk Douglas role in *Detective Story* (1951) and to take a share of his films' profits in lieu of salary (between 1941 and 1951 Ladd made twenty-six films which earned $60 million for the studio) led to his split with Paramount.

Ladd returned to work with the old team of Lake and Bendix in *The Blue Dahlia* (1946), a taut thriller, scripted by Raymond Chandler, which has since become a classic of the genre. He made fourteen films over the next seven years of which the two that stand out most in retrospect were not among the most popular at the box-office. *Two Years Before the Mast* (1946) was a powerful adaptation of Henry Dana's novel about the hardship of life aboard the sailing clippers; Ladd fought injustice and suffered beautifully. His supporting cast was very good too – Bendix and Barry Fitzgerald were fellow seamen and Howard Da Silva, the brutal captain. Da Silva was also in *The Great Gatsby* (1949), playing Wilson, the garage proprietor. The film fell between two stools at the time of its release. Critics disliked it (Scott

Fitzgerald had not then been rediscovered) and the public did not want to see such an unfamiliar Alan Ladd. He was, in fact, physically an amazingly 'right' Jay Gatsby, and his impassivity and sense of suspended emotional animation gave his performance a quality which seems in many respects very close to Fitzgerald's concept of his hero.

By the early 'fifties his box-office drawing-power, at least in the States, seemed to be diminishing. Ladd switched to Warners and made his first film for them in 1952, *The Iron Mistress*, about the inventor of the Bowie knife. He then made *Desert Legion* (1953) for Universal before returning to Paramount to make the film with which more than any other (even *This Gun for Hire*) his name was to be linked. *Shane* (1953), directed by George Stevens, was one of the key Westerns of the early 'fifties; together with films like *High Noon* (1952) and *The Gunfighter* (1950), it deeply influenced all successive explorations of the Western myth. Beautifully photographed (the film won an Academy Award for its cinematographer, Loyal Griggs), it was an unforgettable exposition of the Mysterious Stranger theme. Ladd, beautiful in fringed buckskin and powerfully enigmatic, rides into town, sides with the homesteaders (Van Johnson, Jean Arthur, and Brandon de Wilde as the boy who hero-worships him), overcomes the bad guys led by Jack Palance, and rides off again as quietly and mysteriously as he arrived. The film is his great monument. It grossed $9 million and put him right back on top in 1953 and 1954.

From then on, however, it was a slow but steady decline. He made twenty-one more films before his death (a lethal mixture of sedatives and alcohol) in January 1964, most of them unmemorable. An honourable exception was *The Proud Rebel* (1958), in which his own son David played his screen son struck dumb by shock of his mother's death. It was a gentle, touching film and his performance is good – low-key and sincere – but unfortunately did not do well at the box-office. By the time he made his last film, *The Carpetbaggers* (1964) directed by Edward Dmytryk, he was drinking heavily (one writer suggests that perhaps the loss of his looks triggered this off). The film – a bad but thoroughly enjoyable adaptation of Harold Robbins's *roman à clef* novel about Hollywood in the 'thirties – looked as if it might have launched him on a new up-swing in his film-career. A sequel centred on his screen character, Nevada Smith, was planned by producer Joe Levine (and made later with Steve McQueen) and there was even talk of a television series, but Ladd was, apparently, dubious about his chances of making a comeback. Sadly he did not have the time even to try. Sadly, too, he seems since his death to have attracted very little serious critical attention. He was no great actor, but in his films with Veronica Lake and in *Shane* he left a fine cinematic legacy. As Dilys Powell wrote in The Sunday Times, 'He had the gift of creating a durable popular image. And the cinema can ill afford to lose its idols.'

Like Gary Cooper, it was a two-handkerchief death-scene which started Ladd on the road to stardom. The film was *Joan of Paris* (1942) with Michèle Morgan and Paul Henreid (behind the pillar).

'Alan Ladd was a superb psychopathic killer,' wrote Veronica Lake (seen here) of his performance as Raven in *This Gun for Hire* (1942). The image was to dog him for a decade.

What a marvellous screen
couple Lake and Ladd
were, and never better
than when exchanging
cold, clever wisecracks in
The Glass Key
(1942).

Ladd was on more familiar territory in *Salty O'Rourke* (1945), a tough little film about the crooked side of the racing racket. With him here are Gail Russell and Bruce Cabot.

Howard da Silva spent most of *Two Years Before the Mast* (1946) either needling Ladd or having him flogged. The film, despite its grimness, was one of the top grossers of 1946.

Although his role in *China* (1943) was that of an oil man, Ladd was still essentially playing a gangster. His co-stars were Loretta Young and William Bendix.

And Now Tomorrow (1944) was Ladd's first move away from his tough-guy image. Loretta Young was again his co-star in this melodrama about a miracle cure and high-society manners.

George Stevens, director of *Shane* (1953), said of Alan Ladd in this film that he gave 'one of the classic performances of the screen'. Brandon de Wilde played the boy who hero-worshipped him.

The 1949 version of *The Great Gatsby* was a curiously flawed film. Betty Field was even less successful as Daisy than Mia Farrow twenty-five years later, but Ladd's Gatsby had a strange sense of secretive intensity.

Alan Ladd

Once in a Lifetime. 1932. UNIVERSAL. Russell Mack. With Jack Oakie, Aline MacMahon, Sidney Fox, ZaSu Pitts.
Pigskin Parade (UK title: **Harmony Parade**). 1936. TWENTIETH CENTURY-FOX. David Butler. With Patsy Kelly, Stuart Erwin, Jack Haley, Betty Grable, Judy Garland.
Last Train from Madrid. 1937. PARAMOUNT. James Hogan. With Dorothy Lamour, Anthony Quinn, Gilbert Roland, Lew Ayres.
Souls at Sea. 1937. PARAMOUNT. Henry Hathaway. With Gary Cooper, George Raft, Henry Wilcoxon.
Hold 'Em Navy. 1937. PARAMOUNT. Kurt Neumann. Unbilled performance. With Lew Ayres, Mary Carlisle, John Howard, Elizabeth Patterson, Richard Denning.
The Goldwyn Follies. 1938. UNITED ARTISTS. George Marshall. Unbilled performance. With Adolphe Menjou, Zorina, Andrea Leeds, Kenny Baker, Edgar Bergen.
Come On Leathernecks. 1938. REPUBLIC. James Cruze. Unbilled appearance. With Richard Cromwell, Marsha Hunt, Leon Ames.
The Green Hornet. 1939. UNIVERSAL. Ford Beebe and Ray Taylor. With Gordon Jones, Wade Boteler, Keye Luke, Ann Nagel.
Rulers of the Sea. 1939. PARAMOUNT. Frank Lloyd. With Douglas Fairbanks Jr, Margaret Lockwood, Will Fyffe, George Bancroft, Montagu Love.
Beast of Berlin (also known as **Hitler, Beast of Berlin**; UK title: **The Goose Step**). 1939. PATHÉ/ GRAND NATIONAL. Sherman Scott. With Roland Drew, Steffi Duna, Greta Granstedt, Lucien Prival.
Light of Western Stars. 1940. PARAMOUNT. Leslie Selander. With Victor Jory, Jo Ann Sayers, Russell Hayden, Noah Beery Jr.
Gangs of Chicago. 1940. REPUBLIC. Arthur Lubin. With Lloyd Nolan, Barton MacLane.
In Old Missouri. 1940. REPUBLIC. Frank McDonald. With Leon Weaver, June Weaver, Loretta Weaver, Thurston Hall, Mildred Shay.
The Howards of Virginia (UK title: **The Tree of Liberty**). 1940. COLUMBIA. Frank Lloyd. With Cary Grant, Martha Scott, Sir Cedric Hardwicke, Richard Carlson.
Those Were the Days. 1940. PARAMOUNT. J. Theodore Reid. Billed as

Alan Laird. With William Holden, Bonita Granville, Ezra Stone, Richard Denning.
Captain Caution. 1940. UNITED ARTISTS. Richard Wallace. With Victor Mature, Louise Platt, Leo Carrillo, Bruce Cabot, Pat O'Malley.
Wildcat Bus. 1940. RKO. Frank Woodruff. Unbilled appearance. With Fay Wray, Charles Lang, Paul Guilfoyle, Don Costello.
Meet the Missus. 1940. REPUBLIC. Mal St Clair. With Roscoe Karns, Ruth Donnelly, Spencer Charters George Ernest.
Her First Romance. 1940. MONOGRAM. Edward Dmytryk. With Edith Fellows, Wilbur Evans, Jacqueline Wells, Judith Linden.
Great Guns. 1941. TWENTIETH CENTURY-FOX. Monty Banks. With Stan Laurel, Oliver Hardy, Dick Nelson, Sheila Ryan.
Citizen Kane. 1941. RKO/ MERCURY. Orson Welles. With Orson Welles, Joseph Cotten, Agnes Moorehead, Everett Sloane.
Cadet Girl. 1941. TWENTIETH CENTURY-FOX. Ray McCarey. With Carole Landis, George Montgomery, John Sheppard.
Petticoat Politics. 1941. REPUBLIC. Earle C. Kenton. With Roscoe Karns, Ruth Donnelly, Spencer Charters.
The Black Cat. 1941. UNIVERSAL. Albert S. Rogell. With Basil Rathbone, Hugh Herbert, Bela Lugosi, Broderick Crawford, Gale Sondergaard, Gladys Cooper.
The Reluctant Dragon. 1941. RKO/WALT DISNEY. Alfred Werker. With Robert Benchley, Frances Gifford, Nana Bryant, Barnett Parker.
Gangs Inc (UK title: **Paper Bullets**). 1941. PRODUCERS RELEASING CORPORATION/KOZINSKY. Phil Rosen. With Joan Woodbury, Jack La Rue, Linda Ware, John Archer.
Joan of Paris. 1942. RKO. Robert Stevenson. With Michèle Morgan, Paul Henreid, Thomas Mitchell, Laird Cregar, May Robson.
This Gun for Hire. 1942. PARAMOUNT. Frank Tuttle. With Veronica Lake, Laird Cregar, Robert Preston, Tully Marshall.
The Glass Key. 1942. PARAMOUNT. Stuart Heisler. With Brian Donlevy, Veronica Lake, Bonita Granville, Richard Denning. William Bendix.
Lucky Jordan. 1942. PARAMOUNT. Frank Tuttle. With Helen Walker, Marie McDonald, Mabel Paige, Sheldon Leonard.
Star Spangled Rhythm. 1942. PARAMOUNT. George Marshall. Ladd made a

guest appearance. With Victor Moore, Betty Hutton, Eddie Bracken, Walter Abel, Cass Daley, Anne Revere.

China. 1943. PARAMOUNT. John Farrow. With Loretta Young, William Bendix, Philip Ann, Richard Loo.

And Now Tomorrow. 1944. PARAMOUNT. Irving Pichel. With Loretta Young, Susan Hayward, Barry Sullivan, Beulah Bondi, Cecil Kellaway.

Salty O'Rourke. 1945. PARAMOUNT. Raoul Walsh. With Gail Russell, William Demarest, Bruce Cabot, Spring Byington, Darryl Hickman.

Duffy's Tavern. 1945. PARAMOUNT. Hal Walker. Ladd spoofed himself in a guest role. With Ed 'Archie' Gardiner, Charlie Cantor, Barry Sullivan, Victor Moore, Marjorie Reynolds, Veronica Lake, Howard da Silva.

The Blue Dahlia. 1946. PARAMOUNT. George Marshall. With Veronica Lake, William Bendix, Howard da Silva, Don Costello.

OSS. 1946. PARAMOUNT. Irving Pichel. With Geraldine Fitzgerald, Patric Knowles, John Hoyt.

Two Years Before the Mast. 1946. PARAMOUNT. John Farrow. With Brian Donlevy, William Bendix, Barry Fitzgerald, Howard da Silva, Darryl Hickman.

Calcutta. 1947. PARAMOUNT. John Farrow. With Gail Russell, June Duprez, William Bendix.

Variety Girl. 1947. PARAMOUNT. George Marshall. Ladd made a guest appearance. With Mary Hatcher, Olga San Juan, DeForest Kelly, Bob Hope, Bing Crosby, Dorothy Lamour.

Wild Harvest. 1947. PARAMOUNT. Tay Garnett. With Dorothy Lamour, Robert Preston, Lloyd Nolan, Allen Jenkins, Dick Erdman.

Saigon. 1948. PARAMOUNT. Leslie Fenton. With Veronica Lake, Luther Adler, Douglas Dick.

Beyond Glory. 1948. PARAMOUNT. John Farrow. With Donna Reed, George Macready, George Colouris, Henry Travers, Audie Murphy.

Whispering Smith. 1948. PARAMOUNT. Leslie Fenton. With Robert Preston, Brenda Marshall, Donald Crisp, William Demarest.

The Great Gatsby. 1949. PARAMOUNT. Elliot Nugent. With Betty Field, Barry Sullivan, MacDonald Carey, Ruth Hussey, Shelley Winters, Howard da Silva, Elisha Cook Jr.

Chicago Deadline. 1949. PARAMOUNT. Lewis Allen. With Donna Reed, June Havoc, Arthur Kennedy.

Captain Carey USA. 1950. PARAMOUNT. Mitchell

Leisen. With Wanda Hendrix, Francis Lederer, Celia Lovsky, Angela Clarke, Roland Winters, Rusty Tamblyn.

Branded. 1950. PARAMOUNT. Rudolph Mate. With Mona Freeman, Charles Bickford, Robert Keith, Joseph Calleia, Tom Tully.

Appointment with Danger. 1951. PARAMOUNT. Lewis Allen. With Phyllis Calvert, Paul Stewart, Jan Sterling, Jack Webb.

Red Mountain. 1951. PARAMOUNT. William Dieterle. With Lizabeth Scott, Arthur Kennedy, John Ireland, Jeff Corey, James Bell, Bert Freed.

The Iron Mistress. 1952. WARNER BROTHERS. Gordon Douglas. With Virginia Mayo, Joseph Calleia, Phyllis Kirk.

Thunder in the East. 1952. PARAMOUNT. Charles Vidor. With Deborah Kerr, Charles Boyer, Corinne Calvert, Cecil Kellaway.

Desert Legion. 1953. UNIVERSAL. Joseph Pevney. With Richard Conte, Arlene Dahl, Akim Tamiroff, Leon Askin.

Shane. 1953. PARAMOUNT. George Stevens. With Jean Arthur, Van Heflin, Brandon De Wilde, Jack Palance.

Botany Bay. 1953. PARAMOUNT. John Farrow. With James Mason, Patricia Medina, Sir Cedric Hardwicke, Murray Matheson, Dorothy Patten.

Paratrooper (UK title: **The Red Beret**). 1953. COLUMBIA/WARWICK. Terence Young. With Leo Genn, Susan Stephen, Harry Andrews, Donald Houston, Stanley Baker.

Saskatchewan. 1954. UNIVERSAL. Raoul Walsh. With Shelley Winters, J. Carrol Naish, Hugh O'Brien, Robert Douglas.

Hell Below Zero. 1954. COLUMBIA/WARWICK. Mark Robson. With Jill Bennett, Joan Tetzel, Stanley Baker, Basil Sydney.

The Black Knight. 1954. COLUMBIA/WARWICK. Tay Garnett. With Patricia Medina, André Morrell, Harry Andrews, Peter Cushing.

Drum Beat. 1954. WARNER BROTHERS/JAGUAR (Ladd's own company). Delmer Daves. With Audrey Dalton, Marisa Pavan, Robert Keith, Charles Bronson.

The McConnell Story. 1955. WARNER BROTHERS. Gordon Douglas. With June Allyson, James Whitmore, Frank Faylen, Robert Ellis.

Hell on Frisco Bay. 1955. WARNER BROTHERS/JAGUAR. Frank Tuttle. With Edward G. Robinson, Joanne Dru, William Demarest, Fay Wray.

Santiago. 1956. WARNER BROTHERS. Gordon Douglas. With Rosanna Podesta,

Lloyd Nolan, Chill Wills, Paul Fix.

The Big Land. 1957. WARNER BROTHERS. Gordon Douglas. With Virginia Mayo, Edmund O'Brien, Anthony Caruso, Julie Bishop, David Ladd.

Boy on a Dolphin. 1957. TWENTIETH CENTURY-FOX. Jean Negulesco. With Sophia Loren, Clifton Webb, Alexis Minotis.

The Deep Six. 1958. WARNER BROTHERS/JAGUAR. Rudolph Mate. With Dianne Foster, William Bendix, Keenan Wynn, James Whitmore, Efrem Zimbalist Jr, Joey Bishop.

The Proud Rebel. 1958. BUENA-VISTA-FORMOSA. Michael Curtiz. With Olivia de Havilland, Dean Jagger, David Ladd, Cecil Kellaway, John Carradine.

The Badlanders. 1958. MGM/ARCOLA. Delmer Daves. With Ernest Borgnine, Katy Jurado, Claire Kelly, Kent Smith.

The Man in the Net. 1959. UNITED ARTISTS. Michael Curtiz. With Carolyn Jones, Diane Brewster, John Lupton, Charles McGraw.

Guns of the Timberland. 1960. WARNER BROTHERS/ JAGUAR. Robert D. Webb. With Jeanne Crain, Gilbert Roland, Frankie Avalon, Noah Beery, Alana Ladd.

All the Young Men. 1960. COLUMBIA. Hall Bartlett. With Sidney Poitier, James Darren, Glen Corbett, Mort Sahl, Anna St Clair.

One Foot in Hell. 1960. TWENTIETH CENTURY-FOX. James B. Clark. With Don Murray, Dan O'Herlihy, Dolores Michaels, Barry Coe.

Duel of Champions (Italian title: **Orazi e Curiazi**). 1961 (not released in US until 1964). TIBERIUS FILMS/GRAND NATIONAL. Terence Young. With Jacques Sernas, Luciano Marin, Robert Keith, Franco Fabrizi, Franca Bettoja, Alana Ladd.

13 West Street. 1962. COLUMBIA/LADD ENTERPRISES. Philip Leacock. With Rod Steiger, Michael Callan, Dolores Dorn.

The Carpetbaggers. 1964. PARAMOUNT. Edward Dmytryk. With George Peppard, Carroll Baker, Martha Hyer, Tony Bill.

Ladd also appeared in **Unfinished Rainbows** (1940); **Letter from a Friend** (1943); and **My Favourite Brunette** (1947).

Marlon Brando in *Mutiny on the Bounty* (1962) with (left) Trevor Howard.

Clint Eastwood in *The Beguiled* (1971), with Elizabeth Hartman.

Tyrone Power

Like Robert Taylor, Tyrone Power was also a creation of a studio – in his case Twentieth Century-Fox. However, whereas Taylor undoubtedly needed the studio and his long-term contract to maintain his position as a leading male star once the thrills of delight over his physical appeal had died down, it is much more debatable how Power might have fared without Fox to pick his roles and structure his career. He was certainly as beautiful as Taylor – perhaps the more so for having a slightly less-than-perfect profile, a crop of dark curls, and a touch of the Irish about the eyes. Initially, too, he was as docile as Taylor in his relationship with the studio, but his period under contract was shorter – only eighteen years, and towards the end he began to get restive. Talking to critic Cecil Wilson in the late 'fifties he said, 'It was fifteen years before they suspended me. They wanted me to play one of those colourless parts I'd played too often before. So I struck.'

In fact, Tyrone Power was one of the last of the studio-owned stars, and obviously felt the constraints very sharply towards the end of his eighteen years. 'I'm sick of all these knight-in-shining armour parts,' he said. 'I want to do something worthwhile, like plays and films that have something to say.'

Films in Review, a film journal without which it must be acknowledged this book (and a great deal of other writing about films) would not have been possible, always has a subtitle to its biographical articles which is intended to encapsulate the star's career. For Tyrone Power the legend reads, 'His Good Looks Kept Him In Parts That Thwarted His Acting Growth.' Despite the slight risibility of the capital letters and the simple dogmatism of the statement, the writer (Robert C. Roman) does seem to have had a point. After he left Fox in 1954, Power went through a run of films and gave performances which, if not outstanding, were in many ways improvements on the succession of dull parts with which Fox had furnished him. They at least allowed him opportunities to exercise his acting ability, a talent that was undeniable, but sadly underdeveloped. He said of his years with Fox that he had done 'an awful lot of stuff that's a monument to public patience', but in such films as John Ford's *The Long Gray Line* (1955), *The Eddie Duchin Story* (1956) and *Witness for the Prosecution* (1958) he gave performances that were more than adequate in films that, whatever their shortcomings (*pace* the Spectator critic's dictum that Ford's film was 'the longest and greyest film' she had even seen), were not boring and instantly forgettable. It really does seem possible that had he lived longer (he was only forty-four when he died) his acting ability, so relatively recently allowed to stretch its wings, might well have been much more widely acknowledged by industry and public alike.

Tyrone Power in fact came from a family with a long tradition of theatrical connections. His father, Tyrone Power II, found success as a matinée-idol on the American stage, though born and educated in England. He also made films, signing with Famous Players in New York shortly after the birth of Tyrone Power III, in May 1914. The family moved to Hollywood when the child was just a year old, and there his parents made films for the Selig Company before moving back to New York, where the elder Power played the lead in 'Chu Chin Chow'.

Young Tyrone began his acting career in earnest in 1931, when he joined his father in a Chicago Shakespearean repertory company and made his professional stage début in 'The Merchant of Venice'. The following year Power Sr was offered the lead in a new film, *The Miracle Man*, and he took his son with him to Hollywood. Sadly, however, he died of a heart-attack while filming. His son stayed on, trying to find work as an actor, but only managed a couple of bit parts during his two-year stay, in *Tom Brown of Culver* (1932) and *Flirtation Walk* (1934). Disheartened, he returned to Chicago, where he ironically landed a job at the World Fair in an exhibition which showed how movies were made. He had to pretend to act in front of an empty camera. A fellow demonstrator was a young radio-actor, Don Ameche, and the two became lifelong friends. After this Power won several small parts in Chicago stage productions and then moved to New York, where by a real stroke of luck he attracted the interest of top actress Katherine Cornell and her husband/producer Guthrie McClintic and joined their company. He was playing a lead part in 'St Joan' when a Twentieth Century-Fox talent scout spotted him and offered him a screen-test. In fact Power made two tests and the second impressed Darryl F. Zanuck sufficiently to give him a contract.

His first two films, *Girls' Dormitory* (1936) with Simone Simon and *Ladies in Love* (1936) with Loretta Young, showed off his looks and personality extremely well. The fan-mail began to pour in and Zanuck, most impressed both by his acting and star potential, decided to give him the lead in *Lloyd's of London* (1936), a period piece about the famous insurance syndicate, directed by Hollywood veteran Henry King (he directed his first film in 1916 and his last in 1961, and went on to make ten more films with Power). His performance was strong and competent and his love-scenes with Madeleine Carroll have assurance and a definite sex-appeal. He became a star virtually overnight and, when he travelled to London shortly after its British release, he was greeted by a screaming crowd of adoring women some five thousand strong. No doubt, as with Robert Taylor, the studio publicity department was not a million miles away from the start of this particular riot, but equally certainly the charm of this tall, dark and handsome screen personality had a lot to do with it too.

Power in *Captain from Castile* (1947).

Zanuck's hunch had paid off and he promptly capitalized on Power's enormous box-office popularity. He made four films in 1937 and another four in 1938 – chicken feed compared to the incredible early output of stars like Gable and Grant, but in the less hectic days of the late 'thirties not an inconsiderable amount of work for a star. Three of the 1937 films co-starred him with Loretta Young, *Love Is News*, *Cafe Metropole* and *Second Honeymoon*, and his other leading lady was Sonja Henie, in a film aptly titled *Thin Ice*. His star was still rising and his first two 1938 films were extremely successful at the box-office. *In Old Chicago* he was reunited with Don Ameche (who had played his boss in *Love Is News*), both playing sons of the legendary Mrs O'Leary in a drama of town-hall corruption which culminated in a magnificent re-creation of the great Chicago fire. They competed for the hand of a singer (Alice Faye) and Power won (Ameche having conveniently died a noble death). The trio re-appeared in *Alexander's Ragtime Band* (1938) in the same combination and with the same popular success. At this stage Power was No. 10 in the Hollywood top ten.

Then, foolishly, Fox lent him out – to MGM, to play opposite Norma Shearer in *Marie Antoinette* (1938). It was not so much the array of talent (Shearer, John Barrymore, Robert Morley and Anita Louise) that overshadowed him, as the towering overblown sets and spec-tacular costumes. Fox were so horrified at his fate that they refused to loan him out again for fifteen years and he thus lost parts in Columbia's *Golden Boy* (1939), which made William Holden a star, and Warner's *King's Row* (1942). They promptly starred him in their own historical extravaganza, *Suez* (1938), in which he played Ferdinand de Lesseps, who (according to the script and certainly *not* history) falls in love with the Empress Eugénie (Loretta Young). French actress Annabella was also in the film and she and Tyrone Power married in 1939 – with the ever-present Ameche as best man.

By this time Tyrone Power was almost at the very top. Only Mickey Rooney stood between him and No. 1 in the popularity polls and he had overtaken even Gable. In the next four years, before he went off to war, he made fourteen films and, while none of them did a great deal to enhance his reputation as an actor, most of them did very well at the box-office. The high points were his two films with Rouben Mamoulian, both remakes of Silent successes, and *This Above All* (1942), a wartime romance directed by Anatole Litvak, in which he played a cynical young soldier redeemed by the love of a fine woman (Joan Fontaine). The two Mamoulian films were *The Mark of Zorro* (1940), in which he swashbuckled with spirit but lacked the ultimate panache and athleticism of Fairbanks Sr, and *Blood and Sand* (1941), in which his performance as the matador called forth favourable comparisons with Valentino from critics and the public. He also appeared to advantage in *The Black Swan* (1942), a beautiful if unoriginal pirate film based on a Sabatini

Tyrone Power – third-generation actor and second-generation heart-throb, his genuine acting ability was frustrated by his studio contract.

novel. In 1941 he returned briefly to the stage and appeared with his wife in 'Liliom' at Westport, Connecticut. He got good notices, many of them commenting on a talent that went well beyond opportunities offered by his film roles.

The following year, in August, he enlisted as a private in the US Marine Corps, and after qualifying for officer candidate school (from which he emerged as a second lieutenant) he trained as a pilot. Later he joined Marine Transport Command, flying missions in the South Pacific, and was one of the first pilots to fly supplies, under fire, to the US troops at Iwo Jima. He was discharged early in 1946 and returned to Hollywood to find that both he and the movie business had changed. Later he com-mented 'There was a feeling of fear and tension in the air . . . people went round in fear of losing their jobs. . . .'

He had high hopes that his comeback film, based on Somerset Maugham's novel *The Razor's Edge* (1946), would be a good start to a new career as an actor rather than simply a box-office attraction. In the event he was proved still to have considerable drawing-power but the film was badly scripted (Cukor turned down the direction on these grounds) and Power made little dramatic impact in an impossible part. His next film, *Nightmare Alley* (1947), was a complete and tragic reversal of this situation. Power gave the best performance of his career as an arrogant opportunist using women to climb to the top of his profession as a carnival operator and finally being destroyed by a woman even more cold and calculating than himself. He asked for the part and it should have changed his career but the public, perhaps because they were simply not prepared to see him in such an unsympathetic role, stayed away in droves.

After this Fox played it safe, putting him into costume-dramas such as *Captain from Castile* (1947), *The Prince of Foxes* (1949) and *The Black Rose* (1950) and romances like *The Luck of the Irish* (1948) and *That Wonderful Urge* (1948), a remake of *Love Is News*, with Gene Tierney.

It was during the filming of *Captain from Castile* that he first met his second wife, Linda Christian. She had been brought to Hollywood from her native Mexico by Errol Flynn (according to his autobiography) and was working as an extra in the film. They married in Rome in January 1949 amidst scenes of riot and hysteria as a mob of fans several thousand strong got so carried away that the police riot squads were called out. Giornale d'Italia referred to the event as 'a little bit of Hollywood in a Roman church' and the prelate who conducted the service was alleged to be incensed by the fact that the ceremony was scarcely audible above the whirring and clicking of cameras and the screaming outside the church. Power was thirty-five, she was twenty-two and the marriage lasted for five years.

The Black Rose was made in Britain and Power stayed in London to do another stage part, playing the title-role in 'Mister Roberts'. Harold Hobson, then theatre critic of The Christian Science Monitor, described his performance as 'beautifully quiet and well judged', but after this it was back to the nondescript roles in boring films that Fox kept on coming up with. Life must have been very difficult for Tyrone Power at this time. His excursions into straight theatre had proved that he had a genuine acting ability but contractual obligations and the need not only to support a wife and family (he and Linda Christian had two daughters) but also to live in the accepted style of a star, must have caused him a great deal of tension and unhappiness. He made eight more films (seven for Fox and one, *Mississippi Gambler* (1953), on loan-out to Universal) before he terminated his contract with Fox in 1954. None of them offered him anything more than inconsequential and unmemorable roles. A return to the stage in 1953 in the company of Judith Anderson, Raymond Massey and Charles Laughton must have been a much-welcomed relief. Laughton directed the other three in a dramatized reading of parts of Stephen Vincent Benet's Civil War poem 'John Brown's Body' and they toured 118 US cities before opening to the sound of enthusiastic cheers on Broadway. Life said of Power's performance that it came as a surprise to those who, 'having seen him only in overstuffed costume movies, could never discover what an uncommonly able actor he is'.

During the last four years of his life Tyrone Power was at last able to fulfil his ambition of doing 'something worthwhile'. The quality of his film and stage acting in this period is not consistent. 'The Devil's Disciple' on the London stage was only partially successful, but a British television version of 'Miss Julie' with Mai Zetterling showed him in fine acting form. Similarly, his return to Twentieth to play Jake Barnes in Zanuck's production of Hemingway's *The Sun Also Rises* (1957) was an unwise choice – he was directed again by Henry King and performed adequately, but the film was not good. However, in *Witness For the Prosecution* (1958) he showed just how fine an actor he could be given the right vehicle. Billy Wilder directed and his co-stars were Charles Laughton and Marlene Dietrich.

He married for the third time in May 1958 and it was sad that just as things seemed to be going right for him he died. Like Gable he desperately wanted a son, and his wife gave birth to a boy three months after his death. In a tragic parallel to his own father's death twenty-seven years earlier, he collapsed and died of a heart-attack while filming *Solomon and Sheba* (1959) in Spain in November 1958.

Power and Don Ameche were old friends from way back. *In Old Chicago* (1937) saw them competing for the hand of Alice Faye. No prizes for guessing who won.

Power with Madeleine Carroll in *Lloyd's of London* (1936), the film which took him to the top.

Sand everywhere! *Suez* (1938) was a highly fictionalized account of Ferdinand de Lesseps and the building of the canal. Part of the love interest was provided by French actress Annabella, who promptly became Mrs Power.

Power gave his best performance in *Nightmare Alley* (1947) but his fans didn't like him in an unsympathetic part. Colleen Gray is the girl in the fish-net tights.

Another remake was *Blood and Sand* (1941) and this time Power was following in Valentino's footsteps as the doomed bull-fighter.

Power was, after Flynn, the most attractive swashbuckler of the late 'thirties and early 'forties. *The Mark of Zorro* (1939) was a good and exciting remake of the earlier Fairbanks film. With Power here are Eugene Pallette (far left) and Montagu Love.

The Black Swan (1942) was an adaptation of yet another Sabatini novel – with Power as a benevolent pirate, seen here with Maureen O'Hara.

Tyrone Power

Tom Brown of Culver. 1932. UNIVERSAL. William Wyler. With Tom Brown, H.B. Warner, Slim Summerville, Andy Devine.

Flirtation Walk. 1934. WARNER BROTHERS (FIRST NATIONAL). Frank Borzage. With Dick Powell, Ruby Keeler, Pat O'Brien, Ross Alexander.

Girls' Dormitory. 1936. TWENTIETH CENTURY-FOX. Irving Cummings. With Herbert Marshall, Ruth Chatterton, Simone Simon, Constance Collier, J. Edward Bromberg.

Ladies in Love. 1936. TWENTIETH CENTURY-FOX. Edward H. Griffith. With Janet Gaynor, Loretta Young, Constance Bennett, Simone Simon. Don Ameche, Paul Lukas, Alan Mowbray.

Lloyd's of London. 1936. TWENTIETH CENTURY-FOX. Henry King. With Freddie Bartholomew, Madeleine Carroll, Sir Guy Standing, C. Aubrey Smith, Virginia Field, George Sanders.

Love Is News. 1937. TWENTIETH CENTURY-FOX. Tay Garnett. With Loretta Young, Don Ameche, Slim Summerville, Dudley Digges, Walter Catlett, George Sanders, Jane Darwell.

Cafe Metropole. 1937. TWENTIETH CENTURY-FOX. Edward H. Griffith. With Loretta Young, Adolphe Menjou, Gregory Ratoff, Charles Winninger.

Thin Ice. 1937. TWENTIETH CENTURY-FOX. Sidney Lanfield. With Sonja Henie, Arthur Treacher, Raymond Walburn, Joan Davis, Sig Rumann, Alan Hale.

Second Honeymoon. 1937. TWENTIETH CENTURY-FOX. Walter Lang. With Loretta Young, Stuart Erwin, Claire Trevor, Marjorie Weaver, Lyle Talbot, J. Edward Bromberg, Paul Hurst.

In Old Chicago. 1938. TWENTIETH CENTURY-FOX. Henry King. With Alice Faye, Don Ameche, Alice Brady, Andy Devine, Brian Donlevy.

Alexander's Ragtime Band. 1938. TWENTIETH CENTURY-FOX. Henry King. With Alice Faye, Don Ameche, Ethel Merman, Jack Haley, Jean Hersholt.

Marie Antoinette. 1938. MGM. W.S. Van Dyke. With Norma Shearer, John Barrymore, Robert Morley, Anita Louise, Joseph Schildkraut, Gladys George, Henry Stephenson.

Suez. 1938. TWENTIETH CENTURY-FOX. Alan Dwan. With Loretta Young, Annabella, J. Edward Bromberg, Joseph Schildkraut, Henry Stephenson.

Jesse James. 1939. TWENTIETH CENTURY-FOX. Henry King. With Henry Fonda, Nancy Kelly, Randolph Scott, Slim Summerville, Brian Donlevy, John Carradine.

Rose of Washington Square. 1939. TWENTIETH CENTURY-FOX. Gregory Ratoff. With Alice Faye, Al Jolson, William Frawley, Joyce Compton.

Second Fiddle. 1939. TWENTIETH CENTURY-FOX. Sidney Lanfield. With Sonja Henie, Rudy Vallee, Edna May Oliver.

The Rains Came. 1939. TWENTIETH CENTURY-FOX. Clarence Brown. With Myrna Loy, George Brent, Brenda Joyce, Nigel Bruce, Maria Ouspenskaya, Joseph Schildkraut.

Daytime Wife. 1939. TWENTIETH CENTURY-FOX. Gregory Ratoff. With Linda Darnell, Warren William, Binnie Barnes, Wendy Barrie, Joan Davis.

Johnny Apollo. 1940. TWENTIETH CENTURY-FOX. Henry Hathaway. With Dorothy Lamour, Edward Arnold, Lloyd Nolan, Lionel Atwill.

Brigham Young. 1940. TWENTIETH CENTURY-FOX. Henry Hathaway. With Linda Darnell, Dean Jagger, Brian Donlevy, Jane Darwell, John Carradine, Mary Astor, Vincent Price.

Mark of Zorro. 1940. TWENTIETH CENTURY-FOX. Rouben Mamoulian. With Linda Darnell, Basil Rathbone, J. Edward Bromberg, Eugene Pallette, Gale Sondergaard.

Blood and Sand. 1941. TWENTIETH CENTURY-FOX. Rouben Mamoulian. With Linda Darnell, Rita Hayworth, Nazimova, Laird Cregar, Anthony Quinn.

A Yank in the RAF. 1941. TWENTIETH CENTURY-FOX. Henry King. With Betty Grable, John Sutton, Reginald Gardiner.

Son of Fury. 1942. TWENTIETH CENTURY-FOX. John Cromwell. With Gene Tierney, George Sanders, Frances Farmer, Elsa Lanchester, Harry Davenport, John Carradine, Roddy MacDowell.

This Above All. 1942. TWENTIETH CENTURY-FOX. Anatole Litvak. With Joan Fontaine, Thomas Mitchell, Henry Stephenson, Nigel Bruce, Gladys Cooper, Alexander Knox.

The Black Swan. 1942. TWENTIETH CENTURY-FOX. Henry King. With Maureen O'Hara, Laird Cregar, Thomas Mitchell, George Sanders, Anthony Quinn.

Crash Dive. 1943. TWENTIETH CENTURY-FOX. Archie Mayo. With Anne Baxter, Dana Andrews, James Gleason, Charley Grapewin, Dame May Whitty.

The Razor's Edge. 1946. TWENTIETH CENTURY-FOX. Edmund Goulding. With Gene Tierney, John Payne, Anne Baxter, Clifton Webb, Herbert Marshall.

Nightmare Alley. 1947. TWENTIETH CENTURY-FOX. Edmund Goulding. With Joan Blondell, Helen Walker, Coleen Gray.

Captain from Castile. 1947. TWENTIETH CENTURY-FOX. Henry King. With Jean Peters, Cesar Romero, Lee J. Cobb, John Sutton, Thomas Gomez.

The Luck of the Irish. 1948. TWENTIETH CENTURY-FOX. Henry Koster. With Anne Baxter, Cecil Kellaway, Lee J. Cobb, Jayne Meadows.

That Wonderful Urge. 1948. TWENTIETH CENTURY-FOX. Robert Sinclair. With Gene Tierney, Reginald Gardiner, Arlene Whelan, Gene Lockhart.

The Prince of Foxes. 1949. TWENTIETH CENTURY-FOX. Henry King. With Orson Welles, Wanda Hendrix, Katina Paxinou, Marina Berti, Everett Sloane.

The Black Rose. 1950. TWENTIETH CENTURY-FOX. Henry Hathaway. With Orson Welles, Cecile Aubry, Jack Hawkins, Michael Rennie, Finlay Currie, Herbert Lom, Laurence Harvey.

An American Guerilla in the Philippines. 1950. TWENTIETH CENTURY-FOX. Fritz Lang. With Micheline Presle, Tom Ewell, Bob Patten, Robert Barrat.

Rawhide. 1951. TWENTIETH CENTURY-FOX. Henry Hathaway. With Susan Hayward, Hugh Marlowe, Dean Jagger, Edgar Buchanan, George Tobias, Jeff Corey.

I'll Never Forget You. 1951. TWENTIETH CENTURY-FOX. Roy Baker. With Ann Blyth, Michael Rennie, Dennis Price, Beatrice Campbell, Kathleen Byron.

Diplomatic Courier. 1952. TWENTIETH CENTURY-FOX. Henry Hathaway. With Patricia Neal, Hildegarde Neff, Stephen McNally, Karl Malden.

Pony Soldier (UK title: **MacDonald of the Canadian Mounties**). 1952. TWENTIETH CENTURY-FOX. Joseph Newman. With Cameron Mitchell, Thomas Gomez, Penny Edwards, Robert Horton.

Mississippi Gambler. 1953. UNIVERSAL-INTERNATIONAL. Rudolph Mate. With Piper Laurie, Julie Adams, John McIntire, Paul Cavanagh.

King of the Khyber Rifles. 1953. TWENTIETH CENTURY-FOX. Henry King. With Terry Moore, Michael Rennie, John Justin, Guy Rolfe.

The Long Gray Line. 1955. COLUMBIA. John Ford. With Maureen O'Hara, Robert Francis, Donald Crisp, Ward Bond, Betsy Palmer, Phil Carey.

Untamed. 1955. TWENTIETH CENTURY-FOX. Henry King. With Susan Hayward, Richard Egan, Agnes Moorehead, John Justin, Rita Moreno.

The Eddy Duchin Story. 1956. COLUMBIA. George Sidney. With Kim Novak, Victoria Shaw, Rex Thompson, James Whitmore.

Abandon Ship (UK title: **Seven Waves Away**). 1957. COLUMBIA. Richard Sale. Power produced. With Mai Zetterling, Lloyd Nolan, Stephen Boyd, Moira Lister, James Hayter.

The Sun Also Rises. 1957. TWENTIETH CENTURY-FOX. Henry King. With Ava Gardner, Mel Ferrer, Errol Flynn, Eddie Albert, Juliette Greco, Robert Evans.

Witness for the Prosecution. 1958. UNITED ARTISTS. Billy Wilder. With Marlene Dietrich, Charles Laughton, Elsa Lanchester, John Williams, Henry Daniell.

Power introduced **The Rising of the Moon** (1957).

In a tragic echo of his father's death over a quarter of a century earlier, Power died of a heart-attack while filming *Solomon and Sheba*.

Robert Mitchum

Robert Mitchum is a Hollywood original in a way that even Bogart, with all his quirks and idiosyncrasies, was not. Partly because of this, one suspects that he may eventually come to have a reputation and a following approaching that of Bogey despite the fact that he has nothing like the solid achievement of Bogart's later films behind him. They certainly share a number of contradictory and immensely appealing traits of character. Both have the screen image of loners – cynical, embittered and tough, but at the same time sensitive, humane and potentially very tender. Like Bogart, too, Mitchum spent several journeyman years making pictures before he really broke through – though this is almost too violent a phrase to describe what has proved to be a very low-key, gradual and long-drawn-out progress to the reputation and popularity he now enjoys. As David Shipman says in 'The Great Stars', 'Robert Mitchum has sort of crept up on us.'

Most of the screen personalities discussed in this book have become stars because at a certain point in their careers they enter a halcyon period. Suddenly, things go right – they make the right films with the right directors and leading ladies. They establish in one or more pictures a film persona with sufficiently strong audience-appeal to sustain them in leaner years when the vehicles are not so good and the chemistry doesn't always work with their female co-stars. Mitchum has never had this kind of 'establishing' experience. He is not, and has never claimed to be, a great actor and has, in fact, made more bad and run-of-the-mill pictures than any other actor of his stature and popularity. Yet he has become, and remains, a major Hollywood star, a monolithic screen presence in a world where most of the giants are dead, retired or trying their hands at producing.

He was undoubtedly one of the sexiest of the post-war Hollywood heart-throbs – not beautiful in the Flynn tradition, not even particularly handsome, but immensely sexy. His powerful, almost animal, appeal looks back to Gable in its lazy potentially brutal cynicism and forward to Brando in its sense of sheer physical strength and reserves of unexpressed but smouldering emotion. He made his greatest impact in a single film, *The Night of the Hunter* (1955), in an intriguing and ambiguous role compounded largely of sex, violence and puritanical repression. After this revelation, even in the weakest and least memorable of films his strong sensual image stands out and remains in the memory, long after other characters and plot details have faded.

Robert Mitchum was born in August 1917 in Bridgeport, Connecticut, to an Irish father and the daughter of a Norwegian seaman. His father died when he was two and it seems to have been his mother's remarriage eight years later that was the root cause of his turbulent and troubled teenage years. These seem to have been spent in a constant battle with school-teachers, social workers and the 'authorities' generally, until he ran away from home at the age of fourteen. Then followed a period of riding freight-trains, dish-washing, rolling drunks and vagrancy – the charge for which he spent six days' hard-labour on the chain gang till his true age was discovered and he was released. After this he worked as a ditch-digger, coal-miner, punch-press operator, professional boxer and, with the help of his elder sister (a nightclub singer, living in Long Beach, California), as a stage-hand and later actor with the Long Beach Theater Guild. It was there that he started writing children's plays. A little later, again through his sister, he tried his hand successfully at writing material for nightclub acts, but in 1940 he married his wife Dorothy and got a job in the Lockheed Aircraft plant at Burbank. His partner on the workbench was a man called Jim Dougherty, whose wife Norma turned up years later to co-star with Mitchum in *River of No Return* (1954) – as Marilyn Monroe. Ill-health forced him to quit and live off unemployment benefit until he found a job in a shoe-shop. While he was working there one of his sister's contacts, a booking agent, suggested that he should try his luck in the movies. He laid fictional claim to riding and stunting experience and was hired by United Artists, who promptly used him in very small parts in three Hopalong Cassidy films, all released early in 1943. In fact, that year saw the release of sixteen or seventeen pictures in which Mitchum

There is something infinitely sensual about Robert Mitchum's heavy-lidded, slightly cynical expression – it has made him one of the most enduring stars to come out of Hollywood.

appeared. Most of his performances were in bit parts in such films as *Follow the Band* and *Doughboys in Ireland* (musicals), *Corvette K-225* and *Gung Ho!* (war films), Clarence Brown's *The Human Comedy*, and a Laurel and Hardy romp called *The Dancing Masters*. In two Westerns, however, he had larger parts – a reformed outlaw in Republic's *Beyond the Last Frontier* and a rancher in *Bar 20*, another Hopalong Cassidy adventure.

He first began to make his mark in *When Strangers Marry* (1944), playing second lead in this murder mystery, and, although his role in Mervyn Le Roy's war film *Thirty Seconds Over Tokyo* (1944) was small, RKO were impressed by it, put him under contract and gave him the romantic lead in *The Girl Rush* (1944), a B-musical. After this, there were plans to star him in a film version of 'The Robe', the historico-religious novel by Lloyd C. Douglas, the rights to which had just been purchased by RKO, but the production had to be shelved till after the war. Instead he starred in the remakes of two Zane Grey stories, *Nevada* (1944) and *West of the Pecos* (1945), both B-pictures but both very popular. Then he was loaned out to United Artists to play the part of the tough and beloved Lieutenant Walker in William Wellman's *The Story of GI Joe* (1945). The film tells the story of an actual infantry company in Italy, seen through the eyes of war correspondent Ernie Pyle (played by Burgess Meredith). Mitchum's performance was outstanding and won him an Academy Award nomination for Best Supporting Actor.

During the making of the film he was drafted but obtained a deferment till the film was finished. He did eight months as a private in the army before returning to Hollywood. The success of *GI Joe* and Mitchum in particular enabled his agent to negotiate a new contract during his absence. He was in future to be shared by RKO and Selznick although, as it happened, Selznick never used him, preferring to loan him out.

His first film after his war service was as a war-veteran in *Till the End of Time* (1946), a slick melodrama, and he was then loaned to MGM to play Robert Taylor's stepbrother in *Undercurrent* (1946) with Katharine Hepburn. Mitchum apparently attempted to amuse her with practical and off-colour jokes, which elicited from her the comment, 'You know you can't act and if you hadn't been good-looking you would never have gotten a picture.' He frequently quotes this. He was then in two good films, Raoul Walsh's Western *Pursued* (1947) and Edward Dmytryk's anti-anti-Semitism thriller *Crossfire* (1947), and made five more films before Fate removed him temporarily from the film business. These included *Out of the Past* (1947), a good private-eye thriller with Jane Greer, Robert Wise's powerful Western, *Blood on the Moon* (1948), and *The Red Pony* (1949), a rather weak adaptation by Steinbeck from his own novella, directed by Lewis Milestone.

Then, in August 1948, he was arrested and charged with possessing marijuana. The newspapers had a field day and Mitchum hired the best lawyer he could – Jerry Giesler, who had defended Flynn six years earlier. RKO seemed relatively unmoved by the event and as soon as he was released on bail started him on a new film, *The Big Steal* (1949), another thriller with Jane Greer, directed by Don Siegel. At his trial, Mitchum offered no defence and was found guilty and sentenced to sixty days in jail and two years' probation. He served his time uncomplainingly and immediately after his release (in March 1949) he returned to RKO to complete the film. His standing, both with the studio and the public, seemed unaffected. They apparently respected him for being honest and having taken his punishment without whining. He actually said, 'I got what I deserved', but a curious postscript to the affair occurred in January 1951 when his conviction was reviewed by a Los Angeles Court and the verdict of guilty set aside. His popularity, anyway, was undimmed and he went on to make a string of entertaining, if undistinguished, films for Howard Hughes, the first of which was a romantic comedy with Janet Leigh called *Holiday Affair* (1949).

While the movie-going public obviously liked Mitchum and found him an acceptable hero, there is little evidence that at this stage he was considered sure-fire heart-throb material. Howard Hughes, however, was not slow to latch on to this potential and the next few years saw a couple of ill-fated attempts on his part to make Mitchum part of a Great Team, like Bogart and Bacall. The first Hughes protégée tried out in this way was Faith Domergue, who played an insane society lady opposite Mitchum in *Where Danger Lives* (1950). The partnership, and ultimately Miss Domergue, sank without trace and the next candidate was Jane Russell, by then, thanks to Hughes's engineering skills, the leading lady at RKO. *His Kind of Woman* (1951) and *Macao* (1952) did not do the trick either, largely because Jane Russell just didn't have enough presence for a believable *femme fatale*. However, *His Kind of Woman* made a great deal of money – perhaps because of a delightful performance from Vincent Price as a ham actor, and some good songs (including 'One for My Baby').

Mitchum made ten more films before his RKO contract expired. In the first half-dozen he shared his favours equally between Susan Hayward – *The Lusty Men* (1952) and *White Witch Doctor* (1953) – and Jean Simmons – *Angel Face* (1952) and *She Couldn't Say No* (1954) – and refused a third film with Russell. This was part of a bigger row with Hughes and he made his last four contract films on loan-out. They were a patchy foursome, but this period was the nearest he came to the *anni mirabili* of the other heart-throbs and these films certainly played a large part in establishing him critically, and as a major box-office attraction. Otto Preminger's *River of No Return* (1954) co-starred him with Monroe and though their partnership did not set anything on fire

The Story of GI Joe (1945) was a grimly realistic account of battle conditions in the Second World War, and Mitchum won praise for his performance as the young officer who dies fighting beside his men.

it was a major step forward. Wellman's *Track of the Cat* (1954), in which he played a tough frontiersman, was most notable for its innovatory use of colour – perversely, to achieve black and white effects, and *Not as a Stranger* (1955), the story of an ambitious intern who marries an older nurse for money, was not a critical success. However, the latter was a personal triumph for Mitchum, who gave a finely understated performance and proved a great box-office attraction. The best of the quartet, by far, was the last – *The Night of the Hunter* (1955), directed by Charles Laughton and scripted by James Agee. This unforgettable mixture of allegory, black comedy, sex, violence and sentiment remains one of the most original and stimulating films to come out of Hollywood, and its success rests largely on Mitchum's overwhelming portrayal of the sexy, sadistic backwoods preacher, marrying and murdering his way around the countryside. He was the anti-hero personified and on this performance rests the greater part of his reputation, both as screen-actor and heart-throb.

There has been nothing comparable in his screen-career since, though through the late 'fifties, 'sixties and into the 'seventies he has continued to make a string of interesting and profitable movies. The best of them in the late 'fifties was *The Enemy Below* (1957), directed by Dick Powell and co-starring Curt Jurgens, the story of a tense struggle between a German U-boat and an American battleship. It didn't do terribly well at the box-office, unlike *Heaven Knows Mr Allison* (1957), which had him stranded on a desert island with a nun (Deborah Kerr). This was a real piece of hokum, but directed by John Huston, it proved to be commercially very successful.

He was teamed again with Deborah Kerr in Fred Zinnemann's *The Sundowners* (1960) and, although the film itself elicited only lukewarm reviews, it did good business and won for Mitchum extremely complimentary notices for his portrayal of the wandering Australian sheep-shearer. After an unsuccessful comedy, *The Last Time I Saw Archie* (1961) with Jack Webb, *Cape Fear* (1962), an unpleasant melodrama with Gregory Peck, and a small part in *The Longest Day* (1962), he was back on form again in *Two For the See-Saw* (1962). This story of an out-of-town businessman's affair with an insecure, odd-ball girl (Shirley MacLaine) gave him a chance to play an attractive, sympathetic, lovable man – and he did it to perfection. In 1967 he returned again (as he has done throughout his career) to the Western, to make *El Dorado* for Howard Hawks. He and John Wayne were splendid as two ageing gunmen. By the late 'sixties, Mitchum was right at the top of the Hollywood tree, pulling in fees of nearly a quarter of a million dollars a picture plus a percentage. His box-office appeal was tremendous too and has remained so into the 'seventies. His appearance in David Lean's *Ryan's Daughter* (1970) was the only performance that offered any competition to the spectacular scenery and weather. 'Mitchum,' wrote film critic Derek Malcolm, 'is simply and gloriously himself.' He was talking about Mitchum's role as the wronged husband in the film, but the comment could well stand as a summing up of the man and the actor.

An article in Time magazine in 1968 referred to Mitchum's 'personal colour – and his professional drabness' and herein perhaps lies at least a partial answer to the Robert Mitchum enigma. Both as a personality and in terms of his background and attitudes towards Holly-

The Mitchum/Russell screen partnership never really took off, but in *His Kind of Woman* (1951) it very nearly did.

Mitchum started his screen-career in Westerns and has returned to them intermittently throughout his life. This one is *Blood on the Moon* (1948) with Walter Brennan (left) and George Cooper.

wood, his originality is evident. He was, and is, one of the genuine Hollywood non-conformers, a man who has never become phoney or pretentious. Bogart undoubtedly exploited his screen personality to reinforce, project and sustain his star-appeal and, later, Brando's was exploited for him by the studio and the press. Mitchum, on the other hand, gives the clear impression of honestly not giving a damn. In the summer of 1974 he walked off the set of Otto Preminger's *Rosebud* after a row with the director. His private life has been amazingly untypical of a Hollywood star. He has been married for thirty-four years to the same wife – Dorothy, whom he first met when he was sixteen – and for several years of his film-career they lived 3,000 miles away from Hollywood, on a farm in Maryland. Perhaps the most remarkable thing about him, however, is his genuinely relaxed, but shrewd attitude towards his acting and career. 'Every two or three years, I knock off for a while. That way I'm always the new girl in the whorehouse,' he once said in typical Mitchum idiom.

Three young medical students in *Not as a Stranger* (1955): Lee Marvin, Frank Sinatra and Mitchum. Imagine the stampede if they ever started a group practice.
→

Nuns, especially nuns in potentially sexual situations, have always been good box-office. *Heaven Knows Mr Allison* (1957), with Deborah Kerr in the wimple and Mitchum as a tough marine, was no exception.

In *River of No Return* (1954) Mitchum played a backwoods farmer who guides his son and a dance-hall girl (Marilyn Monroe) through wild country and Indian attacks to safety.

Mitchum as the compelling psychopathic preacher in *The Night of the Hunter* (1955). The word 'Love' is tattooed on the fingers of his right hand, 'Hate' on his left.

Curiously, the screen chemistry between Mitchum and Deborah Kerr, while not of the surging passionate type, was far more effective than anything Howard Hughes tried to fix up. It worked particularly well in *The Sundowners* (1960) and with them here (left to right) are Michael Anderson Jr, Peter Ustinov and Glynis Johns.

Robert Mitchum

Hoppy Serves a Writ. 1943. UNITED ARTISTS. George Archainbaud. With William Boyd, Andy Clyde, Jay Kirby, Victor Jory, George Reeves, Jan Christy.
The Leather Burners. 1943. UNITED ARTISTS. Joseph E. Henabery. With William Boyd, Andy Clyde, Jay Kirby, Victor Jory, George Givot, Shelley Spencer.
Border Patrol. 1943. UNITED ARTISTS. Lesley Selander. With William Boyd, Jay Kirby, Claudia Drake, Russell Simpson, Duncan Renaldo, Andy Clyde.
Follow the Band. 1943. UNIVERSAL. Jean Yarbrough. With Leon Errol, Mary Beth Hughes, Eddie Quillan, Skinnay Ennis, Anne Rooney, Samuel S. Hinds, Leo Carrillo.
Colt Comrades. 1943. UNITED ARTISTS. Lesley Selander. With William Boyd, Andy Clyde, Jay Kirby, George Reeves, Gayle Lord, Earl Hodgins.
The Human Comedy. 1943. MGM. Clarence Brown. With Mickey Rooney, James Craig, Frank Morgan, Fay Bainter, Marsha Hunt, Van Johnson, Donna Reed, Dorothy Morris.
We've Never Been Licked (UK title: **Texas to Tokyo**). 1943. WANGER-UNIVERSAL. John Rawlins. With Richard Quine, Noah Beery Jr, Anne Gwynne, Martha O'Driscoll, Samuel S. Hinds, Harry Davenport.
Beyond the Last Frontier. 1943. REPUBLIC. Howard Bretherton. With Eddie Dew, Smiley Burnette, Lorraine Miller, Richard Clarke, Harry Woods, Ernie Adams.
Bar 20. 1943. UNITED ARTISTS. Lesley Selander. With William Boyd, Andy Clyde, George Reeves, Dustine Farnum, Victor Jory, Douglas Fowler, Betty Blythe.
Doughboys in Ireland. 1943. COLUMBIA. Lew Landers. With Jeff Donnell, Lynn Merrick, Guy Bonham, Red Latham, Wamp Carlson, Kenny Baker.
Corvette K-225. 1943. UNIVERSAL. Richard Rosson. With Randolph Scott, James Brown, Ella Raines, Barry Fitzgerald, Andy Devine, Richard Lane.
Aerial Gunner. 1943. PARAMOUNT. William H. Pine. With Richard Arlen, Chester Morris, Lisa Ward.
The Lone Star Trail. 1943. UNIVERSAL. Ray Taylor. With Johnny

Mack Brown, Tex Ritter, Fuzzy Knight, Jennifer Holt, George Eldredge, Harry Strong.
False Colours. 1943. UNITED ARTISTS. George Archainbaud. With William Boyd, Andy Clyde, Jimmy Rogers, Tom Seidel, Claudia Drake, Douglass Dumbrille.
The Dancing Masters. 1943. TWENTIETH CENTURY-FOX. Mal St Clair. With Stan Laurel, Oliver Hardy, Trudy Marshall, Robert Bailey, Matt Briggs, Margaret Dumont.
Riders of the Deadline. 1943. UNITED ARTISTS. Lesley Selander. With William Boyd, Andy Clyde, Jimmy Rogers, Richard Crane, Frances Woodward, Tony Ward.
Cry Havoc. 1943. MGM. Richard Thorpe. With Margaret Sullavan, Ann Sothern, Joan Blondell.
Gung Ho! 1943. WANGER-UNIVERSAL. Ray Enright. With Randolph Scott, Grace McDonald, Alan Curtis, Noah Beery Jr, J. Carrol Naish, David Bruce.
Johnny Doesn't Live Here Any More. 1944. MONOGRAM. Joe May. With James Ellison, Simone Simon, William Terry, Monna Gombell, Chick Chandler, Alan Dinehart.
When Strangers Marry (UK title: **Betrayed**). 1944. MONOGRAM. William Castle. With Dean Jagger, Kim Hunter, Neil Hamilton, Lou Lubin, Milt Kibbee, Dewey Robinson.
The Girl Rush. 1944. RKO. Gordon Douglas. With Wally Brown, Alan Carney, Frances Langford, Vera Vague, Paul Hurst, Patti Brill.
Thirty Seconds Over Tokyo. 1944. MGM. Mervyn Le Roy. With Van Johnson, Robert Walker, Spencer Tracy, Phyllis Thaxter, Tim Murdock, Scott McKay.
Nevada. 1944. RKO. Ed Killy. With Anne Jeffreys, Guinn 'Big Boy' Williams, Nancy Gates, Richard Martin, Craig Reynolds, Harry Woods.
West of the Pecos. 1945. RKO. Ed Killy. With Barbara Hale, Richard Martin, Thurston Hall, Rita Corday, Russell Hopton, Bill Williams.
GI Joe (also known as **The Story of GI Joe**). 1945. COWAN-UNITED ARTISTS. William A. Wellman. With Burgess Meredith, Freddie Steele, Wally Cassell, Jimmy Lloyd, Jack Reilly, Bill Murphy.
Till the End of Time. 1946. RKO. Edward Dmytryk. With Dorothy McGuire, Guy Madison, Bill Williams, Tom Tully, William Gargan, Jean Porter.
Undercurrent. 1946. MGM.

Vincente Minnelli. With Katharine Hepburn, Robert Taylor, Edmund Gwenn, Marjorie Main, Jayne Meadows, Clinton Sundberg.
The Locket. 1946. RKO. John Brahm. With Laraine Day, Brian Aherne, Gene Raymond, Sharyn Moffet, Ricardo Cortez, Henry Stephenson, Reginald Denny.
Pursued. 1947. WARNER BROTHERS. Raoul Walsh. With Teresa Wright, Judith Anderson, Dean Jagger, John Rodney, Harry Carey Jr, Clifton Young, Alan Hale.
Crossfire. 1947. RKO. Edward Dmytryk. With Robert Young, Robert Ryan, Gloria Grahame, Paul Kelly, Richard Benedict, Sam Levene.
Desire Me. 1947. MGM. Arthur Hornblow Jr. With Greer Garson, Richard Hart, George Zucco, Morris Ankrum, Florence Bates, Richard Humphreys.
Out of the Past (UK title: **Build My Gallows High**). 1947. RKO. Jacques Tourneur. With Jane Greer, Kirk Douglas, Rhonda Fleming, Richard Webb, Steve Brodie, Paul Valentine.
Rachel and the Stranger. 1948. RKO. Norman Foster. With Loretta Young, William Holden, Gary Gray, Tom Tully, Sarah Haden, Frank Ferguson.
Blood on the Moon. 1948. RKO. Robert Wise. With Barbara Bel Geddes, Robert Preston, Phyllis Thaxter, Walter Brennan, Frank Faylen, Tom Tully.
The Red Pony. 1949. REPUBLIC. Lewis Milestone. With Myrna Loy, Louis Calhern, Sheppard Strudwick, Peter Miles, Margaret Hamilton, Patty King, Beau Bridges.
The Big Steal. 1949. RKO. Don Siegel. With Jane Greer, William Bendix, Patric Knowles, Ramon Novarro, Don Alvarado, Pascual Garcia Pina.
Holiday Affair. 1949. RKO. Don Hartman. With Janet Leigh, Wendell Corey, Gordon Gebert, Griff Barnett, Esther Dale, Henry O'Neill.
Where Danger Lives. 1950. RKO. John Farrow. With Faith Domergue, Claude Rains, Maureen O'Sullivan, Harry Shannon, Ralph Dumke.
My Forbidden Past. 1951. RKO. Robert Stevenson. With Ava Gardner, Melvyn Douglas, Janis Carter, Lucile Watson, Basil Ruysdael, Gordon Oliver.
His Kind of Woman. 1951. RKO. John Farrow. With Jane Russell, Vincent Price, Tim Holt, Charles McGraw, Raymond Burr, Marjorie Reynolds, Jim Backus.
The Racket. 1951. RKO. John Cromwell. With

Lizabeth Scott, Robert Ryan, William Talman, Ray Collins, Joyce MacKenzie, Robert Hutton.

Macao. 1952. RKO. Josef von Sternberg. With Jane Russell, William Bendix, Gloria Grahame, Brad Dexter, Ed Ashley.

One Minute to Zero. 1952. RKO. Tay Garnett. With Ann Blyth, William Talman, Charles McGraw, Margaret Sheridan, Richard Egan, Eduard Franz.

The Lusty Men. 1952. RKO. Nicholas Ray. With Susan Hayward, Arthur Kennedy, Arthur Hunnicutt, Frank Faylen, Walter Coy, Carol Nugent.

Angel Face. 1952. RKO. Otto Preminger. With Jean Simmons, Mona Freeman, Herbert Marshall, Leon Ames, Barbara O'Neill, Kenneth Tobey.

White Witch Doctor. 1953. TWENTIETH CENTURY-FOX. Henry Hathaway. With Susan Hayward, Walter Slezak, Mashood Ajala, Timothy Carey, Joseph C. Norcisse, Elzie Emanuel.

Second Chance. 1953. RKO. Rudolph Mate. With Linda Darnell, Jack Palance, Sandro Giglio, Rodolfo Hayes Jr, Reginald Sheffield, Margaret Brewster.

She Couldn't Say No (UK title: **Beautiful but Dangerous**). 1954. RKO. Lloyd Bacon. With Jean Simmons, Arthur Hunnicutt, Edgar Buchanan, Wallace Ford, Raymond Walburn, Jimmy Hunt.

River of No Return. 1954. TWENTIETH CENTURY-FOX. Otto Preminger. With Marilyn Monroe, Rory Calhoun, Tommy Rettig, Douglas Spencer.

Track of the Cat. 1954. WARNER BROTHERS. William A. Wellman, With Teresa Wright, Tab Hunter, Diana Lynn, Beulah Bondi, Carl Switzer, Phillip Tonge.

Not As a Stranger. 1955. UNITED ARTISTS. Stanley Kramer. With Olivia de Havilland, Frank Sinatra, Gloria Grahame, Broderick Crawford, Charles Bickford, Myron McCormick, Lon Chaney, Jesse White, Harry Morgan, Lee Marvin.

The Night of the Hunter. 1955. UNITED ARTISTS. Charles Laughton. With Shelley Winters, Lillian Gish, Evelyn Varden, Peter Graves, Billy Chaplin, Sally Jane Bruce.

Man With the Gun (UK title: **The Trouble Shooter**). 1955. UNITED ARTISTS. Richard Wilson. With Jan Sterling, Henry Hull, Emile Meyer, Barbara Lawrence, Karen Sharpe, Angie Dickinson, John Lupton.

Foreign Intrigue. 1956. UNITED ARTISTS. Sheldon Reynolds. With Genevieve Page, Ingrid Thulin, Frederick O'Brady, Eugene Decker, Ingrid Tidblad, John Parovano, Peter Copley.

Bandido. 1956. UNITED ARTISTS. Richard Fleischer. With Ursula Theiss, Gilbert Roland, Zachary Scott, Rodolfo Acosta, Henry Brandon, Douglas Fowley.

Heaven Knows, Mr Allison. 1957. TWENTIETH CENTURY-FOX. John Huston. With Deborah Kerr.

Fire Down Below. 1957. COLUMBIA. Robert Parrish. With Rita Hayworth, Jack Lemmon, Herbert Lom, Bernard Lee, Bonar Colleano.

The Enemy Below. 1957. TWENTIETH CENTURY-FOX. Dick Powell. With Curt Jurgens, Al Hedison, Theodore Bikel, Russell Collins, Kurt Kreuger, Frank Albertson.

Thunder Road. 1958. UNITED ARTISTS. Arthur Ripley. Based on a story by Mitchum. With Gene Barry, Jacques Aubuchon, Keely Smith, Trevor Bardette, Sandra Knight, Jim Mitchum, Betsy Holt.

The Hunters. 1958. TWENTIETH CENTURY-FOX. Dick Powell. With Robert Wagner, Richard Egan, May Britt, John Gabriel, Lee Phillips, Stacy Harris.

The Angry Hills. 1959. MGM. Robert Aldrich. With Elizabeth Mueller, Stanley Baker, Gia Scala, Theodore Bikel, Sebastian Cabot, Peter Illing, Leslie Phillips, Donald Wolfit, Marius Goring, Jackie Lane, Kieron Moore.

The Wonderful Country. 1959. UNITED ARTISTS. Robert Parrish. With Julie London, Gary Merrill, Jack Oakie, Albert Dekker, Charles McGraw, Pedro Armendariz.

Home From the Hill. 1960. MGM. Vincente Minnelli. With Eleanor Parker, George Peppard, George Hamilton, Everett Sloane, Luana Patten, Anne Seymour.

The Night Fighters (UK title: **A Terrible Beauty**). 1960. UNITED ARTISTS. Tay Garnett. Mitchum co-produced. With Anne Heywood, Dan O'Herlihy, Cyril Cusack, Richard Harris, Marianne Benet, Niall MacGinnis.

The Grass Is Greener. 1960. UNIVERSAL-INTERNATIONAL. Stanley Donen. With Cary Grant, Deborah Kerr, Jean Simmons, Moray Watson.

The Sundowners. 1960. WARNER BROTHERS. Fred Zinnemann. With Deborah Kerr, Peter Ustinov, Glynis Johns, Dina Merrill, Chips Rafferty, Michael Anderson Jr, Mervyn Johns, Lola Brooks, Ronald Fraser, John Meillon, Willie Watson.

The Last Time I Saw Archie. 1961. UNITED ARTISTS. Jack Webb. With Jack Webb, Martha Hyer, France Nuyen, Joe Flynn, James Lydon, Del Moore, Richard Arlen.

Cape Fear. 1962. UNIVERSAL-INTERNATIONAL. J. Lee Thompson. With Gregory Peck, Polly Bergen, Lois Martin, Martin Balsam, Jack Kruschen, Telly Savalas, Barrie Chase.

The Longest Day. 1962. TWENTIETH CENTURY-FOX. Ken Annakin, Bernard Wicki, Andrew Marton. With John Wayne, Eddie Albert, Paul Anka, Arletty, Richard Beymer, Bourvil, Red Buttons, Sean Connery, Ray Danton, Fabian, Mel Ferrer, Henry Fonda, etc.

Two For the See-Saw. 1962. UNITED ARTISTS. Robert Wise. With Shirley MacLaine, Edmond Ryan, Elizabeth Fraser, Billy Gray, Eddie Firestone.

The List of Adrian Messenger. 1963. UNIVERSAL-INTERNATIONAL. John Huston. With George C. Scott, Dana Wynter, Clive Brook, Kirk Douglas, Frank Sinatra, Burt Lancaster, Tony Curtis.

Rampage. 1963. WARNER BROTHERS. Phil Karlson. With Elsa Martinelli, Jack Hawkins, Sabu, Cely Carrillo.

Man in the Middle. 1964. TWENTIETH CENTURY-FOX. Guy Hamilton, With France Nuyen, Barry Sullivan, Trevor Howard, Keenan Wynn, Sam Wanamaker, Alexander Knox, Robert Nicholls.

What A Way To Go! 1964. TWENTIETH CENTURY-FOX. J. Lee Thompson. With Shirley MacLaine, Paul Newman, Dean Martin, Dick Van Dyke, Gene Kelly, Robert Cummings.

Mr Moses. 1965. UNITED ARTISTS. Ronald Neame. With Carroll Baker, Alexander Knox, Ian Bannen.

The Way West. 1967. UNITED ARTISTS. Andrew V. McLaglen. With Kirk Douglas, Richard Widmark, Lola Albright, Michael Witney, Stubby Kaye, Sally Field.

El Dorado. 1967. PARAMOUNT. Howard Hawks. With John Wayne, James Caan, Charlene Holt, Paul Fix, Arthur Hunnicutt, Michele Carey.

Anzio (UK title: **The Battle for Anzio**). 1968. COLUMBIA. Edward Dmytryk. With Peter Falk, Earl Holliman, Mark Damon, Arthur Kennedy, Robert Ryan, Reni Santoni, Anthony Steel.

Villa Rides. 1968. PARAMOUNT. Buzz Kulick. With Yul Brynner, Charles Bronson, Grazia Buccella, Herbert Lom, Frank Wolff, Alexander Knox.

5 Card Stud. 1968. PARAMOUNT. Henry Hathaway. With Dean Martin, Inger Stevens, Roddy McDowall, Katherine Justice, John Anderson.

Secret Ceremony. 1969. UNIVERSAL. Joseph Losey. With Elizabeth Taylor, Mia Farrow, Pamela Brown, Peggy Ashcroft.

Young Billy Young. 1969. UNITED ARTISTS. Burt Kennedy. With Angie Dickinson, Robert Walker, David Carradine, Jack Kelly, John Anderson, Deana Martin.

The Good Guys and the Bad Guys. 1969. WARNER BROTHERS-SEVEN ARTS. Burt Kennedy. With George Kennedy, Martin Balsam, David Carradine, Tina Louise.

Ryan's Daughter. 1970. MGM. David Lean. With Trevor Howard, Christopher Jones, John Mills, Leo McKern, Sarah Miles, Barry Foster, Arthur O'Sullivan, Marie Kean.

Going Home. 1972. MGM (TALBOT/LEONARD PRODUCTION). Herbert B. Leonard. With Brenda Vaccaro, Jan-Michael Vincent, Sylvia Miles, Lou Gilbert, Josh Mostel.

The Wrath of God. 1972. MGM. Ralph Nelson. With Frank Langella, Rita Hayworth, John Colicos, Victor Buono, Paula Pritchett.

The Friends of Eddie Coyle. 1973. PARAMOUNT. Peter Boyle, Richard Jordan, Steven Keats, Alex Rocco.

The Yakuza. 1974. WARNER BROTHERS. Sydney Pollack. With Herb Edelman, Brian Keith, Richard Jordan, James Shigeta, Christina Kokubo, Takakura Ken, Kishi Keiko, Okada Eiji and Machida Kyosukk.

Two for the See-Saw (1962) was that rare animal amongst Mitchum films, a straight (well, fairly) love-story. Shirley MacLaine as an aspiring modern dancer gave it a slightly zany flavour.

Rock Hudson

Rock Hudson was the last of the old-time Hollywood male stars, discovered, developed, protected and exploited by a studio. Billed as 'Baron of Beefcake' and (along with Tab Hunter and various other contemporary and oddly named young men) 'Hollywood's most eligible bachelor', he was indeed the last of the old-fashioned romantic leading-men – a handsome hero in a world of rugged and off-beat anti-heroes. His career, in its early and middle stages, brought to a close the tradition of the beautiful but bland male star which had begun to change as far back as the early 'thirties with Gable and Cooper, which had taken a trouncing at the hands of Humphrey Bogart, and which was being stood on its head by Brando and his successors. Rock Hudson took on the mantle of Robert Taylor and Tyrone Power in an era when their type of appeal and screen image were beginning to look antediluvian. That he managed none the less to fill it – and eventually to transcend it – is a tribute not to his acting ability, but to his extremely good looks and instinct for self-preservation.

A recent article about Rock Hudson in Playgirl (February 1974) played down his physical effect. According to the interview he seemed 'average even ordinary' in appearance. Given that one woman's meat, etc., this is still a remarkable understatement. Whatever else one thinks about Hudson, there is little doubt that even nearing fifty he is physically a stunning man in an almost classic sense. Six foot plus tall, broad of shoulder, handsome but diffident, and fashionably hirsute (he was sporting a fine Zapata moustache and side-burns when spotted in Mayfair a few years ago), he is frankly a knock-out in person. Certainly he impressed female film-goers that way in the early 'fifties, and fan-mail began to pour in, to the tune of two thousand letters a week. Most were offers of marriage, or requests for bits of clothing – an Arkansas housewife proudly grew flowers in a pair of his cast-off shoes. According to a 1954 article by Jonathan Routh, his most persistent wooer in those days was a lady rancher in Texas who wrote him six letters a week beseeching him to give up his 'Hollywood foolishness' and settle down with her as the Cattle King of the Panhandle – a prophetic offer in the light of his subsequent role in George Stevens's film Giant (1956).

'Rock Hudson is to most women what Marilyn Monroe is to most men,' wrote Routh and, if there was a suspicion at this stage that it was not all quite as simple and straightforward as that, it certainly wasn't voiced very loudly. Hudson has always guarded his privacy jealously, never granting interviews unless a press agent is present and shying away from probes into his personal life – an odd worry, as Ken Martin pointed out in an article in TV Times in October 1972, 'because audiences these days are too intelligent to care if a star's private life is different from his on-screen roles'. During his early years at Universal, actress Marylin Maxwell acted as his hostess and companion and he was married, briefly, to his agent's secretary, Phyllis Gates. Throughout his contract years he dutifully 'dated', but when he finally left the system behind and began to freelance in 1966 he gave this up. The Playgirl article (which despite its liberated context displays an amazingly conventional set of attitudes) speaks of his apparent reverence for Woman – he 'idolizes her and cannot bear to be disenchanted'.

If this seems rather a wishy-washy reaction for a screen heart-throb, it none the less accords well with his screen persona for even at the height of his popularity he was one of the least distinctive and individual of Hollywood male stars. Even at his most risqué, in films like *A Very Special Favor* (1965) and *Strange Bedfellows* (1964), he retains a wholesome and ingenuous quality that is as American as apple pie and just about as unmemorable – though at the time it satisfies and is enjoyable in a mild sort of way. It is just this quality that made him such a successful protagonist in the American sex comedies of the late 'fifties and early 'sixties for it adds all kinds of indefinable ironies and ambiguities to his playing of the all-American bachelor/husband.

Rock Hudson was born Roy Fitzgerald in Winnetka, Illinois, in November 1925, of Swiss-Irish parentage (which undoubtedly explains both the dark good looks and the determination of purpose). He joined the navy after leaving high school in 1944. He started off as an aviation mechanic, but, after some confusion with the engines of a B-29, he was demoted to Laundry-man 3rd Class. He had ambitions to attend the University of Southern California, but the entrance exams proved an insuperable obstacle

Rock Hudson – the ex-baron of beefcake who became, if not a great actor, then at least the chief exponent of a new type of American folklore, the Hollywood sex comedy.

and so he took to truck-driving, and later found a job as a postman – in Hollywood. Whether he did this because he had aspirations to go into films, or whether these developed as he did his rounds is not clear, but, which ever way round it was, he did break into movies through this unlikely profession. One of the people to whom he daily delivered letters was an agent called Henry Willson – whose other discoveries included Rory Calhoun, Robert Wagner and John Saxon. Willson saw potential in Roy Fitzgerald and arranged some screen-tests. Director Raoul Walsh was sufficiently taken with him to offer him a tiny part in *Fighter Squadron* (1948), which he was making for Warners. They, in fact, later offered him a contract but he signed instead with Willson and Walsh who, a year later, sold his contract to Universal-International Studios. So Roy Fitzgerald became Rock Hudson and was enrolled in the studio's Talent Development Programme (fellow pupils included Piper Laurie and Tony Curtis). Here he learned the basic techniques of acting, singing and dancing. Diction and horse-riding were also part of the curriculum and there was a health club with a gym and steam-room where the soon-to-be famous physique was brought to the peak of perfection. Chary of his inexperience, though alive to his possibilities, Universal put Hudson in a number of small roles in B-pictures, like *Undertow* (1949) and *I Was a Shoplifter* (1950), both starring Scott Brady. He made over twenty programmers for the studio before he got his big chance in the 1954 remake of *Magnificent Obsession*, most of them in his own phraseology 'Tits and Sand epics – Arabian nights-type pictures with Maria Montez and Yvonne de Carlo'. He also played Red Indians in *Winchester '73* (1950) and *Taza, Son of Cochise* (1954) as Young Bull and Taza respectively, and was on the other side in Raoul Walsh's *The Lawless Breed* (1952) and two Bud Boetticher Westerns, *Horizons West* (1952) and *Seminole* (1953).

His longest and best role during this period came when Walsh borrowed him for RKO's adaptation of Victor Hugo's 'Toilers of the Sea', *Sea Devils* (1953), but it was in Robert Taylor's old role of playboy-turned-devoted-lover in *Magnificent Obsession* (1954) that he really struck a responsive chord in the hearts of women cinema-goers. Even then, it has rather unkindly been said, his impact was only truly felt when he took his shirt off to wash his hands! In fact as weepies go, it isn't that bad a film. Jane Wyman suffers stoically and beautifully and Hudson reforms equally beautifully – and most important of all it made music at the box-office. Rock Hudson was on his way up. After a few more formula pictures he was reunited with Jane Wyman, by public demand according to Universal, in another tear-stained melodrama. *All That Heaven Allows* (1955) was a milk-and-water and highly moral version of 'Lady Chatterley's Lover', with Hudson in the Mellors role (as Ron the gardener) and Wyman, respectably widowed, playing the lady. Like *Obsession* it was directed by Hollywood veteran

Douglas Sirk and again it was a great box-office success and marked the signing of a second seven-year contract with Universal, this time at $3,000 a week.

He had made the big breakthrough in terms of fan-mail and public popularity but it took two more years and two more tear-jerkers before he made his mark as an actor, in George Stevens's film of the Edna Ferber novel, *Giant* (1956). Most people in the film business were surprised when it became known that Warners had borrowed Hudson for the lead part, that of Bick Benedict a Texan cattle-rancher. It was a much-coveted part in an expensive, prestige production (Elizabeth Taylor and James Dean played the other leads). What clinched the part for Hudson was the fact that the character has to age from mid-twenties to seventy in the course of the film and Stevens had seen Hudson ageing most successfully in *The Lawless Breed*. *Giant* is Hudson's own favourite film and not only did it do well (it was the year's biggest grosser) but it established him as a competent actor rather than just another piece of beefcake, and gained him a fresh crop of fans.

Back with Universal he found himself playing in productions with more prestige, although the material was not always too different from his pre-*Giant* days. He did two more melodramas with Douglas Sirk, *Written on the Wind* (1956) with Lauren Bacall as co-star and Dorothy Malone in a supporting role for which she won an Oscar, and *The Tarnished Angels* (1957) again with Malone. By now his popularity was tremendous – in 1957 exhibitors voted him the biggest star of the year. Doubtless this knowledge influenced David Selznick's decision to star him in a remake of Hemingway's *A Farewell to Arms* (1957), first made in 1932 with Gary Cooper and Helen Hayes. Hudson's co-star was Mrs Selznick (Jennifer Jones), and although he doesn't measure up to Cooper, his performance is good, reflecting perhaps a new confidence in his ability and appeal. The film was another box-office success.

It was, however, a lightweight sex comedy that marked the start of the golden period of his stardom. In *Pillow Talk* (1959) with Doris Day, he played a philanderer sharing a party line with a career girl (Day). The film was an unexpected box-office smash and during the next half-dozen years he made six more similar comedies, two of which teamed him again with Doris Day, *Lover Come Back* (1961) and *Send Me No Flowers* (1964). This run of highly stylized and glossily superficial films kept him right at the top in the annual box-office polls – he was at No. 1 in 1959, No. 2 in 1960, 1961 and 1963 and No. 3 in 1964 and 1965. Not only did Hudson achieve an outstanding popularity during this period, but he played a large part in the creation of a new genre of the American cinema – the sex comedy of the late 'fifties and early 'sixties which can be seen in Alexander Walker's phrase, as 'a form of American folk culture'.

The sex comedy, as Mr Walker has pointed out in his perceptive chapter on the subject in

Hudson with Judith Braun in Boetticher's *Horizons West* (1952). The teeth are positively dazzling.

'Sex in the Movies', is essentially a writer's genre. It is formula cinema, with a fairly inflexible set of stereotyped attitudes and situations. The skill involved in the creation of new and amusing permutations of the two basic themes – sex and the single man and sex and the married man – rests largely on inventiveness of dialogue and minor plot variations – hence the dominance of such writers as Stanley Shapiro and George Axelrod. It is the lines which are the real stars of such films. There is no room for overwhelming star presence, acting ability or even strong individuality in the protagonists – they are of secondary importance.

This is why Hudson was so apt for the male leads in these films. His (and Doris Day's) 'homogenized' quality allowed the ingenuity and humour of the script to operate unhindered, and his good looks and basically likeable persona enabled him to retain audiences' sympathy, even when playing every mean trick possible in the sex war. All to no avail, as it turns out, for in the end the woman (complying with box-office demands and the realities of American society) always wins. The 'hero' gets to seduce her, but only after they are married. Before this, however, he manages to subject her to all sorts of embarrassment and ridicule. A favourite ploy is for the hero to radically undermine the heroine's belief in her own sexuality – or even gender – and then, by feigning innocence, impotence, or worse, to trick her into throwing herself whole-heartedly into seducing him as an act of social or emotional samaritanism. The handsome bounder may lose the war, but he wins most of the battles *en route*.

Other stars tried their hands in the genre, notably Jack Lemmon in *How to Murder Your Wife* (1965) and Cary Grant in *Indiscreet* (1958), but Hudson remained the chief exponent of what was to prove, in the increasingly enlightened and outspoken 'sixties, a fairly short-lived and extremely artificial phenomenon. He made *Come September* (1961) and *Strange Bedfellows* (1964) with Gina Lollobrigida, *Man's Favorite Sport?* (1964), directed by Howard Hawks, with Paula Prentiss, and *A Very Special Favor* (1965) with Leslie Caron. Then in 1966 he made a comedy-thriller with Claudia Cardinale called *Blindfold* (1966), which flopped, before turning his back on comedy to make what was to be, artistically speaking, his second significant film.

Seconds (1966) was the first film he made after leaving the shelter – and the confines – of his long sojourn at Universal. Directed by John Frankenheimer it is an ingenious and frightening story of rejuvenation and a second chance in life – at a horrifying price. Frankenheimer apparently wanted Olivier for the part, but in the event Hudson more than justified his taking up of the lead. Although the American box-office was not too good, the film has subsequently become something of a cult film, especially in Britain and Europe. He returned to Universal to make *Tobruk* (1967), which

again didn't do very well, but with *Ice Station Zebra* (1968), based on Alistair McLean's adventure novel, his stock began to rise again. It was, however, a temporary boost and Hudson was well into a decline by the end of the decade. Such had been his earlier popularity though, that in the Motion Picture Herald poll of the 'sixties' top ten money-making stars he tied for third place with Cary Grant and Elizabeth Taylor.

In 1970 Hudson was seen in *Darling Lili*, with Julie Andrews playing a wholesome and fresh-faced version of Mata Hari, and he later appeared in Roger Vadim's first American film, *Pretty Maids All in a Row* (1971), as a promiscuous and homicidal college sports-coach. Since then, however, he has pretty well confined himself to working, most successfully and lucratively, in television (except for *Showdown* (1972), a Western with Dean Martin). His series, 'McMillan and Wife', with Susan St James has been shown on both sides of the Atlantic and he is reported to have received $1,600,000 for six ninety-minute shows in NBC's 'Mystery Theater' series. Universal produces all his television material, so the break in the umbilical cord was only a temporary one. In view of his experience in the late 'sixties, Hudson is probably glad to be back. ●

Hudson as *Taza, Son of Cochise* (1954). He divided his time equally between cowboys and Indians at this stage in his career.

Magnificent Obsession (1954) did for Rock Hudson what the earlier version had done for Robert Taylor. Here he agonizes over a bandaged Jane Wyman.

Two perfect profiles of the 'fifties: Elizabeth Taylor and Hudson as husband and wife in *Giant* (1956). His performance won him an Oscar nomination.

Hudson in *All That Heaven Allows* (1955), with Jane Wyman.

Robert Mitchum in 1951.

Robert Redford in
Downhill Racer
(1969).

Tarnished Angels (1967) was an adaptation of William Faulkner's novel, 'Pylon', and reunited Hudson and Dorothy Malone. The previous year had seen them together in *Written on the Wind.*

Hudson with Doris Day during the filming of *Pillow Talk* (1959). Pasteurized and homogenized, bland and beautiful, and positively no sex before marriage – they made a perfect couple.

An embarrassing incident in Howard Hawks's *Man's Favorite Sport?* (1965), the only one of Rock Hudson's seduction comedies to take to the great outdoors. The lady is Charlene Holt.

Rock Hudson

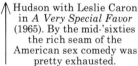
Hudson with Leslie Caron in *A Very Special Favor* (1965). By the mid-'sixties the rich seam of the American sex comedy was pretty exhausted.

The horrifying final sequence in *Seconds* (1966), one of Hudson's favourite films.

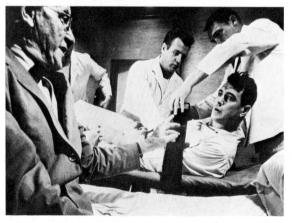

Fighter Squadron. 1948. WARNER BROTHERS. Raoul Walsh. With Edmund O'Brien, Robert Stack, John Rodney, Tom D'Andrea, Henry Hull.
Undertow. 1949. UNIVERSAL-INTERNATIONAL. William Castle. With Scott Brady, John Russell, Dorothy Hart, Peggy Dow, Bruce Bennett.
I Was a Shoplifter. 1950. UNIVERSAL. Charles Lamont. With Scott Brady, Mona Freeman, Andrea King.
One Way Street. 1950. UNIVERSAL. Hugo Fregonese. With James Mason, Marta Toren, Dan Duryea.
Winchester '73. 1950. UNIVERSAL-INTERNATIONAL. Anthony Mann. With James Stewart, Shelley Winters, Dan Duryea, Stephen McNally, Millard Mitchell, Charles Drake.
Peggy. 1950. UNIVERSAL-INTERNATIONAL. Frederick De Cordova. With Diana Lynn, Charles Coburn, Charles Drake, Charlotte Greenwood, Barbara Lawrence.
The Desert Hawk. 1950. UNIVERSAL-INTERNATIONAL. Frederick De Cordova. With Yvonne de Carlo, Richard Greene, George Macready, Jackie Gleason.
Shakedown. 1950. UNIVERSAL-INTERNATIONAL. Joseph Pevney. With Howard Duff, Brian Donlevy.
Double Crossbones. 1950. UNIVERSAL-INTERNATIONAL. Charles T. Barton. With Donald O'Connor, Helen Carter.
Tomahawk. 1951. UNIVERSAL-INTERNATIONAL. George Sherman. With Van Heflin, Yvonne de Carlo, Alex Nicol, Preston Foster, Jack Oakie, Tom Tully.
Air Cadet. 1951. UNIVERSAL-INTERNATIONAL. Joseph Pevney. With Stephen McNally, Gail Russell, Alex Nicol, Richard Long, Charles Drake.
The Fat Man. 1951. UNIVERSAL-INTERNATIONAL. William Castle. With Julie London, J. Scott Smart, Clinto Sundberg, Jayne Meadows.
The Iron Man. 1951. UNIVERSAL-INTERNATIONAL. Joseph Pevney. With Stephen McNally, Evelyn Keyes, Jeff Chandler, Joyce Holden, Jim Backus, Jim Arness.
Bright Victory. 1951. UNIVERSAL-INTERNATIONAL. Mark Robson. With Arthur Kennedy, Peggy Dow, Julie Adams.
Here Comes the Nelsons. 1951. UNIVERSAL-INTER-

NATIONAL. Frederick De Cordova. With Ozzie and Harriet Nelson and family.
Bend of the River. 1952. UNIVERSAL-INTERNATIONAL. Anthony Mann. With James Stewart, Arthur Kennedy, Julie Adams, Jay C. Flippen, Lori Nelson, Henry Morgan.
Scarlet Angel. 1952. UNIVERSAL-INTERNATIONAL. Sidney Salkow. With Yvonne de Carlo, Richard Denning, Bodil Miller, Amanda Blake.
Has Anybody Seen My Gal? 1952. UNIVERSAL-INTERNATIONAL. Douglas Sirk. With Charles Coburn, Piper Laurie, Gigi Perreau, Lynn Bari.
Horizons West. 1952. UNIVERSAL-INTERNATIONAL. Budd Boetticher. With Robert Ryan, Julie Adams, John McIntire, Raymond Burr.
The Lawless Breed. 1952. UNIVERSAL. Raoul Walsh. With Julie Adams, Barry Castle, John McIntire.
Seminole. 1953. UNIVERSAL. Budd Boetticher. With Barbara Hale, Anthony Quinn.
Sea Devils. 1953. RKO. Raoul Walsh. With Yvonne de Carlo, Maxwell Reed, Dennis O'Dea, Michael Goodliffe, Bryan Forbes, Gerard Oury.
The Golden Blade. 1953. UNIVERSAL. Nathan Juran. With Piper Laurie, Gene Evans, Kathleen Hughes, George Macready, Steven Geray.
Gun Fury. 1953. COLUMBIA. Raoul Walsh. With Donna Reed, Phil Carey, Roberta Haynes, Lee Marvin.
Back to God's Country. 1953. UNIVERSAL. Joseph Pevney. With Marcia Henderson, Steve Cochran, Hugh O'Brien, Chubby Johnson.
Taza, Son of Cochise. 1954. UNIVERSAL. Douglas Sirk. With Barbara Rush, Gregg Palmer, Bart Roberts, Morris Ankrum.
Magnificent Obsession. 1954. UNIVERSAL-INTERNATIONAL. Douglas Sirk. With Jame Wyman, Barbara Rush, Agnes Moorehead, Otto Kruger.
Bengal Brigade. 1954. UNIVERSAL-INTERNATIONAL. Lazslo Benedek. With Arlene Dahl, Ursula Thiess, Torin Thatcher, Arnold Moss, Dan O'Herlihy.
Captain Lightfoot. 1955. UNIVERSAL. Douglas Sirk. With Barbara Rush, Jeff Morrow, Kathleen Ryan, Finlay Currie, Dennis O'Dea.
One Desire. 1955. UNIVERSAL-INTERNATIONAL. Jerry Hopper. With Anne Baxter, Julie Adams, Carl Benton Reid, Natalie Wood, William Hopper, Betty Garde.
Never Say Goodbye. 1955. UNIVERSAL-INTERNATIONAL. Jerry

Hopper. With Cornell Borchers, George Sanders, Ray Collins, David Janssen, Shelley Fabares.
All That Heaven Allows. 1955. UNIVERSAL-INTERNATIONAL. Douglas Sirk. With Jane Wyman, Agnes Moorehead, Conrad Nagel, Virginia Grey, Gloria Talbot, William Reynolds, Charles Drake.
Giant. 1956. WARNER BROTHERS. George Stevens. With Elizabeth Taylor, James Dean, Carroll Baker, Jane Withers, Chill Wills, Mercedes McCambridge, Sal Mineo, Dennis Hopper.
Written on the Wind. 1956. UNIVERSAL. Douglas Sirk. With Lauren Bacall, Robert Stack, Dorothy Malone, Robert Keith, Grant Williams.
Battle Hymn. 1957. UNIVERSAL-INTERNATIONAL. Douglas Sirk. With Anna Kashfi, Dan Duryea, Don DeFore, Martha Hyer, Jock Mahoney, Alan Hale.
Something of Value. 1957. MGM. Richard Brooke. With Dana Wynter, Sidney Poitier, Wendy Hiller, Juano Hernandez.
The Tarnished Angels. 1957. UNIVERSAL-INTERNATIONAL. Douglas Sirk. With Dorothy Malone, Robert Stack, Jack Carson, Robert Middleton.
A Farewell to Arms. 1957. SELZNICK/TWENTIETH CENTURY-FOX. Charles Vidor. With Jennifer Jones, Vittorio De Sica, Alberto Sordi, Kurt Kasznar, Mercedes McCambridge, Oscar Homolka, Elaine Stritch.
Twilight for the Gods. 1958. UNIVERSAL-INTERNATIONAL. Joseph Pevney. With Cyd Charisse, Arthur Kennedy, Leif Erickson, Ernest Truex, Richard Haydn, Vladimir Sokoloff, Wallace Ford.
This Earth Is Mine. 1959. UNIVERSAL-INTERNATIONAL. Henry King. With Jean Simmons, Dorothy McGuire, Claude Rains, Kent Smith, Anna Lee, Cindy Robbins.
Pillow Talk. 1959. UNIVERSAL-INTERNATIONAL. Michael Gordon. With Doris Day, Tony Randall, Thelma Ritter, Nick Adams, Julia Meade, Allen Jenkins.
The Last Sunset. 1961. UNIVERSAL-INTERNATIONAL. Robert Aldrich. With Kirk Douglas, Dorothy Malone, Joseph Cotten, Carol Lynley.
Come September. 1961. UNIVERSAL-INTERNATIONAL. Robert Mulligan. With Gina Lollobrigida, Sandra Dee, Bobby Darin, Walter Slezak, Brenda De Banzie, Joel Grey.
Lover Come Back. 1961. UNIVERSAL-INTERNATIONAL.

Delbert Mann. With Doris Day, Tony Randall, Edie Adams, Jack Oakie.
The Spiral Road. 1962. UNIVERSAL-INTERNATIONAL. Robert Mulligan. With Burl Ives, Gena Rowlands, Geoffrey Keen, Neva Patterson.
A Gathering of Eagles. 1963. UNIVERSAL. Delbert Mann. With Rod Taylor, Mary Peach, Barry Sullivan, Kevin McCarthy, Henry Silva, Leif Erickson.
Man's Favorite Sport? 1964. UNIVERSAL. Howard Hawks. With Paula Prentiss, Maria Perschy, John McGiver, Charlene Holt, Roscoe Karns, Regis Toomey.
Send Me No Flowers. 1964. UNIVERSAL. Norman Jewison. With Doris Day, Tony Randall, Paul Lynde, Hal March, Clint Walker.
Strange Bedfellows. 1964. UNIVERSAL. Melvin Frank. With Gina Lollobrigida, Gig Young, Edward Judd, Terry-Thomas, Howard St John.
A Very Special Favor. 1965. UNIVERSAL-LANKERSHIM. Michael Gordon. With Leslie Caron, Charles Boyer, Walter Slezak, Dick Shawn.
Blindfold. 1966. UNIVERSAL-SEVEN PICTURES. Philip Dunne. With Claudia Cardinale, Jack Waldron, Guy Stockwell, Anne Seymour.
Seconds. 1966. PARAMOUNT. John Frankenheimer. With Salome Jens, John Randolph, Will Geer, Jeff Corey, Frances Reid, Murray Hamilton.
Tobruk. 1967. UNIVERSAL. Arthur Hiller. With George Peppard, Nigel Green, Guy Stockwell, Jack Watson, Norman Rossington, Percy Herbert.
Ice Station Zebra. 1968. MGM. John Sturges. With Ernest Borgnine, Patrick McGoohan, Jim Brown, Tony Bill, Lloyd Nolan.
The Quiet Couple (UK title: **A Fine Pair**). 1969. WARNER PATHÉ. Francesco Maselli. With Claudia Cardinale, Tomas Milian, Leon Askin, Ellen Corby.
The Undefeated. 1969. TWENTIETH CENTURY-FOX. Andrew V. McLaglen. With John Wayne, Tony Aguilar, Roman Gabriel, Marian McCargo, Lee Meriwether, Melissa Newman, Bruce Cabot.
The Hornet's Nest. 1969. UNITED ARTISTS. Phil Karlson. With Sergio Fantoni, Sylvia Koscina, Jacques Sernas, Mark Colleano.
Darling Lili. 1970. PARAMOUNT. Blake Edwards. With Julie Andrews, Jeremy Kemp, Lance Percival, Jacques Marin.
Pretty Maids All in a Row. 1971. MGM. Roger

Vadim. With Angie Dickinson, Telly Savalas, John David Carson, Roddy McDowall, Keenan Wynn.
Showdown. 1972. UNIVERSAL. George Seaton. With Dean Martin, Susan Clark, Donald Moffat, John McLiam.

Hudson now concentrates almost exclusively on television and his series 'McMillan and Wife', but he did narrate **Marilyn** (1963).

Marlon Brando

In 1966 Pauline Kael, doyenne of American film-critics, wrote, 'Brando is still the most exciting American actor on the screen.' The timing of this statement was surprising for three reasons. Firstly it was made fifteen years after Brando became a truly great star with the screen version of *A Streetcar Named Desire*. Secondly it was made when his career was, to put it mildly, in the doldrums, and had been wallowing there for five years or more, and, thirdly, with a Cassandra-like gift of prophecy, Miss Kael articulated this judgement a good six years before Brando returned triumphantly to the heights both as a star and as an actor.

There is, however, less to surprise in what Miss Kael said. From his Broadway début as Stan Kowalski in December 1947, it was clear that Marlon Brando was a very special and potentially very great actor. Not only that, but as the years passed it became apparent that the quality which set him apart from the mainstream of the American acting tradition was precisely what made him such a distinctive and distinguished screen-actor. Brando's great strength and force as an actor lies in his unerring ability to express emotions, raw or complex, through his body rather than simply through his face, in motion rather than in words. This ability (his 'sense of revelation in reflex' one biographer has called it) was electrifying enough on-stage, according to those who saw it (Walter Matthau once confessed to seeing Brando in the stage 'Streetcar' 186 times), but transferred to the screen it found its true home. The emphasis which Brando placed on his body as an acting medium helped him to establish a totally new, powerful and spontaneous type of film-acting. His disturbing physical presence and his technique made him that almost unique creature, the great actor who is also a great star – and a great male sex symbol. Early in his rapid rise to fame he was variously labelled by journalists as 'the male Garbo', 'the walking hormone factory' and 'the Valentino of the Bop Generation'. The last phrase is apposite for not since Valentino had there been such emphasis on the sensuality of the body – only with Brando the impact was even more shattering because of his naturalism. What had been stylized sexuality in Silent films, in his performances became a powerful, almost primitive, masculinity. And it made him a tremendous box-office attraction as well as an actor who participated in some of the outstanding American films of the third quarter of the twentieth century.

Perhaps the very grandeur of his achievement has been partly, at least, to blame for his constant vulnerability to all kinds of attack and for the low and difficult periods in his career. His immense talent was apparent so early on that too much was expected of him and

an apparent falling-off in terms of ability and success was inevitable. Brando himself has contributed to this feeling of disappointment in two ways. Firstly he seems to have deliberately courted attack and criticism. Unlike Mitchum, who quite simply turned his back on the whole Hollywood scene, Brando came out to meet it, leading with his chin. He started off well by calling Hollywood 'a cultural boneyard' and announcing that he didn't have the moral strength to refuse the $40,000 for his first film. He was, in the opinion of the Hollywood columnists, rude, unco-operative and vulgar – and they labelled him 'The Slob'. On a more serious level, his prolonged 'down' period was also due to his attempts to play an extraordinarily wide range of roles. He has always cared less about protecting his image than making worthwhile films which really stretch his acting ability. After *Streetcar*, and *Viva Zapata!* (1952), he could undoubtedly have stayed a box-office favourite for years, playing either mean, sexy anti-heroes or sympathetic, sexy heroes, but he never seems to have considered the possibility. Instead he went on to play an extraordinarily wide range of roles which in many instances, especially in the 'sixties, failed to win him critical acclaim or much popularity at the box-office, and caused a general wariness on the part of Hollywood about his future. The last few years, however, have proved the cynics and his detractors wrong. With *The Godfather* and *Last Tango in Paris* Brando has shown that he still has the ability to surprise, delight, and shock cinema audiences.

He was born in Omaha, Nebraska, in 1924, into a prosperous mid-Western family with some artistic pretensions. The prosperity came from his father, a manufacturer of chemical feeds and pesticides, and the artistic temperament was apparent in his mother, Dorothy, and his two elder sisters Joceyln and Frances, who became an actress and a painter respectively. Dorothy was an intelligent, lively and sensitive woman who wrote, painted and sculpted. The Brando family moved around the country quite a bit and it may have been a sense of rootlessness that made 'Bud' Brando such a difficult and competitive youngster. His father thought to bring him to heel in traditional manner by sending him to a military academy but it was a disastrous experiment and made Brando, if anything, more rebellious. He got himself expelled in 1943 and volunteered for the army but a trick knee, the result of a football injury, disqualified him. His two sisters were already established in New York and he decided to join them.

Brando has always insisted that he drifted into acting, but it's possible that he was inspired by Jocelyn's example or that of Henry Fonda, once a protégé of his mother in the Omaha Playhouse, of which she was a leading light. They visited him in Hollywood, when Brando was in his mid-teens. Whatever the reson, shortly after his arrival in New York he enrolled at Erwin Piscator's Dramatic Workshop, where he became the pupil of Stella Adler, member of a famous Broadway family and a follower of Stanislavsky. The workshop later became the famous Actors' Studio and, though Brando remains its most respected product, other notable graduates have included Shelley Winters, Rod Steiger, Tony Curtis, Walter Matthau and Elaine Stritch. During a season of summer stock organized by Piscator at Sayville, Long Island, he acquired an agent, Maynard Morris, who got him a small part in John Van Druten's 'I Remember Mama', which opened in 1944, was a great success and ran for ages. After a year he left the cast and went on to take a larger part in Maxwell Anderson's 'Truckline Cafe', which joined him, professionally, for the first time with Elia Kazan and Karl Malden. The play closed after thirteen performances, and, though in neither role had Brando attracted much critical attention, he was beginning to be talked and enthused about by theatre people, and audiences. He went on to play the young poet Marchbanks in a Cornell/McClintic production of Shaw's 'Candida' and a Jewish refugee in Ben Hecht's 'A Flag is Born' (a Zionist propaganda piece calling attention to the Jewish plight in Palestine). After a disastrous mismating with Tallulah Bankhead in Cocteau's 'The Eagle Has Two Heads', from which he withdrew before the play's Broadway opening, he landed the part that was to be the making of him – Stanley Kowalski in Tennessee Williams's play 'A Streetcar Named Desire'. The play got rave reviews but they were overshadowed by the triumph of Brando's performance as the inarticulate, violent, sexy husband (John Garfield was originally announced for the part) who rapes his nymphomaniac sister-in-law.

Film offers flooded in, but the only one to tempt him was from Stanley Kramer, whose speciality had become socially significant dramas like *Home of the Brave* (1949). He offered Brando the part of a paraplegic war veteran who comes to terms with life in *The Men* (1950) and Brando accepted. He prepared for the role by spending four weeks living in the paraplegic ward of the Birmingham Veterans' Hospital, Van Nuys, and turned in a fine performance, which brought him very good reviews. The film won qualified critical plaudits – the script, by Carl Foreman, was a bit too manipulative and tidy but Zinnemann's direction was masterly. By the time the film was released Brando was already Hollywood's favourite rebel – he referred to Louella Parsons as 'the fat one' and Hedda Hopper as 'the one with the hats', kept a pet raccoon called Russell, and lived off peanut butter and pomegranates.

Despite the implicit threat in all this eccentricity, he was offered another film – the screen version of *Streetcar* (1951) with Vivien Leigh replacing Jessica Tandy as Blanche Dubois. Kim Hunter and Karl Malden retained their Broadway roles in the film, which was directed, as the play had been, by Elia Kazan.

The film was, of necessity, less explicit than the play. The Hays Office would not allow too obvious a rape, and the ending was trimmed so that Stanley's wife is seen to abandon him, though such is the weight of emotion in the film that the audience knows that her desertion will be only temporary. Acting within these limitations, and with a very different Blanche, Brando is magnificent – bettering, according to those who saw both, his stage performance. He was strongly favoured to win the Best Actor Oscar, but lost it to Bogart for *The African Queen*. The film, however, was a box-office sensation and put him fairly and squarely into the top echelons of Hollywood stars. Later he said that he considered it his most satisfactory film.

Brando went on to do a second film for Kazan – for a fee of $100,000. *Viva Zapata!* (1952) is the story of the Mexican peasant-revolutionary who took over where Pancho Villa left off. It was a daring enterprise in the days when HUAC was still busy ferreting out Reds from under every possible Hollywood bed, and Kazan had his work cut out convincing Twentieth Century-Fox that the film would be politically respectable. Anthony Quinn played Zapata's brother (and won a Best Supporting Actor Award) and Jean Peters his wife. Brando

'Two more actors like Brando and television can crawl back into its tube' (anonymous film-producer, *c.* 1955). He was over-optimistic about Brando's effect on the fortunes of the film industry but absolutely accurate about his general impact – it was terrific.

147

adopted an elaborate make-up for Zapata – and a painful one – taping his eyelids and flaring his nostrils with plastic rings. He is hardly the handsome, sexy figure of *Streetcar* in this guise, but his love-scenes with Jean Peters have a tender, humorous quality. The public's cool reception of *Viva Zapata!* was partly due to Kazan's subsequent co-operation with HUAC but also to the intrinsically 'arty' quality of the film – the John Steinbeck script has several very bombastic and rather risible moments. During filming, Brando met Movita, the Mexican actress who was to become the second Mrs Brando. Movita had played Clark Gable's girl friend in the 1935 version of *Mutiny on the Bounty* when she was seventeen. She remained for many years an important but largely hidden part of Brando's life, bearing him a son shortly after their marriage in 1960. They finally separated in 1967, after having another child.

As if to prove his versatility, Brando's next role was that of Mark Antony in an MGM-Mankiewicz production of *Julius Caesar* (1953) with John Gielgud as Cassius and James Mason as Brutus. 'Et Tu, Kowalski?' was the headline on one showbiz journal when this was announced. In the event, despite gloomy prophecies of mumbled and mangled lines, Brando acted admirably and won his third Best Actor nomination. His vocal style was rather at odds with the other actors, and, as always, he was most eloquent when allowing his body to speak for him – but it is a powerful and commanding performance.

After a brief return to the theatre in a summer-stock production of Shaw's 'Arms and the Man', he reinforced Hollywood's characterization of him as The Slob by playing the leader of a motor-cycle gang that terrorizes a small town in *The Wild One* (1953). Banned in Britain until 1968, the film now seems incredibly dated. The spectacle of Lee Marvin as a young terrorist can only cause amusement to a generation more accustomed to juvenile delinquents who are barely into their teens. It was designed purely as a star-vehicle for Brando, however, and despite its failure as film was a great box-office success. His sullen sex-appeal was at its height and, although the film itself verges on caricature for much of the time, his portrayal of Johnny, tough yet vulnerable, inarticulate, rebellious and violent, is totally memorable. He began a legion of leather-jacketed imitators from Dean through to the protagonists of *Easy Rider* (1969).

His next film was again for Kazan and brought him right to the top. In *On the Waterfront* (1954) he plays Terry Malloy, a battered ex-boxer caught up in the corruption of the longshoremen's unions who finally turns against the system. Eva Marie Saint made her screen début as his girl and Rod Steiger played his brother. Terry's speech to his brother when he says, 'Oh, Charlie, Charlie . . . you don't understand. I could have had class. I could have been a contender. I could have been somebody, instead of a bum, which is what I am,' is one of the most powerful and poignant moments on

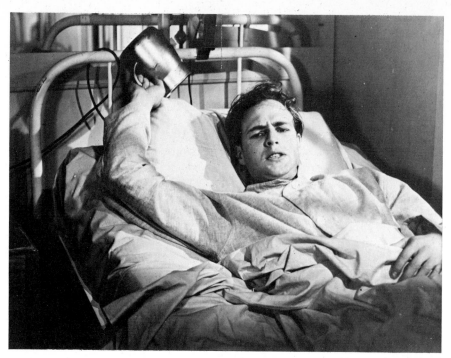

film. Brando here laid the ghost of Kowalski too, for his love scenes with Eva Marie Saint, though immensely erotic, are also very gentle and tender. He won the Oscar for Best Actor for his performance.

Immediately after this he ran into big trouble by refusing to make *The Egyptian* (1954) for Twentieth Century, as he was bound to do by contract. Edmund Purdom played the part and the film proved how accurate Brando's misgivings had been. However, he did penance for his rebellion in the form of *Désirée* (1954), playing Napoleon to Jean Simmons's eponymous role as the girl he loved who became Queen of Sweden. 'I let the make-up play it,' he said after the film was made. Jean Simmons was again his love interest in *Guys and Dolls* (1955), as a Salvation Army girl to his singing-and-dancing gambler. Sinatra and Vivien Blaine were the other couple involved and apparently the two male leads got on together not at all. Not entirely successful, it was none the less a brave try, as was his wheeler-dealing Japanese interpreter in *The Teahouse of the August Moon* (1956). Japan was again the setting for *Sayonara* (1957), which had him as a USAF colonel in love with a Japanese actress. Then he portrayed a young Nazi officer in Preminger's film of Irwin Shaw's novel *The Young Lions* (1958). All these films did very good box-office business and in 1955 and 1958 Brando was voted among the ten most popular stars. He married for the first time in October 1957, but the marriage, which produced a son, Christian Devi, foundered quickly. A possible cause was the revelation that his allegedly Indian bride, Anna Kashfi, was in fact Joanna O'Callaghan, a British girl from Cardiff, Wales.

His next three films, however, did very badly financially. *The Fugitive Kind* (1960) with Anna Magnani was another Tennessee Williams play, this time written expressly for him. It should all have come together, but it

Brando's weeks in a wheel-chair, preparing for his part in *The Men* (1950), were at first written off as a publicity stunt, but he was serious about it and this showed in his performance.

Brando's towering performance as Stanley Kowalski in *A Streetcar Named Desire* (1951) brought him superlative reviews and an ambiguous popular success which tended to ignore his acting ability and concentrate on his sex-appeal. Vivien Leigh's Blanche Dubois was just as powerful.

doesn't and the memory of *Streetcar* rounds off an unsuccessful venture. The film was made while Brando's own independent production *One-Eyed Jacks* (1961) was being re-edited for the umpteenth time. Intended as an anti-cliché Western to end all Westerns, *One-Eyed Jacks* was nothing of the kind. A moderately good film, it did quite well at the box-office but even as a smash hit could never have hoped to recoup its huge costs (around $6 million). This figure, though, is a mere bagatelle compared to the final cost of Brando's next picture, *Mutiny on the Bounty* (1962). This cost $26 million, took just over two years to produce, and its history would fill a large tome. Suffice it to say that Brando's portrayal of Fletcher Christian, especially in the earlier part of the film, as a foppish, aristocratic young man was splendid. However, since he had both a contractual control over artistic content and the reputation of a rebel in the film world it was almost inevitable that he should be the scapegoat for the series of mishaps which made the project such an expensive disaster – and he was undoubtedly responsible for a considerable amount of delay while he tinkered with the script. The film made a lot of money, but not nearly enough to cover costs and after this Brando was a marked man in Hollywood. *Mutiny* marks the start of a long downhill slide, in terms of popularity and the over-all quality of his films.

His performances, however, were never less than interesting in *The Ugly American* (1963), *Bedtime Story* (1964), *The Saboteur: Code Name – Morituri* (1965), Arthur Penn's *The Chase* (1966) and Sidney Furie's *The Appaloosa* (1966). The year 1967 was a turning-point for him in that it saw the nadir of his career in Chaplin's disastrous *A Countess from Hong Kong* (1967), with Sophia Loren, and the be-

ginning of an upward swing in his portrayal of the homosexual army captain in Huston's *Reflections in a Golden Eye* (1967). He replaced Montgomery Clift (who had died earlier) and, although the film made no great splash, his performance is superb, full of nice observation and delicate nuances of feeling.

During the next five years he worked fitfully in films, becoming increasingly involved in the American Civil Rights movement. This ideological commitment lay behind his part in Gillo Pontecorvo's film *Queimada!* (1970) as a British agent provocateur involved in a Caribbean revolution. He made one more film after this, Michael Winner's *The Nightcomers* (1971), before his triumphant renaissance as actor and star in Francis Ford Coppola's immensely successful version of *The Godfather* (1972). Don Corleone, however, was an old man, and Brando's playing of him indicated perhaps a future of superbly wrought character performances. His next film, Bernardo Bertolucci's *Last Tango in Paris* (1972), proved how dangerous it had always been to try and predict anything about Brando. In the person of Paul, he gives an amazingly self-revelatory portrait of himself, and in his relationship with Maria Schneider the powerful, brutal animal quality of his early years is back in full force. Pauline Kael, who kept faith with Brando during the lean years of his career, wrote of the film, 'This must be the most powerful erotic movie ever made and it may turn out to be the most liberating movie ever made ... Bertolucci and Brando have altered the face of an art form.'

Viva Zapata! (1953) was tendentious in places and very consciously a serious film, but Brando's scenes with Jean Peters (the future Mrs Howard Hughes) were a redeeming feature.

Seen now, *The Wild One* (1954) teeters constantly on the verge of self-parody. The improbably named Britches was played by Yvonne Doughty.

One-Eyed Jacks (1961) undoubtedly started life as an exciting and original project. By the end, however, it was vastly expensive and an only reasonably entertaining piece of self-indulgence.

Tarita seems to have been the only good thing Brando salvaged from the wreck of *Mutiny on the Bounty* (1962). It did his career and reputation no good at all.

Terry Malloy in Kazan's *On the Waterfront* (1954) was a powerful, inarticulate figure and Brando gave him the dimensions of a Greek tragic hero. Eva Marie Saint's role in the film, as his girl-friend, was small but telling.

Many people found the thought of Brando in Shakespeare fairly risible. In the event his performance in *Julius Caesar* (1953) was much more than just adequate.

Marlon Brando

Last Tango in Paris (1972) rocketed Brando the Sex-Symbol back into the public eye with scenes like this one with Maria Schneider. In 1973 at least five new books on Brando were published – the last one had appeared in 1962.

The Men. 1950. UNITED ARTISTS. Fred Zinnemann. With Teresa Wright, Everett Sloane, Jack Webb, Richard Erdman, Arthur Jurado, Virginia Farmer.

A Streetcar Named Desire. 1951. WARNER BROTHERS. Elia Kazan. With Vivien Leigh, Kim Hunter, Karl Malden.

Viva Zapata! 1952. TWENTIETH CENTURY-FOX. Elia Kazan. With Jean Peters, Anthony Quinn, Joseph Wiseman, Arnold Moss, Alan Reed, Mildred Dunnock.

Julius Caesar. 1953. MGM. Joseph L. Mankiewicz. With Louis Calhern, James Mason, John Gielgud, Edmond O'Brien, Greer Garson, Deborah Kerr, George MacReady, Michael Pate.

The Wild One. 1953. COLUMBIA. Laslo Benedek. With Mary Murphy, Robert Keith, Lee Marvin, Jay C. Flippen.

On the Waterfront. 1954. COLUMBIA. Elia Kazan. Brando won Best Actor Oscar. With Karl Malden, Lee J. Cobb, Rod Steiger, Pat Henning, Eva Marie Saint, Leif Erickson, James Westerfield.

Désirée. 1952. TWENTIETH CENTURY-FOX. Henry Koster. With Jean Simmons, Merle Oberon, Michael Rennie, Cameron Mitchell, Elizabeth Sellars, Charlotte Austin, Cathleen Nesbitt, Carolyn Jones.

Guys and Dolls. 1955. MGM. Joseph L. Mankiewicz. With Jean Simmons, Frank Sinatra, Vivian Blaine, Robert Keith, Stubby Kaye, B.S. Pully, Johnny Silver, Sheldon Leonard, Veda Ann Borg, Regis Toomey.

The Teahouse of the August Moon. 1956. MGM. Daniel Mann. With Glenn Ford, Machiko Kyo, Eddie Albert, Paul Ford.

Sayonara. 1957. WARNER BROTHERS. Joshua Logan. With Patricia Owens, Red Buttons, Ricardo Montalban, Martha Scott, James Garner, Miiko Taka, Miyoshi Umeki.

The Young Lions. 1958. TWENTIETH CENTURY-FOX. Edward Dmytryk. With Montgomery Clift, Dean Martin, Hope Lange, Barbara Rush, May Britt, Maximilian Schell, Dora Doll, Lee Van Cleef.

The Fugitive Kind. 1960. UNITED ARTISTS. Sidney Lumet. With Anna Magnani, Joanne Woodward, Maureen Stapleton, Victor Jory.

One-Eyed Jacks. 1961. PARAMOUNT. Marlon Brando. With Karl

Malden, Pina Pellicer, Katy Jurado, Ben Johnson, Slim Pickens, Larry Duran, Sam Gilman, Timothy Carey, Miriam Colon.

Mutiny on the Bounty. 1962. MGM. Lewis Milestone. With Tarita, Trevor Howard, Richard Harris, Hugh Griffith, Richard Haydn, Tim Seely, Percy Herbert, Gordon Jackson, Noel Purcell, Chips Rafferty.

The Ugly American. 1963. UNIVERSAL. George Englund. With Eiji Okada, Sandra Church, Pat Hingle, Arthur Hill, Jocelyn Brando, Kurrit Pramoj, Philip Ober.

Bedtime Story. 1964. UNIVERSAL. Ralph Levy. With David Niven, Shirley Jones, Dody Goodman, Aram Stephan, Parley Baer, Marie Windsor, Rebecca Sand, Frances Robinson.

Morituri (UK title: **The Saboteur: Code Name – Morituri**). 1965. TWENTIETH CENTURY-FOX. Bernard Wicki. With Yul Brynner, Janet Margolin, Trevor Howard, Martin Benrath, Hans Christian Blech, Wally Cox, Max Haufler, Gary Crosby.

The Chase. 1966. COLUMBIA. Arthur Penn. With Jane Fonda, Robert Redford, E. G. Marshall, Angie Dickinson, Janice Rule, Miriam Hopkins, Martha Hyer, Robert Duvall, Richard Bradford, James Fox, Diana Hyland, Jocelyn Brando.

The Appaloosa. 1966. UNIVERSAL. Sidney J. Furie. With Anjanette Comer, John Saxon, Emilio Fernandez, Alex Montoya, Miriam Colon, Rafael Compos, Frank Silvera.

A Countess from Hong Kong. 1967. UNIVERSAL. Charles Chaplin. With Sophia Loren, Sydney Chaplin, Tippi Hedren, Patrick Cargill, Margaret Rutherford, Michael Medwin, Charles Chaplin.

Reflections in a Golden Eye. 1967. WARNER BROTHERS-SEVEN ARTS. John Huston. With Elizabeth Taylor, Brian Keith, Julie Harris, Robert Forster, Zorro David, Gordon Mitchell, Irvin Dugan.

Candy. 1968. CINERAMA RELEASING CORPORATION. Christian Marquand. With Eva Aulin, Charles Aznavour, Richard Burton, James Coburn, John Huston, Walter Matthau, Ringo Starr, John Astin, Elsa Martinelli, Sugar Ray Robinson.

The Night of the Following Day. 1969. UNIVERSAL. Hubert Cornfield. With Richard Boone, Rita Moreno, Pamela Franklin, Jess Hahn, Gerard Buhr, Hughes Wanner, Jacques Marin.

Queimada! 1970. UNITED ARTISTS. Gillo Pontecorvo. With Evaristo Marques, Renato Salvatori, Norman Hill, Tom Lyons, Wanani, Cecily Browne, Dana Ghia.

The Nightcomers. 1972. AVCO-EMBASSY. Michael Winner. With Stephanie Beacham, Thora Hird, Verna Harvey, Christopher Ellis, Harry Andrews, Anna Palk.

The Godfather. 1972. PARAMOUNT. Francis Ford Coppola. Brando won Best Actor Oscar. With Al Pacino, James Caan, Richard Castellano, Robert Duvall, Sterling Hayden, Richard Conte, Diane Keaton, John Marley.

Last Tango in Paris. 1972. UNITED ARTISTS. Bernardo Bertolucci. With Maria Schneider, Darling Legitmus, Jean-Pierre Leaud.

Paul Newman

Paul Newman was, and remains, a fascinating amalgam of the old and the new. Unlike Brando he is no great actor – good, but not outstanding – but his screen presence, his acting techniques (especially early in his career), and his off-screen political activities have had very definite echoes of Brando. His sheer good looks, however, with their clean-cut American aura clearly continued the Gable tradition of the handsome hunk of man who remains essentially appealing whatever his role. In David Shipman's words, he is 'too handsome and too limited to be just an actor', but he has enough genuine acting ability and more than enough sex-appeal to be a great star.

Newman's rise to fame began in the late 'fifties, got into its stride during the early 'sixties, and by the end of the decade he was undoubtedly the most popular and best-known screen-actor in the world. *Butch Cassidy and the Sundance Kid* (1969) was the world's biggest ever grosser – until *The Sting* (1973), which teamed him again with Robert Redford and broke box-office records everywhere. To charges of cashing in on the success of the partnership, Newman has replied somewhat crisply that 'nobody complained when Tracy and Hepburn tried to follow up their successes'. If, to purists, the comparison seems presumptuous, it shouldn't, for Newman and Redford really are the nearest thing that present-day Hollywood has to the classic partnerships of the golden years. They have the light-hearted but sustained camaraderie of Hepburn and Tracy, enough good looks and sexiness between them to sink a battleship, a highly entertaining line in banter and backchat, and an immense likeability which is much more than simply the sum of its two parts. In a sense it is almost too easy for Newman now. In the laconic, jokey, sexy persona which he created and which has ripened in these two films, he probably has his meal ticket (if indeed he still needs one) for the rest of his career and it is perhaps the knowledge of this that has driven him to try his hand at directing, and has led him to be so selective in his choice of parts. 'More than once,' he told an interviewer in 1973, 'I have left my business manager whimpering in the bathroom because I'd turned down a lot of loot maybe to do a play for the Actors' Studio or just not work at all.' No studio support, no hindrance, for him – he bought himself out of his one and only studio contract (with Warners) in 1959 for a reputed $500,000. In this respect he is a long way distant from the earlier generation of stars. There is also the question of his off-screen image and it is perhaps here that he differs most from the big names of the 'thirties. Radical rather than conservative in his social and political attitudes (contrasting sharply with such staunch right-wingers as Gable, Wayne and Cooper), it is the stability of his private life which is at the same time one of his most endearing and surprising characteristics. He shares this with other contemporary heart-throbs – Redford, Eastwood and, until recently, McQueen – and curiously it does not seem to have affected his appeal for women at all. Indeed it may help to explain his great popularity. The spectacle of his happy and long-standing marriage to Joanne Woodward can only have helped to create his particularly powerful charisma. He has made stable and happy marriages seem glamorous – no mean feat in this day and age. 'There's no reason to roam,' he once told a reporter. 'I have steak at home – why go out for a hamburger?' The enduring stars have always been the ones who appealed to men as well as women, and it is the relaxed self-possession, the twinkle in the eye and the sure knowledge of being his own master that makes Newman something special.

He was born in January 1925 in Cleveland, Ohio, the son of the wealthy proprietor of a sports-goods store. His childhood and adolescence seem to have been spent happily as a round peg in a round hole and in 1944 he left college (where he had gone on an athletic scholarship) to enlist in the navy. Colour-blindness rather unromantically kept him as a Radioman 3rd Class in the Pacific, and after his discharge in 1946 he returned to college, graduating in 1949 with a degree in drama and economics. Apart from doing a certain amount of acting, he had the doubtful distinction of founding the first student laundry and developed a lifelong passion for beer – graduating, according to his own version of the Newman story, 'magnum cum lager'. He spent the summer with a stock-company in Williams

153

Bay, Wisconsin, and then joined a repertory company in Woodstock, Illinois, where he appeared in sixteen plays and met and married his first wife, actress Jackie Witt. They had three children and divorced in 1957.

In 1950 Newman's father died and he temporarily deserted acting to manage the family store, but a year later could stand no more of life as a small businessman and took his wife, son and life-savings to Yale, where he enrolled in the school of drama. He stayed a year, winning a master's degree in drama and attracting a certain amount of attention from New York talent scouts. In 1952 he was in New York, where he got a part in a television series called 'The Aldrich Family'. During the early and middle 'fifties he worked extensively and fairly constantly in television before his film-career really took off. It was an exciting time to be working in this particular medium. Most television was live and this caused not only a certain number of alarums and excursions, but also an aura of creativity and experiment which produced among other things such talents as John Frankenheimer, Sidney Lumet and Robert Mulligan in the directorial field. It was a period of consolidation, too, for Newman was studying hard at the Actors' Studio with Lee Strasberg.

In 1953 he read for a part in the Theater Guild's production of William Inge's 'Picnic', directed by Joshua Logan. He started off playing a very small part, but rehearsed the larger part of the rich boy who loses his girl to his more dynamic class-mate, and finally got to play it. His notices were good and it was at this time that he first met Joanne Woodward, who was understudying both Janice Rule and Kim Stanley. During the run of the play, Warners offered him a contract – and in early 1954 he went to Hollywood, where he made his large-screen début in *The Silver Chalice* (1954), an expensive religio-costume drama which flopped badly. Newman is still embarrassed by the memory and, when the film was re-run on a Los Angeles television station ten years later, he took out ads in all the papers apologizing for it – with the unlooked-for (but probably predictable) result that it notched up a very high rating. Despite his horror, Warners persuaded him to sign a seven-year contract at two films a year and in exchange let him return to Broadway to do 'The Desperate Hours' in the part Bogart played in the screen version. His good notices for this must have helped him get over *The Silver Chalice*, and he was busy too with the Actors' Studio and television work. The Warner contract had to be honoured, however, and he returned to Hollywood to make *The Rack* (1956) on loan-out to MGM. His performance as a young captain on trial for treason did not get him rave reviews, and already he was being labelled as the new Brando, a tag which annoyed him intensely. The film was withdrawn and only released after the success of his next film, also with MGM, Robert Wise's version of Rocky Graziano's life-story *Somebody Up There Likes Me* (1956). In this rags-to-riches story of the boxer's career he at last made his mark with both critics and audiences and was hailed as a new star. He made a third film for Metro, *Until They Sail* (1957), with Jean Simmons as the love interest, and then returned to Warners to play Ann Blyth's gangster lover in *The Helen Morgan Story* (1957). Neither film was particularly memorable but in both – and especially the latter – Newman attracted a considerable amount of female fan-worship. He played Larry Maddux with just the right amount of sexual arrogance, toughness and magnetism – assisted not a little by director Michael Curtiz.

In 1958 he and Joanne Woodward were married. She had gone to Hollywood at about the same time as him, under contract to Twentieth Century-Fox. It was for this studio that Newman made *The Long Hot Summer* (1958), in which he and Woodward appeared together on-screen for the first time. It was also his first film with Martin Ritt, a director with whom he was to work most successfully later in his career. Newman was awarded the Cannes Prize as Best Actor for his performance and returned to Warners to make *The Left-Handed Gun* (1958) with director Arthur Penn. This realistic and unromantic view of Billy the Kid as an illiterate juvenile delinquent contrasts strikingly with the standard Hollywood version of the legend (especially the Robert Taylor film) and, although reviews were mixed when it opened, it has subsequently been much admired.

Newman's career was on the upswing now, and for his next performance, that of Brick in the film version of Tennessee Williams's *Cat on a Hot Tin Roof* (1958), he won his first Academy Award nomination. The film, as with all Williams's works that transferred from stage to screen, was considerably toned down but both Newman and his co-star, Elizabeth Taylor, gave remarkable performances, backed by a strong cast led by Burl Ives and Judith Anderson. Then he went to Fox to make a comedy with his wife called *Rally Round the Flag, Boys!* (1958), which indicated fairly strongly that his gift for comedy was strictly limited, before returning to Warners to make his last contract film for them, *The Young Philadelphians* (1959). This was an old-fashioned, poor-boy-makes-good film, in which he played a sexy, go-getting, cynical young man on the make, and at the time it was regarded as an archetypal Newman picture.

Once released from his contract he returned to Broadway to do Williams's 'Sweet Bird of Youth' with Geraldine Page. The play was a great success, and during the run he was also making *From the Terrace* (1960) with Joanne Woodward – their third film together. It was another young-man-on-the-make story and did not do very well, but his next film *Exodus* (1960), although not critically well received, made a lot of money. Artistically it was something of a setback for Newman, but with Robert Rossen's *The Hustler* (1961) he was right back on form and won his second Oscar nomination for his impressive portrayal of the obsessive pool-player. He was teamed again with his wife and Martin Ritt in *Paris Blues* (1961), a film really only memorable for some splendid music from Armstrong and Ellington, and his last 1961 film was a screen version of *Sweet Bird of Youth*, again with Geraldine Page, and again in an emasculated version which particularly affected his role as the spoilt kept-boy.

Since then Newman has made twenty films and directed three. He went into the box-office top ten in 1963 at No. 9 and apart from 1965, which saw two of his least successful films, *Lady L* with Sophia Loren and *The Outrage* (*Rashomon* set in Mexico, directed by Ritt), has been there ever since. The highlights of this immensely successful career have demonstrated not only Newman's power at the box-office but also the extent of his acting ability. He has obviously learned to live with his limitations – except perhaps his lack of comic talent. While undoubtedly a very witty, funny man off-screen, he has consistently flopped in screen comedies throughout his career – notable films include *A New Kind of Love* (1963) and *The Secret War of Harry Frigg* (1968). On stage he seemed to have found his comic feet in Frank Corsaro's play 'Baby Want a Kiss' (1964), but on film his sense of fun and wit show best in films like *Butch Cassidy* and *The Sting* which are not primarily comedies.

Although Newman's acting does not have tremendous range (compared, for example, with Brando), he has shown himself an actor of distinction and power in films like *Hud* (1963), *Harper* (1966), *Hombre* (1967), *Cool Hand Luke* (1967), *Winning* (1969) and *WUSA* (1970). Apart from the two recent smash hits with Redford, the best-known and most admired Newman film is probably *Hud* – with which he won his third Academy nomination, for his portrayal of the charming, cold-hearted and opportunistic young rancher. Ironically he did not win an Oscar, but his co-stars Patricia Neal and Melvyn Douglas did. Running it a close second is *Cool Hand Luke*, a powerful story of life in a Southern prison camp, which brought him his fourth nomination.

In 1968 Newman directed his first feature (he had previously directed a half-hour Chekhov monologue on film at the Actors' Studio in 1959). Shot in five weeks in Connecticut and starring Joanne Woodward, *Rachel, Rachel* (1968) won plaudits for both director and star. He won the New York Film Critics' Award for Best Director and she for Best Actress in addition to an Academy Award nomination. Newman's other directorial stints since then have been on *Sometimes a Great Notion* (1971), when he replaced director Richard Colla, and then with Woodward again on *The Effect of Gamma Rays on Man-in-the-Moon Marigolds* (1972), which won her the Best Actress Award at Cannes in 1973.

In 1971, together with Barbra Streisand and Sidney Poitier, he formed the First Artists Production Company (later Steve McQueen joined them), thus extending his interests to producing as well. Despite both the producing and directing, he still seems to want to stay in front of the camera. Recently he has worked happily, but not altogether successfully, with director John Huston. Neither *The Life and Times of Judge Roy Bean* (1972) or *The Mackintosh Man* (1973) did a great deal for him – but since these were followed by *The Sting*, it hardly looks as if his position of starry pre-eminence is in any danger. He is still the world's most popular male star.

Newman's part of Basil, the Greek sculptor, in *The Silver Chalice* (1954) caused him terrible embarrassment both at the time and in subsequent years. Virginia Mayo (the one with heavy make-up) shared the love interest with Pier Angeli.

The Helen Morgan Story (1957) set the seal on Newman as a heart-throb in the story of singer Morgan's unhappy life in the Prohibition era. Ann Blyth played the female lead.

Newman's portrayal of Billy the Kid in Arthur Penn's first feature, *The Left-Handed Gun* (1958), was far removed from the figure of Hollywood tradition. He first played Billy on television earlier in the decade.

Mr and Mrs Newman in *WUSA* (1970), their seventh film together. It was a downbeat but intriguing story, with Newman as a hard-drinking, disillusioned radio reporter and Joanne Woodward as the girl he drifts into an affair with.

The Young Philadelphians (1959) offered Newman a meaty part as a rising young lawyer facing and surmounting all kinds of complicated professional and personal problems – this one is played by Alexis Smith.

Newman was mean, moody and sexy in *Hud* (1963). Patricia Neal was magnificent and won an Oscar.

Shelley Winters played an overweight ex-starlet in *Harper* (1966) and was one of several rather formidable ladies who cross Newman's path in this private-eye thriller. Others were Julie Harris, Janet Leigh and Lauren Bacall.

Perhaps the best-remembered image from *Butch Cassidy and the Sundance Kid* (1969). The film was a phenomenal success and the start of a great screen team – Newman insisted on Redford for his co-star.

The part of Brick in *Cat on a Hot Tin Roof* (1958) could have been overshadowed by the more overtly emotional part of Maggie (Elizabeth Taylor) but they were, in the event, very evenly matched.

Paul Newman

The Silver Chalice. 1954. WARNER BROTHERS. Victor Saville. With Virginia Mayo, Pier Angeli, Jack Palance, Natalie Wood, Walter Hampden.
Somebody Up There Likes Me. 1956. MGM. Robert Wise. With Pier Angeli, Sal Mineo, Everett Sloane, Eileen Heckart.
The Rack. 1956. MGM. Arnold Laven. With Wendell Corey, Walter Pidgeon, Edmond O'Brien, Ann Francis, Lee Marvin.
The Helen Morgan Story (UK title: **Both Ends of the Candle**). 1957. WARNER BROTHERS. Michael Curtiz. With Ann Blyth, Richard Carlson, Gene Evans, Alan King, Rudi Vallee, Walter Winchell.
Until They Sail. 1957. MGM. Robert Wise. With Jean Simmons, Joan Fontaine, Piper Laurie, Charles Drake, Sandra Dee.
The Long Hot Summer. 1958. TWENTIETH CENTURY-FOX. Martin Ritt. With Joanne Woodward, Anthony Franciosa, Orson Welles, Lee Remick, Angela Lansbury.
The Left-Handed Gun. 1958. WARNER BROTHERS. Arthur Penn. With Lita Milan, Hurd Hatfield, James Congdon, James Best, John Dehner.
Cat on a Hot Tin Roof. 1958. MGM/AVON. Richard Brooks. With Elizabeth Taylor, Burl Ives, Judith Anderson, Jack Carson, Madeleine Sherwood.
Rally 'Round the Flag, Boys! 1958. MCCAREY/TWENTIETH CENTURY-FOX. Leo McCarey. With Joanne Woodward, Joan Collins, Jack Carson, Dwayne Hickman, Tuesday Weld.
The Young Philadelphians (UK title: **The City Jungle**). 1959. WARNER BROTHERS. Vincent Sherman. With Barbara Rush, Alexis Smith, Brian Keith, Billie Burke, Otto Kruger, Diane Brewster, Robert Vaughn.
From the Terrace. 1960. TWENTIETH CENTURY-FOX/LINEBROOK CORPORATION. Mark Robson. With Joanne Woodward, Myrna Loy, Ina Balin, Leon Ames, Patrick O'Neal, Elizabeth Allan.
Exodus. 1960. UNITED ARTISTS. Otto Preminger. With Eva Marie Saint, Ralph Richardson, Peter Lawford, Lee J. Cobb, Sal Mineo, John Derek, Hugh Griffith.
The Hustler. 1961. TWENTIETH CENTURY-FOX. Robert Rossen. With Jackie Gleason, Piper Laurie, George C. Scott, Myron McCormick.

Paris Blues. 1961. UNITED ARTISTS. Martin Ritt. With Joanne Woodward, Sidney Poitier, Louis Armstrong, Diahann Carroll.
Sweet Bird of Youth. 1962. MGM. Richard Brooks. With Geraldine Page, Shirley Knight, Ed Begley, Rip Torn, Madeleine Sherwood.
Adventures of a Young Man (UK title: **Hemingway's Adventures of a Young Man**). 1962. TWENTIETH CENTURY-FOX. Martin Ritt. With Richard Beymer, Diane Baker, Corinne Calvert, Fred Clark, Dan Dailey, Ricardo Montalban, Susan Strasberg, Eli Wallach.
Hud. 1963. PARAMOUNT. Martin Ritt. With Melvyn Douglas, Patricia Neal, Brandon de Wilde, John Ashley, Whit Bissell.
A New Kind of Love. 1963. PARAMOUNT. Melville Shavelson. With Joanne Woodward, Thelma Ritter, Eva Gabor, George Tobias, Maurice Chevalier.
The Prize. 1963. MGM. Mark Robson. With Edward G. Robinson, Elke Sommer, Diane Baker, Micheline Presle, Leo G. Carroll.
What a Way To Go! 1964. TWENTIETH CENTURY-FOX. J. Lee Thompson. With Shirley MacLaine, Robert Mitchum, Dean Martin, Gene Kelly, Robert Cummings, Dick Van Dyke.
The Outrage. 1964. MGM. Martin Ritt. With Laurence Harvey, Claire Bloom, Edward G. Robinson, Howard da Silva, William Shatner.
Lady L. 1965. MGM. Peter Ustinov. With Sophia Loren, David Niven, Claude Dauphin, Peter Ustinov.
Harper. 1966. WARNER-PATHÉ. Jack Smight. With Lauren Bacall, Julie Harris, Arthur Hill, Janet Leigh, Robert Wagner, Pamela Tiffin, Shelley Winters.
Torn Curtain. 1966. UNIVERSAL. Alfred Hitchcock. With Julie Andrews, Lila Kedrova, Tamara Toumanova, Hansjoerg Felmy.
Hombre. 1967. TWENTIETH CENTURY-FOX. Martin Ritt. With Fredric March, Richard Boone, Diane Cilento, Barbara Rush, Cameron Mitchell.
Cool Hand Luke. 1967. WARNER BROTHERS. Stuart Rosenberg. With George Kennedy, J.D. Cannon, Robert Drivas, Lou Antonio.
The Secret War of Harry Frigg. 1968. UNIVERSAL. Jack Smight. With Sylvia Koscina, Andrew Duggan, Tom Bosley, John Williams.
Winning. 1969. UNIVERSAL/NEWMAN-FOREMAN. James Goldstone. With Joanne

Woodward, Richard Thomas Jr, Robert Wagner, David Sheiner, Clu Gulager.
Butch Cassidy and the Sundance Kid. 1969. TWENTIETH CENTURY-FOX. George Roy Hill. With Robert Redford, Katharine Ross, Strother Martin, Henry Jones.
WUSA. 1970. ROSENBERG/PARAMOUNT. Stuart Rosenberg. With Joanne Woodward, Anthony Perkins, Laurence Harvey, Pat Hingle.
Sometimes a Great Notion (UK title: **Never Give an Inch**). UNIVERSAL/NEWMAN-FOREMAN. Paul Newman. With Henry Fonda, Lee Remick, Michael Sarrazin, Richard Jaekel.
Pocket Money. 1972. FIRST ARTISTS/NATIONAL GENERAL CORPORATION. Stuart Rosenberg. With Lee Marvin, Strother Martin, Christine Belford, Kelly Jean Peters.
The Life and Times of Judge Roy Bean. 1972. FIRST ARTISTS. John Huston. With Jacqueline Bisset, Ava Gardner, Tab Hunter, John Huston, Roddy McDowall, Anthony Perkins.
The Mackintosh Man. 1973. NEWMAN-FOREMAN FOR WARNER BROTHERS. John Huston. With Dominique Sanda, James Mason, Harry Andrews, Ian Bannen.
The Sting. 1973. UNIVERSAL. George Roy Hill. With Robert Redford, Robert Shaw, Eileen Brennan, Charles Durning, Ray Walston.
Towering Inferno. 1974. TWENTIETH CENTURY-FOX/WARNER BROTHERS. John Guillermin. With Steve McQueen, Richard Chamberlain, Jennifer Jones, Fred Astaire.

Newman also appeared in a short, **The Making of Butch Cassidy and the Sundance Kid** (1969), and directed **Rachel Rachel** (1968) and **The Effect of Gamma Rays on Man-in-the-Moon Marigolds** (1972). He and Joanne Woodward provided narration for an American television series called 'The Wild Places' (1974).

Newman in *Butch Cassidy and the Sundance Kid* (1969).

Steve McQueen

Steve McQueen is, and always has been, his own man. This is not only evident in the practical aspects of his career but, interestingly, in the independence of spirit which informs his screen personality to a very high, and very appealing degree. In film after film he has played the Loner – wary, resourceful, true to his own personal set of values and totally self-contained. From *The Great Escape* (1963) through films like *The Cincinnati Kid* (1965), *Bullitt* (1968) and *The Thomas Crown Affair* (1968), this image has been predominant, finding its clearest, though not its most successful, expression in *Papillon* (1973), whose hero must qualify, if only in factual terms, as the loneliest loner McQueen has even played.

This quality is hardly unique among male stars. Bogart, Mitchum, Cooper and more recently Redford and Eastwood, have all, in their different ways, possessed it. Where McQueen is pre-eminent among his contemporaries and where he differs from earlier exponents is in the detachment ('his special kind of aware, existential cool' The New York Times once called it) which appears to be a spontaneous and essential part of his own character. His screen persona emerged full-blown – it seems to a straightforward extension of his personality. Unlike Bogart, for example, it didn't take him years to build it up – it's a very natural quality, which Bogart somehow never achieved, for all his greatness. This 'cool' is not like the cynicism of Bogart, although it implies a degree of world-weariness, but it does involve a high degree of self-awareness. Like the cat that walked by itself, McQueen, whatever the film, goes his own casual, but cautious way – and he has walked his way into the superstar bracket.

Like so many of the men whose lives have been outlined here, Steve McQueen had an unsettled, and unsettling, childhood. He was born in March 1930 in Beach Grove, Indiana, but went to live with his grandparents in Missouri after his father deserted the family. He stayed there till he was eleven when his mother remarried and had him back to live with her and her new husband in California. He was a wild and difficult boy, probably because of the instability and insecurity of his childhood, and as a result spent two years in a home for delinquent boys, the Boys' Republic in Chino, California. He still visits the home and has founded the Steve McQueen Scholarship there.

Shortly after moving to New York with his mother, towards the end of the war, he ran away from the family and became a merchant seaman on board a tanker. There followed a succession of drifters' jobs, among them working in the Texas oil-fields and for a travelling carnival. He joined the Marines in 1947 and after a brush with the authorities that cost him forty-one days in the brig, he settled down and was honourably discharged in 1950.

Then there were more odd jobs – docker, bartender, salesman and television repairman. It was while he was in this last job that he made the contact that got him into New York's Neighborhood Playhouse. When he left there in 1952 he had decided to have a real try at acting as a career and enrolled at the Uta Hagen-Herbert Berghof school of acting. His first professional stage appearance was in summer stock – the play was 'Peg O'My Heart' with Margaret O'Brien. He did quite a bit of stock and some television work before his break came in 1956, when he replaced Ben Gazzara in the Broadway production of 'A Hatful of Rain', began to be noticed and to do a lot of television. That year, 1956, was a notable year for McQueen in two other respects. He met and married Neile Adams, an actress and dancer who was then appearing in 'The Pajama Game', and he started to work in films – as a $19-a-day extra in *Somebody Up There Likes Me* (1956).

The newly-weds separated almost immediately, Neile to appear in a Las Vegas revue and Steve to take up a part in the Allied Artists' production of a Harold Robbins story, *Never Love a Stranger* (1957). When her contract ended Neile joined him in Hollywood, where she appeared in MGM's *This Could Be the Night* (1957) before giving up her career to have a family (they had a son and daughter). The Harold Robbins story cast him as a nice Jewish boy from a rough neighbourhood who makes good. It was a grave misuse of his talents but he stood out from the rest like a good deed in a naughty world. The film was held back for

McQueen in *The Cincinnati Kid* (1965), with Tuesday Weld.

release for two years, during which McQueen was kept busy with film and television work.

Still billed as Steven McQueen, he appeared in a sci-fi quickie called *The Blob* (1958) to no great effect, but his next film, *The Great St Louis Bank Robbery* (1959), was a much happier venture. He played an ex-campus football hero who drifts into a life of crime, and though the film was badly cut (to shorten it rather than for any other reason) what remained of his performance looked good enough to get him enthusiastic personal notices.

At this point in his career he switched back to television. Dick Powell, who had gone into television production, cast him as the hero of a pilot television Western which became a popular series throughout the States, making McQueen a household name. It was this television work that brought him back to films. Sinatra and his clan were just about to start another of their rather self-indulgent film projects, a war story this time, when Sinatra quarrelled with Sammy Davis Jr and his part, that of a GI sergeant, suddenly became vacant. Sinatra had seen McQueen in 'Wanted – Dead or Alive' and asked him to step into the role. *Never So Few* (1959) was not a very good war film, despite having John Sturges for its director, but McQueen gave a powerful performance which led to his being given the part of Yul Brynner's first recruit and right-hand man (and third billing) in *The Magnificent Seven* (1960), also directed by John Sturges. Based on Akira Kurosawa's truly magnificent screen classic *The Seven Samurai* (1954), the film was a tremendous success and if McQueen did not leap to instant stardom after appearing in it, then this was undoubtedly because it displayed such a plethora of stylish acting and attractive masculinity – quite apart from Yul Brynner and Eli Wallach as chief Good Guy and Bad Guy respectively. The competition included James Coburn, Brad Dexter, Robert Vaughn, Horst Buchholz and Charles Bronson. He was, however, sufficiently outstanding to be offered star billing in an MGM comedy *The Honeymoon Machine* (1961) with Paula Prentiss, Dean Jagger and Jack Weston. Like Newman before him, McQueen did not seem at ease, or show to advantage in slick, moderately sophisticated comedy. He returned to a war setting for his next film, *Hell Is For Heroes* (1962), directed by Don Siegel, still waiting for *Dirty Harry* to bring him to prominence and cult-status. It was not a great box-office success but it was a thoughtful and well-made film and McQueen gave a competent performance as an unstable and bitter GI, whose apparently dangerous foolhardiness proves invaluable in a combat situation. He was another wartime psychopath in *The War Lover* (1962), a made-in-Britain adaptation of John Hersey's novel about a mean but heroic pilot out to seduce his best friend's girl (Robert Wagner and Shirley Anne Field). It was a pretty silly film, but McQueen carried it somehow, ironically turning in an even better performance than he did in the Siegel film. His third war film in a row was the

best of all. *The Great Escape* (1963) not only established him as a star box-office attraction, but was also a great money-maker. In this adaptation of Paul Brickhill's story about escaping POWs, he played his first loner, Hilts the 'Cooler King', whose insolence and indifference to his German captors earns him long spells in solitary. His exciting, but doomed, motor-cycle dash to freedom was the first screen manifestation of his private passion for motor-bikes, racing and speed.

The next three films, although very different, still showed McQueen as essentially a loner. Two of them were made for the talented producer/director team of Alan Pakula and Robert Mulligan, and it is surely due to Mulligan's sensitive and disciplined direction that in *Love With the Proper Stranger* (1963) and *Baby the Rain Must Fall* (1965) McQueen gives two of the finest and most thoughtful performances of his career. In the first film, with Natalie Wood, he played a feckless but charming freelance musician shaken into embarrassment, responsibility and finally a kind of loving when he discovers that a one-night stand has caused a pregnancy. *Baby the Rain Must Fall* presented even more of a challenge and tragically was savagely cut before being shown in Britain, so that, until Robert Mulligan himself arranged a screening of the uncut version at London's

Steve McQueen has a tremendous intensity on-screen which contrasts sharply with the relaxed casualness of his looks. More than any other contemporary male star he brings out women's protective instincts – his essential loneliness is a challenge.

National Film Theatre in 1972, it was impossible to judge the film properly. With a screenplay by Horton Foote and Lee Remick as his co-star, he achieved a subtle and very sad portrayal of an introverted, inadequate drifter, at odds with life and doomed despite his loving and patient wife. Apart from the cuts, the film showed a McQueen that, however good his acting, his fans – and they were growing in number all the time – were not particularly keen to see. It was not a commercial success and nor was the film he made between the two Mulligan movies – *Soldier in the Rain* (1963) with Jackie Gleason and Tuesday Weld, a comedy about the relationship between two soldiers, directed by Ralph Nelson.

Happily, his next film combined both box-office appeal and a chance to do some acting. *The Cincinnati Kid* (1965) was the poker version of *The Hustler*, and did as well both in terms of money and boosting McQueen's popularity. His co-stars were Tuesday Weld again, Karl Malden and the inimitable Edward G. Robinson, and Norman Jewison directed (replacing Sam Peckinpah – which is an interesting thought). It was a taut, suspenseful film, full of good characterizations, not least of which was McQueen's. He went straight into his first big screen Western after this, a spin-off from *The Carpetbaggers* (1964) centred on one of that film's lesser characters. *Nevada Smith* (1966) had him in the title-role (the character was played by Alan Ladd in the earlier film) and despite Henry Hathaway's direction, and some good moments, was basically rather a dull film, though it did well at the box-office. So did his next film, *The Sand Pebbles* (1966), a tale of political brinkmanship set on a US gun-boat in war-ridden China in the 1920s. McQueen played a classic loner, the ship's engineer who feels more at home with his machines than he does with his fellow men. It made $13 million.

He played another solitary character in *The Thomas Crown Affair* (1968), but this time with a difference. Here he was elegant, sophisticated, super-cool, his arrogance and stylish self-possession beautifully matched by that of his co-star, Faye Dunaway. It took him to No. 7 and No. 3 in the US and British lists of the ten top stars, and made a great deal of money, but an even bigger and better bonanza was just around the corner.

Bullitt (1969) started off life as a routine cops-and-robbers movie. McQueen, apparently, had doubts about doing the film but wound up not only starring in it, but producing it too through his company, Solar. What lifted it out of the rut, apart from McQueen's portrayal of Frank Bullitt, was the magnificent car-chase sequence, bumping and leaping up and down the hills of San Francisco, often imitated but never excelled. McQueen had seen an exciting chase in *Robbery*, Peter Yates's film about Britain's Great Train Robbery, and asked him to come over to the States. Just how wise a move this was was underlined by the $15 million box-office take. McQueen's Bullitt was, despite his

policeman's badge, a Sam Spade for the 'seventies – gritty, determined, independent and watchful. This character combined with his *faux-naïf*, crumpled face, his very blue eyes and his air of aloof but exciting sex-appeal took him to new heights, and, despite the ballyhoo surrounding *Papillon*, the film remained the highlight of his career in mid 1974.

Since then he has made a varied batch of films. *The Reivers* (1969) was an adaptation of an autobiographical William Faulkner story about his childhood in Mississippi and his friendship with the family's hired hand, a likeable rogue played by McQueen with relaxed amiability. His next film, *Le Mans* (1971), was an indulgence of his passion for racing, all action (very impressive) and not much else. This obsession seems to have played a part in the break-up of his fifteen-year marriage. He and Neile separated in 1971.

In 1972 he appeared in *Junior Bonner,* directed by Peckinpah, one of a crop of films about rodeo-riders (others were *J. W. Coop* and *When the Legends Die*). McQueen played the title-role, a rodeo-star who returns home for a family reunion to find little but faded nostalgia. The film was not very successful commercially but offered him an opportunity to give a gentle, sensitive performance which harked back to his finer moments with Robert Mulligan. Peckinpah also directed his next film, *The Getaway* (1972), with far more characteristic action, violence and gore. This fast-paced thriller starred him opposite Ali MacGraw, recently divorced from Paramount executive Robert Evans. They married in July 1973 while he was making *Papillon*, Franklin Schaeffner's adaptation of Henri Charrière's best-selling autobiography. *Papillon* is an epic film (it runs for two and a half hours) superbly shot on West Indian locations and full of magnificent stunt work. However, it all hinges very much on the portrayal of Papillon, the convict condemned to a lifetime in the French penal colonies. McQueen works immensely hard at it, but in the last analysis his own star image is against him. He is too indelibly Steve McQueen to be really plausible as Papillon. With the evidence of the Mulligan films and *Junior Bonner* to hand, it would be sad to think that the superstar was limiting the actor.

McQueen as Thomas Crown, the smoothest bank robber in the business. *The Thomas Crown Affair* (1968) was one of that year's biggest grossers.

McQueen with Tuesday Weld in a non-poker-playing moment from *The Cincinnati Kid* (1965).

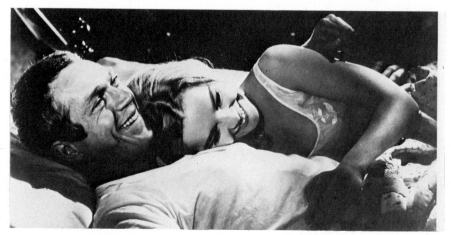

The Great St Louis Bank Robbery (1959) was McQueen's first billing as Steve – he played the driver of the gang's getaway car.

Baby the Rain Must Fall (1965) was a moody and emotionally complex film in which McQueen and Lee Remick gave fine performances. The child is Kimberly Block.

The Cooler King is let out. The Great Escape (1963) had an interesting line-up of incipient stars – apart from McQueen there were James Garner, James Coburn and Charles Bronson. James Donald is the man with the stick.

Bullitt (1969) has been imitated so often, in part or as a whole, that one forgets just how exciting it really was.

Le Mans (1971) was a classic piece of self-indulgence on McQueen's part. Fine if you liked motor-racing, but otherwise definitely a minor work in the McQueen canon.

With Peckinpah directing, one might have expected *Junior Bonner* (1972) to be a bloody, violent affair. In fact it was a low-key sensitive film with a matching performance from McQueen.

Steve McQueen

Never Love a Stranger. 1958. HAROLD ROBBINS/ALLIED ARTISTS. Robert Stevens. With John Drew Barrymore, Lita Milan, Robert Bray, Saelm Ludwig, R. G. Armstrong.
The Blob. 1958. PARAMOUNT. Irvin S. Yeaworth Jr. With Aneta Corseaut, Earl Rowe, Olin Howlin.
The Great St Louis Bank Robbery. 1959. UNITED ARTISTS. John Stix and Charles Guggenheim. With David Clarke, Graham Denton, Molly McCarthy, James Dukas.
Never So Few. 1959. MGM. John Sturges. With Frank Sinatra, Gina Lollobrigida, Peter Lawford, Richard Johnson, Paul Henreid, Brian Donlevy, Dean Jones, Charles Bronson.
The Magnificent Seven. 1960. UNITED ARTISTS. John Sturges. With Yul Brynner, Horst Buchholz, Eli Wallach, James Coburn, Charles Bronson, Robert Vaughn, Brad Dexter.
The Honeymoon Machine. 1961. MGM. Richard Thorpe. With Brigid Baslen, Jim Hutton, Paula Prentiss, Dean Jagger, Jack Weston.
Hell Is For Heroes. 1962. PARAMOUNT. Don Siegel. With Bobby Darin, Fess Parker, Nick Adams, Bob Newhart, James Coburn, Harry Guardino, Mike Kellin.
The War Lover. 1962. BLC/COLUMBIA. Philip Leacock. With Robert Wagner, Shirley Ann Field, Gary Cockrell, Michael Crawford, Bill Edwards, Chuck Julian.
The Great Escape. 1963. UNITED ARTISTS. John Sturges. With James Garner, Richard Attenborough, James Donald, Charles Bronson, Donald Pleasence, James Coburn, David McCallum.
Love With the Proper Stranger. 1963. PARAMOUNT. Robert Mulligan. With Natalie Wood, Edie Adams, Herschel Bernadi, Tom Bosley, Harvey Lembeck, Nick Alexander.
Soldier in the Rain. 1963. WARNER-PATHÉ. Ralph Nelson. With Jackie Gleason, Tuesday Weld, Tony Bill, Tom Posten, Ed Nelson.
Baby the Rain Must Fall. 1965. BLC/COLUMBIA. Robert Mulligan. With Lee Remick, Don Murray, Paul Fix, Josephine Hitchinson, Ruth White.
The Cincinatti Kid. 1965. MGM. Norman Jewison. With Edward G. Robinson, Karl Malden, Tuesday Weld, Ann-Margret, Joan Blondell, Rip Torn, Jack Weston.

Nevada Smith. 1966. PARAMOUNT. Henry Hathaway. With Karl Malden, Brian Keith, Suzanne Pleshette, Arthur Kennedy, Howard da Silva, Paul Fix.
The Sand Pebbles. 1966. TWENTIETH CENTURY-FOX. Robert Wise. With Richard Attenborough, Richard Crenna, Candice Bergen, Marayat Andrianne, Mako, Larry Gates.
The Thomas Crown Affair. 1968. UNITED ARTISTS. Norman Jewison. With Faye Dunaway, Paul Burke, Jack Weston, Yaphet Kotto, Todd Martin.
Bullitt. 1968. WARNER-PATHÉ. Peter Yates. With Robert Vaughn, Jacqueline Bisset, Don Gordon, Robert Duvall, Simon Oakland.
The Reivers. 1969. WARNER-PATHÉ. Mark Rydell. With Sharon Farrell, Will Gee, Rupert Crosse, Mitch Vogel, Michael Constantine, Lonny Chapman.
Le Mans. 1971. TWENTIETH CENTURY-FOX. Lee H. Katzin. With Siegfried Rauch, Elga Andersen, Ronald Leigh-Hunt, Fred Haltiner, Luc Merenda.
On Any Sunday. 1971. TIGON. Bruce Brown. With Mert Lawwill, Malcolm Smith, Bruce Brown.
Junior Bonner. 1972. CINERAMA. Sam Peckinpah. With Robert Preston, Ida Lupino, Joe Don Baker, Barbara Leigh, Mary Murphy, Ben Johnson.
The Getaway. 1972. CINERAMA. Sam Peckinpah. With Ali MacGraw, Ben Johnson, Sally Struthers, Al Lettieri, Slim Pickens.
Papillon. 1973. ALLIED ARTISTS. Franklin J. Schaffner. With Dustin Hoffman, Robert Deman, Don Gordon, Fred Brookfield, Dar Robinson.

Towering Inferno. 1974. TWENTIETH CENTURY-FOX/WARNER BROTHERS. John Guillermin. With Paul Newman, Richard Chamberlain, Jennifer Jones, Fred Astaire.

The second Mrs McQueen (Ali MacGraw) prophetically played McQueen's wife in *The Getaway* (1972). They were married during the filming of *Papillon* (1973).

Robert Redford

Robert Redford has become a superstar almost in spite of himself. Although his tremendously good looks gave him a head start, he was from the beginning an unlikely candidate for popular success and remained for many years in the second rank of Hollywood stars. He has maintained an air of obstinate individuality throughout his career and has, in consequence, become something of an enigmatic figure.

His reaction to the values and attitudes of the Hollywood Establishment has been one of disdainful disregard – 'I look upon going into Hollywood a little like making a mission behind the enemy lines.' Above all he has a deep dislike of publicity and intrusions into his private life. He still feels that he owes the public a performance and nothing more. 'I have no obligation to share my private life with the public,' he said in 1973.

Ironically, however, in his dedicated avoidance of one kind of Hollywood stardom, he has unwittingly participated in the creation of another, almost more potent, variation. His very inaccessibility has helped to create the myth of Robert Redford, so that even before his breakthrough into the superstar bracket with *Butch Cassidy and the Sundance Kid* in 1969 he had begun to develop a powerful and rather mysterious image. This tends to operate on the donkey-and-carrot principle as far as his popularity is concerned. The more widely known and admired he is, the more people want to know about him – and the more reticent and resentful of prying he becomes. The public, faced with this intriguing lack of information, becomes even more curious about him and his status as a star is enhanced accordingly.

As an actor, he has proved to be even more intransigent than Newman over his choice of roles. Perhaps the moment that the Hollywood powers realized they had a genuine maverick on their hands was when he walked out of the lead part in *Blue* a week before shooting was due to start and left town with his wife and children. In his time he turned down the George Segal part in *Who's Afraid of Virginia Woolf?*, the Dustin Hoffman role in *The Graduate* and the John Cassavetes part in *Rosemary's Baby*. Even with a film like Abraham Polonsky's *Tell Them Willie Boy Is Here*, of which he approved in principle, his uncompromising artistic criteria made him unhappy with the finished product. He felt strongly that the Indian characters should have been played by Indians. He himself was initially offered the title-role – eventually played by Robert Blake of *Electra Glide in Blue* (1973) and *Busting* (1974) – but preferred the more ambiguous and interesting role of the sheriff who hunts Willie Boy down. *A propos* this performance he later said, 'I liked that part because of the man's neutral position . . . it was in the grey area I'm rather fond of in films.' In fact, it is in his characterizations of men who operate emotionally, intellectually and morally in the 'grey area' that he excels. From his deft and unobtrusive portrayal of Natalie Wood's homosexual husband in *Inside Daisy Clover* (1965) to his delicate and understated Jay Gatsby, he has consistently exposed shades of moral and emotional ambiguity which are particularly striking when revealed beneath the charming and handsome exterior of such a patently perfect WASP specimen. He manages to suggest these nuances even in an overtly commercial film like *The Way We Were*, despite being hamstrung by an amazingly heavy-handed story-line, but has given his best performances in films which, sadly, have not reached a very wide public. Redford now seems to accept this as an inevitability. 'I have to resign myself to the fact that the films I want to make are probably not going to be commercial', he told a reporter from Show magazine in September 1972. It is perhaps a hopeful sign that his two best and most personal films, *Downhill Racer* and *The Candidate*, were made after his entry into the really big time with *Butch Cassidy*. Popular success, rather than simply subverting his creative aims and principles, seems to have been used by him as leverage to make, where possible, his own kind of film.

Redford's rather cavalier attitude to the filmworld undoubtedly springs from the fact that he spent his childhood in close, unglamorous proximity to Hollywood. He was born in August 1937 in Santa Monica, California, and spent an uneventful childhood and adolescence there. The glories of the capital of the motion-

Robert Redford – an intensely private man in a very public profession, and a superstar in spite of himself.

picture world were revealed to him as sham from an early age. Seeing the backdrop of a set on the edge of a back-lot made an indelible impression on him – '. . . there was this painted sky . . . things in the movies were not real. How could I take them seriously?'

At high school he was very much the golden boy and star athlete – in fact he went to the University of Colorado on a baseball scholarship and thought seriously for a time of taking up sport professionally. However, he was already a little too perceptive to accept unquestioningly the all-American athlete as the middle-class hero. 'We just took what was given to us second-hand and changed it a bit,' he commented later to an interviewer. 'It was boring and maddening and it bothered me.' He was already feeling the crushing weight of the competitive ethos and seeing through the popular platitude that it's not whether you win or lose but how you play the game that matters. This, he decided, was '. . . a load of crap. Who remembers or cares about the good guy who came in second? It's the creep who wins whom we tolerate.'

This was a theme which came to obsess him creatively over the years. *Downhill Racer, The Candidate* and, to a certain extent, *Little Fauss and Big Halsy,* all explore the conventional attitudes to competing and winning and the less pleasant realities that underlie them. At this stage though, the realization simply resulted in him dropping out of college and into a life of travel (both in the States and Europe) and painting, paid for by a stint in the Los Angeles oil-fields. He wound up studying art direction in New York and was increasingly attracted to acting. He switched to this and began to get walk-on parts on Broadway. In 1958 he married – he was twenty-one and his wife Lola was seventeen. They are still together and now have three children.

Redford soon acquired an agent and began to get increasingly sizeable roles in Broadway productions like 'The Highest Tree' and 'Little Moon of Alban'. In 1961 he made his film début in a low-budget, independent movie called *War Hunt* (1962). This was an examination of front-line tensions during the Korean War and John Saxon was the only 'name' film-actor in it. Lower down the cast list was Sydney Pollack, with whom Redford was to work fruitfully in later years when Pollack turned to directing – and Francis Ford Coppola drove one of the army trucks used in the film. The budget was rock bottom and Redford said later that it did not feel like a film at all – 'it was a good feeling but it wasn't a feeling of being related to Hollywood'. His performance as the good guy was thoughtful and revealing but the film did not do very well and he returned to the stage. The real breakthrough came when he played the lead in one of Neil Simon's smash-hit Broadway comedies, 'Barefoot in the Park', in 1963. Film offers began to roll in but unfortunately the one he chose to accept turned out to be a disaster. *Situation Hopeless But Not Serious* (1965) was adapted from Robert Shaw's

story about an eccentric German chemist (played by Sir Alec Guinness) who keeps two American airmen in his cellar for years after the end of the war because he cannot bear to part with them. The film centred very nearly exclusively on Sir Alec, and dropped like a stone almost as soon as it was released (four years later in Britain).

Redford's next film was altogether more propitious. Robert Mulligan and Alan Pakula (who had known him from his theatre days) asked him to appear in *Inside Daisy Clover* (1965), their 'thirties version of Gavin Lambert's incisive novel about Hollywood in the 'fifties. His portrayal of the Hollywood heart-throb who deserts Daisy on their wedding night because he is queer is handled with immense delicacy and he made a definite impact. Unfortunately the film was shown in Britain in a savagely cut (by the distributors) version so audiences had no real chance to appreciate his performance. The film was not a commercial success and nor were his next two ventures. In Arthur Penn's *The Chase* (1966) he was originally offered the key role of the sheriff. He turned it down (Marlon Brando eventually took it), preferring the part of Bubber Reeves, the escaped convict desperate to get back to his wife (Jane Fonda). Despite the relative smallness of the part, he was singled out for praise in many of the reviews. Then he decided to make *This Property Is Condemned* (1966) for Sydney Pollack, now turned director. It was rather like old-home week on the film – Natalie Wood co-starred and Francis Ford Coppola was one of the three writers who adapted the Tennessee Williams one-acter for the screen. Redford played a Southern railroad boss and Wood the daughter of the proprietor of a boarding-house which he visits to lay off workers. Both received good notices, but the film did not do well at the box-office.

The *Blue* fiasco followed shortly afterwards. It was a year before he returned to make a film – the screen version of his Broadway success *Barefoot in the Park* (1967), which reunited him with Jane Fonda as his scatty wife. He was reluctant to re-create his stage role, feeling that it was pretty stale by then, but this didn't show in the finished product, which was a great popular success. His stuffy young lawyer and Fonda's starry-eyed and over-enthusiastic young bride made good screen chemistry and they were well supported by Charles Boyer and Mildred Natwick. He followed this with *Willie Boy* (although it was not released in Britain until after *Butch Cassidy*). His decision was largely based on an empathy with the film's director, Abraham Polonsky, who had been black-listed during the HUAC investigations. Despite the tremendous success of *Butch Cassidy* and its own not inconsiderable merits, the film did not do well at the time of its release, though it has subsequently become something of a cult film.

So far Redford had achieved laudatory notices for roles in good but uncommercial films, one box-office hit in the remake of his

Redford's role as golden boy Wade Lewis in Mulligan's *Inside Daisy Clover* (1965) was small but important. Natalie Wood's choirboy outfit is in honour of an old-fashioned, schmaltzy Hollywood Christmas party.

big Broadway success, and a growing reputation both with the Hollywood hierarchy and the showbusiness press as a difficult and uncooperative individual. He was hovering on the brink of the big break. It came when Paul Newman decided to have him as his co-star in *Butch Cassidy* and stuck to his choice in the face of studio opposition. At the time the two men did not know each other. Now, not surprisingly, they are close friends. Redford's performance both in this film and its later companion piece (also directed by George Roy Hill), *The Sting*, lacked the depth and subtlety of many of his other characterizations but made up for this with its relaxed, witty nonchalance and beautifully timed switches from high drama to low comedy. The film not only won for him a Best Actor Award from the British Film Academy, but it also, because of its overwhelming box-office success, enabled his own company to set up his next film, *Downhill Racer* (1969).

With the assistance of director Michael Ritchie he was able at last to explore the psychology of what he has called 'the Norman Rockwell picture of America', the man who as long as he is winning is tolerated, however unpleasant he really is. The public seemed to think it was just a film about sport and gave it a miss, which is sad since it contains one of Redford's best performances – he makes his skiing champion deeply unlikeable yet totally fascinating in his dedication to the competitive philosophy.

Little Fauss and Big Halsy (1970), directed by Sidney J. Furie, was also about sport – this time the more popular one of motor-cycle racing. Redford and Michael J. Pollard played two itinerant racers and Redford again portrayed a superficially attractive but basically unpleasant character. The film was, however, more coarsely conceived than *Downhill Racer* and he really did not show to great advantage in it. His next film saw him back with Sydney Pollack, playing a resourceful, haunted moun-

tain man in *Jeremiah Johnson* (1972). Beautifully shot, in almost overwhelming mountain locations in Utah, where Redford has his home, the film must have had a special appeal for the side of his personality which craves solitude and open spaces. In spite of the scenic competition, his portrayal of the grim frontiersman dominates the film.

Despite the commercial failure of *Downhill Racer*, he returned to the winning/competitive theme, again with Ritchie directing, in *The Candidate* (1972), this time placing his protagonist in a political setting. Looking uncannily like a junior member of the Kennedy clan (but better-looking), he depicted the downhill slide of a young, liberal politician, talked into running for office in order to air the issues close to his heart, but becoming increasingly intoxicated by the actual process of gaining and wielding power. It is a more complex, more subtle and more satisfying film than *Racer*, but unfortunately did no better at the box-office.

As if to compensate, he went next into an out-and-out commercial vehicle, *The Hot Rock* (1972), with George Segal. Known in Britain as *How to Steal a Diamond in Four Uneasy Lessons*, this was a light-hearted 'caper' movie directed by Peter (*Bullitt*) Yates. Although funny, it could not equal the chemistry generated by the Newman/Redford/Roy Hill combination, which swung into action again with *The Sting* (1973), beautifully aided and abetted by Robert Shaw, cinematographer Robert Surtees and a wonderful Scott Joplin ragtime score. This story of a confidence trick to outclass all others, pulled off by Newman and Redford against a big-time gambler and bullyboy from Chicago (Shaw), showed that the quirky relationship of the earlier film was not simply a one-off phenomenon.

The attempt to create some kind of chemistry

Barefoot in the Park (1967) was a reluctant repeat of his earlier stage success, with Jane Fonda as the dizzy bride. 'It was very difficult to do . . . it's so tough to keep it fresh.' The strain didn't show in the film.

between Redford and Barbra Streisand in Sydney Pollack's *The Way We Were* (1973) was a signal failure, though their combined star-power has made the film a commercial success. The two protagonists seem almost to be acting in different films. Streisand (quite distinct from the part she is playing) turns in a strident and, apart from one moving telephone conversation, unsubtle performance, while he imbues his role with a sense of desperate but suppressed emotional contradictions. The same kind of imbalance exists between the leading characters in Redford's most recent film, Jack Clayton's *The Great Gatsby* (1974), though here it is, if anything, lack of definition rather than over-statement which afflicts Mia Farrow's playing of Daisy. Overburdened by exquisite period re-

creation, the film is a valiant attempt to embody the delicate moral and emotional ambiguities of Scott Fitzgerald's prose. In the end it sinks beneath the weight of its own fidelity to the text. Redford, however, comes as close as anyone could to capturing the enigmatic insubstantiality of Gatsby's life and love, hinting, as he has done throughout his screen career, at resources and complexities beneath his handsome exterior.

It must have seemed like a great idea – teaming Redford and Streisand in a big, glossy romantic picture. Despite Sydney Pollack's direction, however, *The Way We Were* (1973) was not very memorable, though it did good box-office business.

Downhill Racer (1969) 'wasn't a picture about skiing . . . it was a portrait of an athlete, a certain kind of person in American society', according to Redford, seen here with Camilla Sparv.

The old Newman/Redford magic worked just as well, if not better, second time round in *The Sting* (1973). In this exercise in fashionable nostalgia, their easy relationship gave the film heart.

Redford Kennedy-style in *The Candidate*. He saw the film as 'a very heavy statement that no politician can be his own man'.

In *Tell Them Willie Boy Is Here* (1969) Redford preferred the part of the enigmatic sheriff to that of the eponymous hero.

Redford as *Jeremiah Johnson* (1972), in the story of a mountain man's struggle for survival in the rugged regions of Utah. Here he and the survivor of an Indian raid contemplate another wild man, Del Gue (Stefan Gierasch), who finds himself in an awkward dilemma.

Fitzgerald wrote of 'Gatsby': 'The worst fault in it, I think, is a big fault ... the lack of any emotional back-bone at the height of it.' Daisy (Mia Farrow) and Gatsby at one of his parties – surface glitter aplenty but a sense of emptiness at the centre of the film.

Redford as Gatsby – 'There was something gorgeous about him, some heightened sensitivity to the promises of life ... an extraordinary gift for hope, a romantic readiness.' (Scott Fitzgerald)

Robert Redford

War Hunt. 1962. T-D ENTERPRISES. Denis Sanders. With John Saxon, Charles Aidman, Sydney Pollack, Gavin MacLeod.
Situation Hopeless But Not Serious. 1965. PARAMOUNT/CASTLE. Gottfried Reinhardt. With Alec Guinness, Michael Connors, Anita Hoefer, Mady Rahl, Paul Dahlke, Frank Wolff.
Inside Daisy Clover. 1965. PAKULA-MULLIGAN/RONA/ WARNER-PATHÉ. Robert Mulligan. With Natalie Wood, Christopher Plummer, Ruth Gordon, Katharine Bard, Roddy McDowall.
The Chase. 1966. COLUMBIA. Arthur Penn. With Jane Fonda, Marlon Brando, E. G. Marshall, Angie Dickinson, Janice Rule, Miriam Hopkins, Martha Hyer, Robert Duvall, Richard Bradford, James Fox, Diana Hyland, Jocelyn Brando.
This Property Is Condemned. 1966. SEVEN ARTS/STARK/PARAMOUNT. Sydney Pollack. With Natalie Wood, Mary Badham, Kate Reid, Charles Bronson.
Barefoot in the Park. 1967. PARAMOUNT. Gene Saks. With Jane Fonda, Charles Boyer, Mildred Natwick, Herbert Edelman.
Butch Cassidy and the Sundance Kid. 1969. TWENTIETH CENTURY-FOX. George Roy Hill. With Paul Newman, Katharine Ross, Strother Martin, Cloris Leachman.
Tell Them Willie Boy Is Here. 1969. UNIVERSAL. Abraham Polonsky. With Katharine Ross, Robert Blake, Susan Clark, Barry Sullivan.
Downhill Racer. 1969. WILDWOOD/PARAMOUNT. Michael Ritchie. With Gene Hackman, Camilla Sparv, Joe Jay Albert, Jim McMullan.
Little Fauss and Big Halsy. 1970. ALFRAN/ FURIE/PARAMOUNT. Sidney J. Furie. With Michael J. Pollard, Lauren Hutton, Noah Beery, Lucille Benson.
The Hot Rock (UK title: **How to Steal a Diamond in Four Uneasy Lessons**). 1972. TWENTIETH CENTURY-FOX. Peter Yates. With George Segal, Zero Mostel, Ron Leibman, Paul Sand, Moses Gunn, William Redfield, Topo Swope, Charlotte Rae.
Jeremiah Johnson. 1972. WARNER BROTHERS. Sidney Pollack. With Will Geer, Stefan Gierasch, Allyn Ann McLerie, Charles Tyner, Paul Benedict.

The Candidate. 1972. REDFORD-RITCHIE/WARNER BROTHERS. Michael Ritchie. With Peter Boyle, Allen Garfield, Don Porter, Karen Carlson, Quinn Redeker, Morgan Upton, Michael Lerner, Kenneth Tobey, Melvyn Douglas.
The Way We Were. 1973. COLUMBIA. Sydney Pollack. With Barbra Streisand, Bradford Dillman, Lois Chiles, Patrick O'Neil, Viveca Lindfors, Allyn Ann McLerie, Murray Hamilton.
The Sting. 1973. UNIVERSAL. George Roy Hill. With Paul Newman, Eileen Brennan, Robert Shaw, Charles Durning, Ray Walston.
The Great Gatsby. 1974. PARAMOUNT. Jack Clayton. With Mia Farrow, Bruce Dern, Sam Waterston, Karen Black.

Redford also appeared in a short, **The Making of Butch Cassidy and the Sundance Kid** (1969).

Clint Eastwood

Clint Eastwood had the dubious distinction of reaching international stardom and popularity with a screen image almost unparalleled in film history for its violence and viciousness. He was very much a child of the times, as indeed most stars are, and it was perhaps both lucky and unlucky for him that the times in which he rose to fame were so appreciative of violent, bloody and amoral films. He is fortunate and clever to have ridden this particular tiger to the point where he was big enough to call the shots and then to have got himself off it with relative ease. While he shares with other major stars the characteristic of having moved from television fame to Hollywood stardom (McQueen, Marvin and James Garner also followed that trail), he is unique in his transition from, and use of, the 'spaghetti' Western in his rise to the top. Clint Eastwood, after a few journeyman years as a contract player in Hollywood and seven years as a television celebrity, emerged as a superstar almost exclusively as the result of the powerful, violent persona he had created in the Man With No Name, protagonist of the three Italian Westerns he made between 1964 and 1966. In *The Good, the Bad and the Ugly* (1966), the last of the trio, he did actually have a name, Joe, but the character by that time was too well established and potent for this to register – he was still the mysterious stranger.

Where his luck, and undoubtedly his own sense of self-promotion and preservation, were particularly remarkable was in the apparently effortless switch away from the brutal side of this image which he effected on his triumphant return to Hollywood. The character which he now projects retains certain aspects of the original. Eastwood, like all the other superstars of the 'sixties and 'seventies, exudes a distinctive and immensely appealing form of cool. Like Newman, McQueen and Redford, he is alert, wary, pleasantly cynical, appealingly tough – and very handsome (known in South America after *For a Fistful of Dollars* as the Gunman with the Green Eyes). The homicidal aloofness and casual sadism have been transmuted through Walt Coogan and Harry Callahan into a personality which presents the obverse side of the image – aloof and casual, yes, but with a sardonic, deadpan streak, an impatience with the restrictions of red-tape and conventional rules, and a definite, if quirky integrity. More than any of his contemporaries, however, he suggests reserves of strength – and violence. Redford's external attractiveness cloaks complex emotional and moral responses, McQueen's a wary, tough loneliness, but Eastwood is like a coiled spring, taut with suppressed energy, and this is what makes him especially sexy. Under his cool and self-sufficient exterior there lurks a threat of violence, sexual toughness and aggression,

even a touch of sadism perhaps.

He was born in San Francisco in May 1931, but spent most of his childhood travelling about the country with his father, an accountant, as he looked for work in Depression-ridden America. The wandering finally ended in Oakland, where he attended the technical high school and distinguished himself in athletics – he was by then six foot four inches tall.

After leaving school, Eastwood worked for a while as a lumberjack in Oregon before he was called up. He became an army swimming-instructor, stationed at Ford Ord, a few miles away from San Francisco. While he was there, a visiting director from Universal spotted him and told him to look him up at the studio when he got out of the army. He did – only to find that the director was no longer there. After toying with the idea of going to Washington University on the GI Bill, he finally decided to enrol at the Los Angeles City College, where he studied business administration. He was also working part-time as a garage mechanic and it was then that he met and married model Maggie Johnson. They have now been married for twenty years and have two children.

He decided to have another try at Universal since a couple of army friends were working there, as a cameraman and director. They helped him make a test and in 1954 Universal signed him to a standard contract guaranteeing him forty weeks' work a year at $75 a week. He

The archetypal Eastwood image – this time from *High Plains Drifter* (1972).

stayed with them for eighteen months appearing, according to their records, in fourteen films, although he only got billing and footage in six, among them *Revenge of the Creature* (1955), *Tarantula* (1955) and *Never Say Goodbye* (1956), a Rock Hudson vehicle. In the others he was a voice off, the back of a head, someone opening a door. Even though Universal did not renew his contract, the experience had been financially rewarding and he had gained confidence in front of the camera.

Eastwood then moved across to RKO, sadly just in time for their closure. He made only two films for them, both in tiny parts, before going freelance. The first decent billing he got was in Twentieth Century's *Ambush at Cimarron Pass* (1958), where he played second lead to Scott Brady in what he later deemed to have been 'the lousiest Western ever made'. Apart from a small role in William Wellman's First World War flying drama *Lafayette Escadrille* (1957) at Warners, he got no further work and spent a large part of 1957–8 digging swimming-pools for a firm of contractors. The Eastwoods moved to New York and Clint began looking for work in television. One or two small parts were forthcoming but the break when it came was a big one.

A chance visit to CBS Television in New York (he was picking up a story-consultant friend for a lunch date) led to him being given the second lead in a new Western series called 'Rawhide'. This became an instant hit when it was premièred in January 1959 and eventually ran for seven years, with Eastwood shifting from second lead to star later on in the run. Initially, however, he was picked for the part of deputy trail-leader or 'ramrod' on a seemingly endless cattle-drive because he made a good contrast with Eric Fleming, the hero. He had a comfortable contract and, for the first couple of years or so, everything went fine, but he found himself increasingly annoyed by the refusal of CBS to allow him to do any other film or television work during the annual breaks in filming the series. Finally he lost his temper and made his grievance public in The Hollywood Reporter in July 1961. Since he was the increasingly popular star of an immensely successful show, CBS, not unnaturally, were anxious not to lose him. They hastily acceded to his request and he began to appear as a guest on chat shows and made it known that he was available for film work.

In the spring of 1964, this outburst of independence paid off at last. He was asked by an Italian production company called Jolly Films to star in one of the new breed of Italian or 'spaghetti' Westerns that was becoming popular in Europe. The part had been offered to several other actors before him and one of them, Richard Harrison, had suggested Clint Eastwood. He accepted for a flat fee of $15,000 (the film's total budget was $200,000) and flew off to Spain in the summer of 1964 to work with director Sergio Leone on *Per un Pugno di Dollari* (1964). Soon to be known as *For a Fistful of Dollars* in English-speaking countries,

the film was a tremendous success. It was (following the popularity of John Sturges's *The Magnificent Seven*, which was based on Kurosawa's *Seven Samurai*) a faithful translation into the Western formula of another Kurosawa Samurai story, *Yojimbo*. Unfortunately the producers failed to acquire the American rights of the Japanese film, so it was three years before it could be shown in the States. By then, Eastwood was an international star.

He played a bounty-hunter and professional killer called The Man with No Name, and though the film itself is not particularly remarkable, except for its violence and Leone's dramatic visual sense, Eastwood made an immediate and powerful impact in the part. What has been called his 'somnambulant manner' contrasted well with the frenetic activity of the other characters, and with what was to become his uniform of a tattered poncho, sheepskin vest and a cheroot clenched between his teeth (he became known as 'El Cigarillo' in Italy) he re-created the image of the traditional cowboy – silent, violent, mysterious and solitary.

Back in America, he continued to record episodes of 'Rawhide', but word began to trickle back of the sensational success of the film in Italy (it outgrossed both *My Fair Lady* and *Mary Poppins* there and finally took $7 million in Europe alone). Eastwood soon gained the tag of 'the fastest draw in the Italian cinema', and Leone offered him the lead in a sequel, *For a Few Dollars More* (1965). Again he played the Man With No Name, joined this time by Lee Van Cleef, playing another bounty-hunter. This time his fee was $50,000 plus a percentage, plus various fringe benefits. In 1966 he returned to Europe to make his third 'spaghetti' Western, *The Good, the Bad and the Ugly* (1966), with Lee Van Cleef and Eli Wallach. For this he was paid $250,000 plus ten per cent of the Western hemisphere profits. Like *Fistful*, both films did enormously well at the box-office in Europe. Ironically, Eastwood was a major film-star in almost every country but his own.

However, on the home-front things were moving. Following an internal upheaval at CBS, 'Rawhide' had been dropped, revived and then finally dropped with seventeen segments to be filmed. Eastwood settled with CBS in February 1966 for $119,000. In 1967 his first two Italian Westerns opened in the USA, followed in 1968 by the third. All were immensely popular, if not critical successes, though Vincent Canby, the film critic of The New York Times, after an initial adverse reaction (his subtitle for *The Good, the Bad and the Ugly* was 'Zane Grey meets the Marquis de Sade') eventually admitted to a sneaking admiration both for Eastwood's image and the films themselves. He spoke of them as 'spare, bloody, nihilistic nightmares', and of Eastwood as 'the perfect physical spectre, haunting a world in which the evil was as commonplace as it was unrelenting'. At last Clint Eastwood was a major American box-office attraction (he rose to No. 5 in the US

In *Coogan's Bluff* (1968), Eastwood exchanged his horse for a motor-bike but retained the stetson and the high-heeled boots and captured perfectly the puzzlement of the man from the wide open spaces coping with urban life.

top ten and No. 7 in Britain in 1968) and United Artists, who had released all three Italian films in the States, decided to cash in on this phenomenon. They offered him $400,000 plus 25 per cent of the net profits to star in that strange creature, an American 'spaghetti' Western, called *Hang 'Em High* (1968). Directed by Ted Post it had all the violent, amoral and sadistic qualities of the Italian originals and was a major money-spinner. The Italians, perhaps indignant at the loss of Eastwood, albeit to his native industry, tried to cash in too, by twice releasing cobbled-together episodes of 'Rawhide' in the guise of new Eastwood films. Prompt recourse to litigation prevented both ventures from taking off.

Eastwood might well have stuck in this particular rut had it not been for two important events in 1968. The first was the formation of his own production company, Malpaso. The second was his and Malpaso's involvement in a film called *Coogan's Bluff* (1968), directed by Don Siegel. The partnership of Siegel and Eastwood has become one of the most exciting creative Hollywood partnerships in recent years – paralleled perhaps by the Redford/Michael Ritchie and the early McQueen/Robert Mulligan relationships, but more commercially successful and therefore, maybe, more sustained than either of these. *Coogan's Bluff* created a new

and more likeable screen persona for Clint Eastwood. As the cowboy sheriff tracking down his man in modern Manhattan, he is a very engaging character – self-sufficient and laconic with a dry wit and an appealing determination not to let the city slickers put one over on him. The film was fast-moving, exciting and thoroughly enjoyable – and it did very well at the box-office.

Then he did a Second World War drama with Richard Burton called *Where Eagles Dare* (1969) and, as if to prove his versatility, a musical, *Paint Your Wagon* (1969) with Lee Marvin and Jean Seberg, performing adequately if not unforgettably in his musical numbers. It was back to the war in *Kelly's Heroes*, a 'caper' movie set in Yugoslavia about robbing a German bank, but first he and Siegel were reunited, not very happily, in *Two Mules for Sister Sarah* (1970). Originally envisaged as a vehicle for Eastwood and Elizabeth Taylor (she had suggested the project when he was filming with Burton), this was the story of a Texan mercenary who helps a nun to escape a variety of fates worse than death only to discover that she is the madam of a brothel in disguise. Elizabeth Taylor was not free to do the film and Shirley MacLaine took her part. Everybody except Eastwood went down with 'flu or Montezuma's Revenge and, all in all, the film

A smiling Clint Eastwood seen here in *Where Eagles Dare* (1969), an Alistair McLean adventure film, with (left to right) Ingrid Pitt, Mary Ure and Richard Burton.

Pardner (Eastwood) and partner (Lee Marvin) in *Paint Your Wagon* (1969). Two more unlikely stars for a musical it would be hard to imagine, but it worked – in parts.

was not a happy experience – a fact which unfortunately makes itself felt on the screen.

However, this failure was quickly followed by what has been acknowledged to be the most successful Eastwood/Siegel collaboration to date. *The Beguiled* (1971) was a triumph for both of them, although sadly it has not been a commercial success. The sinister story of a wounded deserter from the Civil War taking refuge in a Southern ladies' seminary gave Eastwood the best opportunity he had ever had and he took it, turning in a performance quite unlike anything else he had done and exhibiting a remarkable emotional and dramatic range. Universal simply did not know how to handle the film (described by British critic Tom Milne as 'a rarified piece of Southern Gothic') and it virtually sank without trace when it opened in America. In Europe it has become something of a cult movie, playing to packed houses on the rare occasions when it is screened.

However, 1971 was undoubtedly the year of Clint Eastwood. It saw the release not only of *The Beguiled*, but of his own directorial début, *Play Misty for Me*, and his and Siegel's second enormous popular success, *Dirty Harry*. This was the year, too, that he was No. 1 in the USA box-office poll. *Play Misty* is a tense, exciting thriller about a psychotic girl (Jessica Walter)

with whom a disc-jockey (Eastwood) becomes involved as the result of her nightly request to him to 'Play Misty'. In a neat piece of role reversal, Don Siegel took a small part, that of a bar-tender in the film, but left immediately after his scenes had been shot. 'He doesn't need my help,' he said. 'He's in complete command of the situation.' This was a comment which the finished film more than justified, but the two men returned to their more usual roles in *Dirty Harry*, Siegel's fast-paced thriller about an unconventional, ruthless detective, Harry Callahan (Eastwood), who continually bucks the system. The part was originally intended for Frank Sinatra but a hand injury prevented him from playing it, and it gave Eastwood a chance to demonstrate his tough, virile image at its best. It was one of the 1971 top ten films and earned critical applause as well as a great deal of money.

For his next two films Eastwood returned to the Western. *Joe Kidd* (1972), directed by John Sturges, cast him again as a hired gun in a fairly conventional film, but *High Plains Drifter* (1972), which he directed himself, was a very different animal, owing a great deal to Leone. This is a black, surrealistic film (The Stranger, played by Eastwood, has the town painted red and appoints a dwarf as his deputy) and it confirms Eastwood as a director of

Harry Callahan alias *Dirty Harry* (1971), the film that took Eastwood to international superstardom.

In *Kelly's Heroes* Eastwood did trade in the cowboy hat – for a steel helmet in this story of wartime bank raiding.

Disc-jockey Dave Garland (Eastwood) with the girl (Jessica Walter) whose nightly request is *Play Misty* (1971). Garland is beginning to realize that his one-night stand is leading him into deep trouble.

originality and style. His next film as director did not star himself, but William Holden. Called *Breezy* it was released in 1974.

In 1973 Eastwood was Dirty Harry again, in *Magnum Force* (1973) directed by Ted Post (of *Hang 'Em High*). Harry Callahan's unorthodox and violent methods are counterpointed by a sinister murder squad of young policemen who carry his anti-Establishment instincts to their logical and unpleasant conclusion. This time, Harry is on the side of the angels, but the film lacks the tension, pace and interest of its predecessor.

In a sense, with Clint Eastwood the wheel has come full circle. With *Coogan's Bluff* we are back to the 'urban' Westerns of William S. Hart and Douglas Fairbanks Sr, and in the post-spaghetti Eastwood persona we see a male Hollywood star with something of the stillness and monolithic power of the great Western heroes. As early as 1966 Vittorio de Sica – for whom he filmed an episode of *Le Streghe* (1967) with Silvana Mangano – called Eastwood 'absolutely the new Gary Cooper'. Later, Telly Savalas, a fellow actor in *Kelly's Heroes*, said of him, 'Cooper was perhaps more a man of instinct than Clint, but they both project one thing beautifully: pure Americanism.'

↑ *The Beguiled* (1971) was greatly under-rated when it was first released. Happily its reputation is now growing. Here Eastwood, the wounded Civil War deserter, talks with two of the teachers who nurse him back to health at the ladies' seminary, Geraldine Page (left) and Elizabeth Hartman.

Clint Eastwood

Revenge of the Creature. 1955. UNIVERSAL-INTERNATIONAL. Jack Arnold. With John Agar, Lori Nelson, John Bromfield, Nestor Paiva.
Francis in the Navy. 1955. UNIVERSAL-INTERNATIONAL. Arthur Lubin. With Donald O'Connor, Martha Hyer, Richard Erdman, Jim Backus, David Janssen.
Lady Godiva (UK title: **Lady Godiva of Coventry**). 1955. UNIVERSAL-INTERNATIONAL. Arthur Lubin. With Maureen O'Hara, George Nader, Victor McLaglen, Eduard Franz.
Tarantula. 1955. UNIVERSAL-INTERNATIONAL. Jack Arnold. With John Agar, Mara Corday, Leo G. Carroll, Nestor Paiva, Ross Elliott.
Never Say Goodbye. 1956. UNIVERSAL-INTERNATIONAL. Jerry Hopper. With Rock Hudson, Cornell Borchers, George Sanders, Ray Collins, David Janssen, Shelly Fabares.
The First Travelling Saleslady. 1956. RKO. Arthur Lubin. With Ginger Rogers, Barry Nelson, Carol Channing, Brian Keith, James Arness.
Star in the Dust. 1956. UNIVERSAL-INTERNATIONAL. Charles Haas. With John Agar, Mamie Van Doren, Richard Boone, Leif Erickson, Coleen Gray.
Escapade in Japan. 1957. RKO. Arthur Lubin. With Teresa Wright, Cameron Mitchell, Jon Provost, Roger Nakagawa.
Ambush at Cimarron Pass. 1958. TWENTIETH CENTURY-FOX/REGAL. Jodie Copelan. With Scott Brady, Margia Dean, Irving Bacon.
Lafayette Escadrille (UK title: **Hell Bent for Glory**). 1958. WARNER BROTHERS. William A. Wellman. With Tab Hunter, Bill Wellman Jr, Etchika Choreau, David Janssen, Jody McCrea, Paul Fix.
Per un Pugno di Dollari (UK/US title: **For a Fistful of Dollars**). 1964. JOLLY/CONSTANTIN/OCEAN/ UNITED ARTISTS. Sergio Leone. With Gian Maria Volonte, Marianne Koch, Wolfgang Lukschy.
Per Qualche Dollari in Piu (US/UK title: **For a Few Dollars More**). 1965. PRODUZIONI EUROPEE ASSOCIATE/GONZALES/ CONSTANTIN/UNITED ARTISTS. Sergio Leone. With Lee Van Cleef, Gian Maria Volonte, Rosemary Dexter, Klaus Kinski,

Maria Krup.
Il Buono, il Brutto, il Cattivo (US/UK title: **The Good, the Bad and the Ugly**). 1966. PRODUZIONI EUROPEE ASSOCIATE/ UNITED ARTISTS. Sergio Leone. With Eli Wallach, Lee Van Cleef.
Le Streghe (US title: **The Witches**). 1967. DINO DE LAURENTIIS/UNITED ARTISTS. Vittorio De Sica. With Silvana Mangano.
Hang 'Em High. 1968. LEONARD FREEMAN · PRODUCTIONS/UNITED ARTISTS. Ted Post. With Inger Stevens, Ed Begley, Pat Hingle, James MacArthur, Arlene Golonka.
Coogan's Bluff. 1968. UNIVERSAL. Don Siegel. With Lee J. Cobb, Susan Clark, Betty Field, Don Stroud, Tisha Sterling, Tom Tully.
Where Eagles Dare. 1969. WINKAST/MGM. Brian G. Hutton. With Richard Burton, Mary Ure, Patrick Wymark, Michael Hordern, Donald Houston, Anton Diffring.
Paint Your Wagon. 1969. PARAMOUNT/LERNER. Joshua Logan. With Lee Marvin, Jean Seberg, Harve Presnell, Ray Walston.
Kelly's Heroes. 1970. MGM/WARRIORS/AVALA. Brian G. Hutton. With Telly Savalas, Don Rickles, Donald Sutherland, Carroll O'Connor.
Two Mules for Sister Sarah. 1970. UNIVERSAL/ MALPASO. Don Siegel. With Shirley MacLaine, Manolo Fabregas, Alberto Morin, Armando Silvestre, John Kelly.
The Beguiled. 1971. UNIVERSAL/MALPASO. Don Siegel. With Geraldine Page, Elizabeth Hartman, Jo Anne Harris, Mae Mercer.
Play Misty For Me. 1971. UNIVERSAL/MALPASO. Clint Eastwood. With Jessica Walter, Donna Mills, John Larch, Jack Ging, Irene Hervey.
Dirty Harry. 1971. WARNER BROTHERS/ MALPASO. Don Siegel. With Harry Guardino, Reni Santoni, John Vernon, Andy Robinson, John Larch, John Mitchum.
Joe Kidd. 1972. UNIVERSAL/ MALPASO. John Sturges. With Robert Duvall, John Saxon, Don Stroud, Stella Garcia, James Wainwright.
High Plains Drifter. 1972. UNIVERSAL/MALPASO. Clint Eastwood. With Verna Bloom, Mariana Hill, Mitchell Ryan, Jack Ging.
Magnum Force. 1973. MALPASO/COLUMBIA-WARNER. Ted Post. With Hal Holbrook, Felton Perry, Mitchell Ryan, David Soul.
Thunderbolt and Lightfoot. 1974. MALPASO/ UNITED ARTISTS. Michael Cimino. With George

Kennedy, Jeff Bridges.
The Eiger Sanction. 1975 UNIVERSAL/MALPASO. Clint Eastwood. With George Kennedy, Vonetla McGee.

Eastwood also directed **Breezy** (1973).

Bibliography

Although much of the material presented here is already extensively documented, several of the newer stars are too recent in their success to have attracted any thoroughgoing documentation. Nevertheless a special word of appreciation must go to the series of 'Films Of' pamphlets published in Great Britain by Barnden, Castell Williams, without which my task would have been infinitely more difficult. A few of the longer-established names, surprisingly, do not seem to have anything more authoritative than a mountain of press-clippings to offer the researcher.

Because of all this, the sources for the book have often been fragmented and very scattered and it would be a lengthy and impossible task to itemize them all. Listed below are the key works on the stars and the general reference books to which I found myself turning again and again, and without which I could never have written this book. I have quoted from them liberally throughout the text and have found them invaluable reference works.

General reference
'The Celluloid Sacrifice' by Alexander Walker. Michael Joseph, London, 1966.
'The Filmgoer's Companion' by Leslie Halliwell. MacGibbon and Kee, London, 1965 (3rd edition, revised and enlarged).
'The Great Movie Stars: The Golden Years' by David Shipman. Hamlyn, London, 1970.
'The Great Movie Stars: The International Years' by David Shipman. Angus and Robertson, London, 1972.
'A Pictorial History of Westerns' by Michael Parkinson and Clyde Jeavons. Hamlyn, London, 1972.
'Romance in the Cinema' by John Kobal. Studio Vista, London, 1973.
'Stardom: The Hollywood Phenomenon' by Alexander Walker. Michael Joseph, London, 1970.
'Stunt' by John Baxter. Macdonald, London, 1973.
'Underworld USA' by Colin McArthur. Secker & Warburg and the British Film Institute, London, 1972.

Fairbanks
'Douglas Fairbanks: The Fourth Musketeer' by Ralph Hancock and Letitia Fairbanks. Holt, New York, 1953.
'Douglas Fairbanks: The Making of a Screen Character' by Alistair Cooke. Museum of Modern Art, New York, 1940.

Valentino
'Valentino' by Irving Schulman. Trident Press, New York, 1967.
'Valentino: The Man Behind the Myth' by Robert Oberfirst. Citadel Press, New York, 1962.

Novarro
'Ramon Novarro' by DeWitt Bodeen. Films in Review (USA), November 1967.

Barrymore
'The Film Career of John Barrymore' by Spencer M. Berger. Films in Review (USA), December 1952.
'Goodnight, Sweet Prince' by Gene Fowler. Viking Press, New York, 1944.
'John Barrymore and Dolores Costello' by DeWitt Bodeen. Focus on Film (GB), Winter 1972.

Gilbert
'Casualties of Sound' by Julian Fox. Films and Filming (GB), October 1972.
'John Gilbert' by Lawrence J. Quirk. Films in Review (USA), October 1962.

Colman
'Colman' by Julian Fox. Films and Filming (GB), March and April 1972.
'Ronald Colman' by Jack Jacobs. Films in Review (USA), May 1968.
'Ronald Colman and the Cinema of Empire' by Jeffrey Richards. Focus on Film (GB), Autumn 1970.

Howard
'Leslie Howard' by Homer Dickens. Films in Review (USA), April 1959.
'A Quite Remarkable Father' by Leslie Ruth Howard. Longmans, London, 1959.

Cooper
'The Films of Gary Cooper' by Homer Dickens. Citadel Press, New York, 1970.
'Gary Cooper' by Carlos Clarens. Films in Review (USA), December 1959.
'The Gary Cooper Story' by George Carpozi Jr. Arlington House, New York, 1970.

Gable
'Clark Gable' by Carlos Clarens. Films in Review (USA), December 1970.
'Clark Gable: A Personal Portrait' by Kathleen Gable. Prentice-Hall, New Jersey, 1961.
'Dear Mr G' by Jean Garceau and Inez Cocke. Little Brown, Boston, 1961.
'Gable: A Complete Gallery of his Screen Portraits' by Gabe Essoe and Ray Lee. Price, Sloan, Stern, Los Angeles, 1967.
'The King: A Biography of Clark Gable' by Charles Samuels. Coward-McCann. New York, 1962.

Grant
'Cary Grant' by Robert C. Roman. Films in Review (USA), December 1961.
'Cary Grant: An Unauthorized Biography' by Albert Govoni. Henry Regnery, Chicago, 1971.
'The Films of Cary Grant' by Donald Deschner. Citadel Press, New Jersey, 1973.

Flynn
'The Films of Errol Flynn' by Tony Thomas, Rudy Behlmer and Clifford McCarty. Citadel Press, New York, 1969.
'My Wicked, Wicked Ways' by Errol Flynn. Heinemann, London, 1960.
'Requiem for a Swashbuckler' by John Cutts. Films and Filming, October 1970.

Bogart
'Bogey' by Clifford McCarty. Citadel Press, New York, 1965.
'Bogey: The Good Bad Guy' by Ezra Goodman. Lyle Stewart, New York, 1965.
'Bogie: The Biography of Humphrey Bogart' by Joe Hyams. New American Library, New York, 1966.
'Humphrey and Bogey' by Louise Brooks. Sight and Sound (GB), Winter 1966/67.
'Humphrey Bogart' by Alan G. Barbour. Pyramid Publications, New York, 1973.
'Humphrey Bogart' by Bernard Eisenschitz and Eric Losfeld. Le Terrain Vague, Paris, 1967.
'Humphrey Bogart – 1899–1957' by Clifford McCarty. Films in Review (USA), May 1957.

Taylor
'Robert Taylor' by Ronald L. Bowers. Films in Review (USA), January 1967.

Power
'The Great Stars: Tyrone Power' by Mike Tomkies. Photoplay Film Monthly (GB), August 1964.
'Tyrone Power' by Robert C. Roman. Films in Review (USA), January 1959.

Ladd
'Alan Ladd' by Robert C. Roman. Films in Review (USA), April 1964.
'The Good Bad Ladd' by Julian Fox. Films and Filming (GB), June/July 1972.
'The Great Stars: Alan Ladd' by Mike Tomkies. Photoplay Film Monthly (GB), October 1971.

Mitchum
'The Man Everybody calls Mitchum' by Mike Tomkies. Photoplay Film Monthly (GB), January 1972.
'Robert Mitchum' by Gene Ringold. Films in Review (USA), May 1964.

Brando
'Brando' by Gary Carey. Pocket Books, New York, 1973.
'Brando' by Charles Hamblett. Mayfair Publications, London, 1972.
'Brando' by Ron Offen. Henry Regnery, Chicago, 1973.
'Brando: Portrait of the Artist as a Rebel' by Bob Thomas. W.H. Allen, London, 1973.
'Brando: The Unauthorized Biography' by Joe Morella and Edward Z. Epstein. Nelson, London, 1973.
'Marlon Brando' by Rene Jordan. Pyramid Publications, New York, 1973.

Hudson
'Rock Hudson' by Ken Martin. TV Times (GB), 19 October, 1972.
'Rock Hudson, An Interview' by Sandra Shevey. Playgirl (GB), February 1974.

Newman
'The Films of Paul Newman' by Lawrence J. Quirk. Citadel Press, New York, 1971.
'The Films of Paul Newman' by Kenneth Thompson. Barnden, Castell Williams, London, 1973.
'Involvement' by Gordon Gow. Films and Filming (GB), March 1973.

McQueen
'The Films of Steve McQueen' by Joanna Campbell. Barnden, Castell Williams, London, 1973.

Redford
'The Films of Robert Redford' by David Castell. Barnden, Castell Williams, London, 1974.
'Robert Redford on Privacy in Public Life: a transcript of a John Player Interview with Joan Bakewell at the National Film Theatre'. Films Illustrated (GB), December 1973.
'Robert Redford Still Prefers his Privacy' by Lewis Archibald. Show (USA), September 1972.

Eastwood
'The Films of Clint Eastwood' by Mark Whitman. Barnden, Castell Williams, London, 1973.
'A Fistful of Fame – Clint Eastwood' by DeWitt Bodeen. Focus on Film (GB), Summer 1973.

Filmographies
In addition to all the sources listed above, a number of other books and magazines were used to verify what often turned out to be extremely complicated filmographies. A brief alphabetical list follows:
'American Film Institute Catalogs', Bowker, New York; 'The American Movies Reference Book: The Sound Era' by Paul Michael, Prentice Hall, New York, 1969; 'Anthologie du Cinéma', monographs published by L'Avant Scène du Cinéma; The Bioscope; 'The British Film Catalogue – 1895–1970' by Denis Gifford, David & Charles, Newton Abbot, 1973; Classic Film Collector; 'Classics of the Silent Screen' by Joe Franklin, Citadel Press, New York, 1959; Film Fan Monthly; International Screen World; 'The Italian Film Lexicon – 1973', published by Bianco e Néro, Rome; Kine Weekly; Library of Congress Catalog; 'The MGM Stock Company' by James Robert Parrish and Robert L. Bowers, Arlington House, New York, 1973; Monthly Film Bulletin; Motion Picture Herald; New York Film Review; New York Times Film Reviews; 'A Pictorial History of the Talkies' by Daniel Blum, Spring Books, London, 1960; Picturegoer; Picturegoer Index (BFI); Screen Facts; Screen World; Variety; 'World Film Encyclopedia' edited by Clarence Winchester, Gordon Press, New York, 1933.